MW01243133

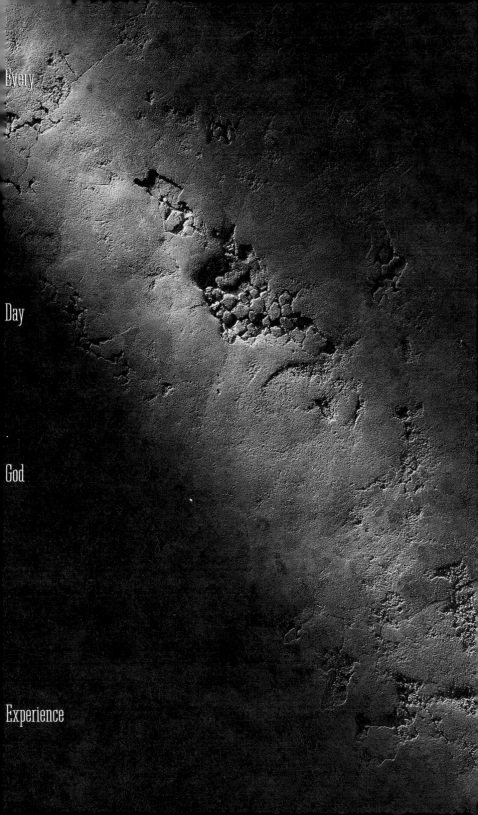

Every

Day

.

God

Experience

Jubilee Publishing Group
Post Office Box 30
Lebanon, Tennessee 37088

Editorial content produced for Jubilee by The Livingstone Corporation.
J. Michael Kendrick, David R. Veerman, Debbie Bible,
Jeremy Funk, Art Moore, Randy Southern, Peter Wallace, Carolyn Williford,
and Len Woods, project staff.
Design and concept execution by Killion McCabe & Associates.
Contributing editors: Rick Dunham, Scott Biggers, Ron Brackin, Donna Lake.
Design: Michael D. Holter.
Youth Advisory Council: Leanna Clayton, Patrick Kent, John Lewis,
Chris Newsom, Claire Nuckels, David White.
Executive Editors, Jubilee: Matthew A. Price, Gary M. Willis.
Executive Editors, World Vision: Douglas R. McGlashan, Kris L. Thompson.

Printed in the United States of America.
First printing, October 1997.

97 98 99 00 01 – 9 8 7 6 5 4 3 2 1

Distributed by Broadman & Holman Publishers
127 Ninth Avenue, North
Nashville, TN 37234
To order, call 1-800-233-1123

ISBN 1-5772-7101-7

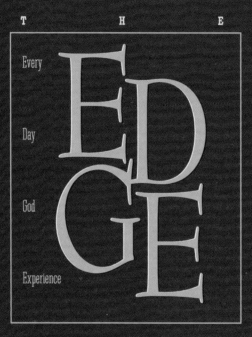

THE

Every

Day

God

Experience

EDGE

THE EVERY DAY GOD EXPERIENCE.
A daily devotional. Created just for you.

We all need an *Every Day God Experience.*

It can happen right after you wake up in the morning. Or maybe late at night. It really doesn't matter what time of day you encounter God through his Word or in prayer.

What matters is that you experience him.

And the book you hold in your hands will help you find those daily, life-changing experiences.

The *Every Day God Experience* is a yearlong devotional. You can read the 260 devotions in this book at your own pace. If you miss a day, you can pick up the next day where you left off without falling behind.

You can also share your *Every Day God Experience*—either with a friend or in a small group setting. The devotions you find in the EDGE can help move you and those you share them with into a more active faith and will serve as a powerful tool for motivation and encouragement.

That's because every devotion is designed to address the *real* issues of the heart you face daily . . . and to challenge your faith.

Not that you'll question your faith—but you'll ask yourself what you're *doing* with it. The EDGE will move you to examine how you show your faith to others. Because, as the old saying goes, that's where the rubber meets the road.

Daily Scripture readings and prayer points in the EDGE are selected so you'll better understand God's heart and how he wants you to live for him—to keep right relationships with your friends, your church, your community . . . and with our world in need.

As you go through the EDGE, you'll be encouraged by the vital truth that God can do tremendous things through you. You'll also be reminded that God is greater than any circumstance you face.

The **testimonies** of artists and others attest to that fact and demonstrate how God is raising up  believers to serve the world and bring light to the darkness. Throughout the book, you'll meet those who have acted on their faith to share hope with thousands of people throughout the world.

Often, these acts of compassion were accomplished through World Vision, one of the world's largest relief and development organizations.

World Vision has also provided you with a number of very cool ideas on how *you* can act on your faith and share Christ's love with others. Jot down your thoughts and action plans on how you can reach out to your community—and keep your journal in the **spiritual journey travel log.**

The EDGE is created to bring you closer to God. Of course, it requires some effort on your part. Commit now to make time in your schedule for him. Sure, it's a challenge. You're busy. And some of your friends may not understand. But there's no more important way to spend your time.

You'll gain a new awareness of your place in the world and in God's Kingdom through the EDGE. You'll see how you can be his hands and feet to those who hurt in the world.

And you'll grow to treasure your *Every Day God Experience.*

May it bless you—and others—as you share in it.

EDGE

GOING OVER THE EDGE

A quick guide to what you'll find in the *Every Day God Experience*.

❧ The EDGE contains 260 days of **devotions** and is designed to be used five days a week.

❧ Each day offers a **Scripture reading** from the *New Living Translation*. It may be just one verse or several. So that you'll get the big picture, you may want to have a Bible nearby to study the verses that apply to the daily selection.

❧ An **application** for your life accompanies each day's passage. Each application offers a contemporary context so you can weave the principle of the Scripture into your daily life. You may find historical context as well, like who the Scripture was specifically addressing or what was going on when it was written.

❧ A **prayer point** complements each day's entry and encourages you to talk with God about issues relevant to the reading . . . and your life.

❧ Most pages offer a **checklist** so you can take notes *and* construct an action list—ways that you can incorporate the day's lesson into your life.

❧ Write about your experiences with God in the **spiritual journey travel log**. Use it to journal . . . to capture how you felt when you read the day's devotion . . . to take notes at church . . . or to keep your own prayer list. *Just use it!*

Sometimes it seems like the entire world is made up of **cliques.** African Americans. Caucasians. Hispanics. Asians. Upper class. Middle class. Lower class. A students. B students. C students. Baby boomers. Generation Xers. Haves. Have nots.

In a society so intent on **emphasizing differences**, it can be tough to find common ground with other people. And yet, in the first chapter of the first book of the Bible, God makes it clear that everyone who draws breath on this planet shares one important characteristic.

Genesis 1:26-27: 26Then God said, "Let us make people¹ in our image, to be like ourselves. They will be masters over all life—the fish in the sea, the birds in the sky, and all the livestock, wild animals,² and small animals." 27So God created people in his own image; God patterned them after himself; male and female he created them.

Most people learn at an early age that the world consists of **"us" and "them."** When one of *us* is in trouble—whether it's a friend, family member, or neighbor we'll usually do our best to help that person. When one of *them* is in trouble—a homeless person who lives in the park, an immigrant family struggling to support themselves without a steady income, or a starving tribe in a foreign land—we're not as motivated to help. Why? Because we don't take their plight personally. We very little connection to them or their situation. We have ing to gain by easing their hardships. Or so we think.

In reality, if we take God's words spoken at creation to we will recognize that **there is no "them"; there is "us."** We are all **created in God's image.** When we

choose to ignore the struggles an difficulties of our neighbors, no m they are, we slight the ones who b imprint of God's marvelous creatio

On the other hand, when we ch get involved in the lives of those wh struggling, when we decide to **focu similarities** rather than differences, reflect not only God's image, but his g as well.

HERE'S WHAT I'M GOI

We are all pencils in the hand of a writing God, who is sending love letters to the world.

Mother Teresa

Us and Them

Day 1

Sometimes it seems like the entire world is made up of **cliques.** African Americans. Irish Americans. Hispanics. Asians. Upper class. Middle class. Lower class. A students. B students. C students. Baby boomers. Generation Xers. Haves. Have nots.

In a society so intent on **emphasizing differences,** it can be tough to find common ground with other people. And yet, in the first chapter of the first book of the Bible, God makes it clear that everyone who draws breath on this planet shares one important characteristic.

Genesis 1:26-27: [26]Then God said, "Let us make people[1] in our image, to be like ourselves. They will be masters over all life—the fish in the sea, the birds in the sky, and all the livestock, wild animals,[2] and small animals." [27]So God created people in his own image; God patterned them after himself; male and female he created them.

Most people learn at an early age that the world consists of **"us" and "them."** When one of *us* is in trouble—whether it's a friend, family member, or neighbor—we'll usually do our best to help that person. When one of *them* is in trouble—a homeless person who lives in the park, an immigrant family struggling to support themselves without a steady income, or a starving tribe in a foreign land—we're not as motivated to help. Why? Because we don't take their plight personally. We feel very little connection to them or their situation. We have nothing to gain by easing their hardships. Or so we think.

In reality, if we take God's words spoken at creation to heart, we will recognize that **there is no "them"; there is only "us."** We are all **created in God's image.** When we

---

[1] **1:26a** Hebrew *man;* also in 1:27.
[2] **1:26b** As in Syriac version; Hebrew reads *all the earth.*

choose to ignore the struggles and difficulties of our neighbors, no matter who they are, we slight the ones who bear the imprint of God's marvelous creation.

On the other hand, when we choose to get involved in the lives of those who are struggling, when we decide to **focus on similarities** rather than differences, we reflect not only God's image, but his grace as well.

HERE'S WHAT I'M GOING TO DO

☐ _____

☐ _____

☐ _____

☐ _____

☐ _____

LARGE AND IN CHARGE

What would happen if your parents decided to take a month-long vacation and left you in charge until they got back? Imagine being the boss of everyone and everything in your house—brothers, sisters, cats, dogs, hamsters, plants. **"Take care of things"** is the only instruction your parents give you before they leave.

How well do you think you'd do? How hard would it be for you to make sure that everyone and everything in your house was taken care of? What would things be like when your parents got back?

Adam and Eve (and their children) knew the feeling of being put in charge. But their responsibilities took on a much larger scope. After God created the earth and everything in it, he invited his human creatures to share in the **joy** and **responsibility** of maintaining it.

> Genesis 1:28: 28God blessed them and told them, "Multiply and fill the earth and subdue it. Be masters over the fish and birds and all the animals."

> Genesis 2:15: 15The LORD God placed the man in the Garden of Eden to tend and care for it.

God tossed us the keys to the earth and said, *You're in charge of the place. Take care of it for me.* That is why we are called *stewards* of God's creation. Stewards are people entrusted with caring for the wealth and property of their master. God has placed us in charge of the earth's resources. We are to use them properly so that everyone can share in its bountiful provision.

How well would you say we have done in fulfilling our

responsibility? When we think about widespread pollution, hunger, and the depletion of resources, such problems often result from being poor stewards. Hoarding resources or taking them without regard for other people or creation itself ultimately harms us all.

While we may be tempted to dismiss such problems as too big for us to tackle, we must keep in mind that **we all have a responsibility to do what we can to manage the earth's resources wisely.** Several small efforts on a local level have the potential to yield large-scale benefits.

HERE'S WHAT I'M GOING TO DO

☐ _____

_____

☐ _____

_____

☐ _____

_____

☐ _____

_____

☐ _____

_____

WILL WORK FOR FOOD?

What is the hardest work you've ever had to do in order to get something to eat? Maybe you've spent an entire day in the kitchen preparing a special meal for someone's birthday. Maybe you've killed and cleaned a turkey for Thanksgiving dinner. Or maybe you've had a bag of potato chips get stuck in a vending machine and had to keep rocking the machine back and forth until the bag fell.

In this era of fast food, convenience stores, and microwaveable meals, **the idea of food being something to work for seems almost foreign.**

Genesis 3:17-19: [17]And to Adam he said, "Because you listened to your wife and ate the fruit I told you not to eat, I have placed a curse on the ground. All your life you will struggle to scratch a living from it. [18]It will grow thorns and thistles for you, though you will eat of its grains. [19]All your life you will sweat to produce food, until your dying day. Then you will return to the ground from which you came. For you were made from dust, and to the dust you will return."

For many of us, the only time we **associate sweat on the brow with food** is when we're eating a spicy burrito. Let's face it, for the majority of Americans, a hot meal is always as close as the local fast-food drive-through.

Because food is so readily available to us, **we have a tendency to take it for granted.** Most of us probably have never gone hungry or had to do much work to get food, so we don't think much of the fact that we're able to eat when we please.

The flip side, of course, is that those who have gone without eating for a long period of time and those who don't know where their next meal is coming from have a much greater appreciation for food.

We're probably all familiar with the image of a homeless person holding a sign that reads WILL WORK FOR FOOD. How about you? **Are you willing to work for food?** Not for yourself, but **for those who do not have enough.** Are you willing to give your time and energy, the sweat of your brow, to collect and deliver food for the needy?

HERE'S WHAT I'M GOING TO DO

☐ _____

_____

☐ _____

_____

☐ _____

_____

☐ _____

_____

☐ _____

_____

RECIPE FOR DISASTER

Greed is good. Or so claims Gordon Gekko, the Wall Street financier played by Michael Douglas in the film *Wall Street*. Gekko argues that **the burning desire to achieve wealth and power for oneself makes American capitalism work.** Greed fuels the machine of free enterprise. And though he makes a fervent (and fairly convincing) speech that proclaims the virtues of greed, Gekko is absolutely wrong. Greed is not good; **greed destroys everything it touches.**

The Bible provides a more accurate assessment of greed and its consequences. One of the earliest examples of greed in Scripture relates the story of Lot and his generous uncle Abraham.

Genesis 13:8-13: 8Then Abram talked it over with Lot. "This arguing between our herdsmen has got to stop," he said. "After all, we are close relatives! 9I'll tell you what we'll do. Take your choice of any section of the land you want, and we will separate. If you want that area over there, then I'll stay here. If you want to stay in this area, then I'll move on to another place."

10Lot took a long look at the fertile plains of the Jordan Valley in the direction of Zoar. The whole area was well watered everywhere, like the garden of the LORD or the beautiful land of Egypt. (This was before the LORD had destroyed Sodom and Gomorrah.) 11Lot chose that land for himself—the Jordan Valley to the east of them. He went there with his flocks and servants and parted company with his uncle Abram. 12So while Abram stayed in the land of Canaan, Lot moved his tents to a place near Sodom, among the cities of the plain. 13The people of this area were unusually wicked and sinned greatly against the LORD.

Lot saw that the plains of Jordan looked fertile and profitable, so he chose that land for himself. In his desire to prosper, Lot **thought only of himself,** leaving the less-desirable land to his uncle Abraham. In short, Lot made a greedy decision. He later **paid dearly for that decision.**

The land that Lot chose bordered on the wicked city of Sodom. Later, when God decided to destroy Sodom, he had to evacuate Lot and his family. Even though they sensed the great danger, they were reluctant to leave their home. As Lot's wife was leaving the city, she looked back (despite God's clear warning) and died. Lot's greedy decision years earlier set in motion a chain of events that eventually tore his family apart.

That's not to say that every greedy decision results in death. And yet when **we choose to satisfy our own desire** for wealth and power and put others second, we can be assured that **we will have to answer to God for it.**

PRAYER POINT

Ask God to remind you of any greedy decisions you've made lately. Ask him to forgive you for those decisions and to give you wisdom and strength to make choices in the future that will honor him.

HERE'S WHAT I'M GOING TO DO

☐ _____

_____

☐ _____

_____

☐ _____

_____

Rights and Privileges

"That's mine!"

"No, it's mine!"

If you have ever been the baby-sitter for children who fought over every toy, you know **frustration.** After quickly intervening and making peace between them, you probably tried to teach the importance of "sharing" and "cooperation." But a few minutes later, they were at it again.

Some people never grow out of their selfishness. In fact, today's passage tells of jealous and spiteful *grown* men.

Genesis 26:20-25: [20]But then the local shepherds came and claimed the spring. "This is our water," they said, and they argued over it with Isaac's herdsmen. So Isaac named the well "Argument,"[1] because they had argued about it with him. [21]Isaac's men then dug another well, but again there was a fight over it. So Isaac named it "Opposition."[2] [22]Abandoning that one, he dug another well, and the local people finally left him alone. So Isaac called it "Room Enough,"[3] for he said, "At last the LORD has made room for us, and we will be able to thrive."

[23]From there Isaac moved to Beersheba, [24]where the LORD appeared to him on the night of his arrival. "I am the God of your father, Abraham," he said. "Do not be afraid, for I am with you and will bless you. I will give you many descendants, and they will become a great nation. I will do this because of my promise to Abraham, my servant." [25]Then Isaac built an altar there and worshiped the LORD. He set up his camp at that place, and his servants dug a well.

Although resources were scarce in the land, God blessed Isaac with an abundance of crops and animals. This only enraged his jealous neighbors, who filled his wells with dirt and told him to leave. Then, after moving and digging a new

[1] **26:20** Hebrew *Esek*.
[2] **26:21** Hebrew *Sitnah*.
[3] **26:22** Hebrew *Rehoboth*.

well, the local shepherds claimed that well as their own. Instead of arguing or fighting, Isaac moved again, **doing what was right** and **trusting God** to provide for him and his family.

The natural human response is to claim what is rightfully ours and then fight for it. When the "bully" yells, "Mine!" we reject his or her claim and hold on tighter. Isaac's lesson, however, is that God has "room enough." That is, God will provide for our needs when we **trust in him** and **live the way he wants us to live.** Isaac had a heritage of faith—remembering God's care for his father, Abraham, in the past, Isaac was confident of God's care in the present. Each time Isaac responded with **love** and **concern** instead of anger toward his enemies, God met his needs.

He'll do the **same** for us. What a great God we have!

PRAYER POINT

Thank God for his continual provision for all your needs and confess any feelings of jealousy or resentment you may be harboring.

HERE'S WHAT I'M GOING TO DO

☐ _____

_____

☐ _____

_____

☐ _____

_____

☐ _____

_____

SPIRITUAL JOURNEY TRAVEL LOG

HOW DO YOU RATE?

I t's the beginning of the semester, and you walk into history class. Your teacher hands out a syllabus, and you notice that you are **responsible** for a term project. It will be counted as 50 percent of your grade. You think to yourself, *I've got plenty of time to work on that. Why, it's not even due for two months.* Then before you know it, the deadline for the project is just one week away, and you haven't even started. *How did this happen?* you wonder.

In this passage, Joseph is assigned a project too. But the stakes are much higher. How he completes it will affect the lives of thousands of people.

Genesis 41:33-36: 33"My suggestion is that you find the wisest man in Egypt and put him in charge of a nationwide program. 34Let Pharaoh appoint officials over the land, and let them collect one-fifth of all the crops during the seven good years. 35Have them gather all the food and grain of these good years into the royal storehouses, and store it away so there will be food in the cities. 36That way there will be enough to eat when the seven years of famine come. Otherwise disaster will surely strike the land, and all the people will die."

God, through Pharaoh, had given Joseph the task of preparing a nation for an upcoming famine. Because God had seen the many times that Joseph had **acted responsibly** in his daily life, God knew that Joseph was the man for the tough job ahead. And Pharaoh obviously sensed that Joseph was someone who could be trusted. By acting responsibly in the arenas where God had placed him, Joseph was also **reflecting a part of God's nature** to those around him.

God, the wisest planner of all, has wonderful plans for your life. And it's important to remember that even something as seemingly small as planning ahead how to complete an assignment is part of God's training for you. **Take advantage of the numerous opportunities you have to grow in being responsible.** Planning classes, completing church and school events, doing assignments, taking care of a pet, and finishing weekly chores will prepare you for the work ahead. Henry Wadsworth Longfellow wrote, "We judge ourselves by what we feel capable of doing, while others judge us by what we have already done." Would people consider you a responsible person?

HERE'S WHAT I'M GOING TO DO

☐ _____

_____

☐ _____

_____

☐ _____

_____

☐ _____

_____

☐ _____

_____

☐ _____

_____

START A REVOLUTION!

The fall of communism in Romania supposedly began with the **courage** of one pastor. He had seen and experienced oppression in its ugliest forms. Because he was **willing to speak out,** he set in motion a wave of discontent and a demand for justice that brought down the heartless regime of an entrenched dictator.

The Egyptians living more than 3,000 years ago confronted a more faceless kind of oppression. Famine ravaged their land, and they were powerless to stop its misery. The crop failure forced the Egyptians to sell their lands and themselves to Pharaoh to buy food. The courage of one man, Joseph, was needed to blunt the impact of the disaster. See how he treats these people who are now the slaves of Pharaoh.

Genesis 47:23-25: ²³Then Joseph said to the people, "See, I have bought you and your land for Pharaoh. I will provide you with seed, so you can plant the fields. ²⁴Then when you harvest it, a fifth of your crop will belong to Pharaoh. Keep four-fifths for yourselves, and use it to plant the next year's crop and to feed yourselves, your households, and your little ones." ²⁵"You have saved our lives!" they exclaimed. "May it please you, sir, to let us be Pharaoh's servants."

Because of his power and position, Joseph could have demanded much more from the Egyptians. But he chose instead to **treat them with kindness.** Oppressed people live among us today. They deserve our kindness as much now as they did then. Who are the oppressed? According to the dictionary, the oppressed are those who have suffered abuse by someone in authority or those who are "weighed down." Can you identify these people in your community? What about people struggling with drug or alcohol addiction? The homeless? Or families who have fled their homelands to avoid starvation or war?

PRAYER POINT

Pray for the courage to act on

behalf of the oppressed.

You may not feel very powerful when it comes to **making a difference in the lives of so many hurting people.** But small steps can lead to giant strides. Rosa Parks started a revolution to improve the lives and self-respect of African Americans by simply refusing to sit at the back of a bus. Patrick Henry, whose words "Give me liberty or give me death" helped ignite the American Revolution, also made a difference. What could you do to start **a kindness revolution** in your neighborhood, church, or school? Think about it.

HERE'S WHAT I'M GOING TO DO

☐ _____

_____

☐ _____

_____

☐ _____

_____

☐ _____

_____

☐ _____

_____

☐ _____

_____

MASTER OF THE CASTLE

H ave you ever wondered what it would be like to be the lord or lady of a great castle? Imagine having hundreds of servants, extensive land holdings, and great numbers of livestock. Think about the storehouses full of food, jewels, and wealth, all at your fingertips. Wouldn't that be something? Believe it or not, you *are* like the owner of a great castle. And **there is much in your storehouses.**

But first, let's reflect on the source of your **treasures.**

Exodus 3:13-17: [13]But Moses protested, "If I go to the people of Israel and tell them, 'The God of your ancestors has sent me to you,' they won't believe me. They will ask, 'Which god are you talking about? What is his name?' Then what should I tell them?" [14]God replied, "I AM THE ONE WHO ALWAYS IS.[1] Just tell them, 'I AM has sent me to you.'" [15]God also said, "Tell them, 'The LORD,[2] the God of your ancestors—the God of Abraham, the God of Isaac, and the God of Jacob—has sent me to you.' This will be my name forever; it has always been my name, and it will be used throughout all generations.

[16]"Now go and call together all the leaders of Israel. Tell them, 'The LORD, the God of your ancestors—the God of Abraham, Isaac, and Jacob— appeared to me in a burning bush. He said, "You can be sure that I am watching over you and have seen what is happening to you in Egypt. [17]I promise to rescue you from the oppression of the Egyptians. I will lead you to the land now occupied by the Canaanites, Hittites, Amorites, Perizzites, Hivites, and Jebusites—a land flowing with milk and honey."' "

We tend to forget that **everything we have comes from God's generosity.** In verse 8 of this same passage, God says, "So I have come to rescue them from the Egyptians

---

[1] **3:14** Or *I AM WHO I AM,* or *I WILL BE WHAT I WILL BE.*
[2] **3:15** Hebrew *Yahweh;* traditionally rendered *Jehovah.*

and lead them out of Egypt into their own good and spacious land. It is a land flowing with milk and honey." Then later, in verses 21 and 22, he says, "And I will see to it that the Egyptians treat you well. They will load you down with gifts, so that you will not leave empty-handed. The Israelite women will ask for silver and gold jewelry and fine clothing from their Egyptian neighbors and their neighbors' guests."

PRAYER POINT

Ask God to remove the blind spots that have kept you from acting in the best interest of others. Confess those sins and, if necessary, make amends to those directly affected.

Whether you realize it or not, you are the master of a castle—the castle of your life. You have been given **time, energy, talents, money, and possessions** to fill your storehouses. What is important to remember is not how much you have, but how you **use what God has given you.** Do you freely share your gifts with others? Are you a generous master or a thoughtless miser? God, who is the master over everything, has been more than generous with us. Shouldn't we be generous to others?

HERE'S WHAT I'M GOING TO DO

☐ _____

_____

☐ _____

_____

☐ _____

_____

THE MAIN ISSUE

If you have ever been in a car that has spun out on an icy road, you have experienced the feeling of **being out of control.** It is a scary feeling. People caught in ecological disasters such as hurricanes, tornadoes, and floods feel the same way. Insurance companies categorize these happenings as "acts of God." But are they really?

Today's passage is about an ecological disaster that happened in Egypt. Read to find out what it was.

> Exodus 10:13-17: ¹³So Moses raised his staff, and the LORD caused an east wind to blow all that day and through the night. When morning arrived, the east wind had brought the locusts. ¹⁴And the locusts swarmed over the land of Egypt from border to border. It was the worst locust plague in Egyptian history, and there has never again been one like it. ¹⁵For the locusts covered the surface of the whole country, making the ground look black. They ate all the plants and all the fruit on the trees that had survived the hailstorm. Not one green thing remained, neither tree nor plant, throughout the land of Egypt. ¹⁶Pharaoh quickly sent for Moses and Aaron. "I confess my sin against the LORD your God and against you," he said to them. ¹⁷"Forgive my sin only this once, and plead with the LORD your God to take away this terrible plague."

Looking at these verses, we see that **God can cause natural disasters to accomplish his will.** Pharaoh had received numerous and clear warnings, but he chose to defy them. God thus showed the Egyptian ruler his great power to soften his hard heart.

But disasters can result from natural causes as well. For example, some countries experience starvation because humans have harmed the environment. By encouraging soil erosion and crop failure, they have created disasters that have harmed millions. Because **the world is fallen and sinful,** people will **suffer,** even the innocent.

People caught up in blaming God for random disasters often fail to see **God at work in the middle of the suffering.** He works through his children, showing mercy and healing to the helpless.

A more important question than *Does God cause ecological disasters?* is *What will be your response to those caught by a natural calamity?* Will you ignore them? Will you try to help? What do you think God would have you to do?

PRAYER POINT

Pray for those organizations involved with disaster relief such as the Red Cross, World Vision, World Relief, and Samaritan's Purse.

HERE'S WHAT I'M GOING TO DO

☐ _____

_____

☐ _____

_____

☐ _____

_____

☐ _____

_____

☐ _____

_____

SHARING

Have you ever had to carry something heavy by yourself? And just as you were ready to drop it, someone came along to help? Or perhaps you had a project to do for school and you were stuck. Then a friend offered to help you. How did it feel? Like a **heavy load was lifted off of you?** Well, that is the way it is with **sharing.** God commands us to share so that we can **help each other** with the heavy loads we all bear.

What types of things does God want us to share? Read today's passage to find out.

Exodus 12:1-5: ¹Now the LORD gave the following instructions to Moses and Aaron while they were still in the land of Egypt: ²"From now on, this month will be the first month of the year for you. ³Announce to the whole community that on the tenth day of this month each family must choose a lamb or a young goat for a sacrifice. ⁴If a family is too small to eat an entire lamb, let them share the lamb with another family in the neighborhood. Whether or not they share in this way depends on the size of each family and how much they can eat. ⁵This animal must be a one-year-old male, either a sheep or a goat, with no physical defects."

These few verses tell us a great deal about God's nature. Notice that God is the one who told the people to share. He required such sharing because he knew it would be difficult for smaller families to afford a lamb. God is in the business of lightening loads, not adding to them. These verses should encourage us to **share our resources** as well: money, time, talents, and material possessions.

Keep in mind that God also commands believers to

share each other's burdens. Galatians 6:2 says, "Share each other's troubles and problems, and in this way obey the law of Christ." People all over the world need **encouragement and help.** God commands us to share. So it is not a question of *Do you share?* but rather *What do you share and with whom?*

HERE'S WHAT I'M GOING TO DO

☐ _____

_____

☐ _____

_____

☐ _____

_____

☐ _____

_____

☐ _____

_____

☐ _____

_____

☐ _____

_____

FRYING PAN FAITH

You have that paper to write for English and the algebra test to study for. Meanwhile, your best friend is mad at you, your parents are upset that you haven't done your chores, and when are you ever going to learn your lines for the church youth play?

If only life were **simple** again. If only you could go back to the way things were **before all this life stuff happened to you.**

Ever feel like that? Well, multiply that feeling by about a hundred and you can identify with the Israelites in the desert wilderness.

Exodus 16:1-3: [1]Then they left Elim and journeyed into the Sin[1] Desert, between Elim and Mount Sinai. They arrived there a month after leaving Egypt.[2] [2]There, too, the whole community of Israel spoke bitterly against Moses and Aaron. [3]"Oh, that we were back in Egypt," they moaned. "It would have been better if the LORD had killed us there! At least there we had plenty to eat. But now you have brought us into this desert to starve us to death."

For more than 400 years, the Israelites lived a horrible life in Egypt. They were slaves. They worked hard under awful conditions and received very little for their labors. But, with Moses as their leader, God had miraculously rescued them from Egypt. Now he was leading them back to their own land.

Just one month after leaving Egypt, the Israelites found themselves in the middle of the Desert of Sin—a huge, barren, mean land. They had jumped out of the frying pan of Egypt. But had they jumped right into the fire of the wilderness? They were surrounded by danger, uncertainty, and fear. And they were hungry.

---

[1] **16:1a** Not to be confused with the English word *sin*.
[2] **16:1b** Hebrew *on the fifteenth day of the second month*. The Exodus had occurred on the fourteenth day of the first month (see Exodus 12:6).

Had they taken the time to **listen,** the people would have heard God calling them. In that barren land, God urged his children to depend solely on him. Yes, they would encounter testing. But God wanted these trials to lead his stubborn people to depend on him. They had to realize that **the only certainty of their lives was God's provision.**

Instead, they complained. They attacked their leaders Moses and Aaron. And they yearned for the past. Sure, they were under tremendous stress, and complaining is a natural reaction to tough circumstances. Unfortunately, their untrusting attitude steered them into even worse problems.

Like the Israelites, you know how it feels to be **stressed out** sometimes. How will you respond the next time you feel overwhelmed by all your responsibilities? If you need to vent, talk to a friend or trusted adult, as well as to God. But don't just complain. **Learn to trust your Provider** every step of the way.

PRAYER POINT

God ultimately provided everything the Israelites needed. He can do the same for you and for anyone else who asks in faith. Talk to him about the pressure points of your life, and ask him to make you sensitive to the many ways he guides and provides for you.

HERE'S WHAT I'M GOING TO DO

☐ _____

_____

☐ _____

_____

_____

PROPER PAYBACKS

If a group of thieves broke into your house and stole your CD player, you'd want to make sure they were punished, right? If a couple of strangers stole your bike, skateboard, or car, you'd want to make sure they got what was coming to them. If somebody ripped your favorite pair of jeans (unless you like them ripped), you'd probably want that person to pay for a pair of new ones.

That's because you want restitution. **Restitution** is the act of making good for loss, damage, or injury. In other words, restitution is **making wrongs right.**

Fairness is essential to justice. And clearly, justice is important to God's heart. Need proof? Read these verses from his law.

Exodus 22:3-8: 3"A thief who is caught must pay in full for everything that was stolen. If payment is not made, the thief must be sold as a slave to pay the debt. 4If someone steals an ox or a donkey or a sheep and it is recovered alive, then the thief must pay double the value. 5If an animal is grazing in a field or vineyard and the owner lets it stray into someone else's field to graze, then the animal's owner must pay damages in the form of high-quality grain or grapes. 6If a fire gets out of control and goes into another person's field, destroying the sheaves or the standing grain, then the one who started the fire must pay for the lost crops. 7Suppose someone entrusts money or goods to a neighbor, and they are stolen from the neighbor's house. If the thief is found, the fine is double the value of what was stolen. 8But if the thief is not found, God[1] will determine whether or not it was the neighbor who stole the property."

This isn't just a list of picky do's and don'ts. These verses are snapshots of God's justice—a few examples regarding how

---

[1] **22:8** Or *the judges.*

justice should be demonstrated in everyday life. Now, you may never have an ox stolen, but chances are you will be treated unjustly a time or two in your life—or even today! Naturally, you'd want the wrongs to be made right.

But consider the other side of the coin. What about when you hurt somebody else, whether intentionally or unintentionally? How strongly are you in favor of justice then?

As a child of God, **you're called to a higher standard.** So consider going beyond what is merely just and fair. Go beyond what's expected. As Jesus put it, go the second mile.

A caring person wants not only to replace what was lost but to ease the pain caused by the loss. By going beyond the "letter of the law," you'll do more to help ease that pain in someone you've hurt. Not only that, but doing so could cause you to think twice before you do anything that could harm another person. **It's an attitude** that will make you more "other-focused" rather than self-focused.

Best of all, you could make a huge impact in the lives of people who have been hurt by lovingly paying them back more than what's expected—in Jesus' name.

HERE'S WHAT I'M GOING TO DO

❑ _____

_____

LOVING STRANGERS

Imagine that you wake up one morning in an unfamiliar room, in a strange house, on an unknown street, in an alien land.

You must get up, get dressed, and go about your day. There are no familiar faces. In fact, you can barely understand a word anyone says.

At lunch, their eating habits surprise you. **You just don't fit in.** What's worse, you can see them looking at you, whispering about you, even laughing with a sneer in your direction.

Not much fun, is it?

Exodus 22:21-27: 21"Do not oppress foreigners in any way. Remember, you yourselves were once foreigners in the land of Egypt. 22Do not exploit widows or orphans. 23If you do and they cry out to me, then I will surely help them. 24My anger will blaze forth against you, and I will kill you with the sword. Your wives will become widows, and your children will become fatherless. 25If you lend money to a fellow Hebrew in need, do not be like a money lender, charging interest. 26If you take your neighbor's cloak as a pledge of repayment, you must return it by nightfall. 27Your neighbor will need it to stay warm during the night. If you do not return it and your neighbor cries out to me for help, then I will hear, for I am very merciful."

Foreigners who wandered into Israel's camp must have been grateful for the kindness they met. God made it a point to tell his people not to mistreat strangers who lived with them. They were to be **treated fairly**—more than fairly—because, after all, the Israelites knew what it was like to suffer in a strange land. **God calls his people to reach out** to "foreigners"—whether they're actually from another land or not. To make them feel welcome. To make them feel at home in their new land. God shows us many times in Scripture that he takes the needs of foreigners, widows, and orphans very seriously. He challenges his people to be just as sensitive.

Perhaps your family has had to move to a new town, maybe even more than once. It's not easy to try to develop new friends or find your way in a new school and neighborhood. It is easy to feel alone, frustrated, and out of place. North America draws hundreds of thousands of refugees and immigrants from other countries. And every year, families move into your community. So there's no doubt **you can have the opportunity to reach out** to these "strangers in a strange land" with God's **love** and **acceptance.**

Open yourself up to them. Be sensitive to the struggles they face. Show them God's kind, generous heart through your own **words** and **actions.**

HERE'S WHAT I'M GOING TO DO

☐ _____

_____

☐ _____

_____

_____

Just Be Just

Day 14

Honesty check: Have you ever fibbed just a little to make yourself look **better** in the eyes of someone else? Maybe you just wanted to be **accepted** by someone you thought was a little better than you—more popular, richer, better looking. You wanted to get on their good side. Did it work? And was it really worth it?

How about people who are not as well off as you—maybe they live in a poorer part of town, they don't wear the coolest clothes, they're not part of the popular cliques. Ever tried to make yourself look good to impress them? Probably not. Why bother, right?

Exodus 23:1-6: [1] "Do not pass along false reports. Do not cooperate with evil people by telling lies on the witness stand.

[2] "Do not join a crowd that intends to do evil. When you are on the witness stand, do not be swayed in your testimony by the opinion of the majority. [3] And do not slant your testimony in favor of a person just because that person is poor.

[4] "If you come upon your enemy's ox or donkey that has strayed away, take it back to its owner. [5] If you see the donkey of someone who hates you struggling beneath a heavy load, do not walk by. Instead, stop and offer to help.

[6] "Do not twist justice against people simply because they are poor."

God's Word is clear: We are supposed to **bother to do right.**

God wants his people to be **authentic. Real. Transparent.** He doesn't want us to put on an act to impress anybody—rich or poor.

In this list of rules and regulations for the Israelites, God makes a strong case for justice by coming at it from both sides: "Do not slant your testimony in favor of a person just because that person is poor. . . . Do not twist justice against people simply because they are poor" (vv. 3, 6).

In other words, **be true** and **do right,** no matter what.

Justice, by definition, is impartial. In fact, the symbol for justice—one you may have seen sculpted on courthouse walls— is a blindfolded woman who holds balanced scales. She's blindfolded because she's impartial. She doesn't care what people look like or how wealthy they are. She treats rich and poor alike, with total fairness.

And so should we. So when it comes to the way you treat a person, **be fair.** That may mean **standing up against the pressure of the crowd,** who may or may not accept a person on the basis of looks, clothes, or the balance in a bank account.

After all, you want to be treated fairly and accepted for who you are. God calls you to do the same for others—rich or poor.

PRAYER POINT

Is an acquaintance of yours being unfairly treated? Accused of something he or she didn't do? Not accepted by the "gang" because of something he or she has done or something he or she is? Pray for that person right now. Ask God to provide an abundance of grace and acceptance. And ask him to make you an instrument of his peace in that person's life.

HERE'S WHAT I'M GOING TO DO

☐ _____

_____

_____

A CARING CROP

A single mother with three small children in tow walked half a mile to a nearby church on a hot Wednesday afternoon. She had heard that this church provided food and other necessities at no charge to the poor. And she was desperate.

Unfortunately, when she arrived at the church she saw a handwritten note on the door. It read, "We're sorry—a large turnout today has already depleted our supplies. Please come back next week."

As she read, a woman walked out of the church. She apologized to the disappointed mother and explained that, for some reason, they just hadn't received as many food donations from their members this week, and what they did have had disappeared fast.

Exodus 23:10-11: [10]"Plant and harvest your crops for six years, [11]but let the land rest and lie fallow during the seventh year. Then let the poor among you harvest any volunteer crop that may come up. Leave the rest for the animals to eat. The same applies to your vineyards and olive groves."

God built into the Israelites' life the concept of **caring for the poor.** In these verses, for instance, God made it clear that he expects his people to care for the poor by helping meet their need for food in various ways.

God established a system of farming in which the people would work the land and harvest crops for six years, then take the seventh year off. During this "sabbath year," no work would be done, no crops would be harvested. This enabled the land to recoup its nutrients and become rich and fertile again.

If the people would obey his commands, God promised that the sixth year's crop would provide enough food not only for that year, but for the seventh year and all the way to the time when the eighth year's crop was harvested. The only thing the people had to do was **trust him to provide,** and he would.

While they let their land rest during that seventh year, some crops would come up on their own. God's people were not to harvest those "voluntary crops." They were to leave them in the fields and allow the poor and hungry to come and harvest whatever they needed. What they didn't take was left for animals to eat. In this way, God would provide for everyone's needs.

Unfortunately, there's no record that Israel ever fully obeyed this command. But you can certainly obey the spirit of it by making sure **the needs of the poor** are regularly **on your mind, in your prayers,** and **in your plans to help.**

PRAYER POINT

Pray for the many ministries designed to provide food and other necessities to poor people in your city, throughout the nation, and around the world. Pray for God's blessing on their work, that he would provide the money and the resources necessary to meet the need. Ask him what part you can play in answering that prayer.

HERE'S WHAT I'M GOING TO DO

☐ _____

_____

☐ _____

_____

☐ _____

_____

Spiritual Journey Travel Log

GIVING TO GOD

DAY 16

If God owns the universe, why does he need anything from us? That thought must have crossed the minds of at least a few Israelites who heard Moses' call to give to the Lord. After all, Moses was not simply urging people to flip a few coins in the offering basket. God asked for the best: gold, silver, and bronze; the finest linens; the most precious stones!

Exodus 35:20-24: [20]So all the people left Moses and went to their tents to prepare their gifts. [21]If their hearts were stirred and they desired to do so, they brought to the LORD their offerings of materials for the Tabernacle[1] and its furnishings and for the holy garments. [22]Both men and women came, all whose hearts were willing. Some brought to the LORD their offerings of gold—medallions, earrings, rings from their fingers, and necklaces. They presented gold objects of every kind to the LORD. [23]Others brought blue, purple, and scarlet yarn, fine linen, or goat hair for cloth. Some gave tanned ram skins or fine goatskin leather. [24]Others brought silver and bronze objects as their offering to the LORD. And those who had acacia wood brought it.

So why does a rich God ask us to give to him? First of all, **giving begins with God.** It is an essential part of his character. The Lord placed the desire to give in the hearts of the Israelites. Nobody's arm was twisted. "If their hearts were stirred and they desired to do so, they brought to the LORD their offerings . . ." (v. 21).

Second, **God is honored by our giving.** By willingly and joyfully sacrificing the best that they had, the Israelites showed their devotion to God. It's one thing to say "I love you" and another to demonstrate it. Words and actions are both important, but by **giving up something precious to us,** we show God that we mean business. In this way,

---

[1] **35:21** Hebrew *Tent of Meeting.*

we teach ourselves to **submit our entire being to the will of God.**

Third, God is very practical: He has a job to do, and **he wants to use us!** We have the privilege of participating in the building of his Kingdom. When we give to the Lord, according to his guidance, we contribute to his work in the world: to clothe and feed the naked and hungry and proclaim salvation through Jesus Christ.

There is no greater joy than living in harmony with how God created us. To be a giver is to **allow God's rich blessings to flow through us** and transform the lives of others.

PRAYER POINT

If you find the thought of giving difficult, ask God to show you if there is anything—a possession or even an ability—that you might value higher than him. God wants to stir your heart and give you the joy of dispensing his blessings.

HERE'S WHAT I'M GOING TO DO

☐ _____

_____

☐ _____

_____

☐ _____

_____

☐ _____

_____

_____

An Offering of Love

Day

17

Have you ever been offered something of value by a poor person? Even if you haven't, you can probably imagine your response. If you're like most people, you would resist taking it. *How*, you might say to yourself, *can he afford it?*

Leviticus 5:7-10: *7"If any of them cannot afford to bring a sheep, they must bring to the Lord two young turtledoves or two young pigeons as the penalty for their sin. One of the birds will be a sin offering, and the other will be a burnt offering. 8They must bring them to the priest, who will offer one of the birds as the sin offering. The priest will wring its neck but without severing its head from the body. 9Then he will sprinkle some of the blood of the sin offering against the sides of the altar, and the rest will be drained out at the base of the altar. 10The priest will offer the second bird as a whole burnt offering, following all the procedures that have been prescribed. In this way, the priest will make atonement for those who are guilty, and they will be forgiven."*

In Leviticus 5, God spells out to the nation of Israel his requirements for **atonement.** In simple terms, atonement means "at-one-ment," or the act of bringing us **back to companionship with God,** in spite of our sin. In verse 6 he describes the kind of sin offering that pleases him—a female sheep or goat. But what about people who are so poor that they can't afford to bring an animal of such value? Are they unable to please God?

God provided a way for the poor to present an appropriate offering by accepting animals of lesser value. Did that in any way diminish the effectiveness of the offering? Definitely not. Leviticus 5:10 says: "In this way, the priest will make atonement for those who are guilty, and they will be forgiven."

Some of the best hospitality you'll find anywhere in the

world is in the poorest of countries. Poor families may not be able to serve the finest foods, but many will offer you **all that they have.** That kind of offering is often far sweeter than the richest foods served in a household that shares only what it can easily do without.

PRAYER POINT

Ask God to increase your

willingness to receive from those

who have less than you.

The amount we give to God *is* important, whether it be money, possessions, or abilities. But **God has a special interest in our willingness to give something that will cost us,** regardless of how much we actually have.

The poor can afford to give, and what they offer is greatly valued and enjoyed by the Great Giver of life.

HERE'S WHAT I'M GOING TO DO

☐ _____

_____

☐ _____

_____

☐ _____

_____

☐ _____

_____

☐ _____

_____

SETTLING THE SCORE

In the spring of 1996, Europe's poorest country, Albania, slid into chaos. Its people rebelled against a corrupt regime. Food soon became scarce as Albanians looted warehouses and stores. A missionary couple roamed the streets of their town looking for food. They were told that looting was the only way to ensure that they had something to eat. Reluctantly, they joined in. Unlike most people, though, they **promised** to find the store owner and pay him for the food they took.

> Leviticus 6:1-7: [1]And the LORD said to Moses, [2]"Suppose some of the people sin against the LORD by falsely telling their neighbor that an item entrusted to their safekeeping has been lost or stolen. Or suppose they have been dishonest with regard to a security deposit, or they have taken something by theft or extortion. [3]Or suppose they find a lost item and lie about it, or they deny something while under oath, or they commit any other similar sin. [4]If they have sinned in any of these ways and are guilty, they must give back whatever they have taken by theft or extortion, whether a security deposit, or property entrusted to them, or a lost object that they claimed as their own, [5]or anything gained by swearing falsely. When they realize their guilt, they must restore the principal amount plus a penalty of 20 percent to the person they have harmed. [6]They must then bring a guilt offering to the priest, who will present it before the LORD. This offering must be a ram with no physical defects or the animal's equivalent value in silver.[1] [7]The priest will then make atonement for them before the LORD, and they will be forgiven."

Saying "sorry" does not make everything better in God's eyes. The missionaries might have tried to **justify** not paying the store owner by pointing out that nobody else did. But the only way that they could maintain a right relationship with

---

[1] **6:6** Or *and the animal must be of the proper value;* Hebrew lacks *in silver;* compare Exodus 5:15.

the owner was to **settle their account** and **pay up.**

It's actually impossible to fully settle our account with God through our own efforts. Just one sin severs the relationship, and **we can do nothing by ourselves to even the score.** In Old Testament times, God provided animals to atone for sin. Today, by trusting in the perfect sacrifice of Jesus Christ, we can settle our account with God forever. But just as in the days of Moses, God requires us to be in good standing with people. **True repentance results in action,** right here in the flesh-and-blood world in which we live.

The act of repayment, or giving back something that was taken, helps **restore** things to their original place. It's also a clear expression of a heart that is truly sorry, enabling the person wronged to more easily accept an apology and restore the relationship.

Our gestures of repayment, even though they seem small, remind us that **God will one day make everything right again** (see Acts 3:21).

PRAYER POINT

Ask God to show you if you need to repay someone, perhaps even for something done a long time ago.

HERE'S WHAT I'M GOING TO DO

☐ _____

_____

☐ _____

_____

☐ _____

_____

WHAT IS FAIR?

That's not fair! How many times while growing up did you hear that exclamation? How often did you say it yourself? By now, most of us have developed a good sense of **what's fair** and **what's not.** Sometimes, however, we fail to understand **what God considers fair.** Take for instance God's instructions for Israelites who had been cured of a contagious skin disease. The payment varied according to a person's financial status.

> Leviticus 14:21-22: [21]"But anyone who cannot afford two lambs must bring one male lamb for a guilt offering, along with two quarts[1] of choice flour mixed with olive oil as a grain offering and three-fifths of a pint of olive oil. The guilt offering will be presented by lifting it up, thus making atonement for the person being cleansed. [22]The person being cleansed must also bring two turtledoves or two young pigeons, whichever the person can afford. One of the pair must be used for a sin offering and the other for a whole burnt offering."

Diseases made a person ceremonially unclean. God required all Israelites, regardless of status, to make an offering before they could rejoin their community. However, he made special provisions for the poor. *If you can't afford two lambs, then bring one.* That was the gist of God's instructions.

God doesn't issue commands without considering who we are and the circumstances we face. **His wisdom produces a fair judgment.** He knows us intimately,

---

[1] **14:21** Hebrew *1/10 of an ephah* [2 liters].

down to the number of hairs on our heads (Matthew 10:30). He knows everything about our past and present situation and has prepared a glorious hope for our future. When we **trust** that divine wisdom and **obey** his commands, we **gain his blessing.**

Fairness is a relative concept. Our assessment of what's fair is based on what happens to others in similar circumstances. But when you trust in God's divine wisdom, you won't worry about what he requires of other people.

PRAYER POINT

Make an effort to pray more specifically for people you see everyday. Learn more about their particular needs and concerns and pray that they will fulfill all that God desires for them.

You may remember after his resurrection, Jesus commanded Peter to follow him, though it would cost Peter his life. Peter looked toward John and said, "What about him, Lord?" Jesus replied, "If I want him to remain alive until I return, what is that to you? You follow me." (See John 21:15-22.)

Peter did what the Lord required of him—and so did John. And faith in the Lord launched a powerful movement of God that continues to this day.

HERE'S WHAT I'M GOING TO DO

❑ _____

_____

❑ _____

_____

_____

GOD'S FAIRNESS

DAY

20

Picture the mad scramble and frenzy of children grabbing for candy freshly spilled from a piñata at Christmas. That's a fairly accurate image of what adults are like. We want to **get as much as we can** before someone else beats us to it. In Leviticus 19, God presented Israel with a radically different model for behavior.

> Leviticus 19:9-16: ⁹"When you harvest your crops, do not harvest the grain along the edges of your fields, and do not pick up what the harvesters drop. ¹⁰It is the same with your grape crop—do not strip every last bunch of grapes from the vines, and do not pick up the grapes that fall to the ground. Leave them for the poor and the foreigners who live among you, for I, the LORD, am your God. ¹¹Do not steal. Do not cheat one another. Do not lie. ¹²Do not use my name to swear a falsehood and so profane the name of your God. I am the LORD. ¹³Do not cheat or rob anyone. Always pay your hired workers promptly. ¹⁴Show your fear of God by treating the deaf with respect and by not taking advantage of the blind. I am the LORD. ¹⁵Always judge your neighbors fairly, neither favoring the poor nor showing deference to the rich. ¹⁶Do not spread slanderous gossip among your people.[1] Do not try to get ahead at the cost of your neighbor's life, for I am the LORD."

God told the Israelites to leave some of their harvest in the field for the poor and the foreigners to collect. The fact that he gave that command suggests that this practice didn't come naturally. Some might call God's command unjust. People should reap what they sow, right?

Yes, hard work should be rewarded, but God's command expresses two desires. One is that **the prosperous should bless those who struggle.** Corporate sin, individual sin, and the fallenness of nature all contribute to poverty. It affects

---

[1] **19:16** Hebrew *Do not act as a merchant toward your own people.*

the just and the unjust. God has a heart of mercy for the poor, regardless of how they got that way.

Also, God's command for the Israelites to leave behind some of their crop makes **a way for the poor to provide for themselves** with dignity. Passing out food is often necessary, especially in emergency situations, but it tends to lower the dignity of the recipient. The method of reaping the remains of the harvest, or gleaning, however, provides a way for the poor to work for what they receive.

In the book of Ruth, we find a well-known story about gleaning. Ruth, a poor widow, was noted for working in the field steadily from morning, collecting unharvested grain. Boaz, the owner of the field, went even beyond the law's requirements to ensure that Ruth collected what she needed. He also took great effort to ensure that she wouldn't be embarrassed.

Boaz reflected the heart of God for the poor: to bless them with **dignity** and **grace.**

> ## PRAYER POINT
>
> Pray for ministries working among the poor—that they will help provide for their needs in a way that builds self-esteem and dignity.

HERE'S WHAT I'M GOING TO DO

☐ _____

_____

☐ _____

_____

_____

PATIENCE, MY DEAR

Do you remember the excitement of sitting next to your family's Christmas tree when you were a child? Surrounded by presents and beautifully decorated, it seemed to invite you to open every gift under its branches. Yet you knew it was better to **wait patiently** until Christmas morning. The passage below, from Leviticus 19, reminds us that showing **patience for the bounty of God's good gifts** is always appropriate for his people.

> Leviticus 19:23-25: 23"When you enter the land and plant fruit trees, leave the fruit unharvested for the first three years and consider it forbidden. 24In the fourth year the entire crop will be devoted to the LORD as an outburst of praise. 25Finally, in the fifth year you may eat the fruit. In this way, its yield will be increased. I, the LORD, am your God."

In verses 23-25 of Leviticus 19, God commands his people to wait five years before eating any fruit from trees they plant in the Promised Land. Why the wait? God offered a reason: "In this way, its yield will be increased" (v. 25). God knew branches have to grow before fruit appears. By the fourth year, enough fruit had grown for the people to give it all back to God "as an outburst of praise" (v. 24). Finally, in the fifth year there was plenty to eat.

Notice God's commands in these verses. After waiting three years, God's people spent another whole year giving the fruit "as an outburst of praise" to him. Like the trees in Leviticus 19, you may be going through a time of **waiting** and **growing,** a time to learn God's Word and talk to him in prayer. God has work for you to do. He promises this. **But while you're waiting, don't be lazy.** Think of all the praising you've got to do! It may be as simple as thanking him for being alive or for all the things he's given you. If you spend time getting to know God and praising him, **he promises to increase** your yield for him.

PRAYER POINT

Pray that as you follow God today, he will increase your patience and trust in him.

Waiting for fruit to grow takes patience. Waiting for Christmas morning took patience too when you were four. Yet when you saw the lighted tree and the growing pile of gifts, you anticipated the joy of the day. And hopefully you had a few nice thoughts about the people who were giving you the gifts. The Israelites waited too. **God wanted the waiting to be a time for them to praise him for his generosity.** And God wants you to wait as well. When it seems like he is not hearing your prayers, wait patiently. The bounty of his blessing will be worth the wait!

HERE'S WHAT I'M GOING TO DO

☐ _____

_____

☐ _____

_____

☐ _____

_____

☐ _____

_____

☐ _____

_____

TAKE A LOAD OFF

DAY 22

You are in the park picnicking with your family. A brass band plays patriotic songs. Later, fireworks flower in the night sky. The Fourth of July is a summer celebration when many leave their work, gather with friends, and remember the birth of the nation. Today we read about a summer celebration of the Hebrew nation called the Festival of Harvest.

Leviticus 23:15-21: [15]"From the day after the Sabbath, the day the bundle of grain was lifted up as an offering, count off seven weeks. [16]Keep counting until the day after the seventh Sabbath, fifty days later, and bring an offering of new grain to the LORD. [17]From wherever you live, bring two loaves of bread to be lifted up before the LORD as an offering. These loaves must be baked from three quarts of choice flour that contains yeast. They will be an offering to the LORD from the first of your crops. [18]Along with this bread, present seven one-year-old lambs with no physical defects, one bull, and two rams as burnt offerings to the LORD. These whole burnt offerings, together with the accompanying grain offerings and drink offerings, will be given to the LORD by fire and will be pleasing to him. [19]Then you must offer one male goat as a sin offering and two one-year-old male lambs as a peace offering.

[20]"The priest will lift up these offerings before the LORD, together with the loaves representing the first of your later crops. These offerings are holy to the LORD and will belong to the priests. [21]That same day, you must stop all your regular work and gather for a sacred assembly. This is a permanent law for you, and it must be observed wherever you live."

The Festival of Harvest happened in May or June. It was a day of thanksgiving at the start of the wheat harvest. Families brought sacrifices to thank God for their crops. Notice that verse 21 says, "That same day, you must stop all your regular work and gather for a sacred assembly." While priests sacrificed to obtain forgiveness for sins and to show thanks to God, Israel **stopped working and rested.** God wasn't talking only about physical rest, like sleeping late. God wanted to give his people **spiritual rest.**

God values rest. And he wants you to value rest as well, both physical and spiritual. Learn to take the time for physical rest. And learn how to rest in him.

PRAYER POINT

Pray for God's rest in your life, whether through emotional peace or physical strengthening. Pray for God's rest in the lives of your friends, relatives, and church leaders.

HERE'S WHAT I'M GOING TO DO

☐ _____

☐ _____

☐ _____

☐ _____

☐ _____

Don't Do Anything!

Kick back, relax, take it easy. In today's passage—as in yesterday's—God tells the Israelites, God's holy people, to **rest, enjoy his blessings, and share these gifts with others.**

Day 23

Leviticus 25:1-7, 20-22: [1]While Moses was on Mount Sinai, the LORD said to him, [2]"Give these instructions to the Israelites: When you have entered the land I am giving you as an inheritance, the land itself must observe a Sabbath to the LORD every seventh year. [3]For six years you may plant your fields and prune your vineyards and harvest your crops, [4]but during the seventh year the land will enjoy a Sabbath year of rest to the LORD. Do not plant your crops or prune your vineyards during that entire year. [5]And don't store away the crops that grow naturally or process the grapes that grow on your unpruned vines. The land is to have a year of total rest. [6]But you, your male and female slaves, your hired servants, and any foreigners who live with you may eat the produce that grows naturally during the Sabbath year. [7]And your livestock and the wild animals will also be allowed to eat of the land's bounty.

[20]"But you might ask, 'What will we eat during the seventh year, since we are not allowed to plant or harvest crops that year?' [21]The answer is, 'I will order my blessing for you in the sixth year, so the land will produce a bumper crop, enough to support you for three years. [22]As you plant the seed in the eighth year, you will still be eating the produce of the previous year. In fact, you will eat from the old crop until the new harvest comes in the ninth year.'"

The Sabbath year came every seven years. "Do not plant your crops or prune your vineyards during that entire year," God said (v. 4). The land and field-workers rested. The Year of Jubilee marked the passing of seven Sabbath years—49 years total. The Jubilee year followed the seventh Sabbath year. That meant there were two consecutive rest years.

How would the people eat during that time? God promised his provision, provision enough even for lowly slaves, servants, and foreigners. Verse 21 highlights this promise.

What does all this have to do with us? First, we should **thank God for his provision.** Living in one of the world's richest countries, God has given us much more than we need. Second, like the Israelites in Leviticus, we should rest in the promise that **he will keep providing for us.** Third, **share with others.** Let's love and feed the "slaves, servants, and foreigners" around us at school, in the gym, next door.

When we love people who don't fit in our group or are hard to get along with, we are doing exactly what Jesus did for us. The first Christians came into a faith that started in the Jewish religion. They didn't fit. Today, people of many races and backgrounds believe in Christ. So Paul says in the New Testament that we are "no longer strangers and foreigners" but now we **rest in Christ and his forgiveness,** just like the Israelites who rested in God's provision in Leviticus 25.

HERE'S WHAT I'M GOING TO DO

☐ _____

_____

☐ _____

_____

A LOAN ARRANGER

For two months, Mark was bothered by the knowledge that one of his favorite shirts was missing from his closet. He didn't care who had borrowed it. He wanted it back. *Whoever took it owes me one*, he thought. Today's passage is about **giving** and **returning** in another family—the children of Israel.

Leviticus 25:35-40: [35]"If any of your Israelite relatives fall into poverty and cannot support themselves, support them as you would a resident foreigner and allow them to live with you. [36]Do not demand an advance or charge interest on the money you lend them. Instead, show your fear of God by letting them live with you as your relatives. [37]Remember, do not charge your relatives interest on anything you lend them, whether money or food. [38]I, the LORD, am your God, who brought you out of Egypt to give you the land of Canaan and to be your God.

[39]"If any of your Israelite relatives go bankrupt and sell themselves to you, do not treat them as slaves. [40]Treat them instead as hired servants or as resident foreigners who live with you, and they will serve you only until the Year of Jubilee."

Verse 36 instructs: "Do not demand an advance or charge interest on the money you lend." Interest is the money paid to "buy" a loan. (For example, if you loaned $5 with a penny of interest every day, you would be entitled to $5.07 after a week.) In verse 38, God teaches that he upholds us and provides for us. The duties and possessions we owe each other should be seen from the perspective of the **source of all generosity, God himself.** We owe God our lives. Jesus said we can't serve both God and money (Matthew 6:24). "The rich and the poor have this in common," Solomon said, "the LORD made them both" (Proverbs 22:2). The lowest common denominator matters most to God.

In ancient times as well as today, God chooses people to do special work. But his choosing is not based on wealth or talent. Jesus ministered to corrupt tax collectors and blind beggars. He gave his life for people from all classes. Now **Christ "lends" us his love and purity in his Holy Spirit.** Our response should always be to **reflect that generosity to others**—without regard to their ability to repay that kindness.

HERE'S WHAT I'M GOING TO DO

☐ _____

_____

☐ _____

_____

☐ _____

_____

☐ _____

_____

SET ASIDE

Our topic this week has been **generosity:** God's generosity to us and our willingness to rest in his abundance and to be generous to "slaves, servants, foreigners," and friends. What better way to thank God for his generosity than by giving back to him?

In today's passage, the Israelites learn to **give back to the Lord.**

> Leviticus 27:30-33: [30]"A tenth of the produce of the land, whether grain or fruit, belongs to the LORD and must be set apart to him as holy. [31]If you want to redeem the LORD's tenth of the fruit or grain, you must pay its value, plus 20 percent. [32]The LORD also owns every tenth animal counted off from your herds and flocks. They are set apart to him as holy. [33]The tenth animal must not be selected on the basis of whether it is good or bad, and no substitutions will be allowed. If any exchange is in fact made, then both the original animal and the substituted one will be considered holy and cannot be redeemed."

Verse 30 says: "A tenth of the produce of the land . . . belongs to the LORD and must be set apart to him as holy." The word *tithe*, which we use today to mean a gift to God, is another way to say *tenth*. In the Old Testament, the amount of "a tenth" was often given to a king—whether to the Lord and his priests and Levites or to an Israelite king. In Genesis 14:20, Abram gave the priest Melchizedek—and to God—a tenth of what he captured after rescuing Lot. In Genesis 28:22, after Jacob's vision of an angel-crowded staircase, he promised God a tenth of everything he had. Still later in Israel's history, Samuel the prophet warned Israel that future kings would "take a tenth

of your grain and of your wine" (see
1 Samuel 8).

We should not rob God of what is
rightfully his. **By giving our money or
time to God, we acknowledge him
as our King.**

Since the Creator God owns
everything—as we saw yesterday—we are
not so much doing God a favor by offering
our gifts. Instead, we are **praising him
for his favor to us.**

HERE'S WHAT I'M GOING TO DO

❑ _____

❑ _____

❑ _____

❑ _____

❑ _____

❑ _____

MORE THAN SORRY

I'm sorry." How many times a week do you hear that sentence? People use the phrase to cover a multitude of offenses—anything from "I'm sorry I stepped on your foot" to "I'm sorry I totaled your brand-new Mercedes." But what does it mean to be **sorry?**

As you might guess, the Bible has a lot to say about **how we should respond when we wrong others.** As the Israelites camped in the wilderness after their exodus from Egypt, God gave them specific instructions as to what they should do after committing an offense against another person.

Numbers 5:5-10: ⁵Then the LORD said to Moses, ⁶"Give these instructions to the people of Israel: If any of the people—men or women—betray the LORD by doing wrong to another person, they are guilty. ⁷They must confess their sin and make full restitution for what they have done, adding a penalty of 20 percent and returning it to the person who was wronged. ⁸But if the person who was wronged is dead, and there are no near relatives to whom restitution can be made, it belongs to the LORD and must be given to the priest, along with a ram for atonement. ⁹All the sacred gifts that the Israelites bring to a priest will belong to him. ¹⁰Each priest may keep the sacred donations that he receives."

In God's system, "I'm sorry" just isn't good enough. When we sin against another person, our first responsibility is to **confess the sin** and **ask for forgiveness.** Our second responsibility is to **make full restitution** or repayment to that person. Suddenly "I'm sorry I ruined your basketball shoes" becomes "Here is the $120 I owe you for a new pair of sneakers."

This principle especially holds true when the wronged people are the poor and needy of our society. Think of the many ways in which the less fortunate are taken advantage of or exploited. When we hear of such exploitation, we may feel twinges of guilt—especially if we've knowingly or unknowingly been involved. But guess what? Guilt is not enough. **We need to make good on our apologies in tangible, measurable ways.**

PRAYER POINT

Ask God to help you recall people who deserve to be paid back for wrongs you've done them. Then ask him for the courage and wisdom to make the situation right.

HERE'S WHAT I'M GOING TO DO

☐ _____

_____

☐ _____

_____

☐ _____

_____

☐ _____

_____

☐ _____

_____

NEED OR WANT?

"Mom, there's nothing to eat!"

The young woman, puzzled by her nine-year-old's statement, walked into the kitchen and opened the refrigerator. Sliding open the cooler drawer, she saw several fresh apples and oranges, a bag of carrot sticks, and strawberries. Looking in the pantry, she found crackers and fruit bars. "What do you mean?" she replied to her daughter. "We have plenty of food!" The girl wandered into the kitchen and made a face. "Not that kind of food!" she whined. "I mean cookies or potato chips!"

When the Israelites left Egypt for the desert wilderness, they needed food to sustain them. **God took care of his people** by sending manna, food from heaven, for them to eat. Every day God sent manna to the Israelites. One day, however, the Israelites decided that they also wanted meat and vegetables in their diet. This request was met by anger from God.

Numbers 11:4-10: [4]Then the foreign rabble who were traveling with the Israelites began to crave the good things of Egypt, and the people of Israel also began to complain. "Oh, for some meat!" they exclaimed. [5]"We remember all the fish we used to eat for free in Egypt. And we had all the cucumbers, melons, leeks, onions, and garlic that we wanted. [6]But now our appetites are gone, and day after day we have nothing to eat but this manna!"

[7]The manna looked like small coriander seeds, pale yellow in color.[1] [8]The people gathered it from the ground and made flour by grinding it with hand mills or pounding it in mortars. Then they boiled it in a pot and made it into flat cakes. These cakes tasted like they had been cooked in olive oil. [9]The manna came down on the camp with the dew during the night.

[1] **11:7** Hebrew *the color of gum resin.*

¹⁰Moses heard all the families standing in front of their tents weeping, and the LORD became extremely angry. Moses was also very aggravated.

The Israelites **confused their needs with their wants.** They needed God and his provision; they wanted more. Mistaking needs for wants is a common problem. In fact, need is one of the most misused words in the English language. "I need a Big Mac." "I need some new clothes." "I need a better stereo system for my car."

Perhaps the best way to tell the difference between a **need** and a **want** is to ask, "What will happen if I don't get it?" Let's use the statement "I need a new jacket" as an example. One person may say, "If I don't get the jacket, I won't look good for my date Friday night." In that case, the jacket is a want. Another person may say, "If I don't get the jacket, I may freeze to death on the street tonight." In that case, the jacket is a need.

The question we must ask ourselves is this: Once our needs are met, should we be more interested in **taking care of our wants or helping others meet their needs?**

PRAYER POINT

Ask God to help you distinguish between your wants and needs, to help you recognize the needs of others, and to help you make some decisions as to what is important to you.

HERE'S WHAT I'M GOING TO DO

☐ _____

☐ _____

Wanting It All

If he were a real person, Montgomery Burns would certainly be the **greediest** person alive. Mr. Burns is Homer Simpson's boss on the animated TV show *The Simpsons*. As the owner of a nuclear power plant, Burns is the wealthiest man in the city of Springfield. Yet, despite his riches, he spends most of his time trying to devise new ways to attain more wealth. He once constructed a device to block out the sun from Springfield so that people would be forced to use more power generated by his plant. Now that's greedy!

The book of Numbers gives us another example of **greed and ambition** run amok. And though it may be less extreme than Mr. Burns' man-made eclipse, it is decidedly more real.

Numbers 16:1-7: ¹"One day Korah son of Izhar, a descendant of Kohath son of Levi, conspired with Dathan and Abiram, the sons of Eliab, and On son of Peleth, from the tribe of Reuben. ²They incited a rebellion against Moses, involving 250 other prominent leaders, all members of the assembly. ³They went to Moses and Aaron and said, "You have gone too far! Everyone in Israel has been set apart by the LORD, and he is with all of us. What right do you have to act as though you are greater than anyone else among all these people of the LORD?"

⁴When Moses heard what they were saying, he threw himself down with his face to the ground. ⁵Then he said to Korah and his followers, "Tomorrow morning the LORD will show us who belongs to him and who is holy. The LORD will allow those who are chosen to enter his holy presence. ⁶You, Korah, and all your followers must do this: Take incense burners, ⁷and burn incense in them tomorrow before the LORD. Then we will see whom the LORD chooses as his holy one. You Levites are the ones who have gone too far!"

Korah was what you might call an ambitious self-starter. Not content with his duties at the tabernacle, he wanted to become a full-fledged priest. Korah was so intent on achieving his goal that he challenged Moses, God's chosen leader for the Israelites. And that's where Korah's ambition and greed got him into trouble.

He and his followers were killed when the earth split open and swallowed them.

So is it wrong to be ambitious? Should those of us who have goals we're trying to achieve keep one eye on the ground to watch for cracks that might open up? No, but we should **constantly assess our ambitions to make sure that they're not motivated by greed.** If we're willing to use, exploit, or damage others in our quest to "get ahead," it's time to **reexamine our goals and motivations.**

HERE'S WHAT I'M GOING TO DO

☐ _____

_____

☐ _____

_____

☐ _____

_____

☐ _____

_____

LAND RUSH

The motion picture *The Field* tells the story of Bull McCabe, a man whose family has farmed a rented field for generations. When the land is suddenly put on the market, McCabe expects to purchase it without difficulty. But to his shock, McCabe is outbid by a rich American. He and his son try to persuade the American to give up the land but end up murdering him when he refuses their offer. The body is soon found, and the gruesome discovery destroys McCabe and his family.

Balak, the king of Moab, was determined to hold onto the land he thought was his. But he was so scared of the Israelites that he hired a sorcerer named Balaam to put a curse on Israel. What Balak didn't count on was God's interference. God refused to allow Balaam to curse Israel. Every time he tried, the curse came out as a blessing. The following passage is Balaam's curse/blessing describing what the Israelites could expect when they settled in the Promised Land.

Numbers 24:5-7: 5"How beautiful are your tents, O Jacob;
how lovely are your homes, O Israel!
6They spread before me like groves of palms,
like fruitful gardens by the riverside.
They are like aloes planted by the LORD,
like cedars beside the waters.
7Water will gush out in buckets;
their offspring are supplied with all they need.
Their king will be greater than Agag;
their kingdom will be exalted."

According to Balaam, the Israelites were looking at a prosperous life in the Promised Land. All they had to do was remain faithful to God. That is not to say that being faithful to

God guarantees material wealth. It doesn't. (Ask any pastor or professional youth worker.) Large investment portfolios, expensive cars, and vacation houses are not necessarily indicators of **spiritual blessing.**

God is the source of all blessings, and yes, there are faithful Christian men and women who are both godly and wealthy. But the important blessings God bestows on his people are spiritual. Our rewards and treasures are **waiting for us in heaven.**

We must remain faithful to God not for the material benefits we will reap, but for the **eternal rewards** that wait for us.

HERE'S WHAT I'M GOING TO DO

☐ _____

☐ _____

☐ _____

☐ _____

☐ _____

Immigration Laws

One of the darker sides to the United States' involvement in World War II was the confinement of thousands of Japanese Americans living on the West Coast. Known as the *Nisei*, these citizens were rounded up and placed in camps for the duration of the war. Their only crime, in most cases, was that they had Japanese ancestry. Only recently has their unfair treatment been redressed.

God wanted to prevent Israel from creating similar injustices. He clearly stated **how his people should treat foreigners.**

Deuteronomy 1:14-18: [14]"You agreed that my plan was a good one. [15]So I took the wise and respected men you had selected from your tribes and appointed them to serve as judges and officials over you. Some were responsible for a thousand people, some for a hundred, some for fifty, and some for ten. [16]I instructed the judges, 'You must be perfectly fair at all times, not only to fellow Israelites, but also to the foreigners living among you. [17]When you make decisions, never favor those who are rich; be fair to lowly and great alike. Don't be afraid of how they will react, for you are judging in the place of God. Bring me any cases that are too difficult for you, and I will handle them.' [18]And at that time I gave you instructions about everything you were to do."

Xenophobia is the fear or mistrust of foreigners. **Racial jokes and stereotypes** are just two of the ways xenophobia is exhibited. In extreme circumstances, xenophobia can result in so-called "hate crimes."

God weighed in on the topic when he urged Hebrew judges to rule fairly in cases involving foreigners. Jesus' solution to the problem of xenophobia is as simple in its wording as it is difficult in its execution: **"Love your**

enemies" (Luke 6:27).

Some of the neediest and most oppressed people in our society today are foreigners. Squalid living conditions, extreme poverty, unsafe neighborhoods, and limited English skills are just a few of the obstacles faced by strangers in our land.

Of course, these same obstacles may deter you from making an effort to show the love Jesus spoke of in Luke 6 to foreign families in your community. They shouldn't. There is a great deal of satisfaction and mutual benefit to be found in **forming relationships with people of other cultures.** Do not allow yourself to miss out on these opportunities.

PRAYER POINT

If you struggle at all with xenophobia, ask God to create in you a spirit of love for the foreigners with whom you come in contact every day.

HERE'S WHAT I'M GOING TO DO

☐ _____

_____

☐ _____

_____

_____

A DOWNSIDE OF PROSPERITY

DAY 31

Born around 600 B.C., Aesop loved to tell clever stories. These stories are known today as Aesop's fables. The fable titled "The Dog and His Reflection" has a good lesson to teach about **prosperity.** It seems that a dog was given a bone. While on his way home, he had to cross a bridge. On crossing, he looked down in the water and noticed what he thought was another dog with a bigger bone. This made him unhappy. It wasn't enough to just have a bone. He wanted a bigger bone. So he opened his mouth to get the bigger bone and lost the one he had. He became greedy. The same thing happens with people. But the worst consequence of greediness is that it causes us to forget God.

Today's passage is a warning to God's people **not to forget him during the times of blessing.**

Deuteronomy 6:10-12: ¹⁰"The LORD your God will soon bring you into the land he swore to give your ancestors Abraham, Isaac, and Jacob. It is a land filled with large, prosperous cities that you did not build. ¹¹The houses will be richly stocked with goods you did not produce. You will draw water from cisterns you did not dig, and you will eat from vineyards and olive trees you did not plant. When you have eaten your fill in this land, ¹²be careful not to forget the LORD, who rescued you from slavery in the land of Egypt."

In these verses, God promised his people many things: a good land, richly stocked houses, and plenty of food and water. But he warned them in verse 12, "Be careful not to forget the LORD." God knew the human tendency to focus on blessings rather than on the One who sends them. Isn't it interesting that human nature is such that the **more we have the more we want?** And the more we get from God the more we forget him? When do you pray the most? When things are going well or when you are in a difficult situation? The answer is probably when you are struggling. Most people act this way. That

may be one reason that **God allows hard things to come into our lives.** He knows **they will draw us closer to him.** Proverbs 30:8-9 states, "Give me neither poverty nor riches! Give me just enough to satisfy my needs! For if I grow rich, I may deny you and say, 'Who is the LORD?' " How about you? Do you forget the Lord in the good times?

HERE'S WHAT I'M GOING TO DO

☐ _____

_____

☐ _____

_____

☐ _____

_____

☐ _____

_____

_____

Just Because

DAY

32

Promises. We hear them all the time. Our friends say, "I promise I won't tell anyone." "I promise I'll pick you up at 8:00." "I promise I'll take you to the junior prom." Parents say things like "I'll be at your play rehearsal tonight" or "I'll come watch your game on Friday." But **sometimes promises are broken,** and someone usually gets hurt in the process. Broken promises are unavoidable in a world of broken people. But **there is one person who will always deliver what he promises.** And that person is God.

In today's passage, **God makes a promise to his people.** Read to discover what this promise is.

Deuteronomy 7:7-12: ⁷"The LORD did not choose you and lavish his love on you because you were larger or greater than other nations, for you were the smallest of all nations! ⁸It was simply because the LORD loves you, and because he was keeping the oath he had sworn to your ancestors. That is why the LORD rescued you with such amazing power from your slavery under Pharaoh in Egypt. ⁹Understand, therefore, that the LORD your God is indeed God. He is the faithful God who keeps his covenant for a thousand generations and constantly loves those who love him and obey his commands. ¹⁰But he does not hesitate to punish and destroy those who hate him. ¹¹Therefore, obey all these commands, laws, and regulations I am giving you today.

¹²"If you listen to these regulations and obey them faithfully, the LORD your God will keep his covenant of unfailing love with you, as he solemnly promised your ancestors."

In these verses, **God promises to care for his people.** He shows his care by delivering them from their slavery in Egypt. How has God shown his care for you? By answering a prayer with a "yes"? By sending along a friend when you needed one? By providing extra money for you to be able to do something that you thought was impossible? God has many ways of providing for us. But if you think about it, the way that **God provides for us most of the time is through other people.** Perhaps God would like to use you to be an answer to someone else's prayer. By helping others, you can reflect the **faithful** and **caring** nature of a loving God.

PRAYER POINT

Recall three incidents in the past week where God's faithfulness was evident to you. Then say a prayer of thanksgiving for his compassion, especially during times when you did not anticipate it.

HERE'S WHAT I'M GOING TO DO

☐ _____

_____

☐ _____

_____

☐ _____

_____

☐ _____

_____

☐ _____

_____

Ravenous

Arnold Schwarzenegger was once asked why he was so successful in his career and how he stayed in such great physical shape. He replied, "I stay hungry." The dictionary defines hunger as "a strong desire or craving." Schwarzenegger defined his hunger as **being eager** for new challenges in his work and in his life. Everybody hungers for something. What do you hunger for? Attention? Friends? Good grades? A special relationship?

Today's passage is also about being hungry. But the hunger God speaks of is **a craving that everyone should have.**

> Deuteronomy 8:1-3: ¹"Be careful to obey all the commands I am giving you today. Then you will live and multiply, and you will enter and occupy the land the LORD swore to give your ancestors. ²Remember how the LORD your God led you through the wilderness for forty years, humbling you and testing you to prove your character, and to find out whether or not you would really obey his commands. ³Yes, he humbled you by letting you go hungry and then feeding you with manna, a food previously unknown to you and your ancestors. He did it to teach you that people need more than bread for their life; real life comes by feeding on every word of the LORD."

These verses tell how God allowed his people to go hungry in the wilderness and then how he met their need for food. But more important, the passage shows how he used their hunger to teach them an eternal lesson: They had a hunger even greater than the hunger for food, **a hunger for God,** which is present in every person. Verse 3 reads "People need more than bread for their life; real life comes by feeding on every word of the LORD."

Sometimes being well fed and having plenty can cause people to ignore **the spiritual hunger.** As a result, they may tend to hunger after things such as wealth, position, and successful careers rather than hungering after God. If when you looked in the mirror tomorrow morning you could see your spirit instead of your physical body, how would it look? Would it be well fed and healthy? **Reading God's Word, fellowshipping with other Christians,** and **sharing God's love** with others are all ways to keep your spirit growing and healthy. What are you doing to **feed your spirit?**

PRAYER POINT

Seek to take God's Word into your soul today through careful study and prayerful thought. Pray that his words will nourish you and cause you to grow.

HERE'S WHAT I'M GOING TO DO

☐ _____

☐ _____

☐ _____

☐ _____

☐ _____

☐ _____

OUT OF THE CHEST

Did you ever read the fable about the mouse in the chest? It seems that a mouse had lived its entire life quite contentedly in an old chest. Then one day the lid of the chest was left open. And the mouse, while playing along the rim, fell out. At first the mouse was scared because it could not get back into the chest. But when the mouse noticed bits of food on the floor, it discovered that there was life outside of the chest as well. Some of us, like the mouse, have a very limited idea of what the world is like. We have been living inside our "chests"—our comfort zones—too long.

In today's verses, God challenges us to **step out of our comfort zones** into the bigger world that needs his love.

Deuteronomy 10:17-19: ¹⁷"The LORD your God is the God of gods and LORD of lords. He is the great God, mighty and awesome, who shows no partiality and takes no bribes. ¹⁸He gives justice to orphans and widows. He shows love to the foreigners living among you and gives them food and clothing. ¹⁹You, too, must show love to foreigners, for you yourselves were once foreigners in the land of Egypt."

Verse 18 says, "He [God] shows love to the foreigners . . . and gives them food and clothing." But you might ask, "Who are the foreigners?" Foreigners can be people who live in other countries and people who live next door to you. They are people who look, think, talk, act, and have beliefs different from you. Christians are called to **imitate** God's nature by showing love to foreigners as well.

Sometimes we are afraid to reach out to those who are different from us because we don't understand their customs, language, or beliefs. But **underneath the differences, we have many similarities.** And who knows, you may be a foreigner some day in need of a helping hand as well.

Stepping out of your comfort zone could mean having dinner with a family that has few friends in your community. It may involve volunteering your time to help them with language skills. Or it could mean simply being a friend at school or at work. **Every act of kindness matters** to someone who stands outside looking in.

PRAYER POINT

Pray that God will help you step out of your comfort zone by giving you a greater awareness of people who are different from you.

HERE'S WHAT I'M GOING TO DO

☐ _____

_____

☐ _____

_____

☐ _____

_____

☐ _____

_____

☐ _____

_____

☐ _____

_____

☐ _____

_____

DO THIS FIRST

Have you ever gotten a package in the mail with PRIORITY marked on it? That red, white, and blue sticker seems to shout, "Open first. Something important is in this package. Don't delay!" If you could sort how you spend your time, money, and talents into slots like the post office sorts packages, what would go into your **PRIORITY** bin?

Yesterday you learned that God wants one of our priorities to be showing love to foreigners. Today's passage is about another priority.

Deuteronomy 14:22-29: ²²"You must set aside a tithe of your crops—one-tenth of all the crops you harvest each year. ²³Bring this tithe to the place the LORD your God chooses for his name to be honored, and eat it there in his presence. This applies to your tithes of grain, new wine, olive oil, and the firstborn males of your flocks and herds. The purpose of tithing is to teach you always to fear the LORD your God. ²⁴Now the place the LORD your God chooses for his name to be honored might be a long way from your home. ²⁵If so, you may sell the tithe portion of your crops and herds and take the money to the place the LORD your God chooses. ²⁶When you arrive, use the money to buy anything you want—an ox, a sheep, some wine, or beer. Then feast there in the presence of the LORD your God and celebrate with your household. ²⁷And do not forget the Levites in your community, for they have no inheritance as you do.

²⁸"At the end of every third year bring the tithe of all your crops and store it in the nearest town. ²⁹Give it to the Levites, who have no inheritance among you, as well as to the foreigners living among you, the orphans, and the widows in your towns, so they can eat and be satisfied. Then the LORD your God will bless you in all your work."

These verses teach us about **tithing.** First we learn that there are two types of tithing. **One tithe goes to God** (v. 23) and **a second goes to help the community,** especially the Levites—the priests and religious officials of Israel (vv. 28-29).

How seriously should we take tithing today? Do the laws given to a people three thousand years ago have anything to say to us today?

In the New Testament, we don't see any specific commands about tithing. That does not mean, however, that we are left with no guidelines for giving. Rather, we are encouraged to **give freely and generously to help other people and the work of the church.** Keep in mind Paul's advice to the Corinthians: "Don't give reluctantly or in response to pressure. For God loves the person who gives cheerfully" (2 Corinthians 9:7).

If you really want to know **how much of a priority God is in your life,** take a look at your giving. How you distribute your time, talents, money, and material goods is a clear indicator of **what your priorities really are.** You might say that God is first in your life, but **do your actions show it?**

HERE'S WHAT I'M GOING TO DO

☐ _____

_____

☐ _____

_____

_____

GODLY GENEROSITY

There are **a lot of excuses for not helping poor people.** How many have you heard yourself make?

- Somebody else will help them.
- I have to take care of my own needs first.
- It's their own fault that they're poor.
- I really don't have enough money to help anyway.
- I have too many other responsibilities to take care of.
- They need to take care of themselves.

Can you think of any others? Keep them in mind as you read this passage.

Deuteronomy 15:7-11: 7"But if there are any poor people in your towns when you arrive in the land the LORD your God is giving you, do not be hard-hearted or tightfisted toward them. 8Instead, be generous and lend them whatever they need. 9Do not be mean-spirited and refuse someone a loan because the year of release is close at hand. If you refuse to make the loan and the needy person cries out to the LORD, you will be considered guilty of sin. 10Give freely without begrudging it, and the LORD your God will bless you in everything you do. 11There will always be some among you who are poor. That is why I am commanding you to share your resources freely with the poor and with other Israelites in need."

In this short passage, God demolishes virtually every excuse that you could come up with for not helping the poor. The Israelites were preparing to enter the land God had promised them—the land they had been forced to wait forty years for because of their disobedience. Would they dare disobey God now?

He tells them that if they found any poor people living in the towns of their new land—the land God was giving them—they were to **generously lend them whatever they**

needed. They were not to be "hard-hearted," "tightfisted," or "mean-spirited." If they refused to loan a needy person what he or she needed, they would "be considered guilty of sin." There's no excuse! The principle stands out clearly: **"Give freely without begrudging it,** and the LORD your God will bless you in everything you do" (v. 10).

Note, however, that God first speaks of loans, then of gifts. The people of God were to be free with loaning their money and materials to help the poor get on their feet. Loans, by definition, are intended to be repaid. And that was the goal of helping the poor: to help them get established so they could repay their loans and prosper.

But then God moves to gifts. Gifts are free, with no strings attached. **Be free with your giving.** Don't expect repayment—**God will repay you with blessings** beyond what money can buy.

HERE'S WHAT I'M GOING TO DO

❑ _____

❑ _____

❑ _____

KEEPING YOUR PROMISE

DAY

37

He stood with a dozen or so of his fellow students at the altar. The hymn had challenged him to go out into the world and take the love of Christ to those who desperately needed it. Together, **they vowed to obey God's command** to "go." He felt excited yet burdened. It was good to stand with his friends and **make this commitment** before God.

Of course, he felt a little guilty too—this was the third time this year he'd gone forward to make the same promise to God. This time, he hoped, he'd have the strength and desire to follow through with it. This time would be different.

When it comes to making promises, what does God think of an attitude like that?

Deuteronomy 23:21-23: [21]"When you make a vow to the LORD your God, be prompt in doing whatever you promised him. For the LORD your God demands that you promptly fulfill all your vows. If you don't, you will be guilty of sin. [22]However, it is not a sin to refrain from making a vow. [23]But once you have voluntarily made a vow, be careful to do as you have said, for you have made a vow to the LORD your God."

God's Word doesn't beat around the bush when it comes to making vows or promises to him. Not only are we to **follow through,** but we're to do so **"promptly."** Vows are serious business. Making a vow or promise is a way of **recognizing God's truth** and **obeying God's will.** It involves mind, heart, and will. It involves standing before the God of the universe. That's why **vows aren't to be made lightly.**

The Scripture goes on to say, "It is not a sin to refrain from making a vow." In other words, it's better not to make one at all than to make one and not keep it. That's not to say, of course, that God won't forgive you if you make a vow in haste or are unable to follow through. But it is to say that **vows are important to God,** and he expects us to do all we can to keep them. Because we're only **as good as our word.**

What vows have you made? Have you promised to follow Christ? Have you promised to be sensitive to the needs of the poor? Have you promised to be open to God's leading in your life? Have you promised to be a witness for him?

God's calling on your life is precious. Handle it with **care** and **commitment.**

HERE'S WHAT I'M GOING TO DO

☐ _____

_____

☐ _____

_____

☐ _____

_____

LOVE THY NEIGHBOR

DAY 38

Who are your neighbors? Certainly, the **people who live in houses or apartments near yours** are your neighbors. But do you really know them? Do you know what kind of people they are? Do you know the struggles they face? Do you know how well off they are or how much they struggle to pay their bills? Or do you really not know your neighbors very well at all?

God's Word consistently encourages us **to love and care for our neighbors.** And today's reading emphasizes how we are to treat our neighbors who are poor.

Deuteronomy 24:10-15: [10]"If you lend anything to your neighbor, do not enter your neighbor's house to claim the security. [11]Stand outside and the owner will bring it out to you. [12]If your neighbor is poor and has only a cloak to give as security, do not keep the cloak overnight. [13]Return the cloak to its owner by sunset so your neighbor can sleep in it and bless you. And the LORD your God will count it as a righteous act.

[14]"Never take advantage of poor laborers, whether fellow Israelites or foreigners living in your towns. [15]Pay them their wages each day before sunset because they are poor and are counting on it. Otherwise they might cry out to the LORD against you, and it would be counted against you as sin."

God must know us pretty well. He keeps repeating the same commands throughout the Scripture. It's as though he knows we have to keep hearing the same challenging truths time and again for them to sink into our hearts and work out into our lives.

In this passage, God again encourages us to **treat our poor neighbors fairly and compassionately.** We are to give and lend freely to our neighbors—and if they're poor, we're not to press for repayment or inconvenience them by taking something they need as a security for a loan. We're supposed to trust God to repay us.

God demands justice for all, especially the poor who receive justice so rarely. Poor people are often taken advantage of. Many are considered lazy or stupid when they are actually victims of oppression. For instance, usually a poor person can only get credit or loans from shyster firms that extract huge amounts of interest. As a result, they end up in an even worse financial condition.

PRAYER POINT

Pray for your neighbors in need today—those who live near you and those who live around the world. Ask God to provide for their needs and to use you in whatever way he can to do so.

God calls us to a higher standard. He challenges us to **do all we can** to help the truly needy. We aren't to demand a profit from them or insist they repay loans quickly. God's laws encourage the poor to improve their place in life. And if they're unable to do so, we are to treat them **compassionately.**

The poor are closer to you than you may think. Perhaps even some of your neighbors are struggling to keep their heads above the financial waters. **Be open and ready to help** in any way you can.

HERE'S WHAT I'M GOING TO DO

☐ _____

_____

☐ _____

_____

A Hunger to Help

DAY 39

Have you ever felt really hungry? Not the time your mom delayed dinner an hour or so. Not the time you were too busy to eat lunch.

Have you ever known **what it feels like not to eat for days at a time?** To search through stinking restaurant dumpsters trying to find edible scraps of food? To stand in line at a food kitchen only to learn the soup had run out and nothing was left to eat? Probably not.

But as you read this passage today, try to put yourself in the place of someone who really is **hungry.**

Deuteronomy 26:10-15: [10]"And now, O LORD, I have brought you a token of the first crops you have given me from the ground." Then place the produce before the LORD your God and worship him. [11]Afterward go and celebrate because of all the good things the LORD your God has given to you and your household. Remember to include the Levites and the foreigners living among you in the celebration.

[12]"Every third year you must offer a special tithe of your crops. You must give these tithes to the Levites, foreigners, orphans, and widows so that they will have enough to eat in your towns. [13]Then you must declare in the presence of the LORD your God, 'I have taken the sacred gift from my house and have given it to the Levites, foreigners, orphans, and widows, just as you commanded me. I have not violated or forgotten any of your commands. [14]I have not eaten any of it while in mourning; I have not touched it while I was ceremonially unclean; and I have not offered any of it to the dead. I have obeyed the LORD my God and have done everything you commanded me. [15]Look down from your holy dwelling place in heaven and bless your people Israel and the land you have given us—a land flowing with milk and honey—just as you solemnly promised our ancestors.' "

God set up an entire system of offerings and feasts for the

Israelites to observe so they might better understand who he was, who they were, and how he intended them to live in this world.

As part of this system, they were to bring part of their first crops of the season, place them before the Lord God, and worship him.

Then, as a way of thanking God, they were to have a party—not only with their friends and families, but with the Levites (the religious leaders) and foreigners who weren't even Jewish. Not only that, but every third year they were to give a special offering of crops. This bonus gift was to help the town's Levites, foreigners, orphans, and widows to make sure they had enough to eat. The principle behind these offerings is clear: God's people are to **keep the poor and needy in mind** and help **provide food for them on a consistent basis.**

PRAYER POINT

Learn about some of the various soup kitchens, homeless ministries, and other programs that help feed the poor in your community. Then pray for them, their leaders, and their volunteers—today and regularly—that God would bless and use them—and you—to meet this desperate need.

Do you know of programs and ministries in your town that help feed the poor? If they're like most such ministries, they operate "hand to mouth." In other words, whatever food or monetary gifts they take in are used immediately to help those who are in need.

You can reach out to the needy through programs like **World Vision's 30 Hour Famine.** Turn to the back of your book to read about the Famine and World Vision's ministry.

HERE'S WHAT I'M GOING TO DO

☐ _____

_____

THE BEST GIFTS ARE USED

At Christmastime or on your birthday, what are your **favorite kinds of gifts?** You may receive some gifts from people who don't really know you. They may even spend a lot of money on your gift, but if it isn't your size or doesn't fit your needs or reflect your interests, it isn't worth very much to you, is it?

On the other hand, a gift from someone who **knows you** and **loves you** is gratefully received. It may even be inexpensive, but you know you will enjoy it because you know you will use it. It fits you . . . in more ways than one.

Deuteronomy 33:13-16: [13]Moses said this about the tribes of Joseph:

"May their land be blessed by the LORD
with the choice gift of rain from the heavens,
and water from beneath the earth;
[14]with the riches that grow in the sun,
and the bounty produced each month;
[15]with the finest crops of the ancient mountains,
and the abundance from the everlasting hills;
[16]with the best gifts of the earth and its fullness,
and the favor of the one who appeared in the burning bush.
May these blessings rest on Joseph's head,
crowning the brow of the prince among his brothers."

God is a gift-giver beyond compare. He knows exactly who you are, what you need, and what you can use. For instance, in today's passage you read about the gift of God's blessings for each tribe of Israel, which he makes through Moses, their leader, who now faces the end of his days as they prepare to enter the Promised Land. Moses acknowledges the amazing work of God in their midst, then goes through each of the twelve tribes, offering a blessing in God's name—long life to one, strength against their enemies for another, safety for a third, and so on. God knew each tribe intimately, and he knew how best to **bless them.** He knew exactly what to give them.

God gives **different people different gifts.** He has given you certain gifts, talents, and abilities to use for his glory. Some people may not have discovered their gifts yet. God desires that all of his children discover and use their gifts.

After all, the best gifts are **those that are used.** And you can tell that a gift is gratefully received when it is wisely used. When God looks at your life, does he see a grateful heart? Does he delight in seeing the gifts he has lavished on you put to work in loving service in his name? That's his desire. So **open your gift from him today,** and **put it to good use.**

HERE'S WHAT I'M GOING TO DO

☐ _____

_____

☐ _____

_____

BEYOND THE COMFORT ZONE

Steven Curtis Chapman

I have always wanted to move beyond the comfort zone in which I have been so fortunate to live. I can get very comfortable in my world. So I've always had the desire to force myself outside and get involved in the lives of those who are much less fortunate.

So here I sit in Honduras, definitely having had my life changed in many ways in just the few hours that I have been here. It's a process, of course—a process that needs to continue after I return home. As I walked through this community, however, the one truth that continued to emerge was that Jesus is here. Actually, that was my prayer as I traveled to meet the children that my family and I are

sponsoring. I wanted to find Jesus here, and looking in the eyes of the children, I wanted to be assured that I am responding to the call of my Savior. The Lord has met me here; he has broken my heart and encouraged me.

One of my first thoughts was that these people really have a sense of peace and a sense of family. They have so much that I need to learn. I need to glean from them and from their culture. So it wasn't a sense of my coming and saying, "These poor, pitiful people are missing out in life." It's more like realizing that they have so much to teach me. After all, these children and their families are fighting for survival, yet they have hope because people have reached out and ministered to them.

I also was encouraged by seeing how so many of the desperate needs are being met by Christian relief organizations. These organizations teach people how to raise the food they need year-round and how to purify their drinking water.

Education stands as another big need of the families and the children whom I help to sponsor. Most of the parents said that they hoped and dreamed that their children would be able to continue their education.

One of the neatest experiences of this trip was meeting a nurse at a clinic. She was a native of the community and had been trained by World Vision. She actually works in seven communities in the area. Looking into the eyes of Luis, Luz, and my other sponsored children, I saw nurses 15 to 20 years from now, or leaders who will rise up and help their own people.

I thank God for the opportunity to help these children. Organizations like World Vision help my arms reach beyond my home and community to make a difference in the world. They help me reach beyond my comfort zone.

Lord, make me an instrument of thy peace:

Where there is hatred, let me sow love;

Where there is injury, pardon;

Where there is doubt, faith;

Where there is despair, hope;

Where there is darkness, light;

Where there is sadness, joy.

O Divine Master, grant that I may not so

much seek to be consoled as to console,

To be understood as to understand,

To be loved as to love;

For it is in giving that we receive;

It is in pardoning that we are pardoned;

It is in dying that we are born to eternal life!

St. Francis of Assisi

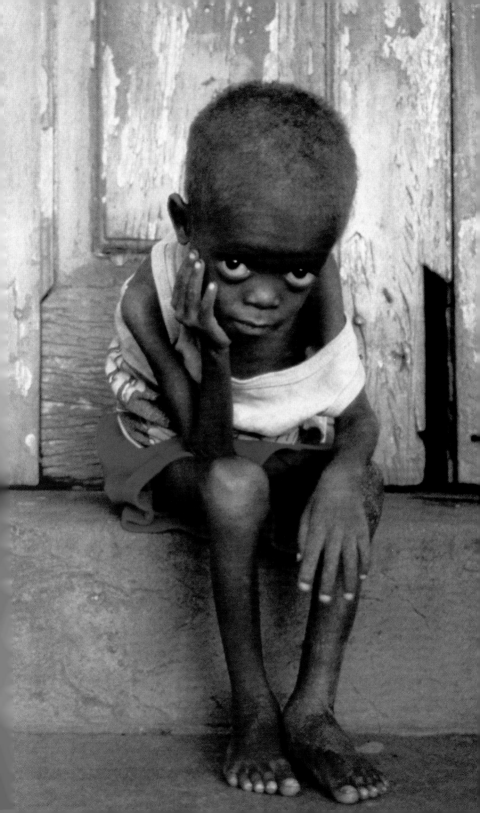

A Chosen Generation!

Torey Parm, 16, is a senior at Reynoldsburg High School in Reynoldsburg, Ohio. He enjoys American history, loves football, and is partial to chicken over other noshes. And Alex Haley's Roots *is his favorite read. Torey was one of World Vision's 30 Hour Famine Study Tour participants in 1996, experiencing rural life in Ethiopia. His heart is for young people, and he hopes to become an American history teacher and football coach. Actually, he's already coaching young people, but for a much greater goal than a touchdown.*

I think young people are getting stronger, and if there's going to be a stirring and explosion in the church in the United States, it will come through the youth first and then spread throughout the whole church.

As a teenager, God definitely wants you to be a champion. Many teenagers were called out in the Bible and asked to step up and do things because older people wouldn't or couldn't. We have strength, and that's why we're definitely needed.

You need to always remember that you have a Father in heaven who loves you very much and loves to see you do great things, to do anything you can possibly imagine that he would want for you. For example, the biggest story in my life is the 30 Hour Famine. I never thought I would have the chance to go to Africa. But I did, and just by the grace of God.

In my church, we recently had our Youth Vision Sunday. It's stirring up our church. You feel it every Sunday. Just more and more of God every week. I mean, we just had an explosion in our city, an outreach at a Dairy Queen, and that's got our whole church stirring. We're in a 21-day prayer vigil, and three of the events we're praying for are youth events. There are about 50 youth in our church of about 400 people. And they're all involved in the programs.

Remember, the sky's the limit. Reach for your goals because, through Christ, you can do anything.

SHAME ON YOU

"Shame on you!" That phrase sends a chill down the spine of the guilty.

"Shame on you" reminds the offender that he or she should **feel bad about the offense,** guilty as charged. Certainly shame can serve a useful purpose, **motivating the person to change** his or her ways. But shame and guilt can also weigh us down, as though we trudge slowly under a heavy burden.

The people of Israel were not strangers to shame and guilt. For centuries they had carried this suffocating weight. But now, after four hundred years of slavery and forty years of wandering in the desert, God was about to lift the load from their backs.

Joshua 5:2-9: ²At that time the LORD told Joshua, "Use knives of flint to make the Israelites a circumcised people again." ³So Joshua made flint knives and circumcised the entire male population of Israel at Gibeath-haaraloth.¹

⁴Joshua had to circumcise them because all the men who were old enough to bear arms when they left Egypt had died in the wilderness. ⁵Those who left Egypt had all been circumcised, but none of those born after the Exodus, during the years in the wilderness, had been circumcised. ⁶The Israelites wandered in the wilderness for forty years until all the men who were old enough to bear arms when they left Egypt had died. For they had disobeyed the LORD, and the LORD vowed he would not let them enter the land he had sworn to give us—a land flowing with milk and honey. ⁷So Joshua circumcised their sons who had not been circumcised on the way to the Promised Land—those who had grown up to take their fathers' places. ⁸After all the males had been circumcised, they rested in the camp until

---

¹ 5:3 *Gibeath-haaraloth* means "hill of foreskins."
² 5:9 *Gilgal* sounds like the Hebrew word *galal*, meaning "to roll."

they were healed.

⁹Then the LORD said to Joshua. "Today I have rolled away the shame of your slavery in Egypt." So that place has been called Gilgal[2] to this day.

Circumcision was a sign of God's covenant relationship with Israel. And on that day—when Israel's men became circumcised—God sent a clear message to his people: "I am **removing the shame of your past** and **renewing my relationship** with you. I want you to look and move forward."

Today, many people suffer from various forms of shame. And to each person with head hung low and eyes cast downward, God says, "Look up." Hebrews 12:2 tells us to keep "our eyes on Jesus," who was "willing to die a shameful death on the cross." The Bible speaks of Jesus scorning the shame of the Cross. Jesus essentially laughed in the face of shame, declaring that it would no longer have power over those who put their trust in him.

God replaced the shame of the Israelites with the renewal of his magnificent plan to bring them into "a land flowing with milk and honey." Today he replaces the shame of innocent victims as well as guilty sinners with the love and forgiveness in Christ.

PRAYER POINT

Pray that God will help you deal with any shame or guilt you have been carrying and that you will understand his unconditional love.

HERE'S WHAT I'M GOING TO DO

☐ _____

_____

_____

COMRADES IN ARMS

God gave Israel the Promised Land. It belonged to them. But in order for them to fully possess the land, they had to **cooperate.** Interestingly, two and a half tribes received land on the east side of the Jordan, where no enemies lived. Yet God required these fighting men to share the blessings and the burdens that the other tribes faced. Put another way, God told them, "I have been generous with you. I have given you food, shelter, and peace. Won't you follow my example and help your brothers and sisters?" The eastern tribes were to withhold nothing:

> Joshua 22:8: ⁸"Share with your relatives back home the great wealth you have taken from your enemies. Share with them your large herds of cattle, your silver and gold, your bronze and iron, and your clothing."

A life truly devoted to God is not a life lived alone. God didn't allow the eastern tribes to simply revel in their blessings and say to the others, "God bless you and give you success." They had to fight alongside their neighbors, helping them possess their land.

Salvation has a similar dynamic. God gives us salvation **without merit, but we must engage in the "battles" of this life in order to fully "possess" it.** We can easily focus on ourselves and revel in our own spiritual success, but that isn't the picture that God gives us of life in the Kingdom of God. The eastern tribes were entrusted with much, so they were expected to give much. They also had a role within their own tribes by sharing the wealth that they gained from their enemies.

Mature Christians have something to give out of the abundance of spiritual blessings they have received through their relationship with Christ. God calls them to **come**

alongside others, to **encourage** and **strengthen** them in their faith and fight next to them in the spiritual battles they face.

Likewise, we can participate in others' lives through **generous giving of our material resources.** Joshua reminded the people of Israel before his death that every blessing they possessed, going back many generations, came from the Lord. God tells them, "I gave you land you had not worked for, and I gave you cities you did not build—the cities in which you are now living. I gave you vineyards and olive groves for food, though you did not plant them" (Joshua 24:13). When we consider his faithfulness to so many generations, we realize that **returning his kindness to others** is a fully appropriate response.

PRAYER POINT

Ask God to remind you of the ways he has blessed you, and then resolve, with the help of the Holy Spirit, to share generously with others.

HERE'S WHAT I'M GOING TO DO

☐ _____

_____

☐ _____

_____

☐ _____

_____

☐ _____

_____

WHAT'S THE HARM?

DAY

43

Just a few generations ago, cigarette advertisers promoted the idea that smoking was actually good for you. "Healthful!" "Refreshing!" "Adds vigor!" boasted the ads that appeared in magazines and on the radio. And many accepted that notion without question. Today, we look at the thousands of lives rubbed out by heart disease and cancer and shake our heads, wondering how anyone could have **believed such nonsense.**

It seems the people of Israel in the time of the judges had accepted some pretty foolish ideas as well. Despite repeated warnings from Moses and Joshua, they no longer saw **the urgency of stamping out dangerous influences.** Their live-and-let-live policy allowed some pretty dangerous people to creep into their lives:

> Judges 1:19-21, 27-28: ¹⁹The LORD was with the people of Judah, and they took possession of the hill country. But they failed to drive out the people living in the plains because the people there had iron chariots. ²⁰The city of Hebron was given to Caleb as Moses had promised. And Caleb drove out the people living there, who were descendants of the three sons of Anak. ²¹The tribe of Benjamin, however, failed to drive out the Jebusites, who were living in Jerusalem. So to this day the Jebusites live in Jerusalem among the people of Benjamin. . . .
>
> ²⁷The tribe of Manasseh failed to drive out the people living in Beth-shan,¹ Taanach, Dor, Ibleam, Megiddo, and their surrounding villages, because the Canaanites were determined to stay in that region. ²⁸When the Israelites grew stronger, they forced the Canaanites to work as slaves, but they never did drive them out of the land.

When God commanded the Israelites to take over the Promised Land, he gave clear instructions regarding the

---

¹ **1:27** Hebrew *Beth-shean*, a variant name for Beth-shan.

people occupying those lands: "You must destroy them totally. Make no treaty with them, and show them no mercy." That may seem harsh at first glance, but the idolatry and corruption of the Canaanites were so intense that Israel would surely turn away from God if they didn't remove them from the land. Despite the warnings, the Israelites became careless. They made treaties with the Canaanites. They mingled with them, and some men took Canaanite wives. Some tribes even took advantage of the situation, using the Canaanites as slaves. Eventually, just as God predicted, the "harmless" Canaanites passed their **corrupt ways** to the **unsuspecting** Israelites.

We find two sobering lessons in the book of Judges. First, **we must take God at his word.** When he issues a warning, we must believe it. We cannot make judgments based on our limited, short-term perspectives. Second, **we have to choose our friends carefully.** We must avoid the temptation of hanging out with people just because they are popular, fun, or just nice. The Israelites made that mistake, and **so can we.**

HERE'S WHAT I'M GOING TO DO

❑ _____

_____

❑ _____

_____

_____

THE STRONG SURVIVE

Samson would be quite a celebrity if he lived in our culture. Agents would beat a path to his door, clamoring for book and movie rights to his life story. He would make the talk show circuit, discussing again and again his superhuman feats—ripping apart a lion with his bare hands, lifting the city gates of Gaza and carrying them to the top of a nearby hill.

But God didn't give Samson action-hero-like strength to make him a celebrity; he **empowered** the man from Dan to save Israel from its oppressors, the Philistines. Tragically, Samson's energies went astray. He had a weakness for the wrong kind of women, and this led to his downfall.

Judges 16:15-17: [15]Then Delilah pouted, "How can you say you love me when you don't confide in me? You've made fun of me three times now, and you still haven't told me what makes you so strong!" [16]So day after day she nagged him until he couldn't stand it any longer. [17]Finally, Samson told her his secret. "My hair has never been cut," he confessed, "for I was dedicated to God as a Nazirite from birth. If my head were shaved, my strength would leave me, and I would become as weak as anyone else."

Samson's life, as judge over Israel for 20 years, highlights several important facts about **God's dispensing of gifts.** One is that **God gives them to flawed people.** Another is that **character does matter.**

God chose Samson before he was born. Samson had nothing to do with his calling—it was God's initiation. The angel of the Lord shocked Samson's barren mother with an appearance, promising that she would bear a son who would rescue Israel from the Philistines. To fulfill that purpose, God gave Samson supernatural strength.

Samson, however, was not a robot. God gave him a free

will. With that freedom, Samson often chose to use God's gifts to satisfy his own needs and desires. His eyes wandered toward Philistine women, prostitutes, and eventually to the devilish Delilah. With such careless behavior, Samson despised the gifts God had so graciously given him.

But **God's purposes are never thwarted,** and by his grace he used even the sensual Samson. Though God didn't condone Samson's impetuous acts, he used them to humble the Philistines and eventually bring catastrophic judgment on the enemies of Israel (Judges 16:23-31). One has to wonder how much greater Samson could have been and how much more good he could have done if only he had lived a righteous life.

God longs for people who will **subject their desires to his will.** Samson's last heroic feat, great as it was, pales in comparison to the humble deeds of service carried out by **obedient, willing believers.**

PRAYER POINT

Ask God to increase your ability to appreciate all that he has given you and to strengthen your love for him so that it is more powerful than your desire to do wrong.

HERE'S WHAT I'M GOING TO DO

❑ _____

_____

❑ _____

_____

❑ _____

_____

A PROMISE IS A PROMISE

In Disney's *Mary Poppins*, the Banks children ask their new nanny how long she'll stay. Her reply: "Until the wind changes." She introduces Jane and Michael to the "pie-crust promise": easily made, easily broken. While she may help the medicine go down, the lady with the magic umbrella doesn't keep promises very well.

The Israelites knew that **keeping promises** was important, though they often failed to keep their end of their agreements with God. During the shameful war between Israel and Benjamin, which began with the brutal murder of a concubine, the Israelites swore they would never give their women in marriage to the Benjaminites. When the fighting was over, Benjamin lay in ruins, and only a few warriors survived. The people of Israel came up with a roundabout way to repopulate the tribe while keeping their vows.

Judges 21:19-25: [19]Then they thought of the annual festival of the LORD held in Shiloh, between Lebonah and Bethel, along the east side of the road that goes from Bethel to Shechem. [20]They told the men of Benjamin who still needed wives, "Go and hide in the vineyards. [21]When the women of Shiloh come out for their dances, rush out from the vineyards, and each of you can take one of them home to be your wife! [22]And when their fathers and brothers come to us in protest, we will tell them, 'Please be understanding. Let them have your daughters, for we didn't find enough wives for them when we destroyed Jabesh-gilead. And you are not guilty of breaking the vow since you did not give your daughters in marriage to them.'"

[23]So the men of Benjamin did as they were told. They kidnapped the women who took part in the celebration and carried them off to the land of their own inheritance. Then they rebuilt their towns and lived in them.

²⁴So the assembly of Israel departed by tribes and families, and they returned to their own homes.

²⁵In those days Israel had no king, so the people did whatever seemed right in their own eyes.

God sanctioned the fight to punish Benjamin for rape and murder (Judges 20:23). When the campaign finally ended, only six hundred Benjaminites had survived (Judges 20:47). Victorious Israelites didn't want to annihilate Benjamin completely, so they found wives for the living. Instead of breaking their vow, the Israelites permitted Benjaminites themselves to nab festival dancers. Since fathers of these dancers had not given their daughters voluntarily, the fathers had not broken the vow (Judges 21:22).

The Israelites barely got by that time, you might say. But they still technically avoided breaking their vow. For the Hebrews, a verbal promise meant a lot. Jesus tells us to **stick by plain words** without using vows or oaths (Matthew 5:33-37).

We learn from the Israelites the importance of keeping our word. To do rightly in the Lord's eyes means to **keep promises to him and to others.** There should be no "pie-crust promises" made by Christians.

HERE'S WHAT I'M GOING TO DO

☐ _____

_____

SPIRITUAL JOURNEY TRAVEL LOG

A HABIT OF KINDNESS

The young family arrived at *Oma* (Grandma) Struber's Salzburg apartment, where they were to live while in Austria. Oma greeted them in German and accented English. That night the old lady with dark gentle eyes cooked *wiener schnitzel*, an Austrian specialty. For five months she left her apartment to them, living in her own guest room. Her **kindness** made them feel right at home.

In the passage for today, kind Boaz makes the Moabite Ruth feel right at home in Israel.

Ruth 2:1-10: ¹Now there was a wealthy and influential man in Bethlehem named Boaz, who was a relative of Naomi's husband, Elimelech.

²One day Ruth said to Naomi, "Let me go out into the fields to gather leftover grain behind anyone who will let me do it."

And Naomi said, "All right, my daughter, go ahead." ³So Ruth went out to gather grain behind the harvesters. And as it happened, she found herself working in a field that belonged to Boaz, the relative of her father-in-law, Elimelech.

⁴While she was there, Boaz arrived from Bethlehem and greeted the harvesters. "The LORD be with you!" he said.

"The LORD bless you!" the harvesters replied.

⁵Then Boaz asked his foreman, "Who is that girl over there?"

⁶And the foreman replied, "She is the young woman from Moab who came back with Naomi. ⁷She asked me this morning if she could gather grain behind the harvesters. She has been hard at work ever since, except for a few minutes' rest over there in the shelter."

⁸Boaz went over and said to Ruth, "Listen, my daughter. Stay right here with us when you gather grain; don't go to any other fields. Stay right

behind the women working in my field. ⁹See which part of the field they are harvesting, and then follow them. I have warned the young men not to bother you. And when you are thirsty, help yourself to the water they have drawn from the well."

PRAYER POINT

Ask God to help you stand out by your offers of kindness to others.

¹⁰Ruth fell at his feet and thanked him warmly. "Why are you being so kind to me?" she asked. "I am only a foreigner."

Boaz's kindness to Ruth was surprising only because Israel and Moab were enemies (Genesis 19:30-38; Numbers 22–25). Still, as one commentator puts it, Boaz showed his kindness by blessing his workers (Ruth 2:4).

We need to model Boaz's kindness. Boaz not only helped Naomi and Ruth out of poverty, but he also treated them **respectfully.** Boaz never looked down on them. In fact, Boaz calls Ruth his "daughter" and eventually marries her, giving Ruth a real home. When we run into people different or less fortunate than us, **we must treat them with dignity,** just as Boaz treated Ruth.

HERE'S WHAT I'M GOING TO DO

☐ _____

_____

☐ _____

_____

☐ _____

_____

PETITIONS

Prayer belongs to everyone. Regardless of our social status, race, or background, regardless of the offenses we have committed or the wounds we have caused, we may come to God with our requests. Knowing that he **hears** them is marvelous in itself; seeing him **respond** fills us with joy and wonder. Hannah, who had lived for years in shame for her childlessness, humiliated by her husband's other wife, knew no other recourse but prayer. And at last her request was granted.

1 Samuel 1:9-18: [9]Once when they were at Shiloh, Hannah went over to the Tabernacle[1] after supper to pray to the LORD. Eli the priest was sitting at his customary place beside the entrance. [10]Hannah was in deep anguish, crying bitterly as she prayed to the LORD. [11]And she made this vow: "O LORD Almighty, if you will look down upon my sorrow and answer my prayer and give me a son, then I will give him back to you. He will be yours for his entire lifetime, and as a sign that he has been dedicated to the LORD, his hair will never be cut."[2]

[12]As she was praying to the LORD, Eli watched her. [13]Seeing her lips moving but hearing no sound, he thought she had been drinking. [14]"Must you come here drunk?" he demanded. "Throw away your wine!"

[15]"Oh no, sir!" she replied, "I'm not drunk! But I am very sad, and I was pouring out my heart to the LORD. [16]Please don't think I am a wicked woman! For I have been praying out of great anguish and sorrow."

[17]"In that case," Eli said, "cheer up! May the God of Israel grant the request you have asked of him."

[18]"Oh, thank you, sir!" she exclaimed. Then she went back and began to eat again, and she was no longer sad.

---

[1] **1:9** Hebrew *the Temple of the LORD*.
[2] **1:11** Some manuscripts add *He will drink neither wine nor intoxicants.*

The first thing to note about this prayer is that it happened at a specific time. Hannah was at Shiloh at God's Tabernacle after supper (v. 9). Although Jesus taught that it doesn't matter where we pray or worship (John 4:21), **it is important to develop a regular habit of prayer throughout the day.** Next, we see that "Hannah was in deep anguish, crying bitterly" (1 Samuel 1:10). We should not be afraid to show our emotions to God! After all, he made us and knows us better than anyone. God wants us to be **transparent** with him.

Third, Hannah dedicates her all to God (v. 11). Dedicating Samuel to God was not merely a bargain to obtain a child; it was a beautiful act of faith.

You can know Hannah's happiness: God's blessings on your prayers. **Pray honestly. Pray consistently.** Your heart counts the most. Let your whole being enter your prayer, just as Hannah demonstrated.

PRAYER POINT

Be transparent with God in your prayers. And be consistent in your prayer time.

HERE'S WHAT I'M GOING TO DO

☐ _____

_____

☐ _____

_____

☐ _____

_____

SOLID GROUND

The swarms of reporters sent to cover the first game of the 1989 World Series had no idea that they would spend little time talking about baseball that evening. The skies were clear, the temperature ideal. But during batting practice, while fans were filing into Candlestick Park, the earth began to tremble. Within seconds, the city was paralyzed by a powerful earthquake that cracked foundations, collapsed freeways, and opened canyons in the earth. Although the stadium suffered little damage, the fans who left that evening surely thought for many days about their brush with the uncontrollable forces of nature.

In today's reading, Hannah affirms **God's control over everything**—not only the forces of nature, but the destiny of his chosen people.

1 Samuel 2:5-8: ⁵Those who were well fed are now starving;
and those who were starving are now full.
The barren woman now has seven children;
but the woman with many children will have no more.
⁶The LORD brings both death and life;
he brings some down to the grave but raises others up
⁷The LORD makes one poor and another rich;
he brings one down and lifts another up.
⁸He lifts the poor from the dust—
yes, from a pile of ashes!
He treats them like princes,
placing them in seats of honor.
"For all the earth is the LORD's,
and he has set the world in order."

Verse 8 declares: "For all the earth is the LORD's, and he

has set the world in order." Or as another translation puts it: "For the foundations of the earth are the LORD's; upon them he has set the world." The "foundations of the earth" are the base of his whole creation. **God controls everything from the ground up.**

PRAYER POINT

Thank the Creator-God for being

in control. Thank him for

blessing you.

Hannah praises God for surprising changes that reveal his control. She is no longer barren but "full" with "seven children" (v. 5). Seven is a number signifying completeness and God's richest blessings. Verse 7 says: "The LORD makes one poor and another rich; he brings one down and lifts another up." God does not endorse poverty or favor inequality. In verse 8, God gives the poor back their dignity: "He lifts the poor from the dust—yes, from a pile of ashes! He treats them like princes, placing them in seats of honor."

HERE'S WHAT I'M GOING TO DO

☐ _____

_____

☐ _____

_____

☐ _____

_____

☐ _____

_____

POWER CORRUPTS

Lord Acton, a noted scholar in the nineteenth century, coined a famous phrase that is often repeated today: **"Power tends to corrupt,** and absolute power corrupts absolutely."

Looking back at the miserable history of Israel's monarchy, we see that principle in action. Sadly, the prophet Samuel had warned Israel of the dangers that would come with giving such wide-reaching power to an earthly ruler. Samuel had foreseen the corruption of future kings, so he begged the people not to pursue such a plan.

> 1 Samuel 8:10-18: ¹⁰So Samuel passed on the LORD's warning to the people. ¹¹"This is how a king will treat you," Samuel said. "The king will draft your sons into his army and make them run before his chariots. ¹²Some will be commanders of his troops, while others will be slave laborers. Some will be forced to plow in his fields and harvest his crops, while others will make his weapons and chariot equipment. ¹³The king will take your daughters from you and force them to cook and bake and make perfumes for him. ¹⁴He will take away the best of your fields and vineyards and olive groves and give them to his own servants. ¹⁵He will take a tenth of your harvest and distribute it among his officers and attendants. ¹⁶He will want your male and female slaves and demand the finest of your cattle¹ and donkeys for his own use. ¹⁷He will demand a tenth of your flocks, and you will be his slaves. ¹⁸When that day comes, you will beg for relief from this king you are demanding, but the LORD will not help you."

The prophet's words were, well, prophetic! This is precisely what happened. To build kingdoms, kings need money and servants—lots and lots of both. Kings, Samuel warned, are very greedy. Look at all the possessive verbs:

---

¹ **8:16** As in Greek version; Hebrew reads *young men*.

"take," "take away," "want," "demand." Before long, the people of Israel were complaining about high taxes (1 Kings 12:4)!

With such **power** to demand money and command subjects comes **kingly pride.** Almost all of Israel's leaders yielded to the alluring trappings of power. Even the godly King David occasionally forgot that he was under God's authority. Such **failures by power-intoxicated leaders always produce unhappiness among the populace.**

PRAYER POINT

Pray for wisdom to avoid an ego trip of pride, no matter your success.

You can learn a couple of truths from this chapter of Israel's history. First, remember that **while humans are corrupted by power, God is not.** His ability to do anything and everything is rooted in his inherent goodness. He will never act selfishly or ruthlessly. He rules the world with absolute fairness and kindness. Thus, we can have full confidence that he will govern our lives in ways that are **good.**

Second, be extremely careful that you don't get tripped up by pride if and when you find yourself in a position of prominence or power. Depend on his wisdom. Rely on his guidance. "When you **bow down** before the Lord and admit your dependence on him, he will **lift you up** and **give you honor"** (James 4:10).

HERE'S WHAT I'M GOING TO DO

☐ _____

_____

_____

IN GOD WE TRUST?

In the last few years, **American Christians have become a vital part of the political process.** Some argue that this is a healthy trend—that believers elected to positions of influence can be salt and light in a decaying, darkening culture. That is, Christian politicians can enact laws that will return the country to its righteous roots.

Others believe that spending so much money, time, and effort to bring about mere political change is a waste. Their argument is that the nation as a whole will never change until individual hearts are transformed spiritually. Both arguments have merit, but each side needs to remember the timeless truth taught by the ancient prophet Samuel in his farewell address to the nation of Israel:

> 1 Samuel 12:12-15, 24: ¹²"But when you were afraid of Nahash, the king of Ammon, you came to me and said that you wanted a king to reign over you, even though the LORD your God was already your king. ¹³All right, here is the king you have chosen. Look him over. You asked for him, and the LORD has granted your request.
>
> ¹⁴"Now if you will fear and worship the LORD and listen to his voice, and if you do not rebel against the LORD's commands, and if you and your king follow the LORD your God, then all will be well. ¹⁵But if you rebel against the LORD's commands and refuse to listen to him, then his hand will be as heavy upon you as it was upon your ancestors.
>
> ²⁴"But be sure to fear the LORD and sincerely worship him. Think of all the wonderful things he has done for you."

In essence, Samuel was warning Israel against forgetting that God was their **true King.** In order for their new system of government to work, the people had to maintain **a primary trust in and fear of God.** He is the ultimate

Ruler. He is the only one who deserves full confidence and allegiance.

Samuel was saying that **when God is revered and remembered** and **when his laws are followed carefully,** things would go well in the nation. We need this same warning today. The temptation is for us to put our hope in whatever political party or candidate claims to represent "traditional values." We get all worked up over particular bills, as if a single legislative act can bring about godliness in the nation. We fret over judicial decisions, viewing the Supreme Court as though it were, in fact, "supreme." We tend to rely heavily on economic forecasts and reports. Each of these is important, but **the greater truth is that God is in control,** and we need to trust him and nothing else.

PRAYER POINT

Pray that you and other believers would place the hope for justice in the hands of the Lord instead of in world leaders and governments.

HERE'S WHAT I'M GOING TO DO

❑ _____

_____

❑ _____

_____

❑ _____

_____

❑ _____

_____

Fast Food

Victor Hugo's *Les Miserables* tells the story of Jean Valjean, a man who is sentenced to hard labor after stealing a loaf of bread to feed his starving family. Even after his release, he is pursued by a cruel police official named Javert, who will stop at nothing to keep Valjean in his power. Valjean, by his wits and courage, eventually overcomes his adversary.

Today's passage concerns another fugitive running from a vengeful pursuer. Like Valjean, David takes bread to survive his ordeal with the insanely jealous Saul.

1 Samuel 21:1-6: [1]David went to the city of Nob to see Ahimelech the priest. Ahimelech trembled when he saw him. "Why are you alone?" he asked. "Why is no one with you?"

[2]"The king has sent me on a private matter," David said. "He told me not to tell anyone why I am here. I have told my men where to meet me later. [3]Now, what is there to eat? Give me five loaves of bread or anything else you have."

[4]"We don't have any regular bread," the priest replied. "But there is the holy bread, which I guess you can have if your young men have not slept with any women recently."

[5]"Don't worry," David replied. "I never allow my men to be with women when they are on a campaign. And since they stay clean even on ordinary trips, how much more on this one!"

[6]So, since there was no other food available, the priest gave him the holy bread—the Bread of the Presence that was placed before the LORD in the Tabernacle. It had just been replaced that day with fresh bread.

The loaves—one representing each tribe—belonged to priests and symbolized **God's provision** for Israel (Leviticus 24:5-9). In this story, David needs God's provision. He is running away from Saul, though he hides that secret from others (1 Samuel 21:2). Knowing his life is in danger, David asks for help. Despite God's regulations against it, Ahimelech gives David the holy bread for food because it was the only food available (v. 6).

Jesus cites this event to criticize the Pharisees for keeping religious customs while forsaking God. In Jesus' mind, saving a godly but starving David had been more important than keeping religious law. Healing someone was better than "not working" on the Sabbath. Jesus didn't condone lawbreaking but urged **acting with a spirit of goodness** that the law endorsed. **Compassion** matters more than custom to Jesus (Luke 6:1-11).

PRAYER POINT

Ask God for a compassionate heart toward people. Ask the Holy Spirit to reveal areas of spiritual pride or arrogance. Confess any ways you have made certain religious practices more important than caring for others.

HERE'S WHAT I'M GOING TO DO

❑ _____

_____

❑ _____

_____

❑ _____

_____

❑ _____

_____

SHARE YOUR BLESSINGS

DAY 52

Imagine that you're a companion of David, the man who would become king of Israel. You and six hundred other Israelites are in hot pursuit of the Amalekites, who have taken your wife and children (along with everyone else's family) captive. Day and night you ride, on the verge of exhaustion. When you reach the Besor Ravine, two hundred of the men in your group decide they can't go any further and give up the chase. You and the other four hundred continue on until you finally catch the Amalekites, defeat them in battle, and head for home with the spoils of victory.

As you approach the Besor Ravine and the men who stayed behind, some of the guys around you start grumbling, saying that the plunder should not be split with those who did not fight. Do you agree with them? Why or why not? How do you think David will respond to such grumbling?

1 Samuel 30:23-25: ²³But David said, "No, my brothers! Don't be selfish with what the LORD has given us. He has kept us safe and helped us defeat the enemy. ²⁴Do you think anyone will listen to you when you talk like this? We share and share alike—those who go to battle and those who guard the equipment." ²⁵From then on David made this a law for all of Israel, and it is still followed.

Like David, we often hear from people who have ideas about **what we should or shouldn't do with our material possessions.** "It's your money," they say. "You earned it. Why should you give it to someone else?"

We would do well to learn what David understood: **Every blessing we receive—material or otherwise—**

comes from the Lord. It is not ours; it is his. We are merely stewards or caretakers of God's riches. When we start trying to determine who "deserves" to share our blessings, we are ignoring the fact that **we ourselves are undeserving of those blessings.**

Think about it: What did we do to earn the privilege of being born in one of the wealthiest and most advanced countries in the world? What makes us so special that we don't have to worry about dying of starvation or finding a safe place to spend the night?

We have been blessed by the Lord. Who will you allow to **share your blessings?**

PRAYER POINT

Spend some time thanking God for blessings that you may have taken for granted or believed you deserved in the past. Ask him to help you be a wise steward of those blessings.

HERE'S WHAT I'M GOING TO DO

❏ _____

_____

❏ _____

_____

❏ _____

_____

❏ _____

_____

GIVE UP WHAT?

Think of all the things that could possibly cause you to miss a meal. Sickness, of course, could do it. People on crash diets often skip meals, although it isn't recommended. Surgery and other medical procedures require **abstinence from food** for a certain period of time. A more extreme circumstance is not having access to food, whether as a result of poverty or famine.

What about **prayer** and **meditation?** Could they be added to the list? Is it likely or even possible that you would give up one or more meals in order to **focus your thoughts on the Lord** or a special request that you were bringing to him?

Both the Old and New Testaments offer several accounts of people fasting, abstaining from food, for various reasons. Let's look at an example from the life of King David.

2 Samuel 3:31-37: [31]Then David said to Joab and all those who were with him, "Tear your clothes and put on sackcloth. Go into deep mourning for Abner." And King David himself walked behind the procession to the grave. [32]They buried Abner in Hebron, and the king and all the people wept at his graveside. [33]Then the king sang this funeral song for Abner:

"Should Abner have died as fools die? [34]Your hands were not bound; your feet were not chained. No, you were murdered—the victim of a wicked plot."

All the people wept again for Abner. [35]David had refused to eat anything the day of the funeral, and now everyone begged him to eat. But David had made a vow, saying, "May God kill me if I eat anything before sundown." [36]This pleased the people very much. In fact, everything the king did pleased them! [37]So everyone in Judah and Israel knew that David was not responsible for Abner's death.

David fasted out of grief. Abstaining from food was his way of showing his sorrow over Abner's death.

Though fasting today is not as prevalent as it was during biblical times, it is still an **important spiritual discipline.** Fasts can last eight or more hours. (World Vision, for instance, sponsors the 30 Hour Famine to raise money to feed hungry kids and as a way of heightening awareness of hunger.) Fasting allows believers to **shift their focus** from their **physical needs** to their **spiritual needs.**

Fasting is an intensely private issue; it's between you and the Lord. However, if you have a personal issue or societal concern (such as homelessness in your area or a famine in a foreign land) that you would like to bring to the Lord in a special way, you might consider, after discussing it with your parents, embarking on a fast.

PRAYER POINT

If you're not sure about fasting, ask the Lord to give you some direction. Talk to some mature Christians and read some Bible passages about fasting; then ask the Lord whether fasting is a spiritual discipline that you should add to your life.

HERE'S WHAT I'M GOING TO DO

☐ _____

_____

☐ _____

_____

☐ _____

_____

WHY ME?

DAY

54

Most people who experience tragedy firsthand—whether it be the loss of a loved one, a devastating accident, or a physical ailment—invariably ask the same question: "Why me?" **Some feel as though they've been singled out** for punishment or "testing" and can't understand why.

King David himself asked the Lord, "Why me?" shortly after he took the throne. However, David's question had a much different tone to it.

> 2 Samuel 7:18-24: ¹⁸Then King David went in and sat before the LORD and prayed, "Who am I, O Sovereign LORD, and what is my family, that you have brought me this far? ¹⁹And now, Sovereign LORD, in addition to everything else, you speak of giving me a lasting dynasty! Do you deal with everyone this way,¹ O Sovereign LORD? ²⁰What more can I say? You know what I am really like, Sovereign LORD. ²¹For the sake of your promise and according to your will, you have done all these great things and have shown them to me.
>
> ²²"How great you are, O Sovereign LORD! There is no one like you—there is no other God. We have never even heard of another god like you! ²³What other nation on earth is like Israel? What other nation, O God, have you redeemed from slavery to be your own people? You made a great name for yourself when you rescued your people from Egypt. You performed awesome miracles and drove out the nations and gods that stood in their way. ²⁴You made Israel your people forever, and you, O LORD, became their God."

You can almost hear the surprise and wonder in David's voice in this passage: "Who am I, O Sovereign LORD . . . ?" (v. 18). Out of all the people in Israel, God selected David to be the leader of his chosen nation. In response, David was equal parts amazed, humbled, and thankful that the Lord

¹ **7:19** The meaning of the Hebrew is uncertain.

was so **gracious** to him.

Do you ever feel like David? Are you ever amazed at what the Lord has done for you? Do you ever consider yourself unworthy of God's blessings?

If you answered "no" to these questions, you're not alone. The truth is, our society conditions us to expect the best for ourselves. Because we're so focused on what we don't have—whether it's a new car, a high-paying job, or professional-level athletic skills—**it's easy for us to ignore or take for granted the things we do have.**

Rather than expecting the best for ourselves, we need to cultivate the spirit of amazement, humility, and thankfulness that David possessed. We need to recognize that there are people around us in much more dire circumstances than we face. We need to recognize that our (relatively) privileged lifestyle is not some sort of birthright but an inexplicable **blessing from God.** We need not only to praise him for his blessings but to **use those blessings to help others.**

"Who are we, O Sovereign Lord, that you have chosen to bless us?"

PRAYER POINT

Spend time in prayer, asking God, "Why me?" Thank him for the blessings he has bestowed on you. Name as many of these blessings as you can think of in your prayer.

HERE'S WHAT I'M GOING TO DO

☐ _____

_____

☐ _____

_____

HAVE MERCY

"Everybody's crying mercy when they don't know the meaning of the word."—*Mose Allison*

Mercy might be defined most simply as **"kind and compassionate treatment."** Yet mercy also involves choice. Being merciful means choosing not to repay others for how they have hurt you.

A good example of mercy can be found in the Old Testament account of David's return to Jerusalem after his son Absalom's rebellion.

2 Samuel 19:18-23: [18]They all crossed the ford and worked hard ferrying the king's household across the river, helping them in every way they could.

As the king was about to cross the river, Shimei fell down before him. [19]"My lord the king, please forgive me," he pleaded. "Forget the terrible thing I did when you left Jerusalem. [20]I know how much I sinned. That is why I have come here today, the very first person in all Israel[1] to greet you."

[21]Then Abishai son of Zeruiah said, "Shimei should die, for he cursed the LORD's anointed king!"

[22]"What am I going to do with you sons of Zeruiah!" David exclaimed. "This is not a day for execution but for celebration! I am once again the king of Israel!" [23]Then, turning to Shimei, David vowed, "Your life will be spared."

We don't know for sure what David was thinking when Shimei made his requests, but it's quite likely that he put himself in the other man's position. Shimei, who had earlier cursed the king and hurled dirt and rocks at him, had realized the horrible mistake he had made. **The key to showing**

---

[1] **19:20** Hebrew *the house of Joseph.*

mercy to another person is to ask, "What would I like that person to do for me if our situations were reversed?"

Hard as it may be to do, we can gain a great deal of perspective by putting ourselves in the place of those who may have wronged us. When we are able to **empathize with others,** we are much more likely **to respond to them in a merciful and God-honoring way.**

HERE'S WHAT I'M GOING TO DO

☐ _____

_____

☐ _____

_____

☐ _____

_____

☐ _____

_____

☐ _____

_____

☐ _____

_____

THE HANDS OF THE LORD

O ne of the first things many children learn about God is that "he's got the whole world in his hands." If you went to Sunday school or vacation Bible school as a kid, you probably sang (or at least heard) this song. If so, did you ever wonder what it means? Maybe you pictured God holding the earth in his outstretched hands, cupping it like an egg. Or maybe you envisioned him spinning the earth on his index finger like a celestial Harlem Globetrotter.

Or maybe you were bright enough as a kid to understand that the song refers to the fact that **God takes care of the earth and everyone in it.** This is a principle King David understood very well.

> 2 Samuel 24:14: ¹⁴"This is a desperate situation!" David replied to Gad. "But let us fall into the hands of the LORD, for his mercy is great. Do not let me fall into human hands."

David had sinned against God by ordering an unauthorized census of Israel's army. When David repented of his sin, God gave him a choice of three punishments: three years of famine, three years of being pursued by enemies, or three days of plague in the land. David knew that God, even in his anger, would be more merciful than humans would be, so he chose the plague. David was **confident of the Lord's mercy** because he had personally experienced it many times before.

How about you? Do you have as much faith in God's mercy as David had? Do you see **evidence of God's mercy** in your life or in the world around you? In what ways does God make his mercy known to you? These are all important questions, to be sure.

Here's an even more important question: Do you think

God could use you as **an instrument of his mercy?** In other words, could you use your time, resources, and talents to make a difference in someone else's life on behalf of the Lord? Think about it.

PRAYER POINT

Ask the Lord to make you an instrument of his mercy. Ask him to prepare your heart and spirit so that you might make a difference in someone else's life.

HERE'S WHAT I'M GOING TO DO

- ☐ _____

- ☐ _____

- ☐ _____

- ☐ _____

- ☐ _____

- ☐ _____

GENEROSITY UNLIMITED

Sheila always treasured her Christmas memories of shopping with her granddad. Every year in mid-December, he would pick a night to take Sheila and her sisters into the city. They loved this event, for they knew that once at the toy store, they would hear the words, "You may pick out anything you want." Granddad put no limit on their choices. After each girl had made a selection, he would purchase the toy. Sheila can still remember the smile on his face and the joy in his eyes as he would hand out the gifts. She thought Granddad was the most generous person in the world.

In today's passage, God shows his **great generosity** by going one step further. He gives Solomon what he asks for and more besides.

1 Kings 3:9-14: ⁹"Give me an understanding mind so that I can govern your people well and know the difference between right and wrong. For who by himself is able to govern this great nation of yours?"

¹⁰The LORD was pleased with Solomon's reply and was glad that he had asked for wisdom. ¹¹So God replied, "Because you have asked for wisdom in governing my people and have not asked for a long life or riches for yourself or the death of your enemies—¹²I will give you what you asked for! I will give you a wise and understanding mind such as no one else has ever had or ever will have! ¹³And I will also give you what you did not ask for—riches and honor! No other king in all the world will be compared to you for the rest of your life! ¹⁴And if you follow me and obey my commands as your father, David, did, I will give you a long life."

How surprised Solomon must have been to not only receive what he asked for, but much more. This passage shows **God's heart for his children.** Like Sheila's grandfather, God **delights** in giving. He is at times even extravagant. An extravagant person spends much more than necessary.

Think about all that God has created for us to enjoy: sunsets, rainbows, the myriad of colors, and the variety of animals. He could have just made three colors, one kind of sunset, and five or six animals. But aren't you glad he didn't! In addition, **he promises many more gifts in the Bible.** His most extravagant gift was his Son, Jesus. Yes, God is a generous God. But what delights God more than giving to his children is **when he sees his children imitating his extravagance on others.**

PRAYER POINT

Thank God for his unlimited generosity. Then ask him to show you how you can give extravagantly to a friend, a family member, or a worthy cause this week.

HERE'S WHAT I'M GOING TO DO

☐ _____

☐ _____

☐ _____

☐ _____

☐ _____

IMPOSSIBLE? (NOT)

Imagine that your family has only one frozen pizza left to eat. Your mom has lost her job, and there is no way for her to get more money. She has no idea where she will get tomorrow's food. But she decides to fix the pizza anyway. Your family is so hungry they eat all but one piece. She puts the leftover piece in the fridge for you to eat tomorrow. When you wake up the next morning, you open the refrigerator door expecting to see a piece of pizza. But instead you see a whole pizza. You eat a few slices and put the rest in the fridge. When you arrive home from school, you open the refrigerator for a snack and once again you see a whole pizza. **Wouldn't that be something?**

Today's passage shares many similarities to the story you just read. Only this one really happened.

1 Kings 17:8-16: ⁸Then the LORD said to Elijah, ⁹"Go and live in the village of Zarephath, near the city of Sidon. There is a widow there who will feed you. I have given her my instructions."

¹⁰So he went to Zarephath. As he arrived at the gates of the village, he saw a widow gathering sticks, and he asked her, "Would you please bring me a cup of water?" ¹¹As she was going to get it, he called to her, "Bring me a bite of bread, too."

¹²But she said, "I swear by the LORD your God that I don't have a single piece of bread in the house. And I have only a handful of flour left in the jar and a little cooking oil in the bottom of the jug. I was just gathering a few sticks to cook this last meal, and then my son and I will die."

¹³But Elijah said to her, "Don't be afraid! Go ahead and cook that 'last meal,' but bake me a little loaf of bread first. Afterward there will still be enough food for you and your son. ¹⁴For this is what the LORD, the God of

Israel, says: "There will always be plenty of flour and oil left in your containers until the time when the LORD sends rain and the crops grow again!"

15So she did as Elijah said, and she and Elijah and her son continued to eat from her supply of flour and oil for many days. 16For no matter how much they used, there was always enough left in the containers, just as the LORD had promised through Elijah.

No matter how desperate the situation, **there is always hope when God is in the picture.** Just look at the stories of Gideon and his three hundred warriors, Joshua and the battle of Jericho, or David and Goliath. God seems to enjoy **defying the odds.** In today's story, God miraculously provided food for the widow, her son, and Elijah even though it seemed impossible.

God wants to provide for you too. Philippians 4:19 states, "And this same God who takes care of me will supply all your needs from his glorious riches, which have been given to us in Christ Jesus." Written almost two thousand years ago, this verse is still true today. What is it you need? Money for college? A job? Take your request to God and **watch what happens.**

HERE'S WHAT I'M GOING TO DO

❑ _____

_____

❑ _____

_____

WHAT GOES UP

It seems to be a law of nature and a fact of life that **what goes up must come down.** Often a mountaintop experience is followed by a trip through the valley of despair.

Consider the case of Elijah. If anyone had a reason to celebrate a mountaintop experience, it was this courageous prophet of God. Single-handedly, he had stood against a tyrannical queen and hundreds of pagan prophets and triumphed over them all. His victory on Mount Carmel demonstrated God's power over his enemies in a way that shook Israel to its foundations. Yet where do we find Elijah after his stunning victory? Read today's passage to find out.

1 Kings 19:1-8: ¹When Ahab got home, he told Jezebel what Elijah had done and that he had slaughtered the prophets of Baal. ²So Jezebel sent this message to Elijah: "May the gods also kill me if by this time tomorrow I have failed to take your life like those whom you killed."

³Elijah was afraid and fled for his life. He went to Beersheba, a town in Judah, and he left his servant there. ⁴Then he went on alone into the desert, traveling all day. He sat down under a solitary broom tree and prayed that he might die. "I have had enough, LORD," he said. "Take my life, for I am no better than my ancestors."

⁵Then he lay down and slept under the broom tree. But as he was sleeping, an angel touched him and told him, "Get up and eat!" ⁶He looked around and saw some bread baked on hot stones and a jar of water! So he ate and drank and lay down again.

⁷Then the angel of the LORD came again and touched him and said, "Get up and eat some more, for there is a long journey ahead of you."

⁸So he got up and ate and drank, and the food gave him enough strength to travel forty days and forty nights to Mount Sinai,¹ the mountain of God.

¹ 19:8 Hebrew *Horeb*, another name for Sinai.

Elijah was caught in a wave of depression. Even after all he had seen and done, he declared that his life was no longer worth living. But God helped him by providing food and rest. Away from the noise and turmoil of Ahab's kingdom, he was able to **regain his perspective** and **resume his faithful ministry.**

We need to take this lesson to heart. People who are constantly in motion need **time apart from the turmoil** to be with God. A constant schedule of work—even great work for God's Kingdom—can empty and drain us, leaving us depressed, restless, and unsatisfied. We need to practice the habit of **being still, listening** to God's voice instead of talking, **hearing** instead of doing. If we do, we will find **contentment in all circumstances.**

HERE'S WHAT I'M GOING TO DO

☐ _____

☐ _____

☐ _____

_____

THE RIVER

DAY 60

Living near a river's edge can be wonderful in summer and beautiful in fall. But in the spring, one needs to **keep a close eye on the river** because of the spring melt. If left unmonitored, the lazy summer river can become a raging torrent of destruction and death.

In today's verses, you will read about something else that can destroy lives if left unmonitored.

1 Kings 21:5-10: ⁵"What in the world is the matter?" his wife, Jezebel, asked him. "What has made you so upset that you are not eating?"

⁶"I asked Naboth to sell me his vineyard or to trade it, and he refused!" Ahab told her.

⁷"Are you the king of Israel or not?" Jezebel asked. "Get up and eat and don't worry about it. I'll get you Naboth's vineyard!"

⁸So she wrote letters in Ahab's name, sealed them with his seal, and sent them to the elders and other leaders of the city where Naboth lived. ⁹In her letters she commanded: "Call the citizens together for fasting and prayer and give Naboth a place of honor. ¹⁰Find two scoundrels¹ who will accuse him of cursing God and the king. Then take him out and stone him to death."

Ahab was a king who had everything he wanted. So why did he want a poor man's vineyard enough to kill for it? It was because he had become **the slave of his greed.** While possessions and wealth in and of themselves are not evil, love of them can lead to horrible crimes and injustices, such as the one Ahab encouraged.

¹ **21:10** Hebrew *two sons of Belial*; also in 21:13.

Greed is the same today as it was in Bible times. Left unchecked, **it can push people to do all sorts of senseless things.** Do you ever watch the nightly news? Nations and corporations alike attack each other for very little gain. And not a month goes by that we don't hear of someone being killed or hurt badly during a carjacking or robbery. Greed is indeed **an attitude to take seriously.**

Do you have a problem with greed? Do you long for money, possessions, or popularity? Ask God to help you **surrender** your greedy tendencies to him.

HERE'S WHAT I'M GOING TO DO

☐ _____

☐ _____

☐ _____

☐ _____

☐ _____

☐ _____

PASSIN' THE FAITH ALONG

Karen thought she was being fair. She always made her two sons divide any candy they were sharing. But she noticed one day that nine-year-old Kevin was helping himself to a larger piece of the candy bar and giving the smaller portion to six-year-old Ryan. So Karen made a new rule: Whoever did the breaking would get the last choice of halves. After that, Kevin made sure that the candy bar was **equally** divided!

God expects us to **share fairly with others.** He gives us many resources, but he also expects us to be generous with those gifts. Read this passage to find out about a woman with whom God shared his resources.

2 Kings 4:1-7: [1]One day the widow of one of Elisha's fellow prophets came to Elisha and cried out to him, "My husband who served you is dead, and you know how he feared the LORD. But now a creditor has come, threatening to take my two sons as slaves." [2]"What can I do to help you?" Elisha asked. "Tell me, what do you have in the house?" "Nothing at all, except a flask of olive oil," she replied. [3]And Elisha said, "Borrow as many empty jars as you can from your friends and neighbors. [4]Then go into your house with your sons and shut the door behind you. Pour olive oil from your flask into the jars, setting the jars aside as they are filled." [5]So she did as she was told. Her sons brought many jars to her, and she filled one after another. [6]Soon every container was full to the brim! "Bring me another jar," she said to one of her sons. "There aren't any more!" he told her. And then the olive oil stopped flowing. [7]When she told the man of God what had happened, he said to her, "Now sell the olive oil and pay your debts, and there will be enough money left over to support you and your sons."

In this story, the woman is both obligated and indebted.

She is obligated to her debtors and indebted to God for **his provision** of the means to satisfy the debt. And like this woman, we too are obligated to others and **indebted to God.**

We are like firemen on the line. In the days before fire hoses, the people would line up and pass buckets of water up to the front to help put out the burning buildings. The chain of action had to work efficiently if there was any chance of putting out the fire. A straggler or lazy worker would waste precious time and energy, and someone else—the owner of the house—would pay the price.

It is the same with us. God passes his love and **his blessings** to us so that we can **pass them on to others.** By doing this we can help quench the fires of famine, drought, and starvation, one person at a time. How **generous** are you with **your resources?** What are you doing to pass along God's blessings?

PRAYER POINT

Ask God to stir you to action in any area in which you tend to be a spectator rather than a participant, especially when it comes to helping others.

HERE'S WHAT I'M GOING TO DO

☐ _____

_____

☐ _____

_____

☐ _____

_____

A PASSIONATE GOD

Ever hear something like this on television? "Jeff and Corinne take passion to new limits in an all-new episode of *Santa Monica!* Don't miss it!"

Sad to say, the word "passion" is one of the most abused words in our language today. It is often used to define any strong feeling. And having that "feeling" justifies all kinds of **selfish behavior.** Television and movie advertisers, for example, use this word to put a positive spin on a destructive extramarital affair or abusive behavior. Politicians like the word too, because it expresses deep concern without any accompanying commitment. "I have a passion for the poor!" a senator exclaims to a cable-television camera, while the next day his committee proposes a ten-percent pay hike for his colleagues.

But **passion has a much larger and richer meaning** than the examples just cited. In today's verses, we will discover what God is very passionate about. His take on this word may surprise you.

2 Kings 19:29-31: ²⁹Then Isaiah said to Hezekiah, "Here is the proof that the LORD will protect this city from Assyria's king. This year you will eat only what grows up by itself, and next year you will eat what springs up from that. But in the third year you will plant crops and harvest them; you will tend vineyards and eat their fruit. ³⁰And you who are left in Judah, who have escaped the ravages of the siege, will take root again in your own soil, and you will flourish and multiply. ³¹For a remnant of my people will spread out from Jerusalem, a group of survivors from Mount Zion. The passion of the LORD Almighty will make this happen!"

Did you discover what one of the Lord's passions is? It is people. That's right. Human beings! Passion can be defined as **a powerful emotion** such as love or anger, but it can also be defined as an energetic and unflagging pursuit of an aim or devotion to a cause. **God has a ceaseless devotion toward his people.**

Today's passage tells how God showed his devotion by providing food and hope for the Jewish people. This highlights the two ingredients of passion: emotion and action. Made in God's image, **humans were created with passions,** or the desire to be devoted to a cause too. What are your passions? Art, music, sports, helping people? Ask God to help you discover your passions and use them to further his Kingdom.

PRAYER POINT

Ask God to help you discover

your spiritual passions.

HERE'S WHAT I'M GOING TO DO

☐ _____

_____

☐ _____

_____

☐ _____

_____

☐ _____

_____

☐ _____

_____

☐ _____

_____

For Now and Forever

Some people who really don't understand **Christianity** downplay it as "pie in the sky when you die"—in other words, they think it's just vague, empty promises of sweetness and light in heaven. They assume that the Christian life on earth is tough, hard, and grim. A bunch of do's and don'ts without much joy or excitement.

Sure, life can be tough. And yes, there are limits to our behavior here on earth—which God gave us for our own protection. But there's much more than just the "sweet by and by." There's the **blessed here and now.** As you read today's passage, take note of the ways God rewarded David both in the present and in the future. Because that's just what he'll do for you too.

1 Chronicles 17:7-15: 7"Now go and say to my servant David, 'This is what the LORD Almighty says: I chose you to lead my people Israel when you were just a shepherd boy, tending your sheep out in the pasture. 8I have been with you wherever you have gone, and I have destroyed all your enemies. Now I will make your name famous throughout the earth! 9And I have provided a permanent homeland for my people Israel, a secure place where they will never be disturbed. It will be their own land where wicked nations won't oppress them as they did in the past, 10from the time I appointed judges to rule my people. And I will subdue all your enemies.

" 'And now I declare that the LORD will build a house for you—a dynasty of kings! 11For when you die, I will raise up one of your sons, and I will make his kingdom strong. 12He is the one who will build a house—a temple—for me. And I will establish his throne forever. 13I will be his father, and he will be my son. I will not take my unfailing love from him as I took it from Saul, who ruled before you. 14I will establish him over my dynasty and my kingdom for all time, and his throne will be secure forever.' " ¹⁵So Nathan went back to David and told him everything the LORD had said.

David had been a fabulously successful leader of his nation. Israel was prosperous, peaceful, and promising. In fact, God had given David so many blessings in this life that he was beginning to feel a little guilty! (Check out verses 16-19.) David felt bad that, while he lived in an incredibly beautiful palace, God was still worshiped in a tent. He wanted to build God a proper temple. But God spoke to Nathan, David's trusted advisor. Through Nathan, God assured David that he had been chosen to lead his people Israel. God **promised** he would raise up David's son after him and make him a great king. And that son would be the one to build the temple.

When he heard this message, David was overwhelmed with gratitude. It was almost too good to be true! Yet that's just the kind of God he is. **He wants to lavish on us every blessing in this life**—the blessings of fellowship, freedom, love, joy, peace, and much more.

PRAYER POINT

David prayed. "What more can I say about the way you have honored me? You know what I am really like" (1 Chronicles 17:18).

Recognize that God does know what you are really like, inside and out, and he still loves and treasures you. And he looks forward to spending eternity with you. Take some time to enjoy that truth with God in prayer.

HERE'S WHAT I'M GOING TO DO

☐ _____

☐ _____

_____

OVERWHELMED

You've got a big job ahead of you. Maybe it's a huge term paper or a science project. Maybe it's going through all the steps to get into college. Maybe it's doing your part to fulfill the Great Commission. How do you feel when you face a large task? Overwhelmed . . . inadequate . . . scared . . . weak? You may even **feel like giving up.**

King David was preparing his people—and his son Solomon—for a huge job. Today's passage reveals his very helpful advice.

1 Chronicles 28:11-13, 19-20: 11Then David gave Solomon the plans for the Temple and its surroundings, including the treasuries, the upstairs rooms, the inner rooms, and the inner sanctuary where the Ark's cover—the place of atonement—would be kept. 12David also gave Solomon all the plans he had in mind1 for the courtyards of the LORD's Temple, the outside rooms, the treasuries of God's Temple, and the rooms for the dedicated gifts. 13The king also gave Solomon the instructions concerning the work of the various divisions of priests and Levites in the Temple of the LORD. And he gave specifications for the items in the LORD's Temple which were to be used for worship and sacrifice.

19"Every part of this plan," David told Solomon, "was given to me in writing from the hand of the LORD.2"

20Then David continued, "Be strong and courageous, and do the work. Don't be afraid or discouraged by the size of the task, for the LORD God, my God, is with you. He will not fail you or forsake you. He will see to it that all the work related to the Temple of the LORD is finished correctly."

David had dearly wanted to be the one to build the great and awesome Temple of God in the land of Israel. But God had other plans. So David gave to his son Solomon, who would be

---

1 **28:12** Or *the plans of the spirit that was with him.*
2 **28:19** Or *was written under the direction of the LORD.*

the next king, all the plans God had given him for the Temple and the surrounding areas.

Now, how would you feel if you were young Solomon? Talk about **pressure!** But David passed along some encouraging **words full of God's power.** And Solomon undoubtedly took them to heart.

Prayer Point

Turn 1 Chronicles 28:20 into a prayer asking God to give you the strength and courage to enable you to do his work.

You see, when you face a task given to you by God—no matter what size it is—he stands ready to give you all the strength, wisdom, and help you need to finish it. When you consider the work that must be done for the Kingdom of God, the job can seem overwhelming. But the key is simply to **do your part,** in the power and wisdom of God. Rely on him to guide you and fill you.

So **be strong and courageous,** and trust God to give you everything you need to do **what he has called you to do.**

Here's What I'm Going to Do

☐ _____

_____

☐ _____

_____

☐ _____

_____

☐ _____

_____

THE JOY OF REJOICING

DAY

65

Joy. It's one of the finest feelings humans can experience. How long has it been since you really felt **joyful?** Maybe you haven't had much reason lately to experience the joy of the Lord. You're stuck in life's hassles, in the mundane matters of everyday existence, or wallowing in some painful circumstances. Joy? That may seem like a huge cosmic joke.

No matter how you're feeling right now, **open your heart and your mind** to God's Word today and catch a glimpse of his joyful people.

2 Chronicles 7:1-3, 8, 10: [1]When Solomon finished praying, fire flashed down from heaven and burned up the burnt offerings and sacrifices, and the glorious presence of the LORD filled the Temple. [2]The priests could not even enter the Temple of the LORD because the glorious presence of the LORD filled it. [3]When all the people of Israel saw the fire coming down and the glorious

presence of the LORD filling the Temple, they fell face down on the ground and worshiped and praised the LORD, saying, "He is so good! His faithful love endures forever!"

[8]For the next seven days they celebrated the Festival of Shelters[1]. . . .
[10]Then at the end of the celebration,[2] Solomon sent the people home. They were all joyful and happy because the LORD had been so good to David and Solomon and to his people Israel.

The Temple of God—ornate, gold-laden, and stunningly beautiful—took seven years to build and innumerable hours of labor. Now it was complete. And King Solomon and the people of Israel had dedicated it to the Lord God.

[1] **7:8** Hebrew *the festival.*
[2] **7:10** Hebrew *Then on the twenty-seventh day of the seventh month.* This day of the Hebrew lunar calendar occurs in late September or early October.

As soon as Solomon finished praying, God's glorious presence filled the building. It was so amazing that no one—not even the priests—could enter it. The people were overcome by **praise** and **joy,** falling on their faces and worshiping the Lord. They cried, "He is so good! His faithful love endures forever!" (v. 3).

You may never experience anything so dramatic. And yet the same God is at work in you and through you. **Lift up your eyes—away from your circumstances and onto the Lord.** Recognize how good he has been to you, how faithful his love has been for you. Isn't he worthy of your joyful praise today?

PRAYER POINT

Carve out some time in your schedule just to praise God for the many blessings and gifts he has given you. Make a list of the people, experiences, memories, and possessions that have brought you joy. Think of as many as you can. Then thank God for them one by one.

HERE'S WHAT I'M GOING TO DO

☐ _____

☐ _____

☐ _____

☐ _____

SPIRITUAL JOURNEY TRAVEL LOG

THE FASTING PHENOMENON

In an earlier devotional, we talked about fasting. Yeah, it seems old-fashioned and weird not to eat for a day or two. Should we fast? Why? Read today's awesome story to see how fasting played a role in **an amazing answer to prayer.**

2 Chronicles 20:2-4, 13-17: [2]Messengers came and told Jehoshaphat, "A vast army from Edom[1] is marching against you from beyond the Dead Sea.[2]" [3]Jehoshaphat was alarmed by this news and sought the LORD for guidance. He also gave orders that everyone throughout Judah should observe a fast. [4]So people from all the towns of Judah came to Jerusalem to seek the LORD.

[13]As all the men of Judah stood before the LORD with their little ones, wives, and children, [14]the Spirit of the LORD came upon one of the men standing there. His name was Jahaziel son of Zechariah, son of Benaiah, son of Jeiel, son of Mattaniah, a Levite who was a descendant of Asaph. [15]He said, "Listen, King Jehoshaphat! Listen, all you people of Judah and Jerusalem! This is what the LORD says: Do not be afraid! Don't be discouraged by this mighty army, for the battle is not yours, but God's. [16]Tomorrow, march out against them. You will find them coming up through the ascent of Ziz at the end of the valley that opens into the wilderness of Jeruel. [17]But you will not even need to fight. Take your positions; then stand still and watch the LORD's victory. He is with you, O people of Judah and Jerusalem. Do not be afraid or discouraged. Go out there tomorrow, for the LORD is with you!"

What caused Jehoshaphat and his people to fast? They learned that they were about to be attacked by a large army. The king's response was immediate. He sought God's guidance. He also ordered the people of Judah to observe a fast. They were forced to **depend on God**—and **their**

[1] **20:2a** As in one Hebrew manuscript; most Hebrew manuscripts and ancient versions read *Aram*.
[2] **20:2b** Hebrew *the sea*.

hunger reminded them of that dependence.

These spiritual warriors accomplished more than any army with swords and spears, for the Scripture tells us that the soldiers of Moab and Ammon turned on each other. The end result of Judah's **obedience** was a spectacular victory over the enemy. Why? Because the people of Judah **diligently sought God.** When you need clarity about a decision or you realize that you need to be spiritually cleansed from sin, consider **fasting.** Avoid food for a day, and spend the time you'd normally use eating in prayer instead. Focus on God. Read his Word. Seek his guidance. Let your hunger remind you of your spiritual hunger for him.

PRAYER POINT

As you spend time in fasting and prayer, ask God to show you sins to confess, attitudes to improve, decisions to make, truths to trust, behaviors to change, people to forgive, painful memories to let go of, and callings to obey. Be sure to spend a good amount of time in quiet solitude, and listen carefully to your loving Father.

HERE'S WHAT I'M GOING TO DO

❑ _____

❑ _____

❑ _____

REASON FOR REMEMBERING

Have you ever gotten off track with God? It's easy to let some things slide, like attending church or youth group, reading the Bible every day, or praying whenever you can. **It's easy to let other activities take up your time** so that you no longer do what is most important. As a result, your heart becomes cold and your life becomes **meaningless.**

The whole land of Judah had grown cold to God. They virtually ignored him and his Word. And they had suffered as a result. But King Josiah did what was right in God's eyes. He destroyed the pagan shrines and false idols throughout the land. Years later, he ordered the Temple restored. One of his most important acts was to revive the Passover celebration, which had been almost completely forgotten. Josiah made sure it was celebrated in a big way:

> 2 Chronicles 35:1-6: [1]Then Josiah announced that the Passover of the LORD would be celebrated in Jerusalem on the appointed day in early spring.[1] The Passover lambs were slaughtered at twilight of that day. [2]Josiah also assigned the priests to their duties and encouraged them in their work at the Temple of the LORD. [3]He issued this order to the Levites, who had been set apart to serve the LORD and were teachers in Israel: "Since the Ark is now in Solomon's Temple and you do not need to carry it back and forth on your shoulders, spend your time serving the LORD your God and his people Israel. [4]Report for duty according to the family divisions of your ancestors, following the written instructions of King David of Israel and the instructions of his son Solomon. [5]Then stand in your appointed holy places and help the families assigned to you as they bring their offerings to the Temple. [6]Slaughter the Passover lambs, purify yourselves, and prepare to help those who come. Follow all the instructions that the LORD gave through Moses."

[1] **35:1** Hebrew *on the fourteenth day of the first month.* This day of the Hebrew lunar calendar occurs in late March or early April.

We may be surprised to learn that the people of Judah had forgotten Passover. After all, it was the most important celebration in the life of the nation. Passover looked back to the time that God freed his people from bondage in Egypt. The people remembered the many miraculous things God had done **on their behalf.** But centuries of disobedience and false religion took their toll on the land, and soon everything the people were supposed to hold dear was buried beneath the rubble.

Judah's lesson came too late, however. Despite Josiah's good intentions, his country fell into its bad habits soon after the king died. Not long after that, Judah was carried into captivity. Don't let that happen to you. **Remember what the Lord has done for you.** And keep your will open to his.

HERE'S WHAT I'M GOING TO DO

☐ _____

☐ _____

☐ _____

_____

_____

ON LOAN FROM GOD

Imagine that an army captured everyone in your town and shipped you all to a foreign country. For fifty years, your people lived as slaves under an oppressive government that didn't allow you to fully **practice your faith.** Now you can understand how the Israelites felt during their half-century of exile in Babylon. But when King Cyrus of Persia conquered the Babylonians and ordered the return of all exiled peoples—including the Israelites—to their native lands, the people of Israel were able to reinstate their God. What a breath of fresh air! What an occasion to rejoice!

At this critical moment, God stirred the hearts of the priests and Levites and the leaders of the tribes of Judah and Benjamin to return to Jerusalem to rebuild the Temple of the Lord.

Ezra 2:68-69: 68When they arrived at the Temple of the LORD in Jerusalem, some of the family leaders gave generously toward the rebuilding of God's Temple on its original site, 69and each leader gave as much as he could. The total of their gifts came to 61,000 gold coins,[1] 6,250 pounds[2] of silver, and 100 robes for the priests.

Each family head gave as much as he could for the rebuilding of the Temple, and some gave generously. Ezra explains that these people **freely offered their gifts.** They willingly gave **beyond** what they could actually afford. In reality, the people who gave generously had no ability to give without God's initial generosity. Before the Israelites returned home, something quite remarkable occurred. Their foreign neighbors, in extravagant measure, gave them gifts, including silver and gold and supplies for their journey. So it seemed only fitting that they **give back to God** the unexpected blessing they had received from others.

---

[1] **2:69a** Hebrew *61,000 darics of gold,* about 1,100 pounds or 500 kilograms in weigh
[2] **2:69b** Hebrew *5,000 minas* (3 metric tons).

Giving back to God honors him because it acknowledges that **he is the initiator of good things.** Even our love for him is an offering of what he has given us. First John 4:19 says that "we love each other as a result of his loving us first." When we're inclined to hold back, to say that we don't have enough to give, we need to come back to the reality that God has given richly to us and wants us to **follow his example.**

HERE'S WHAT I'M GOING TO DO

☐ _____

☐ _____

☐ _____

☐ _____

☐ _____

☐ _____

SAD AND HUNGRY

When was the last time you saw a celebrity or politician show remorse for his or her role in a public scandal? Some confess to having made an "error in judgment" or even a "mistake." They may even weep and beg for understanding. But **how many make a fundamental change in their lives?** After they've shaken off the acute embarrassment, many go back to the way they lived before.

Rarely do we see sorrow that **changes lives.** In contrast to today's quick apologies, Ezra's grief for the sin of his people could not be mistaken. Weeping, he threw himself on the ground in front of the Temple of God, drawing a large crowd. The people responded, weeping bitterly and confessing that they had disobeyed God by marrying pagan women. They vowed to do whatever God, through Ezra, commanded.

> Ezra 10:5-6: ⁵So Ezra stood up and demanded that the leaders of the priests and the Levites and all the people of Israel swear that they would do as Shecaniah had said. And they all swore a solemn oath. ⁶Then Ezra left the front of the Temple of God and went to the room of Jehohanan son of Eliashib. He spent the night¹ there, but he did not eat any food or drink. He was still in mourning because of the unfaithfulness of the returned exiles.

Ezra's genuine display of remorse jolted the Israelites. It snapped them back into reality, exposing the true condition of their hearts. By joining Ezra, they were beginning their own restoration. But Ezra did not stop there. He went alone into a temple chamber where he voluntarily abstained from both food and drink.

Ezra's fast showed that he **agreed with God about sin:** It is **serious** and **never to be taken lightly.** Ezra put aside his physical needs for a time and focused on his spiritual

---

¹ **10:6** As in parallel text at 1 Esdras 9:2; Hebrew reads *He went.*

condition. Often during a fast, people find that their spiritual sensitivity is greatly enhanced. They find it easier to hear God's voice and to express to him what is truly on their hearts.

Fasting, in itself, does not make us more spiritual. The Israelites complained to the prophet Isaiah (see Isaiah 58) that God didn't respond favorably to their fasting. Isaiah declared that their fighting and quarreling betrayed their fasting. They were simply "going through the motions of penance." The Lord wants our fasting **to lead to a new awareness of ourselves and others.** Fasting should make us aware of the pressing hardships that millions face every day.

Fasting can help us in many ways. It teaches us self-discipline. It helps us understand the plight of the poor. But sometimes it can be a way of telling God that we are putting everything else aside to get right with him. As Ezra demonstrated, that **reason** alone can have effects that we cannot imagine.

PRAYER POINT

Ask God to help you practice self-sacrifice today as an offering of gratitude for his goodness to you.

HERE'S WHAT I'M GOING TO DO

☐ _____

_____

☐ _____

_____

☐ _____

_____

TAKING A STAND

The world today is full of leaders who take advantage of the poor. A few years ago, the Marcos family ruled the Philippines and lived in splendor at the expense of their fellow citizens, many of whom suffered in abject poverty. One man, Benigno Aquino, stood up and said, "This is not right!" His **tireless campaign for justice** eventually led to his murder by Marcos' henchmen. But three years later, a pro-democracy movement led by Aquino's widow toppled Marcos from power.

Nehemiah, who lived near the end of the Old Testament era, took a similar stand as he called on the carpet some of his own people for exploiting the poor.

Nehemiah 5:1-8: ¹About this time some of the men and their wives raised a cry of protest against their fellow Jews. ²They were saying, "We have such large families. We need more money just so we can buy the food we need to survive." ³Others said, "We have mortgaged our fields, vineyards, and homes to get food during the famine." ⁴And others said, "We have already borrowed to the limit on our fields and vineyards to pay our taxes. ⁵We belong to the same family, and our children are just like theirs. Yet we must sell our children into slavery just to get enough money to live. We have already sold some of our daughters, and we are helpless to do anything about it, for our fields and vineyards are already mortgaged to others."

⁶When I heard their complaints, I was very angry. ⁷After thinking about the situation, I spoke out against these nobles and officials. I told them, "You are oppressing your own relatives by charging them interest when they borrow money!" Then I called a public meeting to deal with the problem.

⁸At the meeting I said to them, "The rest of us are doing all we can to redeem our Jewish relatives who have had to sell themselves to pagan foreigners, but you are selling them back into slavery again. How often must we redeem them?" And they had nothing to say in their defense.

PRAYER POINT

Pray that God will give you the courage to speak out against injustice.

Nehemiah first silenced the accused with a question: How many times will we have to buy back the people you sell into slavery? With shame now falling on them, Nehemiah, fearlessly, got right to the point: "What you are doing is not right!" (v. 9). He then demanded that the poor be reimbursed for all that they had lost. Nehemiah also made the rich take a vow to no longer take advantage of their neighbors.

People like Nehemiah and Benigno Aquino are rare. Aquino lost his life for his stand against injustice. Not everyone is called to lead a resistance against an unjust government, but we can **speak out against the injustice** we encounter in day-to-day life. We can follow Nehemiah's threefold example of **confronting** people with the consequence of their action, forthrightly declaring that it is wrong, then calling for **justice.**

HERE'S WHAT I'M GOING TO DO

☐ _____

_____

☐ _____

_____

BAD MEMORIES

DAY

71

You've probably met a few people who can't seem to **remember** anything. How often do we as Christians act as if we have **no memory of what God has done for us?** We need **reminders to strengthen our faith** in times of weakness and turn us back to God when we rebel.

At a time when Israel had once again turned from God, Ezra led his people in a beautiful prayer that recounted God's love and faithfulness to them from the time of Abraham.

Nehemiah 9:7-16: [7]"You are the LORD God, who chose Abram and brought him from Ur of the Chaldeans and renamed him Abraham. [8]When he had proved himself faithful, you made a covenant with him to give him and his descendants the land of the Canaanites, Hittites, Amorites, Perizzites, Jebusites, and Girgashites. And you have done what you promised, for you are always true to your word.

[9]"You saw the sufferings and sorrows of our ancestors in Egypt, and you heard their cries from beside the Red Sea.[1] [10]You displayed miraculous signs and wonders against Pharaoh, his servants, and all his people, for you knew how arrogantly the Egyptians were treating them. You have a glorious reputation that has never been forgotten. [11]You divided the sea for your people so they could walk through on dry land! And then you hurled their enemies into the depths of the sea. They sank like stones beneath the mighty waters. [12]You led our ancestors by a pillar of cloud during the day and a pillar of fire at night so that they could find their way.

[13]"You came down on Mount Sinai and spoke to them from heaven. You gave them regulations and instructions that were just, and laws and commands that were true. [14]You instructed them concerning the laws of your holy Sabbath. And you commanded them, through Moses your servant, to obey all your commands, laws, and instructions.

---

[1] **9:9** Hebrew *sea of reeds.*

¹⁵"You gave them bread from heaven when they were hungry and water from the rock when they were thirsty. You commanded them to go and take possession of the land you had sworn to give them. ¹⁶But our ancestors were a proud and stubborn lot. and they refused to obey your commands."

God obviously thinks **remembering is important** (see verse 10). Ezra's prayer recalls the Israelites' repeated pattern of rebellion followed by God's mercy, grace, and forgiveness. God showed remarkable patience with his people, refusing to abandon them despite their rejection of him. They needed to remember that fact as they came before him in repentance. Just like Ezra, we need to remember and praise God for all that he has done for us.

PRAYER POINT

Keep a string tied loosely around your finger for one day. When you look at the string. say a prayer of thanks for one blessing God has given you recently.

HERE'S WHAT I'M GOING TO DO

☐ _____

☐ _____

☐ _____

☐ _____

CHOOSING OR SNOOZING?

Think about how many **choices** you make daily: what to wear, what to eat, where to sit, how to spend free time, and so on. Most of these decisions are no big deal. They don't have long-term implications for you or anyone else. But imagine being in a position of power. And suppose the fate of an entire nation hung on your decisions. How would you stand up to such pressure?

That's exactly what Esther faced. A plan had been proposed to wipe out all the Jewish exiles living in Persia. As the queen, Esther was in a position of influence. As a Jew, Esther knew she had to try to save her people. Esther felt scared because requesting an audience with the king, even by the queen, was unheard of. The Persian ruler had a "don't call me, I'll call you!" philosophy. By **taking the initiative to act,** Esther just might lose her head! And yet by standing by and doing nothing, her countrymen might be eradicated! What a choice! Take the path of least resistance, don't rock the boat, give in to peer pressure, say nothing, and live a cushy, carefree life in the palace. Or risk everything. Everything! She thought long and hard. . . .

Esther 4:15-17: 15Then Esther sent this reply to Mordecai: 16"Go and gather together all the Jews of Susa and fast for me. Do not eat or drink for three days, night or day. My maids and I will do the same. And then, though it is against the law, I will go in to see the king. If I must die, I am willing to die." 17So Mordecai went away and did as Esther told him.

If you've ever read the book of Esther, you know the end of the story. In short, God put Esther in a position of influence. God then used Esther's uncle Mordecai to speak words of truth and conviction. Finally, God used Esther's courageous act to save the Jewish people. It's a great story with a happy ending. But before all the smiles and hugs and pats on the back, there were some tense and scary moments.

Chances are you will never face the awesome responsibility of trying to save an entire people. But **you do face tough choices all the time:** Will you look out only for yourself, or also for others? Will you use your gifts and abilities to serve God and others even when it's risky? Will you listen more to the still small voice of God than to the suggestions of friends and your own pounding heart?

Like Esther, you can have a **positive impact.** But to do that you will need to **make seeking and following God your top priority.** You will need others praying for you (as Esther had "all the Jews of Susa" remembering her before God). And you will need someone in your life like Mordecai—someone who can challenge you to do right when you're scared and leaning the other way. Who knows? By living in such a fashion, God may use you to make a huge difference in the lives of those who are right on the edge.

HERE'S WHAT I'M GOING TO DO

☐ _____

_____

☐ _____

_____

☐ _____

_____

THE BLAME GAME

On the nightly news you watch footage of a town devastated by tornadoes. Amidst the wreckage, a few survivors speak to reporters in angry tones. They seem bitter. Others, though clearly sad, project an image of **quiet trust in God.**

Why the different reactions? Why do some people seem to lose their faith during times of intense trial, while others seem to develop **a stronger faith?** And the bigger question: How do *you* react when life gets crazy? The Old Testament book of Job tells the story of a wealthy man whose faith was severely tested. When Job's livestock and children were killed in freakish accidents, his reaction was remarkable:

> Job 1:20-22: ²⁰Job stood up and tore his robe in grief. Then he shaved his head and fell to the ground before God. ²¹He said, "I came naked from my mother's womb, and I will be stripped of everything when I die. The LORD gave me everything I had, and the LORD has taken it away. Praise the name of the LORD!" ²²In all of this, Job did not sin by blaming God.

Notice that Job expressed great grief. He tore his robe and shaved his head (ancient customs of those in mourning). But he also demonstrated **deep trust in God.** He bowed down and prayed. He even worshiped! Was Job nuts? How could he praise God in the midst of such tragedy? Apparently Job understood the fact of God's sovereignty. That is, he recognized that **God is in complete control of everything** in the universe.

It is God who gives and who takes away. In his pain and confusion, Job kept clinging stubbornly to that one truth. He refused to accuse God of being cruel. Notice that he did not demand answers or comfort. Which brings us back to our question: In your life, when the "wheels fall off" or the "roof caves in," how do you react? Do you get angry and yell at God? Do you pout and try to find some way to numb the pain? Do you give God ultimatums, telling him he'd "better" fix your problems, and quick!? Or do you trust in the truth that God's ways are higher than ours and that he is both wise and good? That everything that happens, he allows for reasons we may never understand.

It's important to remember that we can't control what happens to us, but **we can control our response** to what happens. When hard times come, we can (and should) feel sad. We can (and should) be honest with God. Then by choosing to **believe that God will somehow work everything together for good** (Romans 8:28), we can endure.

Like Job, it's possible for us to praise God—even from the pits!

HERE'S WHAT I'M GOING TO DO

☐ _____

_____

☐ _____

_____

☐ _____

_____

COACHING SCHOOL

Perhaps you've seen (or even played for) a coach with a one-size-fits-all approach. In every situation, it's always the same reaction. He yells. Or she criticizes. No matter what you do or how hard you try, you always know what's coming.

On the other hand, you know of coaches who are **master motivators.** They can tailor their actions to the needs of the moment. Today a player needs a pat on the back and a word of encouragement. Tomorrow that player may need a good "chewing out." To bring out the best in people **takes wisdom to know how to respond** to their unique moods and situations.

Job's comforters were graduates of the first "school of coaching." After sitting quietly with him for a week or so (a good and compassionate response!), they eventually gave in to the temptation to preach. Oblivious to Job's pain and insensitive to his feelings, their lectures were more than he could bear.

Job 16:1-6: ¹Then Job spoke again: ²"I have heard all this before. What miserable comforters you are! ³Won't you ever stop your flow of foolish words? What have I said that makes you speak so endlessly? ⁴I could say the same things if you were in my place. I could spout off my criticisms against you and shake my head at you. ⁵But that's not what I would do. I would speak in a way that helps you. I would try to take away your grief. ⁶But as it is, my grief remains no matter how I defend myself. And it does not help if I refuse to speak."

Rather than feeling helped and encouraged, Job felt attacked and misunderstood. If he tried to express his pain and confusion, they jumped on his words. If he said nothing, they criticized that! He couldn't win. No wonder he was so frustrated!

The record of Job and his "comforters" is a good lesson in **how to relate to those in grief.** We need to be extremely sensitive. We need to guard against speaking an endless flow of words— especially "foolish words." It is crucial to **listen** and **share the pain** of those facing trials. At times we eventually may have to speak hard words, but we should not be eager to blast someone with the truth. As one wise counselor has said, "Don't *criticize* a person until you have first *cried* for that person."

HERE'S WHAT I'M GOING TO DO

GOD TO THE RESCUE?

In many fairy tales, poor or cruelly treated people end up "happily ever after." Cinderella leaves behind a miserable life as a maid for a cruel family to marry her prince. A poor miller's daughter becomes queen and outwits Rumpelstiltskin to keep her child. The destitute Aladdin stumbles on a genie's lamp and becomes wealthy and powerful. Adults and children alike still love such rags-to-riches tales.

But do fairy tales bear any resemblance to **real life?** In today's passage, Job wonders why poor people endure **misery without relief.**

Job 24:1-8: ¹"Why doesn't the Almighty open the court and bring judgment? Why must the godly wait for him in vain? ²Evil people steal land by moving the boundary markers. They steal flocks of sheep, ³and they even take donkeys from the poor and fatherless. A poor widow must surrender her valuable ox as collateral for a loan. ⁴The poor are kicked aside; the needy must hide together for safety. ⁵Like the wild donkeys in the desert, the poor must spend all their time just getting enough to keep body and soul together. They go into the desert to search for food for their children. ⁶They harvest a field they do not own, and they glean in the vineyards of the wicked. ⁷All night they lie naked in the cold, without clothing or covering. ⁸They are soaked by mountain showers, and they huddle against the rocks for want of a home."

This passage points out that robbery spreads like an epidemic (vv. 2-3). The poor are hungry (v. 5), naked (v. 7), and homeless (v. 8). " 'Why doesn't the Almighty open the court and bring judgment? Why must the godly wait for him in vain?' " Job asks (v. 1). While answers may be beyond us, hidden in **God's ultimate purposes,** we can know something about his will from readings over the past couple weeks. Again and again we've seen God **bless his people even in tough times.** Our readings have also shown that God blesses those who **trust** him. Faith is trust in God.

PRAYER POINT

Pray for God's justice to prevail in the world and that Christians will be vehicles of his work. Pray for patience to wait and trust in God's good promises.

In the Bible, poor people and widows demonstrate **remarkable faith.** The widow who feeds Elijah with the last of her flour is rewarded with a bottomless jar until the drought ends (1 Kings 17:8-16). Jesus blesses the widow who gives her final coins as a temple offering (Luke 21:1-4). In ancient times and today, many poor people have strong faith because—in their poverty—they understand what it means to be needy. Jesus specifically promises to bless the poor—to fulfill their needs, if not materially at least spiritually (Luke 6:20). Even today, God may use the faith of the poor to humble wealthier followers.

God tackles Job's second complaint in the final verses of chapter 24. He promises to rescue the poor in his own time (v. 21ff). **God's promises are more dependable** than even the happiest fairy tale. Whether we help the poor frequently or pray for God's justice in the world, our mission is to **watch** and **act** as God directs.

HERE'S WHAT I'M GOING TO DO

☐ _____

_____

☐ _____

_____

SPIRITUAL JOURNEY TRAVEL LOG

Dressed for Success

You've been looking forward to the senior prom for several weeks. Because it's a once-in-a-lifetime event, you decide to go all out. You rent an expensive tuxedo and buy new shoes. You arrange for a limousine to pick up your date. You make reservations at the finest restaurant in town. When the special evening comes, you climb into the limo and ride to your date's house. She appears at the door—but what a shock! She's wearing jeans and a polo shirt. You stumble for words, but she responds first: "Why are you so decked out? It's not that big of a deal, is it?"

A special celebration calls for appropriate clothes, doesn't it? Today's passage is about **the splendid clothing God provides for his people.**

Job 29:11-18: [11]"All who heard of me praised me. All who saw me spoke well of me. [12]For I helped the poor in their need and the orphans who had no one to help them. [13]I helped those who had lost hope, and they blessed me. And I caused the widows' hearts to sing for joy. [14]All I did was just and honest. Righteousness covered me like a robe, and I wore justice like a turban. [15]I served as eyes for the blind and feet for the lame. [16]I was a father to the poor and made sure that even strangers received a fair trial. [17]I broke the jaws of godless oppressors and made them release their victims. [18]I thought, 'Surely I will die surrounded by my family after a long, good life.' "

Verse 14 says, "All I did was just and honest. Righteousness covered me like a robe, and I wore justice like a turban."

On one level, righteousness means having **a special standing with the Father because of Christ's purity.** God sees his Son's sinless life in place of our sinful one. On another level, righteousness is the **purity** we ourselves live through the Holy Spirit as we imitate Christ. The key word in verse 14 is "covered." Psalm 85:2 says, "You have forgiven the guilt of your people—yes, you have covered all their sins." God has covered our old sin nature with **the robe of Christ's righteousness.**

We show we are Christians by how we **act.** Job's actions speak for themselves in today's passage. How can we shine righteousness like Job did? By putting on holiness and justice. That's what you wear for **success** in God's Kingdom.

You may feel awkward or overdressed if you wear a new prom outfit to a football game. There is no awkwardness in Christ's righteousness, however. Only awe at the splendor of the robe and crown. Thank the Righteous One, Jesus Christ, for buying your new wardrobe.

PRAYER POINT

Thank the Lord for his righteousness that covers you.

Ask him to show you how you specifically can shine his righteousness where you are.

HERE'S WHAT I'M GOING TO DO

☐ _____

_____

☐ _____

_____

☐ _____

_____

GOOD GUYS AND BAD GUYS

Surfing late-night television, you've probably come across old movies and TV shows. Depending on your taste, you may sit and watch these shows from beginning to end or flip past them as fast as you can. One of the most striking things about these old shows is the way they draw an obvious line between **evil** and **good.** If you're watching a western, you know that the good guy wears the white hat and the bad guy wears the black hat. If you're watching a crime drama, you know that the hero is the square-jawed detective or honest cop and the villain is the snarling punk or oily business executive. And of course, you always know that the good guy will win in the end.

The author of Psalm 1 seems to have had this same mind-set. Take a look at his comparison of a **righteous** person and a **wicked** person.

Psalm 1:3-4: [3][The righteous] are like trees planted along the riverbank, bearing fruit each season without fail. Their leaves never wither, and in all they do, they prosper. [4]But this is not true of the wicked. They are like worthless chaff, scattered by the wind.

Looking around today, it's tough to be as confident as the psalmist was. Much has changed since the days when bad guys always got what was coming to them at the end of a movie. In today's society, the wicked seem to, well, prosper. Inevitably the people who succeed in the corporate and professional world are those who ignore basic Christian concepts such as loving one's enemies and ministering to the poor and needy.

Why is that? Why does God allow those who flout his will and exploit the less fortunate to prosper? The answer is simple: He doesn't—at least not according to his definition of prospering. Exploiters of the poor and weak may benefit financially, but their gains are extremely short lived. In contrast, the righteous—those who minister to the needy and who live according to God's will—can look forward to **eternal prosperity.**

> And in despair I bowed my head
> "There is no peace on earth," I said.
> "For hate is strong and mocks the song
> Of peace on earth, goodwill to men."
> Then pealed the bells more loud and deep,
> God is not dead nor doth he sleep.
> "The wrong shall fail, the right prevail,
> With peace on earth, goodwill to men."

—*Henry Wadsworth Longfellow*, "I Heard the Bells on Christmas Day"

God promises that **his people will claim the ultimate victory over evil.** Let that thought encourage you when you see the proud and arrogant prosper.

PRAYER POINT

Ask God to give you the patience and endurance to confront evil in the world.

HERE'S WHAT I'M GOING TO DO

☐ _____

_____

☐ _____

_____

☐ _____

_____

_____

PRICELESS

How much are you worth? If you had to put a price on yourself, what would it be? There are a couple of different ways to think about this. If you were somehow able to break down the chemicals and compounds that make up your body and sell them on the open market, you might get a couple hundred dollars for yourself. A more profitable route would be to sell your organs and body parts to people in need of transplants. Depending on market demand, you might be able to make five figures. (Of course, you wouldn't be around to spend it.) That's not bad money, but it certainly doesn't qualify you as a priceless artifact.

Except in God's eyes. You see, **God appraises human beings on a much grander scale.** Let's take a look at God's appraisal.

Psalm 8:6-9: ⁶You put us in charge of everything you made, giving us authority over all things—
⁷the sheep and the cattle
and all the wild animals,
⁸the birds in the sky, the fish in the sea,
and everything that swims the ocean currents.
⁹O LORD, our LORD, the majesty of your name fills the earth!

Fortunately, God places a much **higher value** on human beings than we do. For reasons that are beyond our comprehension, we are incredibly valuable in his eyes. Every person with whom we come in contact on a given day is **precious** to God.

On the one hand, that's great news. After all, who wouldn't want to be valuable to God? On the other hand, it places a great deal of responsibility on us to **treat others properly.** When we mistreat God's "valuables"—for instance, the poor and needy—in a sense, we are disrespecting him. How would you feel if someone were to come into your home and start treating your most expensive possessions as though they were junk? Think about how God feels when we treat his most valuable possessions—people—like garbage.

If God says that human beings are valuable, who are we to disagree with him? And if God cares for his precious possessions, who are we to mistreat them?

HERE'S WHAT I'M GOING TO DO

☐ _____

_____

☐ _____

_____

☐ _____

_____

☐ _____

_____

_____

BLOCK THAT KICK

DAY 79

Let's say you're the star player on your high school basketball team. Your team has earned a trip to the state championship game. With three seconds left in the game and your team down by one point, you are fouled as you are taking a shot. So you step to the free throw line with the chance of being the hero. Instead, you miss both shots, and time runs out. You feel pretty low, right? But that's not the worst of it. The next day you get prank phone calls from people who curse you for losing the game and then hang up. Somebody tacks a sign on your locker with the word CHOKE written on it. You hear snickers as you walk to class. Talk about **kicking someone when they're down!**

As you might expect, God frowns on this kind of behavior—especially when those being "kicked" are the poor and needy of the world.

Psalm 10:9-14: 9Like lions they crouch silently, waiting to pounce on the helpless. Like hunters they capture their victims and drag them away in nets.
10The helpless are overwhelmed and collapse; they fall beneath the strength of the wicked.
11The wicked say to themselves, "God isn't watching! He will never notice!"
12Arise, O LORD! Punish the wicked, O God! Do not forget the helpless!
13Why do the wicked get away with cursing God? How can they think, "God will never call us to account"?
14But you do see the trouble and grief they cause. You take note of it and punish them.

The helpless put their trust in you.
You are the defender of orphans.

Of course, these verses don't really apply to us. After all, we're not the type of people who would kick the poor and needy when they're down, are we? We would never make fun of a kid at school whose clothes are ragged and outdated. We would never laughingly yell, "Get a job!" to a homeless person asking for handouts on the street. Right?

PRAYER POINT

Ask God to remind you of situations and circumstances in your life in which you purposefully or inadvertently "kicked" a person when he or she was down.

Truth be told, most of us are **guilty** of kicking people when they're down. And when you think about it, it's a fairly lame excuse to say, "I was just kidding—I didn't mean to hurt anyone." Anytime we **speak or act insensitively toward those less fortunate than us,** we do hurt someone. We hurt the person we're talking about—and **we hurt God.**

Like it or not, we have a responsibility to the poor and needy of this world. God calls us to show them **love, compassion,** and **concern for their well-being.** To do this, we must hold our "foot" in check when we're tempted to lash out at them or have fun at their expense; otherwise, we may end up kicking ourselves later.

HERE'S WHAT I'M GOING TO DO

☐ _____

_____

☐ _____

_____

A Hot Tip

Everybody loves to root for **the underdog.** There's something exciting about seeing the "little guy" prevail in the face of overwhelming odds. The higher those odds are, the harder we cheer. Hollywood certainly recognizes this. If you've ever cheered for Rocky Balboa as he fought for the heavyweight title or grinned goofily at the end of *Hoosiers*, you know what we're talking about.

But here's something you may not know: **God also roots for underdogs.** In fact, he does more than root for them.

> Psalm 12:5-8: 5The LORD replies, "I have seen violence
> done to the helpless,
> and I have heard the groans of the poor.
> Now I will rise up to rescue them,
> as they have longed for me to do."
> 6The LORD's promises are pure,
> like silver refined in a furnace,
> purified seven times over.
> 7Therefore, LORD, we know you will protect the oppressed,
> preserving them forever from this lying generation,
> 8even though the wicked strut about,
> and evil is praised throughout the land.

Talk about your insider tips: If God is rooting for a specific group—in this case, the **weak** and **needy** of the world—sell the house, mortgage the farm, and put everything you've got in that stock. And if God is actually helping that group . . . well, it's a can't-miss situation.

So how can Christians get in on the action? How can we take advantage of this inside information? By doing what God does—**helping the underdogs.** God protects the weak and needy of the world in countless ways. Among the instruments he uses are his Christian servants. In fact, caring for and protecting the less fortunate are **natural extensions of a Christian's relationship with God.**

PRAYER POINT

Ask God to help you understand your responsibility to the needy people in your area. Also ask him to give you wisdom and courage when it comes time for you to act on their behalf.

This care can take many forms. It may involve **physical protection**—not necessarily from threatening people (although that may be the case sometimes), but from the elements. What can we do to make sure that the homeless and disadvantaged people in our corner of the world have sufficient shelter to protect them from the cold and heat?

Care for the needy may also involve **protecting them from political exploitation.** What can you do to make sure that your city (or state) government is committed to helping the poor in your area and is not merely using them as a political platform?

These are just a couple of ideas to get you thinking about your responsibilities. The important thing is not how you care for and protect the needy, but that you do. So get out there and help the underdog.

HERE'S WHAT I'M GOING TO DO

❑ _____

_____

❑ _____

_____

SHOWING HIS LOVE

Danny Stephens,
SMALLTOWN POETS

A s the keyboard player and World Vision spokesman for the modern rock band Smalltown Poets, I have the privilege quite often of getting others involved in the crucial ministry of child sponsorship. Being a voice for hungry children around the world is important to me. Here's why:

A couple of years ago, God began to open my eyes to the fact that something was missing from my relationship with him. This came as a shock to a guy who was saved at age eight and never took a "walk on the wild side." While I certainly hadn't lived a perfect life, I also don't have one of those fascinating testimonies of being saved out of the occult, the Mafia, drug addiction, alcoholism, etc. I praise the Lord for those testimonies, but I've always stayed pretty much close to home when it comes to God.

Largely through World Vision, the Holy Spirit began to impress on me that I wasn't practicing New Testament Christianity. Simply put, Christ mandates that I meet the real, day-to-day needs of others (check out the story of the sheep and the goats in Matthew 25:31-46). The words of the

apostle James echo that command (James 2:14-16). Although we're not saved by the good things we do, we're created to do good works in Jesus' name (Ephesians 2:10). Our acts of mercy lead people to Christ by showing them his love. I had been lazy, selfish, and disobedient. Though I knew Christ, I did not exemplify New Testament Christianity.

Since then, God has opened many doors for me to help others. To God's glory, I have been able to feed a few homeless people, open my home to needy friends, buy things for the poor,

sponsor my precious World Vision child, Daniel, encourage others to sponsor children, and so on. The joy I've found from this is more than worth my efforts, and God continues to bless my obedience to his call.

I challenge you to ask God for opportunities to practice New Testament Christianity, thus impacting lives. God will absolutely open doors if you will ask. Love others as Christ loves you. It will change their lives; it will change your life. I know from experience.

The Hidden Wealth around Us

A junior at the University of Notre Dame in South Bend, Indiana, Rachel Wacker, 20, majors in studio art and philosophy. She loves writing poetry, playing soccer, and sipping cappuccino. Rachel traveled to Ghana, West Africa, in 1995 as one of two 30 Hour Famine Study Tour participants. (She's pictured above with fellow participant Toby Long, in Ghana.) She returned to Ghana again for a month in December 1996. She also recently studied in Italy and served as a volunteer with Mother Teresa's Missionaries of Charity. Rachel says her travels and the relationships she's had overseas have dramatically changed the way she relates to people here at home.

Before I went overseas, it was easy to go into class and do what I had to do. I was in there to take my notes, listen to my teacher, and get my grades. I didn't really notice the people next to me. And I didn't realize how much the things they said, the problems they were having, or the good things they were doing were affecting my life. Or how the things I was saying in class were affecting their lives.

Since I started to look at people more and to notice other people's presence, I realized that I have so much to learn from each person. But in order to learn from them, I have to recognize that each person has something to give to me. And that's recognizing their dignity as a human being.

I found out my life is so much richer because I'm gaining not only from my own personal experience but also from the experiences that all these other people have. When you're willing to share with them, they're likely to share with you.

It's also changed the relationship between God and me. I recognized that I had this dream to see Africa, that the dream could, in fact, be inspired by God, and that it was okay to try to follow this dream and trust in God's plan for me. That really strengthened my personal faith. And it's made me a much more peaceful person. But now my walk with God is also very exciting, because I have a much more active approach to my faith—I'm looking for what he wants instead of just waiting for it to happen to me.

The Power of Respect

Kelly King-Ellison, 21, is a junior pre-med student at Washington University in St. Louis, Missouri, specializing in biomedical engineering. She rows on the varsity crew and is a member of Kappa Kappa Gamma service fraternity. Kelly visited Mozambique in 1994 as one of World Vision's 30 Hour Famine Study Tour participants.

As a volunteer at a hospital, I was warned by my mentor to treat everybody as an equal. He said that if I can't do that, then the hospital doesn't want me as a volunteer. So I've really made a conscious effort of loving everyone and looking at each person as a form of Christ. As a result, I've met some of the most amazing people.

I even met a guy from Mozambique in the hospital's emergency room. An outcast and hard to deal with, he wasn't respected. He hadn't showered, and no one wanted to talk to him.

But when I went to him and started speaking Portuguese, we talked for an hour. It was so much fun! As it turns out, he was an interesting man who had many wonderful stories to share. I learned a lot from him—more than any textbooks could teach me. And it was just by learning to respect that man and actually going over the barrier that no one else would cross. It really benefited my life in many ways.

I hope you will begin to reach out to everyone you possibly can. Go out and work for God. Grasp life. There are so many opportunities and so many people to get to know. Even among the wealthiest people, there is so much hurt and pain in our society from what's going on in the world. Even the simplest things can help somebody. Sometimes all it takes is a smile to make a person's day.

No Deaf Ear

Day

81

Perhaps the most horrific words in the entire Bible are found in Matthew 27:46. As Jesus hung on the cross, with the weight of the world's sins on his shoulders, he cried out, "My God, my God, why have you forsaken me?" At that moment Jesus was completely alone, abandoned even by his heavenly Father.

Is it possible that there are people in the world today who feel similarly **abandoned** by God? Think of the African mother who watches three of her children die slowly and agonizingly of starvation because of a drought in her country. Is it possible that this woman might feel forsaken by God? More to the point, would she be justified in feeling that way?

What is God's attitude toward the **suffering** of his people on earth? What can we expect of him?

Psalm 22:24-28: 24For he has not ignored the suffering of the needy.
He has not turned and walked away.
He has listened to their cries for help.
25I will praise you among all the people;
I will fulfill my vows in the presence of those who worship you.
26The poor will eat and be satisfied.
All who seek the LORD will praise him.
Their hearts will rejoice with everlasting joy.
27The whole earth will acknowledge the LORD and return to him.
People from every nation will bow down before him.
28For the LORD is king!
He rules all the nations.

Let's get the obvious out of the way right now. If God wanted to, he could serve every person on earth a four-course meal morning, noon, and night from now until the end of time. So why doesn't he?

We live in a world cursed by sin. We cannot attempt to understand why God allows tragedies to happen. But David's words in Psalm 22 make it clear that God **cares** about the suffering of the afflicted. He **hears** all cries for help—and he uses a variety of means to **respond** to those cries. As Christians, we must understand that we are among those "means," that **we are instruments of God's grace,** and that we have a responsibility to respond to cries for help.

It's easy to dismiss others' suffering as being beyond our ability to help. Yet nothing is beyond God's ability. If we allow ourselves to be instruments of his healing, there is no limit to what can be accomplished. All it takes is a **decision** on our part to get involved.

PRAYER POINT

Ask God to make you aware of ways in which he can use you to help alleviate suffering.

HERE'S WHAT I'M GOING TO DO

❏ _____

_____

❏ _____

_____

❏ _____

_____

❏ _____

_____

ALL OUR NEEDS

In Mark Twain's novel *The Prince and the Pauper*, a poor young man named Tom is invited into a castle by a prince who befriends him. The prince convinces Tom to switch places with him. Tom agrees. Then, for the first time in his life, Tom has fashionable clothes, rich surroundings, and all the food he can eat. His every need is met by the king.

The children of the heavenly King have even greater privileges, as the writer of the following psalm declares. Read and discover some of **the needs that God meets for us.**

Psalm 34:6-10: ⁶I cried out to the LORD in my suffering, and he heard me.
He set me free from all my fears.
⁷For the angel of the LORD guards all who fear him,
and he rescues them.
⁸Taste and see that the LORD is good.
Oh, the joys of those who trust in him!
⁹Let the LORD's people show him reverence,
for those who honor him will have all they need.
¹⁰Even strong young lions sometimes go hungry,
but those who trust in the LORD will never lack any good thing.

God hears and cares, and David appreciates that fact. Verse 6 states, "I cried . . . and he heard me." God is always available, and he is never too busy to listen. The same verse goes on to say, "He set me free from all my fears." The world is filled with fear. But here God promises **to comfort us and to help us push through our fears.** Verse 7 reminds us that God is our guard

and rescuer. As our guard, he meets our need for security. As our rescuer, he meets our greatest need, the need to be rescued from sin. And verse 9 says that if we **trust** and **honor** God, we will have all that we need.

PRAYER POINT

Thank God for giving you all you

need to live.

What a wonderful King we have. And how fortunate that we who are Christians will enjoy the riches of the King—not just temporarily, but for the rest of our lives. David wrote in another psalm, "Once I was young, and now I am old. Yet I have never seen the godly forsaken" (Psalm 37:25). It's a promise that covers us like a warm coat on the coldest day. **Praise the Lord for his unceasing care for our needs!**

HERE'S WHAT I'M GOING TO DO

☐ _____

_____

☐ _____

_____

☐ _____

_____

☐ _____

_____

☐ _____

_____

SCAN THE HORIZON

DAY
83

It was March. Off the coast of Maine at Hendricks Head lighthouse, an elderly, childless couple watched intently as a ship ran aground on the shoals. Because of the violent snowstorm and the high seas, there was nothing they could do to help the victims but watch and pray.

The next day, they looked for signs of life. They could see the ship's debris floating about, but one item seemed different from the others. It was a mattress that looked as though someone had rolled something up in it. With his wife holding a line, the lighthouse keeper waded out into the sea to retrieve it. Back on the beach, they cut the ropes around the mattress. Inside they found a wooden box. Lying in the box was a weak, helpless, crying baby girl whom they later adopted. In the midst of tragedy, they found a ray of joy that would forever brighten their lives.

Even in the darkest circumstances, **God gives us hope.** His ceaseless care for his people shines through the words of this psalm.

> Psalm 35:9-10: ⁹Then I will rejoice in the LORD.
> I will be glad because he rescues me.
> ¹⁰I will praise him from the bottom of my heart:
> "LORD, who can compare with you?
> Who else rescues the weak and helpless from the strong?
> Who else protects the poor and needy from those who want to rob them?"

Like the lighthouse keeper and his wife, God is always **scanning** the horizon for those who need his help. His vigilant watch locates victims who are lost or adrift, unseen to everyone else. He also **rescues** them from their plight. We should be filled with wonder knowing that **God cares for us** so intimately.

But God's care goes beyond us. It extends to orphans, widows, shut-ins, the homeless, the jobless, those who are ill, the disabled, the starving—the list could go on and on. **God loves those whom the world mistreats and sometimes even forgets.**

Don't forget, however, that you can be God's eyes as well. From whose vantage point do you see the poor, the weak, the needy? Do you scan the horizon for those who need rescue? If not, ask God to give you **a greater vigilance** to see the ones whom no one else notices.

HERE'S WHAT I'M GOING TO DO

❑ _____

_____

❑ _____

_____

❑ _____

_____

❑ _____

_____

_____

Good News/Bad News

Ever hear one of those good news/bad news jokes? They go something like this. A farmer who was on vacation called his farmhand to see how things were going. "Oh, just fine," the farmhand replied. "The good news is the dog's leg should be all healed by the time you get home. The bad news is the truck rolled over it."

"The truck rolled over it?" the farmer asked.

"Yep, the bad news is that someone forgot to set the brake. But the good news is that when the truck rolled over the dog's leg, it slowed the truck down a bit before it hit the barn."

"Hit the barn?!?" shouted the farmer.

"Yep," replied the farmhand. "That's the bad news. But here's the good news. The truck didn't do much damage to the barn because most of it had burned down the day before."

Today's passage shares the **ups and downs** of a good news/bad news message. You can be sure, however, that David, the author of this psalm, didn't find anything funny about the content:

Psalm 37:12-18: ¹²The wicked plot against the godly;
they snarl at them in defiance.
¹³But the LORD just laughs,
for he sees their day of judgment coming.
¹⁴The wicked draw their swords
and string their bows
to kill the poor and the oppressed,
to slaughter those who do right.
¹⁵But they will be stabbed through the heart with their own swords,
and their bows will be broken.
¹⁶It is better to be godly and have little

than to be evil and possess much.
17For the strength of the wicked will be shattered,
but the LORD takes care of the godly.
18Day by day the LORD takes care of the innocent,
and they will receive a reward that lasts forever.

These verses are full of good news and bad news. For **the wicked,** the news is bad. "The wicked . . . string their bows. . . . Their bows will be broken" (vv. 14-15). "The strength of the wicked will be shattered" (v. 17). "The wicked will perish. . . . They will disappear like smoke" (v. 20). But for **believers,** the news is good. "The LORD takes care of the godly" (v. 17). "They will receive a reward that lasts forever" (v. 18).

The information age allows us to witness and read about the evil things that plague our world. But we have **a source of hope that surpasses the world's despair.** By reading the Bible—God's Good News—we can be reminded daily that God has overcome whatever trial we face. Now that *is* good news!

PRAYER POINT

Ask God to make his Word the lens through which you view the world. Ask him to help you study Scripture in a thoughtful, life-changing way.

HERE'S WHAT I'M GOING TO DO

☐ _____

_____

☐ _____

_____

_____

IGNORED

Have you ever felt ignored? Perhaps your parents are divorced and the parent you live with is working so hard to make ends meet that he or she just doesn't seem to have any time for you. Or maybe you're not a part of the popular crowd at school, or any crowd for that matter. And you hate sitting alone at lunch. But no one offers to sit with you. Everyone seems to be **ignoring** you.

Read these verses to find out about someone who is always thinking about those who feel **ignored** and **rejected.**

> Psalm 40:16-17: [16]But may all who search for you
> be filled with joy and gladness.
> May those who love your salvation
> repeatedly shout, "The LORD is great!"
> [17]As for me, I am poor and needy,
> but the LORD is thinking about me right now.
> You are my helper and my savior.
> Do not delay, O my God.

What confidence this passage expresses! It begins with the **most important requirement** for all believers: **They must search for God.** Those who want joy and gladness will not find it apart from him. But if they search, they will find, and their joy will be complete and unshakable. Thus the poor person, who might be inclined to worry or curse his or her situation, waits with quiet confidence in God's goodness. That person may be ignored and despised, but he or she has **a companion in God.** Such favor is worth more than all the friendships in the world.

David is not telling us that God thinks only about the poor and needy; he reminds us, instead, that confidence in God enables us to put earthly troubles in perspective. No matter what happens, no matter who turns a cold shoulder, we have the **friendship** of our heavenly Father. And he will give us **companions** to take the place of those who desert us.

Remind yourself today of the great privilege of friendship God gave you when you came to Christ. Thank him that **you are no longer ignored.** Then think about the needs of those who are ignored and rejected. Commit to pray for them. Then take steps to ease their loneliness. Just as Jesus was known for befriending the friendless, we must be known by the **kindness** we show.

HERE'S WHAT I'M GOING TO DO

❑ _____

_____

❑ _____

_____

❑ _____

_____

❑ _____

_____

❑ _____

_____

SPIRITUAL JOURNEY TRAVEL LOG

WHERE ARE YOU RUNNING?

On New Year's Day, 1929, a packed Rose Bowl Stadium watched the University of California battle Georgia Tech. After a scoreless first quarter, Georgia Tech began to move the ball down the field. The quarterback passed the ball to a running back, but the back fumbled as he was hit. The ball squirted into the hands of a California defensive back, who latched on to the ball and chugged toward the goal line. Everyone began to yell. The California player imagined that the spectators were celebrating his moment of glory. But ten yards from the end zone, he was tackled by one of his own teammates! He realized, to his horror, that he had been **running the wrong way.**

This blunder allowed Georgia Tech to score a safety (two points) moments later when they tackled a California player in the end zone. And the crowning blow was the final score of the game: Georgia Tech 8, California 7. The infamous player became known in sports history as "Wrong Way" Riegels.

Today's passage tells us how running the wrong way in this life can have even more **serious consequences.**

Psalm 49:8-13: [8]Redemption does not come so easily,
for no one can ever pay enough
[9]to live forever
and never see the grave.
[10]Those who are wise must finally die,
just like the foolish and senseless,
leaving all their wealth behind.
[11]The grave is their eternal home,
where they will stay forever.
They may name their estates after themselves,
but they leave their wealth to others.

¹²They will not last long despite their riches—
they will die like the animals.
¹³This is the fate of fools,
though they will be remembered as being so wise.

Wealth may be able to buy a lot of things, but it can't buy freedom from death or a place in heaven. Yet worldly wealth is the goal for many. When we make wealth the goal and our reason for living, we begin running the wrong way. That course ends in exhaustion and despair. Instead, we should be **running after true riches:** life with God and a life of service to others. When we pursue God's path, we are **strengthened** and **encouraged** with every step we take.

As you choose to run after true riches, the crowd may try to convince you that you are running the wrong way. Just remember that God is the one who designed the game and the field. Run his way! Listen for his cheers!

HERE'S WHAT I'M GOING TO DO

☐ _____

_____

☐ _____

_____

☐ _____

_____

_____

WORTHLESS WEALTH

We've all heard stories about eccentric rich people, but John Mytton carried eccentric behavior to new heights. Born in 1797 to a wealthy English squire, Mytton inherited a sizable fortune as a young man, including a regular annual allowance. But Mytton loved his carefree life too much. He drank heavily and spent his days conducting **foolish** experiments, such as seeing if a horse and carriage could jump a toll gate. He hunted even in the worst weather, sometimes wearing no clothing! He often threw bundles of money to servants and friends without concern for the future. Soon he had bankrupted his estate. He died in a debtors' prison at the age of 37.

Mytton's life may be an extreme example, but it does show us that **wealth can be a great trap.** It can insulate us from God's truth and encourage us to indulge ourselves, sometimes to death. David recognized this truth when he wrote the following psalm:

> Psalm 49:16-20: [16]So don't be dismayed when the wicked grow rich, and their homes become ever more splendid.
> [17]For when they die, they carry nothing with them. Their wealth will not follow them into the grave.
> [18]In this life they consider themselves fortunate, and the world loudly applauds their success.
> [19]But they will die like all others before them and never again see the light of day.
> [20]People who boast of their wealth don't understand that they will die like the animals.

The old saying goes, "You'll never see a hearse pulling a U-haul trailer." The truth is, **when people die, they take nothing with them into the afterlife.** That's why the writer of this psalm encourages God's people not to become dismayed when unbelievers get richer and richer and their homes become even more lavish. All that wealth will ultimately gain them **nothing.**

Believers, on the other hand, are promised the "riches" of God forever: **eternal life** with him. And that's worth far, far more than any earthly riches.

One day every person—whether rich or poor on earth—will stand naked and empty-handed before God in heaven. The only rewards we can claim at that time are those we have **stored up in heaven by our actions while on earth** (read Matthew 6:19-21).

How are these rewards built? By **serving God** with our time and talents on earth. By **ministering** to others in his name, even if that costs us something we value. By **setting our priorities in life according to his will,** not according to the world's standards of success. To build treasure in heaven, our faith must be in God, not in money or possessions or power. The more we use our gifts and resources for his glory on earth, the greater our treasure in heaven will be.

HERE'S WHAT I'M GOING TO DO

☐ _____

_____

☐ _____

_____

TRUE SACRIFICE

Why do you go to church? Why do you read your Bible? Why do you give money to charitable causes and ministries? Why do you volunteer for missions trips?

In short, when it comes to being a Christian, **why do you do what you do?** Is it because that's what you're used to doing? Or is it because you genuinely want to love, serve, and know God as best you can?

God is concerned foremost about the **motives** that drive you, as you'll see in today's passage.

> Psalm 50:7-15: ⁷"O my people, listen as I speak.
> Here are my charges against you, O Israel:
> I am God, your God!
> ⁸I have no complaint about your sacrifices
> or the burnt offerings you constantly bring to my altar.
> ⁹But I want no more bulls from your barns;
> I want no more goats from your pens.
> ¹⁰For all the animals of the forest are mine,
> and I own the cattle on a thousand hills.
> ¹¹Every bird of the mountains
> and all the animals of the field belong to me.
> ¹²If I were hungry, I would not mention it to you,
> for all the world is mine and everything in it.
> ¹³I don't need the bulls you sacrifice;
> I don't need the blood of goats.
> ¹⁴What I want instead is your true thanks to God;
> I want you to fulfill your vows to the Most High.
> ¹⁵Trust me in your times of trouble,
> and I will rescue you,

and you will give me glory."

As believers, we're called to serve God out of a heart of thanks. We're called to sacrifice our time and energy for his glory. We're called to know him intimately because we're going to spend eternity with him. We do these things not in order to gain God's favor, but to **reflect the changes he has already made in our lives.**

Even so, those activities can become **hollow** if they're pursued for the wrong purposes. That's what happened to the Israelites with their sacrifices. They were doing the right things, but for the wrong reasons. They were simply going through the motions. They had forgotten why they were doing what they were doing.

God calls them on it. He tells them very clearly that he really doesn't need their bulls or goats or sheep. He wants their hearts. He wants their honest praise. He wants their trust. And he wants them to fulfill their promises to him.

God is pleased with sacrifices that come from true love and obedience. From where are your sacrifices coming?

PRAYER POINT

Examine your own motives before the Lord. Search your heart with the guidance of his Spirit to determine the true reasons why you do what you do as a believer.

HERE'S WHAT I'M GOING TO DO

☐ _____

_____

☐ _____

_____

_____

FATHER TO THE FATHERLESS

Where do you turn when you're **down** and **lonely?** Maybe you call a friend who you know will listen and care and offer some good advice. Maybe you hang out with your family and enjoy the easy interaction you find at home. Maybe you spend extra time with your youth group and share your struggles with them. Or maybe you go to God in prayer. All of these are healthy responses to loneliness. But think about people who don't have families, parents, or even friends. What can they do to heal their hurting hearts?

Today's Scripture gives us a glimpse of **God's grace for the lonely.**

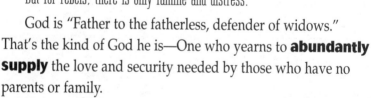

Psalm 68:3-6: ³But let the godly rejoice.
Let them be glad in God's presence.
Let them be filled with joy.
⁴Sing praises to God and to his name!
Sing loud praises to him who rides the clouds.
His name is the LORD—
rejoice in his presence!
⁵Father to the fatherless, defender of widows—
this is God, whose dwelling is holy.
⁶God places the lonely in families;
he sets the prisoners free and gives them joy.
But for rebels, there is only famine and distress.

God is "Father to the fatherless, defender of widows." That's the kind of God he is—One who yearns to **abundantly supply** the love and security needed by those who have no parents or family.

The root of much of our pain and need is **loneliness.** When we feel lonely, we sometimes try to soothe our pain in ways that not only fail to fill our loneliness, but remove us even further from others. **God stands ready to fill up the emptiness in our hearts.**

He will build a support team for each of us, if only we'll take advantage of it. It may be your own family, your youth group, or a group of your closest friends. Whatever it is, God is pleased to provide for your need to "belong."

But we need to make sure that the "family" we rely on is truly one God has provided for us. It's easy to fall into a group and discover that its purposes are counter to God's will. Just consider how influential the gang movement is in cities today to see the deep need for a "family" of some kind to hang out with.

Trust God to fill your loneliness his way. He promises to do just that. Because he loves to hear the praises that result.

HERE'S WHAT I'M GOING TO DO

☐ _____

_____

☐ _____

_____

☐ _____

_____

_____

A POWERFUL PRAYER

You see a homeless man on the street. He's coming your way. **What do you do?** Do you say anything? Do you give him anything? You see a mother with three small children, waiting in front of a church's canned goods distribution center. What do you do?

You hear about starving children in Africa, India, Asia . . . all around the world. You read about Christians in foreign lands who are persecuted for their faith, who lose everything they own, who are rejected by their families and communities. What do you do?

Psalm 74:20-23: [20]Remember your covenant promises,
for the land is full of darkness and violence!
[21]Don't let the downtrodden be constantly disgraced!
Instead, let these poor and needy ones give praise to your name.
[22]Arise, O God, and defend your cause.
Remember how these fools insult you all day long.
[23]Don't overlook these things your enemies have said.
Their uproar of rebellion grows ever louder.

If only you had all the money in the world, you could do a lot to help. If only you were president of the world, you could do much to relieve the suffering. If only . . .

But let's get real here. You barely have pocket change for the week. And you certainly aren't in any position of power. But Someone is. And he is working to help **the oppressed and downtrodden,** not only in your neighborhood but around the world. The truth is, we do have an incredible, even infinite, power available to us: the power of an omnipotent God.

There is one thing our all-powerful and loving God calls us to do. It won't cost us anything but time. **Pray.** Pray for the poor, the needy, the hungry. **Ask God not to let them be constantly disgraced.** Ask God to care for them so that they will give praise to his name. And ask God to **use you** to improve their circumstances and bring encouragement to their souls.

We live in a fallen world. A long time ago, humankind made the choice to go its own way rather than God's. In the Garden of Eden, Adam and Eve chose to blatantly disobey God for their own pleasure. Even today, we live with the consequences of that choice. We must deal with the often horrible results of that selfish attitude. Those consequences include hunger, pain, sickness, crime . . . the list seems endless.

PRAYER POINT

Do you know any poor and needy people by name? Do you know some by their faces, having seen them on the street or at a homeless kitchen? If so, bring them before the Lord in prayer. Pray Psalm 74:21 on their behalf.

But God can and does reach through all that pain and darkness to touch hurting souls with his **love** and **provision.** Let us pray that he will do that for the needy today.

HERE'S WHAT I'M GOING TO DO

☐ _____

_____

☐ _____

_____

☐ _____

_____

_____

SPIRITUAL JOURNEY TRAVEL LOG

Rebellious Hearts

Imagine being rescued from a horrendous situation and released into total freedom. Imagine being led physically by God every day, so you had no question as to which way you were supposed to go and what you were supposed to do. Imagine being protected and provided for day by day. Imagine **every need being met** from God's hand.

And imagine getting **frustrated** by it, **even angry at God.** Imagine complaining bitterly about this kind of treatment. That doesn't make much sense, does it? But it happened. In today's reading, the psalmist describes what happened to the nation of Israel.

Psalm 78:14-22: [14]In the daytime he led them by a cloud,
and at night by a pillar of fire.
[15]He split open the rocks in the wilderness
to give them plenty of water, as from a gushing spring.
[16]He made streams pour from the rock,
making the waters flow down like a river!
[17]Yet they kept on with their sin,
rebelling against the Most High in the desert.
[18]They willfully tested God in their hearts,
demanding the foods they craved.
[19]They even spoke against God himself, saying,
"God can't give us food in the desert.
[20]Yes, he can strike a rock so water gushes out,
but he can't give his people bread and meat."
[21]When the LORD heard them, he was angry.
The fire of his wrath burned against Jacob.
Yes, his anger rose against Israel,
[22]for they did not believe God

or trust him to care for them.

It's amazing to read of the awesome exploits of God on behalf of the Israelites—and then to read of their thanklessness, their bitterness, their unceasing **desire for more** than what they were getting. They were never satisfied. They never seemed to fully trust the God who rescued them. So they blamed him for every problem they encountered, rather than **trusting him** to take them through it his way. Imagine that!

But when we get overwhelmed by the needs and responsibilities of life, isn't it easy for us to **blame God for not making things better for us?** Don't we get upset and even bitter when God doesn't do things exactly the way we think he should for us? The truth is, deep down, we're really not so different from the Israelites. Our hearts can become just as hardened and selfish as theirs, if we're not careful. A regular habit of examining our lives in the light of God's Word will reveal those hardened places and keep us from believing the lies we tell ourselves.

HERE'S WHAT I'M GOING TO DO

❑ _____

_____

❑ _____

_____

❑ _____

_____

JUDGING THE JUDGES

You may be surprised to learn that **God has some pretty high standards** for earthly rulers and judges. Check out some of these standards in Psalm 82.

Psalm 82:1-8: ¹God presides over heaven's court;
he pronounces judgment on the judges:
²"How long will you judges hand down unjust decisions?
How long will you shower special favors on the wicked?
³Give fair judgment to the poor and the orphan;
uphold the rights of the oppressed and the destitute.
⁴Rescue the poor and helpless;
deliver them from the grasp of evil people.
⁵But these oppressors know nothing;
they are so ignorant!
And because they are in darkness,
the whole world is shaken to the core.
⁶I say, 'You are gods
and children of the Most High.
⁷But in death you are mere men.
You will fall as any prince,
for all must die.' "
⁸Rise up, O God, and judge the earth,
for all the nations belong to you.

Court is in session in heaven. The rulers of this world are on trial, and God is the judge. He wants to know one thing: How well did the rulers and judges treat the poor and oppressed of this world? God wants to know **what they have done to help the neglected and needy.**

The psalm writer makes an interesting statement regarding the influence of powerful judges and rulers. He says that because they walk about in darkness, the world is shaken to the core (v. 5). Did you hear that? Mistreatment of the poor and oppressed can have **a worldwide impact!**

Don't think that just because you're not considering a career in law or politics that you're off the hook as far as the poor and needy are concerned either. God may hold those in positions of authority to higher standards, but he still expects all of his children **to show kindness** to those less fortunate than us.

PRAYER POINT

As our country continues to face controversial social issues, pray that judges (and other rulers) will apply wisdom and the fear of God to their decisions.

God's final warning to the judges and rulers in this passage should also serve as a wake-up call to us. Though these people may have great power in our lifetime, God says that in death they are only humans. One day they, like all people, will stand before God with their titles and authority stripped away, facing their Creator as ordinary men and women.

What will you be able to say to the Creator on that day about your treatment of the poor and neglected people in society today?

HERE'S WHAT I'M GOING TO DO

☐ _____

_____

☐ _____

_____

☐ _____

_____

THANKSGIVING ALL YEAR

If you had to come up with a slogan or saying that captures most people's attitude in society today, what would it be? Here's a suggestion: "It's my right." It's hard to find **true thankfulness** in our world today. Sure, we say thanks when someone does something nice for us, but are we really thankful? Many people believe that they are entitled to everything good that happens to them and, therefore, see no need to be thankful. After all, they think, I'm entitled to it.

The writer of Psalm 92, in contrast, displays a much different type of attitude. Let's take a look.

> Psalm 92:1-4: ¹It is good to give thanks to the LORD,
> to sing praises to the Most High.
> ²It is good to proclaim your unfailing love in the morning,
> your faithfulness in the evening,
> ³accompanied by the harp and lute
> and the harmony of the lyre.
> ⁴You thrill me, LORD, with all you have done for me!
> I sing for joy because of what you have done.

Have you ever been so overwhelmed by an emotion or feeling that you just had to blurt it out—regardless of the consequences? That's kind of what David does in this passage. He's got this feeling building up inside of him until he just can't keep it in any longer: "I sing for joy because of what you have done."

Not only is David thankful for **what God has done,** he also reveals a **genuine passion** for God. This is a response that can come only from the heart. As David thinks about God's gracious deeds, he wells up with joy and expresses himself in song. Here is a person who knows that he has received from God much more than he could ever hope to give back.

A grateful person has the right perspective on life. This person recognizes that we have no right to expect anything from God—or from anybody else, for that matter. In fact, if we deserve anything from God, it's judgment and punishment for our sins.

Sometimes it's pretty difficult to maintain an **attitude of thanksgiving** ("Thanks for helping me get an 'F' on this test, God"; "I'm so grateful that I don't have enough money to wear something nice to the prom"). But as hard as it may be to believe, even in times of great hardship we can legitimately **give thanks** to God. That's because no matter how bad things are, the fact remains that God loves us, that he is always present with us, and that he has provided a glorious future with him forever.

PRAYER POINT

Make a list of the things for which you are thankful and pray through them, offering back to God a sacrifice of praise and thanksgiving.

HERE'S WHAT I'M GOING TO DO

☐ _____

_____

☐ _____

_____

☐ _____

_____

☐ _____

_____

THE PURPOSE OF LIFE

DAY 94

Here's one of the most serious questions you'll ever have to answer: What is the **purpose** of your life? In other words, what were you put on this earth to **do** or **accomplish?** Consider the question for a moment before you answer. Some people may think in terms of career and say, "I was created to become a doctor and help sick people." Others may think in terms of family and say, "My purpose is to get married, have kids, and raise a good Christian family." Still others may think patriotically and say, "I was born to pursue life, liberty, and happiness."

Read Psalm 100 and then answer the question again.

Psalm 100:1-5: ¹Shout with joy to the LORD, O earth!
²Worship the LORD with gladness.
Come before him, singing with joy.
³Acknowledge that the LORD is God!
He made us, and we are his.
We are his people, the sheep of his pasture.
⁴Enter his gates with thanksgiving;
go into his courts with praise.
Give thanks to him and bless his name.
⁵For the LORD is good.
His unfailing love continues forever,
and his faithfulness continues to each generation.

Put simply, God made us **to worship him.** It seems like a fairly **simple** purpose, doesn't it—one that shouldn't be too hard to understand. So why is it so difficult for us to fulfill our purpose? Because many of us have convinced ourselves that we need other things in order to be truly happy.

"If I had more money, then I'd be happy." "I'd be happy if

I could just find someone to date." "All I need to be happy is a nice car and some gas money." Wrong, wrong, and wrong. All we need to be happy is **the sense of fulfillment** that comes from pursuing our purpose in life. The apostle Peter spoke of a "glorious, inexpressible joy" that overtakes us when we **focus our desires and energies on God** and **place our trust in him.**

PRAYER POINT

Praise God for the fact that he has created you with an important purpose for your life. Ask him to help you as you seek to fulfill that purpose.

Look at the psalmist's words in verse 3: First we acknowledge that "the LORD is God." Nothing in this world has greater power or significance than him. Then we recognize that "he made us"—and, in the process, gave us purpose for our existence. Finally we see his purpose, that we would be "his people, the sheep of his pasture" (v. 3). As our shepherd or caretaker, God will go to any lengths to ensure that those of us under his care are **safe** and **content.**

Throughout the centuries, people have tried everything under the sun to find fulfillment in their lives—sex, money, possessions, family, careers, fame, drugs, and so on. But the simple fact is that we find fulfillment **only by worshiping our Creator.**

HERE'S WHAT I'M GOING TO DO

☐ _____

_____

☐ _____

_____

LEARNING DEPENDENCY

Perhaps you spend a lot of time dreaming about becoming **independent.** You know—not having to answer to your parents or live by their rules and regulations anymore. Americans place such a high priority on independence that we set aside every Fourth of July to celebrate it. It's one of the most prized possessions in our society. But should it be? The author of Psalm 104 has a lot to say to people who believe they can handle life **on their own.**

Psalm 104:21-29: 21Then the young lions roar for their food,
but they are dependent on God.
22At dawn they slink back
into their dens to rest.
23Then people go off to their work;
they labor until the evening shadows fall again.
24O LORD, what a variety of things you have made!
In wisdom you have made them all.
The earth is full of your creatures.
25Here is the ocean, vast and wide,
teeming with life of every kind,
both great and small.
26See the ships sailing along,
and Leviathan, which you made to play in the sea.
27Every one of these depends on you
to give them their food as they need it.
28When you supply it, they gather it.
You open your hand to feed them, and they are satisfied.
29But if you turn away from them, they panic.
When you take away their breath, they die
and turn again to dust.

Being overly dependent on someone else is usually viewed as a weakness—and, in extreme cases, a mental illness. However, **dependency on God is not a weakness;** in fact, it's really nothing more than **facing reality.** God sustains all life every moment of the day. Apart from him **nothing** can exist.

If we really believe that every breath depends on God, shouldn't our lives reflect that belief? In fact, as extreme as it sounds, we should acknowledge our dependence on God in everything we **do** and **say.** So, instead of trying to accomplish things on our own, we should **submit ourselves to God's agenda** and allow him to **carry it out** through us.

PRAYER POINT

Ask God to make you aware of what he is doing around you.

Notice the issues that should be on your agenda.

HERE'S WHAT I'M GOING TO DO

☐ _____

_____

☐ _____

_____

☐ _____

_____

☐ _____

_____

☐ _____

_____

SPIRITUAL JOURNEY TRAVEL LOG

GOD IS GREAT, GOD IS GOOD

Aslan, the lion in C. S. Lewis' classic children's novel *The Lion, the Witch, and the Wardrobe*, represents Christ. Lucy, a young girl, learns about Aslan from Mr. and Mrs. Beaver of the land of Narnia. Lucy is perplexed to hear of Aslan's fearsome nature. "Then he isn't safe?" Lucy asks Mr. Beaver. "Safe?" replies Mr. Beaver. " 'Course he isn't safe. But he's good."

Psalm 107 offers some stunning examples of **the goodness of God.** Let's take a look at them.

Psalm 107:1-9: ¹Give thanks to the LORD, for he is good!
His faithful love endures forever.
²Has the LORD redeemed you? Then speak out!
Tell others he has saved you from your enemies.
³For he has gathered the exiles from many lands,
from east and west, from north and south.
⁴Some wandered in the desert,
lost and homeless.
⁵Hungry and thirsty,
they nearly died.
⁶"LORD, help!" they cried in their trouble,
and he rescued them from their distress.
⁷He led them straight to safety,
to a city where they could live.
⁸Let them praise the LORD for his great love
and for all his wonderful deeds to them.
⁹For he satisfies the thirsty
and fills the hungry with good things.

This good God described in Psalm 107 is the same fearsome Lord who destroyed the earth with a flood and sent horrible plagues on the land of Egypt. Throughout history,

God's holiness and judgment have struck fear in the hearts of men and women. Even God's angels caused people to tremble. It's no wonder that an angel's first words were often, "Fear not."

PRAYER POINT

Ask God to help you and your friends become instruments of his goodness to the poor and needy in your area.

But according to this psalm, the **redeemed**—those whom God has brought into his family—can declare that God is good. Israel knew of God's goodness through his deeds. He brought the nation back together after it had been scattered by Assyrian and Babylonian conquerors. He rescued them from wandering in the desert and provided food and drink for them. He heard their cries for help and rescued them from their distress.

Sometimes we may not recognize God's goodness. We may become perplexed by his awesome nature. We will never be able to understand God completely—at least not during our time on earth—because we are not God. But regardless of our confusion, we can **rest assured** in the fact that God is good.

HERE'S WHAT I'M GOING TO DO

☐ _____

_____

☐ _____

_____

☐ _____

_____

_____

JUST DESERTS

DAY

97

Y ou're watching a hot new movie. It's got everything—
action, great characters, a spine-tingling plot, and some
funny one-liners. It also features a bad guy who absolutely
personifies evil. You find yourself hoping, almost praying, that
this "beast" will eventually get what he **deserves.**

Sure enough, in the end, it happens. The hero comes on
the scene, the two fight, and the villain is disposed of in
gruesome fashion. You feel like cheering!

This is the same dynamic at work in Psalm 109. David,
speaking of an unidentified enemy, writes:

> Psalm 109:26-30: ²⁶Help me, O LORD my God!
> Save me because of your unfailing love.
> ²⁷Let them see that this is your doing,
> that you yourself have done it, LORD.
> ²⁸Then let them curse me if they like,
> but you will bless me!
> When they attack me, they will be disgraced!
> But I, your servant, will go right on rejoicing!
> ²⁹Make their humiliation obvious to all;
> clothe my accusers with disgrace.
> ³⁰But I will give repeated thanks to the LORD,
> praising him to everyone.

This may not seem like a very godly prayer—to call
down curses on someone—but David was deeply disturbed
and angry. It bothered him that this individual had been so
harsh to the poor and needy. And so David prayed that
the wicked would be judged and **the innocent
vindicated.** David wanted God to be honored and obeyed.
He understood that as long as the powerful mistreated the

powerless, this was not fully possible.

What about you? Does it bother you when you see **injustice?** How do you feel when you see refugees or immigrants being treated unfairly? Are you moved to pray in such situations? When evil governments starve their own people, do you pray for God to bring down those in power?

PRAYER POINT

Ask God to work through you on behalf of the oppressed.

We cannot right every wrong or rectify every unjust situation. But we can do two things. As stated, **we can pray** for God to work on behalf of the oppressed. And we can, in our own lives, **show kindness** to those in trouble. And think about this: If we are callous or cruel to those in need, we may end up being the "bad guys" in a prayer like David's in Psalm 109.

HERE'S WHAT I'M GOING TO DO

☐ _____

☐ _____

☐ _____

☐ _____

☐ _____

GOOD HANDS

Have you dropped anything lately? If so, you know that Murphy (the compiler of the infamous "Murphy's Laws") was right. If you drop a book, it will inevitably fall into a puddle! If you drop a bite of food, it will miss your napkin by a centimeter (or less!) and end up in your lap. If you drop a tool while working on your car, it will roll to that exact spot where you can't reach it without crawling underneath through the grease!

In a spiritual sense, people also sometimes "drop" (that is, we slip or fall). The **good news** of Psalm 113 tells us that God can reach down, pick us up, and put us back where we belong.

> Psalm 113:5-8: ⁵Who can be compared with the LORD our God,
> who is enthroned on high?
> ⁶Far below him are the heavens and the earth.
> He stoops to look,
> ⁷and he lifts the poor from the dirt
> and the needy from the garbage dump.
> ⁸He sets them among princes,
> even the princes of his own people!

According to this hymn of praise, we have real reasons for rejoicing. Our God is an awesome God. He is glorious beyond words. Nothing in all the universe compares with him. Yet God cares for his creatures. He is willing to look down from on high and locate his children in trouble. But not only that, the psalm tells us that he "lifts the poor . . . and the needy . . . [and] he sets them among princes" (vv. 7-8).

What does all this mean? In a spiritual sense, God can **lift us from the depths of sin.** In a physical or material sense, God can also rescue those on the edge. The psalm assures us that those who have fallen, who have slipped through the cracks of society, are **not forgotten** by God.

He sees them. He cares. He acts on their behalf. The fact of the matter is that God wants to use you as his **hands** and **feet** to help pick up those who have fallen. The

prayers you offer to God, the money you give to support a hungry child, the time you volunteer to serve in an inner-city mission—these are just a few of the ways **God can use you to retrieve his precious creatures** who have slipped or fallen.

HERE'S WHAT I'M GOING TO DO

☐ _____

_____

☐ _____

_____

☐ _____

_____

IT KEEPS GOING AND GOING

One of the most effective advertising campaigns of the last few years has been the group of commercials featuring the Energizer Bunny. Nothing can stop (or even slow down) this drum-beating rabbit. It just keeps going and going and going.

Guess what? That's a good (though imperfect) picture of **the love of God.**

Unlike a man-made battery, God's love truly is **inexhaustible.** Throughout history the Lord has hovered over the world, caring for his people and intervening in their lives. That's the message of the jubilant Hebrew poet in this psalm:

Psalm 136:1-5: ¹Give thanks to the LORD, for he is good!
His faithful love endures forever.
²Give thanks to the God of gods.
His faithful love endures forever.
³Give thanks to the LORD of lords.
His faithful love endures forever.
⁴Give thanks to him who alone does mighty miracles.
His faithful love endures forever.
⁵Give thanks to him who made the heavens so skillfully.
His faithful love endures forever.

"His faithful love endures forever." Twenty-six times the writer sings this chorus. In every single verse, the unending love of God is proclaimed. How is God's love demonstrated? In creation, in the way God supernaturally delivered his people from Egypt and brought them into the Promised Land, in the way God provides for everyday needs like food.

And what is the proper response to such perpetual care

and concern? The people of God should be extravagantly thankful! The command to "give thanks" is found twelve times, almost once for every two verses! This is not just a hymn of praise for Old Testament Israelites. Modern-day Christians can rejoice in the same way. Why? Because God still leads his children. He still delivers. He heals and comforts and provides. **He is with you** when you go through "the wilderness."

The love of God never ceases. He is forever patient and loving, eager to forgive us and restore us. And if you let him, he will take you to good places where you can **know him and his love** in deeper ways than ever before.

PRAYER POINT

Thank God for his ceaseless love.

Then express your gratitude for the individual ways he has blessed you, the specific acts of care you have experienced.

HERE'S WHAT I'M GOING TO DO

☐ _____

_____

☐ _____

_____

☐ _____

_____

☐ _____

_____

☐ _____

_____

MIND-BOGGLING

The minute people lose sight of how awesome God is, they get **off track in their thinking and actions.** Question his goodness and you'll doubt. Doubt his power and you'll worry. Forget his mercy and you'll run from him. Perhaps this explains why God included Psalm 139 in the Bible—to help us remember how **mind-boggling** our Maker really is.

Psalm 139:1-6, 13-18: ¹O LORD, you have examined my heart
and know everything about me.
²You know when I sit down or stand up.
You know my every thought when far away.
³You chart the path ahead of me
and tell me where to stop and rest.
Every moment you know where I am.
⁴You know what I am going to say
even before I say it, LORD.
⁵You both precede and follow me.
You place your hand of blessing on my head.
⁶Such knowledge is too wonderful for me,
too great for me to know!
¹³You made all the delicate, inner parts of my body
and knit me together in my mother's womb.
¹⁴Thank you for making me so wonderfully complex!
Your workmanship is marvelous—and how well I know it.
¹⁵You watched me as I was being formed in utter seclusion,
as I was woven together in the dark of the womb.
¹⁶You saw me before I was born.
Every day of my life was recorded in your book.
Every moment was laid out

¹ **139:17** Or *How precious to me are your thoughts.*

before a single day had passed.
[17]How precious are your thoughts about me,[1]
O God! They are innumerable!
[18]I can't even count them;
they outnumber the grains of sand!
And when I wake up in the morning,
you are still with me!

The first six verses of David's prayer celebrate God's omniscience—his knowledge of all things. **God is fully aware** of everything about us—our failures, our futures, even our unspoken thoughts. Nothing is secret with him.

But look at verses 13-18. This section depicts God's wondrous creation of a human being. David paints a word picture of a seamstress tenderly knitting every stitch so as to weave a beautiful garment. Imagine that—the God who knows everything, the God who is everywhere, caring enough to make each individual into a unique masterpiece!

PRAYER POINT

Thank God that he loves you and cares so much about you. Confess any instances in which you have offended God in the past week. Thank him for his tenderness in the details—the fine needlework—of your life.

HERE'S WHAT I'M GOING TO DO

☐ _____

_____

☐ _____

_____

☐ _____

_____

STICKS AND STONES

F̲ew hurts in life can match those inflicted by a **cruel tongue.** The taunting remark made to an overweight person. A teacher's mean-spirited putdown in front of other students. The coach's criticism of another player, reported in a local newspaper.

David knew **the pain of a cutting remark.** Listen to how he describes the words of his violent enemies:

Psalm 140:1-6, 12-13: ¹O LORD, rescue me from evil people.
Preserve me from those who are violent,
²those who plot evil in their hearts
and stir up trouble all day long.
³Their tongues sting like a snake;
the poison of a viper drips from their lips.
⁴O LORD, keep me out of the hands of the wicked.
Preserve me from those who are violent,
for they are plotting against me.
⁵The proud have set a trap to catch me;
they have stretched out a net;
they have placed traps all along the way.
⁶I said to the LORD, "You are my God!"
Listen, O LORD, to my cries for mercy!
¹²But I know the LORD will surely help those they persecute;
he will maintain the rights of the poor.
¹³Surely the godly are praising your name,
for they will live in your presence.

David calls his persecutors "the proud." Proud people—whether individuals or groups or governments—think the best way to flex their muscles is to **put others down.** Proud people, to paraphrase Christian author C. S. Lewis, are always looking down on everything and everybody. Therefore, they cannot see the God who is high above them. David refused to give in to the temptation of pride. Instead of relying on himself and treating others unkindly, he put his trust in God. "I know the LORD will surely help," he exclaimed (v. 12). While the proud are praising themselves and pursuing others with deadly words and force, David **praised the Lord.**

PRAYER POINT

Confess any ways you've put others down. Ask God to help keep you from having a cruel tongue when you are suffering. Give thanks, too, that God hears your prayers.

Have you ever felt discouraged, singled out, or persecuted for being a Christian? Are you facing adversity or feeling helpless? Are you sensing you can't resolve a pressing problem? Know that **you can call on the Lord.** Say with David, "You are my God! Listen, O LORD, to my cries for mercy" (v. 6). God **hears** the prayers of his people!

HERE'S WHAT I'M GOING TO DO

☐ _____

_____

☐ _____

_____

☐ _____

_____

_____

HELP!

You've probably heard the saying "God helps those who help themselves." Maybe you've even thought that's a verse right out of God's Word. Not true. Actually, as Psalm 146 shows, the Bible teaches just the opposite: God helps those who in their helplessness **call to him.**

Psalm 146:3-10: ³Don't put your confidence in powerful people;
there is no help for you there.
⁴When their breathing stops, they return to the earth,
and in a moment all their plans come to an end.
⁵But happy are those who have the God of Israel¹ as their helper,
whose hope is in the Lord their God.
⁶He is the one who made heaven and earth,
the sea, and everything in them.
He is the one who keeps every promise forever,
⁷who gives justice to the oppressed
and food to the hungry.
The Lord frees the prisoners.
⁸The Lord opens the eyes of the blind.
The Lord lifts the burdens of those bent beneath their loads.
The Lord loves the righteous.
⁹The Lord protects the foreigners among us.
He cares for the orphans and widows,
but he frustrates the plans of the wicked.
¹⁰The Lord will reign forever.
O Jerusalem,² your God is King in every generation!
Praise the Lord!

This passage contrasts human nature with God's nature. Verse 4 recalls that humans are mortal and could die at any

---

¹ **146:5** Hebrew *of Jacob.*
² **146:10** Hebrew *Zion.*

time. In a moment all their plans would come to an end. God, on the other hand, is **eternal** and **always carries out his plan** because he has always existed. As mortals, we obviously have no choice about how the world functioned before our birth or how it will operate after our death. We control **very little** of what happens in the world even while we live! God created and regulates the entire universe (v. 6a). In addition to being the Creator, he is **more faithful than a best friend.** He "keeps every promise forever" (v. 6b).

Why would the infinite, all-powerful God care so much about finite and frail creatures? Why would he bother to "give justice to the oppressed and food to the hungry," "free the prisoners," and "open the eyes of the blind" (vv. 7-8)? This is a great mystery. What is clear is that **God simply chooses to love us** and show us **mercy** and **grace.** And he seems to have a special concern for those who are weak and who know it.

This is illustrated beautifully in the Gospels where, time and again, Jesus helped people who could not help themselves. Sick people who could not recuperate became well; blind people saw; demons that trapped people in despair and destruction were cast out. Today, God is waiting and willing to help you. Acknowledge that you can't help yourself and come to him. He is your **helper.**

HERE'S WHAT I'M GOING TO DO

☐ _____

_____

THE ANT AND THE SLUGGARD

You're assigned a group project at school. Your grade for the project is based on how well you **work** with the other members of your group. Even though it is a school assignment, you and the members of your group are pretty excited about it—all but one of you, that is. You've got one guy in your group who absolutely refuses to do anything. While the rest of you slave away to finish the project, this guy sleeps or stares off into space. Your teacher is so impressed with the finished project that she gives everyone in the group an "A"— including Mr. Do-Nothing. How would you feel if this happened to you? What would you do?

The book of Proverbs has a lot to say about people like Mr. Do-Nothing. Let's take a look at one such passage.

> Proverbs 6:6-11: 6Take a lesson from the ants, you lazybones. Learn from their ways and be wise! 7Even though they have no prince, governor, or ruler to make them work, 8they labor hard all summer, gathering food for the winter. 9But you, lazybones, how long will you sleep? When will you wake up? I want you to learn this lesson: 10A little extra sleep, a little more slumber, a little folding of the hands to rest—11and poverty will pounce on you like a bandit; scarcity will attack you like an armed robber.

Humans were created by God **to do work**—it's part of our nature. Unfortunately, work often can be difficult and boring. Some people find work so distasteful that they choose not to do it. These are the "lazybones" the writer of Proverbs refers to; these are the people who need to take a few lessons from the ant.

Let's take Mr. Do-Nothing out of a school setting and put him into the real world. He still sits around all day and lets other people do all of the work. He doesn't suffer, though, because he has people taking care of him—whether they are his parents, his spouse, or the government.

We need to learn to distinguish between those who are **simply lazy** and those who are **true victims.** Too often a suspicion lingers in the minds of many Christians that anyone who doesn't prosper isn't living right. They fail to understand the poverty, lack of opportunity, hostile climate, and scarcity of resources that keep many people from improving their situation. Often their road to recovery begins with **the compassion that others show**—in the form of food, clothing, vaccines, or agricultural skills, to name a few.

It's important to take responsibility to work hard, as that honors God. It's also important **to offer help to those who genuinely need it—who are true victims.**

HERE'S WHAT I'M GOING TO DO

❏ _____

_____

❏ _____

_____

❏ _____

_____

❏ _____

_____

THE PATH TO PROSPERITY

What is the quickest way to prosper in our society today? What is the best route to financial success? The first order of business is choosing the right profession. A career in computers might be a good move. Most doctors have bright financial prospects. Lawyers, for better or worse, are always in demand. If you have the looks and talent, a career in Hollywood might be the ticket. After you've chosen a vocation, you'll need to come up with a financial strategy for your earnings. The stock market can pay big dividends, but it's risky. Mutual funds are safer but less likely to produce huge windfalls. You might also invest in anything from art to classic cars.

So in a nutshell, the quickest way to prosperity in our society today is choosing a well-paying career and then investing your money wisely. Right?

Well, that may seem like a good plan, but the Bible offers an even quicker route to **financial success.**

Proverbs 11:24-25: [24]It is possible to give freely and become more wealthy, but those who are stingy will lose everything.

[25]The generous prosper and are satisfied; those who refresh others will themselves be refreshed.

OK, so God has a **different concept** of financial success than we do. To him, the true measure of prosperity is not how much a person has, but **how generous that person is.** It sounds like a concept from "The Twilight Zone," doesn't it? The more we **give away,** the more we **receive.**

The key to understanding God's "balance sheet" is to look beyond the financial aspects of giving and receiving. The person who gives freely of his or her time, energy, and money is going to **impact** a lot of lives and **gain** a lot of friends. What price can you put on those rewards? On the other hand, the stingy person who withholds money and who chooses not to share with others misses out on some tremendous opportunities for personal fulfillment and prosperity.

The concept is simple: "The one who plants generously will get a generous crop" (2 Corinthians 9:6).

HERE'S WHAT I'M GOING TO DO

☐ _____

_____

☐ _____

_____

☐ _____

_____

☐ _____

_____

THE GREAT PRETENDERS

You've probably never answered a personal ad, but if you ever do, beware. You may be quite surprised at what you find. You see, people who place personal ads have been known to . . . well, creatively **alter the truth** about themselves. So a man who describes himself as a "sports enthusiast who enjoys entertaining in his home" may actually turn out to be a guy who likes sitting around the house all day watching ESPN. A woman who describes herself as "mature, attractive, and a lover of animals" may turn out to be a senior citizen who has 35 cats running around her house and whose mother once told her she was pretty.

Even if you've never taken out a personal ad, chances are you've creatively altered the truth about yourself at least once or twice in your life. Whether we'd care to admit it or not, most of us have **pretended to be someone we're not.**

The book of Proverbs has some interesting things to say about pretending. Let's take a look.

Proverbs 13:7-8: 7Some who are poor pretend to be rich; others who are rich pretend to be poor.

8The rich can pay a ransom, but the poor won't even get threatened.

According to God's accounting method, **money** does not necessarily make a person rich. If a person has a wealth of material possessions but is lacking spiritually and socially, he or she has **nothing.** He or she is only "pretending" to be rich. Likewise, a person who possesses very little materially may have great wealth spiritually and socially. Thus, he or she is only "pretending" to be poor.

The writer of Proverbs also makes one other interesting distinction between the rich and the poor. People who own much material wealth may need to use that money to buy their way out of trouble or to pay off criminals and enemies. A poor person (one with no material wealth), on the other hand, doesn't have to worry about such threats. When was the last time you heard of a homeless person being held hostage while her kidnappers demanded a shopping cart full of old blankets and rags? Bob Dylan said it best: "When you ain't got nothin', you got nothin' to lose."

These rather radical views from the book of Proverbs are important to keep in mind as we decide for ourselves **what kind of wealth we will pursue.**

PRAYER POINT

Ask the Lord to help you shift your focus from material wealth to social and spiritual wealth.

HERE'S WHAT I'M GOING TO DO

☐ _____

_____

☐ _____

_____

☐ _____

_____

☐ _____

_____

☐ _____

_____

_____

SPIRITUAL JOURNEY TRAVEL LOG

Friends in Low Places

"I just don't know who my **real friends** are anymore." How many times have you heard a celebrity say something like that? The pattern is inevitable: When a person becomes rich or famous, he or she is suddenly surrounded by a large group of friends, acquaintances, groupies, and hangers-on. Everybody wants to be your buddy when you're on top.

When you're on the bottom, though, things are different. The poor and anonymous have very little trouble determining who their real friends are—they often don't have any friends.

The book of Proverbs has some strong warnings against this kind of **double standard.** Let's check it out.

Proverbs 14:20-21: 20The poor are despised even by their neighbors, while the rich have many "friends."

21It is sin to despise one's neighbors; blessed are those who help the poor.

It seems cruel that on top of the economic frustrations that come with poverty, poor people have to suffer socially as well. Why do you suppose so many of us feel **uncomfortable** about associating with the poor? Are we afraid that our reputations will suffer? Are we afraid that poverty is contagious and we might "catch" it? It's hard to say, but here's one theory to consider. Perhaps we avoid the poor in an effort to keep them anonymous. **It's easy for us to ignore the plight of the needy** if they're just a faceless group of people. If they're our friends, however, it makes it difficult for us to refuse to help them.

The book of Proverbs is quite clear on the matter: Those who despise their neighbor sin, but **those who are kind to the needy are blessed.** Showing kindness to the needy involves sharing food (Proverbs 22:9), lending money (Proverbs 28:8), and defending their rights (Proverbs 31:9)—

all things that **a good friend** would do.

Are you prepared to become **a friend to the friendless?** Are you prepared to show kindness to the needy?

PRAYER POINT

Ask the Lord to create in you a heart for the needy, a desire to befriend the disadvantaged in your neighborhood or community.

HERE'S WHAT I'M GOING TO DO

☐ _____

_____

☐ _____

_____

☐ _____

_____

WALKING THE TALK

A popular creed among athletes is "If you can't walk the walk, don't talk the talk." The point is, if you're going to talk trash on the court or field—or toot your own horn—you'd better be able to back up your words with actions. If you don't have the skills to match your words, you'll get no respect.

This saying certainly applies to many other areas of life beyond sports, but it is especially relevant to the Christian faith. The author of Proverbs may not use the same phrasing, but he has a lot to say about **matching words with actions.**

> Proverbs 14:31: ³¹Those who oppress the poor insult their Maker, but those who help the poor honor him.

> Proverbs 17:5: ⁵Those who mock the poor insult their Maker; those who rejoice at the misfortune of others will be punished.

> Proverbs 19:17: ¹⁷If you help the poor, you are lending to the LORD—and he will repay you!

We can talk and talk about how much we love the Lord and want to follow his will, but unless we back up our talk with actions—specifically by obeying the Lord's commands—our words are **hollow.** One of the best and most obvious ways to show our love for the Lord is to treat the poor and needy of the world **according to his instructions.**

God identifies himself so closely with the poor and needy that anything we do to (or for) them, we do to (or for) him. If we oppress or mock the poor, we show contempt for God; if we are kind to the needy, we **honor** the Lord and will be **rewarded** for our actions.

God gives us an opportunity **to tangibly show the world how we feel about him.** He also gives us a chance to show our **thankfulness** for all that he has done for us. So helping the poor is not just a matter of being kind and generous to other people; it's a matter of honoring the Lord.

Just like on the basketball court or football field, people are watching us closely to see whether our actions back up our words. If we don't walk the walk, we—and our Christian witness—are going to lose a lot of respect in the eyes of many people.

HERE'S WHAT I'M GOING TO DO

☐ _____

_____

☐ _____

_____

☐ _____

_____

☐ _____

_____

☐ _____

_____

_____

Hearing Aids

Have you ever wished that you could wear a hearing aid? Then you could turn down the volume on little brothers and sisters, parents, teachers, or whoever is bugging you. (A teacher of deaf children once said that her students used to do this when they didn't want to hear what the teacher was asking them to do!) But you would also pay a price for that lack of hearing. You might miss an opportunity to go to an exciting game or concert. You might risk injury because you wouldn't be able to hear a warning.

Unfortunately, humans tend to **tune out** God and **ignore** the cares of needy people. But what is the consequence of this action? Read the following verse to find out.

Proverbs 21:13: 13Those who shut their ears to the cries of the poor will be ignored in their own time of need.

This verse seems to indicate that how we treat the poor will determine in some way how we will be treated. The challenge is to **open our ears and listen**—to be sensitive to people in need. Because such compassion requires time and because our lives already seem filled with activities and interests, it may seem impossible to slow down long enough to listen. But helping the poor is a priority with God, so it needs to be a **priority** with us.

Beyond hearing the cries, the second challenge is to help the poor. We need to follow through with **loving actions!** Remember, God heard our cries and reached out to us in love when we were spiritually destitute. He hears every prayer and is **always ready to help** when we ask. Reflecting God's love, we should **reach out** to help. Are you tuning in or tuning them out?

HERE'S WHAT I'M GOING TO DO

☐ _____

_____

☐ _____

_____

☐ _____

_____

☐ _____

_____

☐ _____

_____

_____

GOD'S INVESTMENT STRATEGY

Those who frequent casinos, buy dozens of lottery tickets weekly, or bet on sporting events all hope for the same thing: easy money. Put a little in, get a whole lot more back. And sometimes, people do. But this rarely happens in any area of life. Usually a good return requires **a sizable investment.** This is true in sports, in school, and in one's spiritual life. The rule also applies to using resources, time, money, and other possessions.

Solomon, no stranger to wealth, offered his own advice on **resource management:**

Proverbs 22:2-9: ²The rich and the poor have this in common: The LORD made them both.

³A prudent person foresees the danger ahead and takes precautions; the simpleton goes blindly on and suffers the consequences.

⁴True humility and fear of the LORD lead to riches, honor, and long life.

⁵The deceitful walk a thorny, treacherous road; whoever values life will stay away.

⁶Teach your children to choose the right path, and when they are older, they will remain upon it.

⁷Just as the rich rule the poor, so the borrower is servant to the lender.

⁸Those who plant seeds of injustice will harvest disaster, and their reign of terror will end.

⁹Blessed are those who are generous, because they feed the poor.

The last two verses here especially speak to us about **the investment we make in other people.** Look at verse 9 again, "Blessed are those who are generous . . ." God blesses those who are generous with true riches such as the joy that comes from helping another, the peace that comes from obeying God, and eternal rewards. Such rewards are not always immediate, and they cannot always be seen right away. We must learn to take God at his word. **When he promises blessing, we can surely expect it.**

Generosity is not just a good feeling, however. We can't call ourselves generous if we merely sympathize with the plight of the poor. Generous people are **sacrificing** people. They surrender convenience, comfort, and luxury so that others will thrive. But if we are willing to take the narrow path, we will find greater rewards than we could ever achieve in a headlong rush for the good life.

PRAYER POINT

Pray for a missionary from your church today, someone who has invested his or her life in sharing the Good News with others.

HERE'S WHAT I'M GOING TO DO

☐ _____

_____

☐ _____

_____

☐ _____

_____

☐ _____

_____

☐ _____

_____

DEFENDER OF THE POOR

According to legend, in the year 1160, a baby boy was born to a woodsman and his wife. Over the years he became quite proficient with a bow. One day, the boy suddenly became an orphan. That's when he chose his life's goal: to steal from the rich and to give to the poor. You've heard of Robin Hood. Even today, he enjoys a legendary reputation as a defender of the oppressed.

But in this passage, you will learn about another defender of the poor. And this person is not a legend. He is **real** and still at work.

Proverbs 22:16-23: ¹⁶A person who gets ahead by oppressing the poor or by showering gifts on the rich will end in poverty.

¹⁷Listen to the words of the wise; apply your heart to my instruction. ¹⁸For it is good to keep these sayings deep within yourself, always ready on your lips. ¹⁹I am teaching you today—yes, you—so you will trust in the LORD. ²⁰I have written thirty sayings for you, filled with advice and knowledge. ²¹In this way, you may know the truth and bring an accurate report to those who sent you.

²²Do not rob the poor because they are poor or exploit the needy in court. ²³For the LORD is their defender. He will injure anyone who injures them.

Now, let's look at these verses a little more closely. Verse 16 contains a promise, "A person who gets ahead by oppressing the poor . . . will end in poverty." Although material poverty may be included, God is referring to something far worse: **spiritual poverty.** Verse 22 contains a commandment, "Do not rob the poor . . . or exploit the needy in court." That's pretty straightforward. God is saying, "Don't do this!" Why? Verse 23 contains the answer: "For the LORD is their defender. He will injure anyone who injures them." Wow! Makes you definitely want to treat the poor with **respect,** doesn't it? From these three verses, it is plain to see that God **highly regards the poor.** So should we. It is not enough to just promise not to hurt or take advantage of them; God wants us to go a step further and **defend** them as well.

PRAYER POINT

Pray for understanding of how to become a defender of the poor.

HERE'S WHAT I'M GOING TO DO

☐ _____

_____

☐ _____

_____

☐ _____

_____

☐ _____

_____

☐ _____

_____

SPIRITUAL JOURNEY TRAVEL LOG

THE SMELL OF SUCCESS

A few years back, two friends went on a camping trip in the mountains of Virginia. They pitched their tent along the banks of the Shenandoah River. For breakfast each morning, they would gather wild blackberries and make pancakes over an open fire. At night they would cook their dinner in the one pot they had brought along. At the end of the long weekend, they packed their car and headed home.

Along the way they stopped for a snack. As they walked into the restaurant, people began to look at them a little strangely. *What were they staring at?* they wondered. Then it hit them: They both smelled like walking campfires. Everyone in the restaurant knew they had been around fire because the smell of smoke was in their hair and on their skin.

Today's passage contains **God's warning** about hanging out with **selfish** and **stingy** people. For just like the campfire, they, too, will leave their "scent" on those nearby.

Proverbs 23:6-8: ⁶Don't eat with people who are stingy; don't desire their delicacies. ⁷"Eat and drink," they say, but they don't mean it. They are always thinking about how much it costs. ⁸You will vomit up the delicious food they serve, and you will have to take back your words of appreciation for their "kindness."

Those close to selfish and stingy people stand in danger of **picking up bad habits, attitudes, and characteristics.** One is the tendency to give mixed messages. Verse 7 reads " 'Eat and drink,' they say, but they don't mean it." God wants us to say what we mean and mean what we say. He is always direct with us, and he wants us to **be direct** with others.

Another pitfall is an obsession with money. They are always thinking about how much money everything costs rather than focusing on the people they are feeding. God wants us to be **people-centered,** not money-centered.

Selfish and stingy people are also discontented. Never satisfied with what they have, they always want more. God warns us to stay away. He knows that if we spend too much time with them we will surely be affected.

PRAYER POINT

Think about your friends and acquaintances. Is there one person in particular who you are concerned about? Pray for that person and ask God to show you whether or not you should be spending time with him or her.

HERE'S WHAT I'M GOING TO DO

☐ _____

_____

☐ _____

_____

☐ _____

_____

☐ _____

_____

☐ _____

_____

How to Retaliate

A classmate keeps putting you down in front of your friends.

- A so-called friend spreads a false and totally embarrassing rumor about you.
- Somebody works behind the scenes to cause problems between you and some of your friends.
- Someone steals the money that you were saving for a big date and had stashed away in your bookbag.

When somebody **intentionally** does something **to hurt** or **embarrass** you, what does it feel like? Not good! You really want to get them back for it. You want to make them pay.

But is that God's way? Read today's verses and find out.

Proverbs 25:21-22: 21If your enemies are hungry, give them food to eat. If they are thirsty, give them water to drink. 22You will heap burning coals on their heads, and the Lord will reward you.

Verse 21 doesn't give much room for excuses, does it? It doesn't say you have every right to seek revenge. It doesn't say, "Sure, you can get back at your enemy the same way he or she got you!"

Instead, it clearly says you are to **go out of your way to serve** your enemies—those who oppose you, at whatever level, in whatever way. So if your enemies are hungry, offer them food. If they're thirsty, make sure they have something to drink.

In other words, **don't hold back doing good.** Rather, take the initiative to reach out and make an effort to meet their needs.

What happens when you do that? Two interesting and surprising things happen, according to verse 22: First, your enemies will feel guilty for what they've done because you've shown them **kindness.** Some scholars think the phrase "heap burning coals on their heads" refers to an ancient Egyptian ritual, in which a guilty person carried a bowl of hot coals on his or her head as a sign of repentance. The point is that, by returning good for evil and showing kindness to those who have hurt you, you could actually win them over and cause them to change.

This doesn't mean that it's all right to manipulate someone. God wants his children to serve others with a pure, honest, giving heart—no matter who they are. The second thing that happens is that God will reward you because you're **trusting** him to take care of the situation. You're letting him be the ultimate Judge who will make things right in the end. That's the way he likes it. Next time you face a situation in which someone has hurt you, remember these verses. It won't be easy, but it will work!

PRAYER POINT

Think of one or more people who have hurt you lately and lift them up to the Lord in prayer. Ask God to bless them abundantly. Ask him to give you the power and grace you need to be kind to those "enemies."

HERE'S WHAT I'M GOING TO DO

☐ _____

_____

☐ _____

_____

_____

THE ROOT OF EVIL

Pick up today's paper or watch a local newscast, and you'll see story after story that illustrates the point of today's Scripture reading. One story may be about a politician who has been caught using campaign money for personal gain. Another may be about a business that scammed the elderly.

On and on it goes—one bad piece of news about our world after another. It all seems **random, out of control,** and **scary.** Why are people so crazy? Read today's proverbs and note the theme: **the root of evil.**

Proverbs 28:2-11: ²When there is moral rot within a nation, its government topples easily. But with wise and knowledgeable leaders, there is stability.

³A poor person who oppresses the poor is like a pounding rain that destroys the crops.

⁴To reject the law is to praise the wicked; to obey the law is to fight them.

⁵Evil people don't understand justice, but those who follow the Lord understand completely.

⁶It is better to be poor and honest than rich and crooked.

⁷Young people who obey the law are wise; those who seek out worthless companions bring shame to their parents.

⁸A person who makes money by charging interest will lose it. It will end up in the hands of someone who is kind to the poor.

⁹The prayers of a person who ignores the law are despised.

¹⁰Those who lead the upright into sin will fall into their own trap, but the honest will inherit good things.

[11]Rich people picture themselves as wise, but their real poverty is evident to the poor.

These proverbs indicate that there are two kinds of people in the world: **evil** people and **godly** people. You see the distinction throughout society among people of all ages and classes.

What causes evil people to do what they do? Think about it: Their ultimate objective is to **promote themselves.** In essence, they are behaving **selfishly.**

Selfish people have one thing on their minds: themselves. Any way they can get more attention, more power, more money, more pleasure for themselves, they will do it. Sadly, the souls of such people can resemble a bottomless pit. Nothing can ever fill it up. Self-centered people are never satisfied.

Selfless people are those whom God honors. People who follow the Lord are honest and kind to the poor. Which type of person are you?

HERE'S WHAT I'M GOING TO DO

☐ _____

_____

☐ _____

_____

☐ _____

_____

☐ _____

_____

GREED VS. GIVING

You need some cash—some "walking around money."
What do you do? Go whine to your mom or dad? Dig
around in the couch cushions or the car seats? Borrow from
your little sister? Give up and stew in self-pity?

How about offering to do a work project around the house,
doing some babysitting, cutting some lawns, or even finding a
part-time job? You see, **your attitude will go a long way**
toward determining how well and how often your needs are
met. Read today's verses from Proverbs and see if you can
figure out how that works.

> Proverbs 28:19-27: ¹⁹Hard workers have plenty of food; playing around
> brings poverty.
>
> ²⁰The trustworthy will get a rich reward. But the person who wants to get
> rich quick will only get into trouble.
>
> ²¹Showing partiality is never good, yet some will do wrong for something
> as small as a piece of bread.
>
> ²²A greedy person tries to get rich quick, but it only leads to poverty.
>
> ²³In the end, people appreciate frankness more than flattery.
>
> ²⁴Robbing your parents and then saying, "What's wrong with that?" is as
> serious as committing murder.
>
> ²⁵Greed causes fighting; trusting the LORD leads to prosperity.
>
> ²⁶Trusting oneself is foolish, but those who walk in wisdom are safe.
>
> ²⁷Whoever gives to the poor will lack nothing. But a curse will come upon
> those who close their eyes to poverty.

God's Word seems to keep hitting us over the head about
our attitude toward money, doesn't it? Notice the

distinction that's made between hard work and playing around . . . being a trustworthy worker and wanting to get rich quick . . . being greedy as opposed to being a giver.

If you have the attitude that the world owes you, that you are entitled to get whatever you want by whatever means you can, then the Bible says you will end up poorer than when you started—not only financially, but emotionally and spiritually as well.

PRAYER POINT

Ask God to show you how you can give generously of your time and resources. Pray that he will keep your heart from being greedy.

But if you have the attitude that the hard work of a wise and trustworthy person will bring great rewards from the hand of God, then **you will surely prosper**—financially, emotionally, and spiritually.

Did you notice the promise in verse 27? "Whoever gives to the poor will lack nothing. But a curse will come upon those who close their eyes to poverty." In the world's eyes, that doesn't make sense—it seems you'd be richer if you kept all your money rather than giving some of it away! But that's just how God's economy works. He promises abundant riches—not necessarily in the wallet but certainly in the heart—to those who live and work according to his will.

HERE'S WHAT I'M GOING TO DO

☐ _____

_____

☐ _____

_____

Just Enough

Congratulations! You've just won $10 million! Now, what are you going to do? What will you buy for yourself? Where will you live? What will you give your friends and family? What will you do for God and his Kingdom?

Maybe you've read stories about people who won great sums of money in the lottery or sweepstakes. Many of these winners may say they don't plan on letting all that money **change their lives.** Some of them say they'll even keep their jobs and try to maintain the lifestyle they're accustomed to.

Follow-up stories, however, often reveal how all that money dramatically changed the winners' lives—for the **worse.** Some of them divorced their mates, lost their friends, frittered away their winnings, and ended up much worse off than before they won. One big winner said, "If I had known what would happen, I never would have entered that contest. I wish I had never won!"

Proverbs 30:7-9: 7O God, I beg two favors from you before I die. 8First, help me never to tell a lie. Second, give me neither poverty nor riches! Give me just enough to satisfy my needs. 9For if I grow rich, I may deny you and say, "Who is the LORD?" And if I am too poor, I may steal and thus insult God's holy name.

If you were given two wishes, what would they be? Agur was a wise teacher who wrote some very smart sayings, one of which is today's reading. He begs God for two favors: first, that he would never tell a lie. Second, that he would get just enough to meet his needs—neither too little nor too much.

Now, how similar were your two wishes to Agur's?

Agur was wise indeed. First, he wanted a life that was totally **open** and **honest** before God and his fellow human beings. That way he'd never have to lie or trick or come up with excuses. Imagine the **freedom of a life that was totally honest!**

Second, he wanted neither poverty nor riches. Now, the first part of that makes sense. Who would ask God for poverty? But the second part may have a lot of people scratching their heads. Why didn't Agur want wealth? Agur knew that if he grew rich, he might put his faith in his money rather than in God. He might even deny the Lord.

Being poor can be hazardous to your physical and spiritual health. On the other hand, Jesus pointed out that rich people have trouble getting into God's Kingdom (Matthew 19:23-24). The apostle Paul learned **to be content** with whatever he had—whether little or much—and in whatever situation he found himself (Philippians 4:12). You can learn that too, as God answers the prayer of Agur on your behalf.

PRAYER POINT

Make Agur's prayer your own. Ask God to make your life one marked by honesty and contentment. Then trust him to answer you.

HERE'S WHAT I'M GOING TO DO

☐ _____

_____

☐ _____

_____

☐ _____

_____

_____

SPIRITUAL JOURNEY TRAVEL LOG

SPEAK UP!

DAY
116

Oskar Schindler—the focus of the blockbuster movie *Schindler's List*—was an unconventional hero. He certainly wasn't a godly do-gooder. In fact, he was a drinker, a gambler, a cheater, and a womanizer. He was driven by greed and lust.

As World War II began, he saw an opportunity to make a lot of money by employing Jews at slave wages in a Polish munitions factory. But by the end of the war, he had risked his life and spent his fortune to save those same Jewish people. He cheated the Nazis for months by billing them for defective bullets and shells that German troops could not use.

What made him change? Why did he turn from selfish victimizer to selfless humanitarian? We may never know. But we can speculate that he **responded to a need.** He helped bring **justice** to those who were perishing. If Oskar Schindler could do that on the life-threatening level that he did, can't we do the same in smaller ways?

Proverbs 31:8-9: ⁸Speak up for those who cannot speak for themselves; ensure justice for those who are perishing. ⁹Yes, speak up for the poor and helpless, and see that they get justice.

King Lemuel is one of the Bible's mystery men. All we know about him is that he was a king. Some scholars think that he ruled the kingdom of Massa in northern Arabia. Wherever Lemuel ruled, he had come to know the one true God. And he followed some wise sayings his mother had taught him.

Today's reading focuses on one of those sayings. Lemuel knew that, as king of his nation, he had **a great responsibility** to make sure the poor and needy got justice.

It was easy to overlook those in poverty and need. It was even easier to abuse them. The poor were often mistreated and mocked for their helplessness. Lemuel knew it was his job not to let that happen. He was **an advocate for the helpless.** This saying, which reflects the heart of God, guided King Lemuel. It can also guide you.

When you learn about an injustice—the homeless being harassed downtown, poor people who are subjected to substandard housing by slum landlords, or another unjust situation—speak up! Be an advocate. Talk to your pastor to see if your church can get involved in helping in some way. Write a letter to the editor of your local paper describing the situation and challenge the readers to do what's right.

In short, **get involved.** After all, wouldn't you want someone on your side if you were in their situation?

HERE'S WHAT I'M GOING TO DO

☐ _____

_____

☐ _____

_____

☐ _____

_____

☐ _____

_____

WINNERS AND LOSERS

More than a hundred years ago, a young woman named Hetty Green inherited nearly $5 million in property and investments. Yet she was determined to have more. Stingy and shrewd, she turned her sizable sum into an even greater fortune. Her appearance and manners matched her frugal ways. She wore faded and tattered clothes and traveled in a rundown carriage that had once been a henhouse. In her old age, she imposed her tightfistedness on others and criticized those who did not heed her advice. She supposedly died during an argument with a servant over a houseguest's spending habits.

Would it surprise you to learn that the author of Ecclesiastes wrote about **the trap of wealth** thousands of years before Hetty Green was born? Take a look.

Ecclesiastes 5:8-11: [8]If you see a poor person being oppressed by the powerful and justice being miscarried throughout the land, don't be surprised! For every official is under orders from higher up, and matters of justice only get lost in red tape and bureaucracy. [9]Even the king milks the land for his own profit![1]

[10]Those who love money will never have enough. How absurd to think that wealth brings true happiness! [11]The more you have, the more people come to help you spend it. So what is the advantage of wealth—except perhaps to watch it run through your fingers!

This **greedy, never-enough attitude** dwells deep in the human heart. Unfortunately, many act on that impulse and increase their wealth at someone else's expense. And more often than not, the victims are the poor and needy.

What can be done about this unfair situation? Plenty. You see, we don't live in the same kind of society the writer of

---

[1] 5:9 The meaning of the Hebrew is uncertain.

Ecclesiastes lived in. Our rulers are not sovereign kings who answer to no one but themselves; our rulers answer to us, the people. **We have a say in what our leaders do.** So when we see the poor and needy being abused, we have a right to do something about it.

PRAYER POINT

Pray for a proper attitude toward wealth.

Actually, we have more than a right; we have a **responsibility.** You see, God tells his people to take care of the less fortunate in society. Those of us who recognize that riches are meaningless compared to people **must take action** when we see the poor hurt.

There are many different ways to take action, but it all starts with a right attitude toward riches. What is your attitude toward wealth?

HERE'S WHAT I'M GOING TO DO

☐ _____

_____

☐ _____

_____

☐ _____

_____

☐ _____

_____

☐ _____

_____

THE ANSWER IS MONEY?

DAY 118

Did you ever wonder where the idea of money came from? Think about it. At some point in history, someone had to decide that a shiny piece of rock or metal was worth something. Can you picture the very first conversation about money? "Hey, Zedediah, I'll tell you what I'm going to do. If you give me two of your sheep and one of your donkeys, I'll give you this shiny rock." The funny thing is, at some point, Zedediah (or someone like him) had to say, "You know, I think that shiny rock is worth two sheep and a donkey." Lo and behold, the concept of money was born.

Solomon has some interesting—and rather startling—things to say about money. Let's take a look.

Ecclesiastes 10:16-20: [16]Destruction is certain for the land whose king is a child[1] and whose leaders feast in the morning. [17]Happy is the land whose king is a nobleman and whose leaders feast only to gain strength for their work, not to get drunk.

[18]Laziness lets the roof leak, and soon the rafters begin to rot.

[19]A party gives laughter, and wine gives happiness, and money gives everything!

[20]Never make light of the king, even in your thoughts. And don't make fun of a rich man, either. A little bird may tell them what you have said.

Wait a minute. Look at the last line of verse 19 again: "Money gives everything." Is Solomon being sarcastic here, or is he being serious?

From a spiritual standpoint, he's certainly being sarcastic. Anyone who believes that money is the answer to personal happiness and ultimate fulfillment is in for a rude shock. It's no coincidence that the wealthiest people in the world are

---

[1] **10:16** Or *whose king is a servant.*

often the most miserable. Anyone who attempts to fill his life with riches and material possessions will ultimately discover that he is empty inside. Only God can provide **ultimate, eternal happiness and fulfillment.**

From a social standpoint, however, Ecclesiastes 10:19b is a pretty accurate statement. Money is the answer for most problems in society today—particularly the problems that face the poor and needy. For better or for worse, money talks—the more you have, the more people will listen.

PRAYER POINT

Ask God to help you become a "craftsperson" with your money, putting it to use in wise ways to help the poor and needy in your community.

Having said that, it's also important to keep in mind that money itself is useless—**it's what you do with it that counts.** The best way to look at money is as a tool—nothing more, nothing less. It's a tool that can be used for good or for evil. Used appropriately, it can bring great blessing to others.

HERE'S WHAT I'M GOING TO DO

☐ _____

☐ _____

☐ _____

☐ _____

SEASONS OF LIFE

DAY 119

Who do you suppose appreciates the warm weather of spring more—people who live in Honolulu or people who live in Chicago? For Hawaiians, warm temperatures and beautiful weather are part of everyday life. People in Illinois, on the other hand, are forced to suffer through five months of brutal cold, vicious winds, and mounds of snow, slush, and freezing rain. With apologies to all Hawaiian citizens, no one appreciates spring more than a Midwesterner.

The Song of Songs talks about this idea of "changing seasons." But as you'll see, weather is the farthest thing from the writer's mind.

> Song of Songs 2:10-13: ¹⁰"My lover said to me, 'Rise up, my beloved, my fair one, and come away. ¹¹For the winter is past, and the rain is over and gone. ¹²The flowers are springing up, and the time of singing birds has come, even the cooing of turtledoves. ¹³The fig trees are budding, and the grapevines are in blossom. How delicious they smell! Yes, spring is here! Arise, my beloved, my fair one, and come away.'"

Life, like nature, has its **seasons.** Those who have endured bitter cold rejoice when spring arrives to warm the earth. In the same way, no one can appreciate security, stability, and happiness as much as those who have endured hardship and misery.

Why are some people able to endure hardship in life? **The secret is hope.** For Midwesterners, the hope of spring helps them endure winter. For Christians, the hope of **eternal life** through Jesus helps them endure life's miseries. If we can recognize that our present "wintertime" suffering—no matter how intense it is—is temporary, we take a big step toward spiritual "springtime."

Christians can also look forward to a more immediate

hope—the assistance of fellow believers. God's people are called **to look after each other, to support one another** in times of suffering and hardship. In a sense, we are called to be spiritual "meteorologists," recognizing the seasons of life of those around us.

Many people in this world (and probably many people in your community) have endured—and are continuing to endure—long, long winters. For them, spring never seems to come. That's where we come in. Our job is to **provide relief for these sufferers,** to help them move from winter to spring. This help may involve personal contact, providing encouragement and emotional support to those who need it. It may also involve financial or material assistance, doing whatever we can to lessen the burden of the poor and the suffering in our community and around the world.

If you're in the midst of a winter in your life, remind yourself that God has prepared an eternal spring for those who **trust** in him. At the same time, remind yourself that you have the ability (and the responsibility) to offer "springtime" relief to others who are facing their own winter in life.

PRAYER POINT

Pray specifically for Christians around the world who are experiencing persecution or hardship. Ask God to help you become a taste of spring for people facing long winters in their lives.

HERE'S WHAT I'M GOING TO DO

☐ _____

_____

☐ _____

_____

Words to Remember

On a chilly November day in 1863, a crowd gathered to hear two prominent speakers dedicate a battlefield memorial. The main speaker was Edward Everett, who spoke for nearly two hours. The man who followed him spoke but a few minutes. No one today remembers Everett's speech, but Abraham Lincoln, the other speaker, recited some of the most famous words in American history—the Gettysburg Address.

Lincoln's speech is famous, in part, because it said **so much** in **so few** words. Well versed in Scripture, Lincoln may have borrowed a page from the prophets of the Old Testament, also famous for their direct, in-your-face style. In the book of Isaiah, God gives his people a few short sentences that pack a punch. Let's take a look at it.

Isaiah 1:17: 17Learn to do good. Seek justice. Help the oppressed. Defend the orphan. Fight for the rights of widows.

Five sentences, but what a message! In that verse, God tells us that we are to take care of our family. God's concern for the oppressed, orphans, and widows seems to indicate that they're part of his wider earthly family. And just as food and safety are the top priorities for our natural brothers and sisters, they're also priority *numero uno* for our spiritual siblings.

The oppressed, the fatherless, and widows don't have a lot of people looking out for them. That's why it's so important for us to assume our **God-given responsibilities** as spiritual fathers, mothers, sisters, and brothers, doing everything we can to defend them and make sure that they are taken care of.

We may not see any earthly payback for fulfilling our responsibilities to the poor and oppressed, but we can rest assured that **our heavenly reward will be something**

special. If we only do what Isaiah tells us in this verse, we will be taking a giant step toward **loving** people the way God has commanded us.

HERE'S WHAT I'M GOING TO DO

☐ _____

_____

☐ _____

_____

☐ _____

_____

☐ _____

_____

☐ _____

_____

THE LEAST OF THESE

Jeff Frankenstein, NEWSBOYS

Last year, our band had the opportunity to perform in a few Third World countries. We learned that we would be traveling to Brazil and Panama to do some missionary work along with our concerts. Although my parents (and many of the other guys' parents) are actively involved in missions work around the world, this was my first time traveling to a Third World country. In the past, friends who had been on similar trips would tell me how much they had been changed by the experience, but for some reason I was usually quite skeptical of their reports. But this was the chance to see for myself.

When we landed in Brazil, all of us were excited about seeing a new country. The longer we stayed there, however, the more we became disturbed. We were stationed in São Paulo, which we didn't realize is the fourth largest city in the world. The city is crammed with poor people. We saw large high-rise buildings where businesspeople work. But attached to each building are tiny shacks where the poor live. In Brazil the people are either very rich or very poor—there is no in between.

Our experience in Panama was very similar. Walking through the villages and seeing the conditions in which these people live was very humbling. I was challenged immediately. We have it so good in the States. We strive to have what we call the "American dream," but these people fight for survival. I guess we've seen so many grim pictures on TV that our minds get numb to the fact that the images are real and so are the people. The more we saw, the more we were challenged.

All of the people we encountered in the towns and villages were so open to the Gospel. They were hungry to learn about Christianity, while we so often take our faith for granted. During this trip, a passage in the Bible that really hit me hard was Matthew 25:41-46: "Then the King will turn to those on the left and say, 'Away with you, you cursed ones, into the eternal fire prepared for the Devil and his demons! For I was hungry, and you didn't feed

me. I was thirsty, and you didn't give me anything to drink. I was a stranger, and you didn't invite me into your home. I was naked, and you gave me no clothing. I was sick and in prison, and you didn't visit me.' Then they will reply, 'Lord, when did we ever see you hungry or thirsty or a stranger or naked or sick or in prison, and not help you?' And he will answer, 'I assure you, when you refused to help the least of these my brothers and sisters, you were refusing to help me.' And they will go away into eternal punishment, but the righteous will go into eternal life."

These "least" people are just like you and me. They are created in God's image too (Genesis 1:27). Often it's easy to ignore them because they are so far away, but as Christians it is our responsibility to do what we can to help. Society constantly tells us that a person's worth is based on his or her financial worth, but the Bible says, "Give as freely as you have received!" (Matthew 10:8).

Proverbs 31:8-9 states: "Speak up for those who cannot speak for themselves; ensure justice for those who are perishing. Yes, speak up for the poor and helpless, and see that they get justice." Our trip challenged me to do just that. I will remember what I saw and experienced for the rest of my life. May we all strive to treat our neighbors fairly, to treat our neighbors as ourselves.

O Jesus,

ever with us stay;

Make all our moments

calm and bright;

Chase the

dark night of sin away;

Shed o'er the world

thy holy light!

Bernard of Clairvaux

THE SAFE PLACE OF GOD'S WILL

Shawn Pendry, 17, is a senior at St. John's Country Dayschool in Orange Park, Florida. His passion is music. He plays the saxophone, oboe, and piano … and sings. He loves jazz, especially the sounds of Miles Davis. Shawn visited Mali, West Africa, as a participant of the 1997 30 Hour Famine Study Tour. He loved going on the trip. He says sometimes God asks him to do things he really doesn't want to do.

Sometimes there are things that you set your heart on because they're things that you really enjoy. But those things aren't always what God intends for you.

There are other times when you are called to go do something that you don't want to do, that may make you feel uncomfortable, like the time after I got back from Mali when I was invited to speak at a retirement community.

The thought of going before the elderly people, quite honestly, made me feel very uncomfortable. But once it was over, I realized that that's where God wanted me to be. So even though sometimes you may not want to do something, consider that maybe God wants you in that place at that time because, a lot of times, it can make a difference in someone else's life—and in your life too.

Community service helps me in that area. I'm involved in my church in drama, puppet, and clown evangelism ministries. And I work with a community food distribution program. I think doing things like that can open something inside us that may make it easier for God to reach us.

Maybe he wants us to go and talk to some person in our class who we don't like, some person who's a jerk or something, and we're not open to that. But community service allows you to work with all sorts of people and teaches you people skills, self-discipline, and patience. And you'll need that when God speaks to you so you're able to go and do what he wants you to do.

BULLIES EVERYWHERE

Every playground and every school in America has its share of bullies. Some of them are named Spike, some are named Mad Dog, and some have less threatening names. But all of them have one thing in common: They love to pick on and **take advantage** of those who are smaller and weaker than they are. Bullies can make life seriously **miserable.**

Unfortunately, there is no age limit for bullies. In fact, some of the meanest bullies are adults. They may not use physical force, but they take advantage of the weak and thrive on other people's misery just the same.

God has some strong words for these bullies. Let's see what he has to say in the book of Isaiah.

Isaiah 3:13-15: [13]The LORD takes his place in court. He is the great prosecuting attorney, presenting his case against his people! [14]The leaders and the princes will be the first to feel the LORD's judgment. "You have ruined Israel, which is my vineyard. You have taken advantage of the poor, filling your barns with grain extorted from helpless people. [15]How dare you grind my people into the dust like that!" demands the LORD, the LORD Almighty.

Notice the words used to describe what these people do—**"ruined"** and **"grinding."** It's not a coincidence that the Lord uses such violent imagery. Even though these bullies may not be putting a *physical* squeeze on the poor, they are doing severe damage nonetheless. **Many, many people are hurt as a result of these bullies' actions.**

Who are the bullies? They're people in positions of power who use their influence to take advantage of others—particularly those who are weaker than they are. They're politicians who use their office and clout to help themselves get richer (perhaps through salary hikes or kickbacks) while turning their backs on the people who need help the most. They're unscrupulous people who harm the environment or deny decent wages to people in order to fatten their own wallets. These opportunists—and others like them—are the modern-day bullies oppressing the poor and needy.

For those of us who look for justice, there's good news: **These bullies will not prevail.** They will have to give an account for the injustices they have created. What's more, they will realize too late that the people they oppressed—the poor and needy—are often the ones who have attained true riches. Indeed, **the first shall be last.**

So while we Christians have a responsibility to do everything we can in this world to relieve the suffering of those who are oppressed, we can also look forward to God's final **justice.**

HERE'S WHAT I'M GOING TO DO

☐ _____

_____

☐ _____

_____

☐ _____

_____

TAKING ADVANTAGE

Ever take advantage of a little kid? Like when you're playing Monopoly: "Hey, how about I give you this pretty orange property, and you give me that ugly blue piece called Park Place?"

Such **trickery** may be "no big deal" in a game. You may get away with it and even prosper. But in real life when the rich or powerful abuse the poor and weak, God gets angry. And he rises to the defense of the afflicted.

Isaiah 10:1-5: ¹Destruction is certain for the unjust judges, for those who issue unfair laws. ²They deprive the poor, the widows, and the orphans of justice. Yes, they rob widows and fatherless children! ³What will you do when I send desolation upon you from a distant land? To whom will you turn for help? Where will your treasures be safe? ⁴I will not help you. You will stumble along as prisoners or lie among the dead. But even then the LORD's anger will not be satisfied. His fist is still poised to strike. ⁵"Destruction is certain for Assyria, the whip of my anger. Its military power is a club in my hand."

A major Bible theme (emphasized again in today's passage) is that **God cares deeply for the helpless.** He becomes angry when the poor are mistreated, exploited, or ignored. This passage condemns judges who twist justice by maligning the poor.

Notice how God in the flesh (i.e., Jesus) reacted when he saw instances of injustice. He criticized Israel's religious leaders for "completely forget[ting] about justice," hoarding things, and ignoring the needy (Luke 11:37-43). The scribes and Pharisees were too busy worrying about all their rules and traditions to care about the less fortunate. They forgot, as did the leaders in Isaiah's time, that God values **caring for the**

poor and **treating people right** far more than he cares about petty rule-keeping. He wants to see changed hearts that love and treat the poor with dignity and justice.

Those who take advantage will be judged. God asks some sobering questions in verse 3 of this passage: "What will you do when I send desolation upon you? . . . Where will your treasures be safe?" The implicit answer to this question is: They won't be safe. History shows that God stripped Israel of her treasure—her special blessings and position. God vented anger against people who cared more about living comfortably than about **living holy lives before him.** He never stopped loving Israel, but he disciplined his wayward people.

He will do the same thing to those who mistreat the poor today. They will have to contend with **the anger of God.**

PRAYER POINT

Confess any instances in which you have ignored the poor or acted selfishly rather than compassionately toward those in need.

HERE'S WHAT I'M GOING TO DO

☐ _____

_____

☐ _____

_____

☐ _____

_____

_____

CRY ME A RIVER

When's the last time you cried? What happened to cause the tears to flow?

In today's passage, Israel parties even though the Lord commands all the Israelites to **mourn.**

Isaiah 22:12-14: ¹²The LORD, the LORD Almighty, called you to weep and mourn. He told you to shave your heads in sorrow for your sins and to wear clothes of sackcloth to show your remorse. ¹³But instead, you dance and play; you slaughter sacrificial animals, feast on meat, and drink wine. "Let's eat, drink, and be merry," you say. "What's the difference, for tomorrow we die." ¹⁴The LORD Almighty has revealed to me that this sin will never be forgiven you until the day you die. That is the judgment of the LORD, the LORD Almighty.

Jerusalem was told to mourn because its sin had offended a holy God. In the biblical way of thinking, full realization of sin should lead to sadness and, perhaps, weeping. David wept when he confessed his affair with Bathsheba (2 Samuel 12:13-23). The Jewish remnant wept when they heard God's law, understood it, and realized how far from it they had strayed (Nehemiah 8:9).

But in Isaiah 22, Jerusalem was one big party. Contrast this behavior with the record of the Ninevites (Jonah 3:6-9). On the verge of destruction, Nineveh recognized its sins and repented, but here Jerusalem did not.

God is not calling us to live sad or guilt-ridden lives. And you don't necessarily have to cry to get right with God. **Confession,** like other prayers, comes about **as a result of the Holy Spirit's work.** By confession we take full responsibility for our wrong choices. We own up completely to our rebellious acts. We come to God humbly for the forgiveness that only he can provide. True confession doesn't leave stains of self-hatred but enables us to experience **a new sense of God's forgiveness.**

Ultimately, confession makes us vulnerable, puts us all in the same boat. When we confess—and sometimes cry—we admit a need, a need for comfort and, in this case, for forgiveness. A good cry from the heart is always honest. However you confess your sins to God, let go of those nagging guilt feelings and remember Christ's firm yet gentle words: God blesses those who mourn, for they will be comforted (Matthew 5:4).

HERE'S WHAT I'M GOING TO DO

❏ _____

❏ _____

❏ _____

❏ _____

FOOLS ON PARADE

DAY

124

In American colonial days, people guilty of irresponsible or foolish behavior were publicly ridiculed. They were put in stocks and made the object of laughter.

Today **foolish people** routinely appear on talk shows and even make millions boasting of their outrageous behavior. It almost seems as though it pays to indulge in preposterous actions . . . until you read what God has said:

Isaiah 32:5-8: ⁵In that day ungodly fools will not be heroes. Wealthy cheaters will not be respected as outstanding citizens. ⁶Everyone will recognize ungodly fools for what they are. They spread lies about the LORD; they deprive the hungry of food and give no water to the thirsty. ⁷The smooth tricks of evil people will be exposed, including all the lies they use to oppress the poor in the courts. ⁸But good people will be generous to others and will be blessed for all they do.

According to the prophet Isaiah, the day is coming when people will once again frown on foolish behavior. Proud sinners—those who make it a habit to lie and mistreat the less fortunate—will be singled out.

According to the Bible, **God is all-knowing.** He not only sees everything people do, but he is fully aware of motives and attitudes. He sees right into the heart and soul of each person. The Scriptures also declare that God is a just judge. Every person will one day stand before God and be required to **give an account** for the life he or she has lived.

But that day seems like a mere fantasy. Here and now, sinful behavior is "no big deal." And so most people live selfishly and thoughtlessly. They take advantage of others and then try to justify their actions. They rationalize their deeds. They make excuses. They blame others. Countless people (including many celebrities) live outrageously. They thumb their noses at rules and decency. They live to shock others. And though they may be treated as heroes in the current culture, they will definitely be **exposed** and **shamed** in God's coming Kingdom. This is a lesson everyone needs to grasp: Because God is an all-knowing, perfect judge, **nobody will get away with anything!**

So what can you do? How can you avoid joining in the foolishness? How can you be different? How can you live the kind of life that will be celebrated and blessed by God? Verse 8 tells us that "good people will be generous." Rather than concentrating on yourself and doing foolish things, God desires that you **think of others** and **do selfless things.** God wants you to make it your aim to be generous.

HERE'S WHAT I'M GOING TO DO

❏ _____

_____

❏ _____

_____

❏ _____

_____

❏ _____

_____

SIGNATURES

You're sitting in your car, casually listening to the radio, when you hear a song you've never heard before. You listen intently because you like what you hear. Then it comes to you—you're hearing the single from the new CD of your favorite group. You know because you **recognize** the guitar riffs, the lead singer's voice, and the style of the lyrics.

If you're a fan of music—whether it's rock, classical, jazz, or country—you can become so familiar with an artist that you can recognize his or her work instantly, even though you may never have heard a particular piece before. That's because all accomplished musicians have a "signature"—a style or trait—that makes their craft stand out.

In the same way, we can recognize **God's work** through his **great miracles,** as Isaiah tells us:

Isaiah 41:17-20: [17]"When the poor and needy search for water and there is none, and their tongues are parched from thirst, then I, the LORD, will answer them. I, the God of Israel, will never forsake them. [18]I will open up rivers for them on high plateaus. I will give them fountains of water in the valleys. In the deserts they will find pools of water. Rivers fed by springs will flow across the dry, parched ground. [19]I will plant trees—cedar, acacia, myrtle, olive, cypress, fir, and pine—on barren land. [20]Everyone will see this miracle and understand that it is the LORD, the Holy One of Israel, who did it."

The poor and needy in this case are the Israelites, God's chosen people. In this figurative passage, they are wandering through the desert, on the verge of dying from thirst. God, however, vows **not to forsake them.** In fact, he uses supernatural means to provide for their needs, causing rivers to flow from barren mountains, springs to emerge from parched ground, and pools of water to appear in the desert.

God went to miraculous lengths to protect his people in Old Testament times. But does he still use supernatural means to help the poor and needy today? He does, but more often he uses **the church** to work in miraculous ways **on his behalf.** The world often fails to notice these quiet wonders carried out by people who love God and take his commandment to love others with great seriousness.

We cannot begin to fathom the awesome power of God and the possibilities of that power as it relates to those who are suffering in the world. We can only **faithfully obey God's instructions** to care for the poor and needy we come in contact with and trust him to take action when he deems it necessary.

HERE'S WHAT I'M GOING TO DO

☐ _____

☐ _____

☐ _____

☐ _____

PROMISES YOU CAN TRUST

The world is full of promises:

- "If elected, I promise to increase the minimum wage to $8.00 an hour."

- "If you use the Tummy Twister ten minutes a day, three times a week, you'll lose fifteen pounds in less than a month!"

- "If you find it cheaper anywhere else, we'll give it to you free!"

- "Satisfaction guaranteed or your money back."

How do you decide whether a promise is **believable** or **not?** It all depends on the person making the promise. If the promise maker is a politician looking to get reelected or an advertiser trying to sell a product, you may want to take the guarantee with a grain of salt.

If, however, the promise maker is someone incapable of lying, someone who is perfectly trustworthy, then you'd better believe that **the promise will be kept.** Let's take a look at one such promise in the book of Isaiah.

Isaiah 49:8-13: 8This is what the LORD says: "At just the right time, I will respond to you. On the day of salvation, I will help you. I will give you as a token and pledge to Israel. This will prove that I will reestablish the land of Israel and reassign it to its own people again. 9Through you I am saying to the prisoners of darkness, 'Come out! I am giving you your freedom!' They will be my sheep, grazing in green pastures and on hills that were previously bare. 10They will neither hunger nor thirst. The searing sun and scorching desert winds will not reach them anymore. For the LORD in his mercy will lead them beside cool waters. 11And I will make my mountains into level paths for them. The highways will be raised above the valleys. 12See, my people will return from far away, from lands

---

[1] **49:12** As in Dead Sea Scrolls, which read *from the region of Aswan*, which is in southern Egypt. Masoretic Text reads *from the region of Sinim*.

to the north and west, and from as far south as Egypt.¹"

¹³Sing for joy, O heavens! Rejoice, O earth! Burst into song, O mountains! For the LORD has comforted his people and will have compassion on them in their sorrow.

God is speaking to Israel in this passage, reassuring the poor and needy Israelites that he will be with them. Look at what the Lord specifically promises his people: He promises that they will **never hunger** or **thirst,** that he will **comfort** them, and that he will have **compassion** on the afflicted ones.

The Israelites knew that the Lord is trustworthy, that he keeps his promises. We should know that too. God has promised to protect the weak and satisfy the needy. That does not mean that the poor and needy will not suffer. However, we must remain confident that the Lord will eventually **fulfill his promises** to the disadvantaged—in his time and in ways that we cannot imagine.

So where do you fit in the picture? Recognize that **you** may be **one of the ways** God accomplishes his work of uplifting others. Are you looking to serve?

HERE'S WHAT I'M GOING TO DO

❑ _____

_____

❑ _____

_____

THE SURPRISE APPEARANCE

How do you picture Jesus during his time on earth? What do you suppose he looked like? How did he act? How did he carry himself? What impression did his physical appearance make on other people? Think about it: This man had the power to change water into wine, the ability to cause the blind to see, and the authority to calm a raging storm. His **teachings** were so unique that **they completely altered the way people have thought of God.** He was so wise and learned that he confounded even the most respected religious leaders of his time.

Yet you may be surprised to learn that people did not necessarily **respond well** to Jesus. Let's take a look at a very interesting description of the Son of God in the book of Isaiah.

Isaiah 53:3-9: ³He was despised and rejected—a man of sorrows, acquainted with bitterest grief. We turned our backs on him and looked the other way when he went by. He was despised, and we did not care.

⁴Yet it was our weaknesses he carried; it was our sorrows¹ that weighed him down. And we thought his troubles were a punishment from God for his own sins! ⁵But he was wounded and crushed for our sins. He was beaten that we might have peace. He was whipped, and we were healed! ⁶All of us have strayed away like sheep. We have left God's paths to follow our own. Yet the LORD laid on him the guilt and sins of us all.

⁷He was oppressed and treated harshly, yet he never said a word. He was led as a lamb to the slaughter. And as a sheep is silent before the shearers, he did not open his mouth. ⁸From prison and trial they led him away to his death. But who among the people realized that he was dying for their sins—that he was suffering their punishment? ⁹He had

¹ **53:4** Or *Yet it was our sicknesses he carried; it was our diseases.*

done no wrong, and he never deceived anyone. But he was buried like a criminal; he was put in a rich man's grave.

As hard as it may be to imagine, the only Son of God came to earth as a servant—a despised, rejected, oppressed, and afflicted servant. He endured the world's hatred and **gave his life** for the human race he loved. How does that description compare with the mental image of Jesus you had earlier?

Actually, Jesus' appearance makes sense when you think about it. If he had taken the form of a wealthy and powerful leader when he came to earth, it would have contradicted God's emphasis throughout the Old Testament. God constantly **identified himself** with the poor and needy of the world, even going so far as to say that those who oppress the poor show contempt for their Maker (Proverbs 14:31). So what other form would Jesus have taken than that of a lowly servant?

The Lord understands what it's like to be looked down on by society. He knows what it means to be poor. He experienced the suffering of the downtrodden. And as a result of this personal experience, the Lord knows exactly how to **help those in need.**

HERE'S WHAT I'M GOING TO DO

☐ _____

_____

_____

A SATISFYING INVITATION

Rock superstar Mick Jagger is famous for the line, "I can't get no satisfaction." Satisfaction is defined as "the fulfillment or gratification of a desire, need, or appetite." With this definition in mind, make a mental list of the things you would need in order to be **completely satisfied.** Be honest here.

When you've finished making your list, take a look at what God has to say about satisfaction in Isaiah 55.

Isaiah 55:1-2: ¹"Is anyone thirsty? Come and drink—even if you have no money! Come, take your choice of wine or milk—it's all free! ²Why spend your money on food that does not give you strength? Why pay for food that does you no good? Listen, and I will tell you where to get food that is good for the soul!"

The Old Testament contains several promises from the Lord to **protect** and **care** for the needs of the poor. This is not one of those promises. The focus here is not on physical needs but on spiritual ones. This is not an invitation to dinner

but an **invitation to salvation.**

The Lord is inviting people to come to him, to trust and rely on him for salvation. He points out that there is no need to pursue anything else in life because he is the **only one who can bring genuine satisfaction.** (Remember that mental list you made earlier? Cross out everything on it except "the Lord.") Neither food nor drink nor riches will ever completely satisfy us; without the Lord and his salvation, we will always be unfulfilled.

How should this knowledge affect how we react to a world filled with need? Is it reasonable to expect people who are wondering where their next meal is coming from to listen to us when we tell them the only thing that will satisfy them is the Lord and his salvation? Probably not. That's why our ministry should **always consider the whole person.** When we help take care of people's physical needs, we are sharing God's love and compassion and often those in need will be more open to considering the **salvation** God offers.

PRAYER POINT

Praise the Lord for the fact that he extended to you an invitation to experience his salvation. Ask him to help you maintain a perspective on helping the whole person— meeting both physical and spiritual needs—in your ministry to those less fortunate than you.

HERE'S WHAT I'M GOING TO DO

☐ _____

_____

☐ _____

_____

☐ _____

_____

☐ _____

_____

GOOD NEWS!

When was the last time you received some really good news? Perhaps it was the morning you found out that the person you'd had a crush on for years actually liked you too. Or maybe it was the afternoon you turned over your graded final exam and saw a bright red "A" at the top of the page. Or perhaps it was the evening your dad announced that your family would be taking a trip to Hawaii.

Do you remember how you reacted when you got the **good news?** Did you scream? Did your mouth drop open in amazement? Did you high-five everyone in a three-block radius? Sometimes it's almost as fun to watch someone else receive good news as it is to get good news ourselves. Almost. The fact is, nothing can brighten a person's day quicker than good news.

The Lord certainly understands **the power of good news.** In fact, one of the most important aspects of the Christian life involves spreading the Good News.

Isaiah 61:1-3: [1]The Spirit of the Sovereign LORD is upon me, because the LORD has appointed me to bring good news to the poor. He has sent me to comfort the brokenhearted and to announce that captives will be released and prisoners will be freed.[1] [2]He has sent me to tell those who mourn that the time of the LORD's favor has come,[2] and with it, the day of God's anger against their enemies. [3]To all who mourn in Israel,[3] he will give beauty for ashes, joy instead of mourning, praise instead of despair. For the LORD has planted them like strong and graceful oaks for his own glory.

Put yourself in the place of a homeless or needy person, and answer this question: "What's the best news you could ever hope to get?" Probably the first answer that comes to mind involves winning the lottery or being given a place

---

[1] **61:1** Greek version reads *and the blind will see.*
[2] **61:2** Or *to proclaim the acceptable year of the LORD.*
[3] **61:3** Hebrew *in Zion.*

to live rent-free.

And yet the news that the Lord gave to Israel in Isaiah 61—the news that was later proclaimed by Jesus himself in Luke 4:18-19—is much more exciting and meaningful. God sent his only Son to **mend** the brokenhearted, to **free** those who are slaves to sin, and to **comfort** those who mourn. Because of the salvation provided by Jesus, all who believe in him can look forward to one day escaping the injustice, suffering, and poverty of this present world.

PRAYER POINT

Ask the Lord to make you aware of opportunities you have to show his care to non-Christian friends and acquaintances.

Working to meet the needs of hurting and broken people may lead to opportunities to talk to them about **the fulfillment of their eternal needs.** How wonderful it is to know that with God's help, we too can turn ashes to beauty, mourning to joy, and despair to praise.

HERE'S WHAT I'M GOING TO DO

☐ _____

_____

☐ _____

_____

☐ _____

_____

☐ _____

_____

CONNED

DAY

130

"If it seems too good to be true, it probably is." Unfortunately, people usually learn the truth of that statement by being taken, conned, or swindled.

Con artists **prey** on the weak, the desperate, and the unsuspecting. Baiting their traps with **extravagant promises,** they draw in their victims. Only when these unscrupulous men and women have left town with the money do the victims realize they've been had.

Read this prophecy in Jeremiah to discover what God says about those who set and spring their traps.

Jeremiah 5:26-31: 26"Among my people are wicked men who lie in wait for victims like a hunter hiding in a blind. They are continually setting traps for other people. 27Like a cage filled with birds, their homes are filled with evil plots. And the result? Now they are great and rich. 28They are well fed and well groomed, and there is no limit to their wicked deeds. They refuse justice to orphans and deny the rights of the poor. 29Should I not punish them for this?" asks the LORD. "Should I not avenge myself against a nation such as this?

30"A horrible and shocking thing has happened in this land—31the prophets give false prophecies, and the priests rule with an iron hand. And worse yet, my people like it that way! But what will you do when the end comes?"

No one likes cheaters. In fact, every society has laws to protect citizens from being lied to and taken advantage of. Thus we have contracts, full disclosure, and "truth in advertising." It comes as no surprise, then, that God would have harsh words for those who get rich off the poor by **cheating** them and **denying** them their rights and justice. What is shocking about this passage, however, is that these "wicked men" are members of the family. God calls them "my people" (v. 26). And he promises to punish them severely.

Those who claim God as Father should live like his sons and daughters. This means **obeying him and caring for each other.** Too often, however, there is very little **discernible difference** between those inside God's family and the rest of the world. They may look good on Sunday, professing to love God, and then live for themselves during the rest of the week. For example, instead of taking care of the poor, they take advantage of them through shady business deals. God warns these people that they **won't escape** his wrath.

PRAYER POINT

Confess those times when you have "set traps" and "plotted" against others for your own benefit. Ask God to show you what you need to change to better represent him to others.

It's easy to judge, identifying business executives, salespeople, politicians, and others who seem to fit the description. But consider the ways that *you* take advantage of others to promote your own agenda. Honestly evaluate your role in this life-drama. Do you exalt yourself by pushing down others? Do you enhance your status at someone else's expense? Do your friends and classmates know you belong to God's family—is there a difference? Determine to be part of God's **solution,** not the problem.

HERE'S WHAT I'M GOING TO DO

☐ _____

_____

☐ _____

_____

NAME DROPPING

Picture this. You're at a party and the loudmouth next to you is bragging about all the cool people he knows. He's dropping names faster than a gossip columnist. Filled with disgust, you probably move to another circle of friends as quickly as possible.

Some people act as though name-dropping is a varsity sport. They met the actor at the mall, saw the starlet on the beach, sat near the pro athlete on the plane. Evidently they feel important by associating themselves with celebrities.

The same thing happens in everyday relationships. People like to associate with those who have achieved a measure of stardom or status. They want to be **part of the in-crowd.**

It's a **waste** of time. Read today's passage to see who is really worthwhile getting to know.

Jeremiah 9:23-24: 23This is what the LORD says: "Let not the wise man gloat in his wisdom, or the mighty man in his might, or the rich man in his riches. 24Let them boast in this alone: that they truly know me and understand that I am the LORD who is just and righteous, whose love is unfailing, and that I delight in these things. I, the LORD, have spoken!"

A lot of people seem to live in the glow of celebrities, boasting about meeting or knowing the rich and famous. But God points out that even those who *are* wise, powerful, and wealthy have nothing to brag about. All of their popularity and status is **meaningless** when compared to our awesome Lord.

Actually, in this passage God is saying, "The only One worth knowing is *ME*, so deal with that!" And when we get to know the Lord, we realize that **he alone is just, righteous, loving, and faithful.** Now that's a name worth "dropping."

Where do you find your identity, your self-concept? If it's from your friends, clique, or gang, think again. Instead of worrying about status and popularity, focus on **knowing the Lord.** He is just, righteous, and loving, and everything comes from him—wisdom, power, and riches.

PRAYER POINT

Ask God to help you get to know him better and to remove anything in your life that stands between you and him.

HERE'S WHAT I'M GOING TO DO

☐ _____

_____

☐ _____

_____

☐ _____

_____

☐ _____

_____

☐ _____

_____

☐ _____

_____

_____

AND THE WINNER IS . . .

The Nobel Peace Prize is one of the world's most prestigious awards. It is awarded annually to people who distinguish themselves in the areas of physics, chemistry, medicine, literature, and the pursuit of peace. Some might say that it is **a sign of true greatness** to be awarded one of these prizes. What is your measure of greatness?

To find out what God thinks, read today's passage.

Jeremiah 22:15-17: 15"But a beautiful palace does not make a great king! Why did your father, Josiah, reign so long? Because he was just and right in all his dealings. That is why God blessed him. 16He made sure that justice and help were given to the poor and needy, and everything went well for him. Isn't that what it means to know me?" asks the LORD. 17"But you! You are full of selfish greed and dishonesty! You murder the innocent, oppress the poor, and reign ruthlessly."

In 1979, one of the Nobel prizes was awarded to a poor woman living in the slums of a huge city. Known for her ministry with lepers and street people, she continues to work with the poorest of the poor. Her name is Mother Teresa. Indeed, she exemplifies true greatness, according to God's definition. Jeremiah sums up this definition in these

words written about King Josiah: "He was **just** and **right** in all his dealings. . . . He made sure that **justice** and **help** were given to the poor and needy" (vv. 15, 16).

You may be thinking, "Hey, I'm no Mother Teresa, so what does God expect me to do?" Look again at what Jeremiah wrote. The actions and qualities of true greatness are doable for *anyone*, with God's help.

Can you be just in your dealings with your friends and family? Can you give help to the poor and needy? Sure you can. **You can make a difference.** Look for how you can win "God's peace prize."

PRAYER POINT

Ask God to help you be just and fair, at home and at school.

HERE'S WHAT I'M GOING TO DO

☐ _____

☐ _____

☐ _____

☐ _____

☐ _____

RESTORING WRECKS

In the United States when there is a serious accident involving cars, the police usually call an ambulance and a wrecker truck. In the United Kingdom, however, in a similar situation the police call an ambulance and a *recovery* truck. Both trucks are basically the same, but their names are quite different. *Wrecker* seems to emphasize the problem, while *recovery* emphasizes **restoration.** Which would you rather have take care of your car?

God is in the restoration business—**life restoration.** Read this passage to see what he promises to restore to his people.

> Jeremiah 33:10-13: ¹⁰"This is what the LORD says: You say, 'This land has been ravaged, and the people and animals have all disappeared.' Yet in the empty streets of Jerusalem and Judah's other towns, there will be heard once more ¹¹the sounds of joy and laughter. The joyful voices of bridegrooms and brides will be heard again, along with the joyous songs of people bringing thanksgiving offerings to the LORD. They will sing,
>
> 'Give thanks to the LORD Almighty, for the LORD is good.
> His faithful love endures forever!'
>
> For I will restore the prosperity of this land to what it was in the past, says the LORD.
>
> ¹²"This is what the LORD Almighty says: This land—though it is now desolate and the people and animals have all disappeared—will once more see shepherds leading sheep and lambs. ¹³Once again their flocks will prosper in the towns of the hill country, the foothills of Judah,¹ the Negev, the land of Benjamin, the vicinity of Jerusalem, and all the towns of Judah. I, the LORD, have spoken!"

Certainly the people of Judah, God's people, and their land

---

¹ **33:13** Hebrew *the Shephelah*.

looked devastated and hopeless. But God saw beyond the devastation to future **prosperity** (v. 11).

Homeless people, alcoholics, and drug addicts are called "human wrecks," with the emphasis on "wreck." But God sees the same needy people with eyes of faith, hope, and love. **God knows that no one is a hopeless wreck.** Recovery is always a possibility with him in the picture. And this is how God wants his people to look at others—not with condemning, judgmental attitudes, but with the eyes of love.

PRAYER POINT

Consider the people in your town whom others view as human wrecks. Ask God to help you see them as precious, the way he does, and pray for them today.

Psychologists have reported that in refugee camps, the sound of laughter is seldom heard, even among the children. With all the trauma of war and loss of hope, children sometimes forget how to connect with their emotions. They totally shut down. But when the sound of laughter is heard, the psychologists know that restoration and healing have begun.

What can you do to restore the "wrecks" in your world? You can provide **hope.** You can bring **laughter.**

HERE'S WHAT I'M GOING TO DO

☐ _____

_____

☐ _____

_____

_____

SUCCESS

Drive through neighborhoods where many wealthy people live, and you'll see spacious and meticulously manicured yards. The ornate and large houses look like palaces. Many of the homes have backyard swimming pools, and the driveways have luxury cars parked in them. Judging from the appearance of things, you might assume that the people living in this neighborhood were **very successful.** But is success just based on what a person has?

Today's passage contains Jeremiah's message to another group of people who looked very successful on the outside—the Babylonians. They were the most affluent and powerful nation on earth. But were they really successful?

Jeremiah 51:45-48: ⁴⁵"Listen, my people, flee from Babylon. Save yourselves! Run from the LORD's fierce anger. ⁴⁶But do not panic when you hear the first rumor of approaching forces. For rumors will keep coming year by year. Then there will be a time of violence as the leaders fight against each other. ⁴⁷For the time is surely coming when I will punish this great city and all her idols. Her whole land will be disgraced, and her dead will lie in the streets. ⁴⁸The heavens and earth will rejoice, for out of the north will come destroying armies against Babylon," says the LORD.

Obviously God was not very happy with the Babylonians. Even though the Babylonians were successful in the eyes of the world, they were **failures** as far as God was concerned. That's because **they valued wealth and possessions over faithfulness to God.**

In contrast, Jeremiah was a total failure in the world's estimation. He had lived most of his life under the rule of evil kings who had no respect for God. He was often rejected by his neighbors and his nation's leaders and even tortured and threatened with death. He had no money or status. In the end, however, Jeremiah and not the Babylonian kings received God's seal of success.

Earthly wealth disappears quickly, but **eternal wealth lasts forever.** Jeremiah made the right choice in being faithful to God although it cost him just about everything.

Determine to be a **success** in God's eyes. He's the only one who really counts.

HERE'S WHAT I'M GOING TO DO

☐ _____

_____

☐ _____

_____

☐ _____

_____

☐ _____

_____

☐ _____

_____

☐ _____

_____

☐ _____

_____

THE RAVAGES OF HUNGER

DAY

135

You see images of hungry children. Their bellies are painfully distended. Their eyes are bottomless pools of pain. They haven't the energy to swat the flies swarming around their eyes and mouths. They haven't the strength to weep.

You see images of inner-city children, neglected by parents, forgotten by the public. They live in squalor. They fight over garbage—if they are able. They die without pity.

You see images like these and shake your head in **sorrow**. And you thank God that you probably will never have to find out firsthand what it must be like to **experience hunger and need that desperately.**

The Bible offers another description of the ravages of hunger. Keep these images in mind as you read these verses.

Lamentations 4:2-10: [2]See how the precious children of Jerusalem,[1] worth their weight in gold, are now treated like pots of clay.

[3]Even the jackals feed their young, but not my people Israel. They ignore their children's cries, like the ostriches of the desert.

[4]The parched tongues of their little ones stick with thirst to the roofs of their mouths. The children cry for bread, but no one has any to give them.

[5]The people who once ate only the richest foods now beg in the streets for anything they can get. Those who once lived in palaces now search the garbage pits for food.

[6]The guilt[2] of my people is greater than that of Sodom, where utter disaster struck in a moment with no one to help them.

[7]Our princes were once glowing with health; they were as clean as snow and as elegant as jewels.

[8]But now their faces are blacker than soot. No one even recognizes them. Their skin sticks to their bones; it is as dry and hard as wood.

---

[1] **4:2** Hebrew *sons of Zion*.
[2] **4:6** Or *punishment*.

⁹Those killed by the sword are far better off than those who die of hunger, wasting away for want of food.

¹⁰Tenderhearted women have cooked their own children and eaten them in order to survive the siege.

PRAYER POINT

If there is sin you are harboring, confess it now so that it won't ravage your life.

The world's hungry today suffer for many reasons—drought, destruction, political turmoil, wars. For the most part, they are innocent victims. But that was not the case with the Israelites. Their hunger **resulted directly from their sin.** After many years of warnings, God was allowing the enemy to lay siege to Jerusalem.

As you read these descriptions of mistreated, crying children . . . people searching garbage pits for scraps of rotting food . . . you get a glimpse of how **devastating** sin can be. It destroys life.

Ask God to help you reach those who are devastated by sin. Turn away from it. Do not let it destroy your life.

HERE'S WHAT I'M GOING TO DO

☐ _____

_____

☐ _____

_____

☐ _____

_____

GETTING WHAT YOU DESERVE

DAY 136

When you were a kid, how many times did your mom have to warn you before you'd do something? How often did you hear threats like these: "If you don't clean those toys up by the time I count to three, you're going to get it!" Or, "Stop all that racket in there or you'll be sent to your room!" Or even, "If you don't stop picking on your sister, I'm going to start picking on you!" What happened if you **kept doing** what you **weren't supposed to be doing?**

Most parents carried through with the disciplinary action they had promised, sometimes with the comment, "Don't say I didn't warn you!" For generations, the Israelites had heard through the prophets all about God's promise of punishment if they didn't straighten up and return to him.

Now Ezekiel describes again the certain desolation of Israel—the **consequences** of years and years of willful disobedience.

Ezekiel 7:14-18, 23-27: ¹⁴"The trumpets call Israel's army to mobilize, but no one listens, for my fury is against them all. ¹⁵Any who leave the city walls will be killed by enemy swords. Those who stay inside will die of famine and disease. ¹⁶The few who survive and escape to the mountains will moan like doves, weeping for their sins. ¹⁷Everyone's hands will be feeble; their knees will be as weak as water. ¹⁸They will dress themselves in sackcloth; horror and shame will cover them. They will shave their heads in sorrow and remorse.

²³"Prepare chains for my people, for the land is bloodied by terrible crimes. Jerusalem is filled with violence. ²⁴I will bring the most ruthless of nations to occupy their homes. I will break down their proud fortresses and defile their sanctuaries. ²⁵Terror and trembling will overcome my people. They will look for peace but will not find it. ²⁶Calamity will follow

calamity; rumor will follow rumor. They will look in vain for a vision from the prophets. They will receive no teaching from the priests and no counsel from the leaders. ²⁷The king and the prince will stand helpless, weeping in despair, and the people's hands will tremble with fear. I will bring against them the evil they have done to others, and they will receive the punishment they so richly deserve. Then they will know that I am the LORD!"

Just like a wise parent, **God's patience is not limitless.** He still expects his children to live obediently, maturely, and wisely. If we don't, there will be consequences—perhaps not on the level the Israelites faced, but painful anyway.

Make sure your heart never hardens like the Israelites' hearts did. Be **open** to God's warnings about sin. Be **diligent** to seek his will. You don't have to experience what the Israelites did to "know that I am the LORD!"

PRAYER POINT

Be honest with God about your

walk with him. What sins have

you committed lately? What bad

attitudes are you harboring? Ask

him to give you the guidance and

strength you need to do right.

HERE'S WHAT I'M GOING TO DO

☐ _____

_____

☐ _____

_____

☐ _____

_____

DAY

137

Some medical experts now say the tendency to become an alcoholic is hereditary. Children of alcoholics potentially face the same struggles their parents and grandparents did because of their genetic makeup. Many people who wrestle with problems like addiction often blame their parents and excuse their own **lack of personal responsibility.**

But don't they have a point? Aren't a lot of the problems we have to deal with personally the fault of our previous generations? And if so, why doesn't God do something about it? That's a good question, but let's have God answer it with today's reading.

Ezekiel 18:1-9: ¹Then another message came to me from the LORD: ²"Why do you quote this proverb in the land of Israel: 'The parents have eaten sour grapes, but their children's mouths pucker at the taste'? ³As surely as I live, says the Sovereign LORD, you will not say this proverb anymore in Israel. ⁴For all people are mine to judge—both parents and children alike. And this is my rule: The person who sins will be the one who dies.

⁵"Suppose a certain man is just and does what is lawful and right, ⁶and he has not feasted in the mountains before Israel's idols or worshiped them. And suppose he does not commit adultery or have intercourse with a woman during her menstrual period. ⁷Suppose he is a merciful creditor, not keeping the items given in pledge by poor debtors, and does not rob the poor but instead gives food to the hungry and provides clothes for people in need. ⁸And suppose he grants loans without interest, stays away from injustice, is honest and fair when judging others, ⁹and faithfully obeys my laws and regulations. Anyone who does these things is just and will surely live, says the Sovereign LORD."

The Israelites used the **excuse** that God was punishing

them because of the sins of their ancestors. It wasn't their fault! True, generation after generation of spiritual decay in Israel had made the situation incredibly bad. But in blaming their parents and grandparents, the Israelites didn't take any responsibility for themselves. **They just gave up.**

But Ezekiel the prophet sets them straight. He explains that God judges each person **individually,** parent and child alike. Then he describes a righteous person—one who does what is "lawful and right." One who doesn't worship idols, but God alone. One who obeys God's laws regarding sex. One who deals honorably and justly in his or her business dealings. One who doesn't mistreat the poor but gives food to the hungry and provides clothes for people who need them. One who is just and fair in all areas. One who faithfully obeys the Lord.

Whether good or bad, each person receives God's fair treatment. Sure, we may suffer the effects of the sins committed by those who came before us. But God doesn't punish us for somebody else's sins. And we shouldn't use their behavior as **an excuse for our sins.**

PRAYER POINT

Pray for yourself as an individual responsible to God. Ask God to make you a more righteous, just person in every area of your life.

HERE'S WHAT I'M GOING TO DO

☐ _____

_____

☐ _____

_____

HEALING THE LAND

Concern about pollution, global warming, and rain forest destruction grabs headlines these days. Yet we hear relatively little about the **spiritual pollution** that threatens to claim just as many lives. Every day, our culture suffers the **increasing consequences of our actions.**

Thousands of years ago, Israel witnessed the slow, steady destruction of their own land. It was directly caused by **generations of sinful behavior.** But through his prophet Ezekiel, God promised a stunning restoration of the land.

Ezekiel 47:1, 6-12: ¹Then the man brought me back to the entrance of the Temple. There I saw a stream flowing eastward from beneath the Temple threshold. This stream then passed to the right of the altar on its south side.

⁶He told me to keep in mind what I had seen; then he led me back along the riverbank. ⁷Suddenly, to my surprise, many trees were now growing on both sides of the river! ⁸Then he said to me, "This river flows east through the desert into the Jordan Valley,¹ where it enters the Dead Sea.² The waters of this stream will heal the salty waters of the Dead Sea and make them fresh and pure. ⁹Everything that touches the water of this river will live. Fish will abound in the Dead Sea, for its waters will be healed. Wherever this water flows, everything will live. ¹⁰Fishermen will stand along the shores of the Dead Sea, fishing all the way from En-gedi to En-eglaim. The shores will be covered with nets drying in the sun. Fish of every kind will fill the Dead Sea, just as they fill the Mediterranean³! ¹¹But the marshes and swamps will not be purified; they will be sources of salt. ¹²All kinds of fruit trees will grow along both sides of the river. The leaves of these trees will never turn brown and fall, and there will always be fruit on their branches. There will be a new crop every month,

---

¹ **47:8a** Hebrew *the Arabah.*
² **47:8b** Hebrew *the sea;* also in 47:10.
³ **47:10** Hebrew *the great sea;* also in 47:15, 17, 19, 20.

without fail! For they are watered by the river flowing from the Temple. The fruit will be for food and the leaves for healing."

After Jerusalem fell, Ezekiel offered the people a message of hope. He explained that God is holy, but Jerusalem—and its Temple—had been defiled. They were dirty. The nation needed to be cleaned up from years of blatant disobedience to God. So God had sent the Israelites into captivity for seventy years in order to **cleanse** the land.

In a vision, Ezekiel returns to the cleansed nation. He comes to the Temple and watches in fascination as a fresh, lively stream flows from the Temple—healing the land, even making the Dead Sea pure and fresh.

It's a beautiful picture of **God's healing touch.** And it will ultimately come true in our earth when **Jesus returns.**

The same way that God heals and restores the land, **he restores individual lives**—even those who have experienced total degradation. When God unleashes his healing power, dry, dusty hearts bubble up with the Spirit of God. Fruit grows abundantly. There is lush and beautiful growth.

HERE'S WHAT I'M GOING TO DO

☐ _____

_____

☐ _____

_____

_____

EAT YOUR VEGGIES

The category is Least Favorite Food. The nominees: peas, spinach, cauliflower, and asparagus. For most people it is some sort of **vegetable,** a nearly forgotten food group in these days of fast-food.

In biblical days, however, vegetables ruled as **a source of everyday nutrition.** In fact, in one Bible story, vegetables were actually an answer to prayer!

Daniel 1:11-20: [11]Daniel talked it over with the attendant who had been appointed by the chief official to look after Daniel, Hananiah, Mishael, and Azariah. [12]"Test us for ten days on a diet of vegetables and water," Daniel said. [13]"At the end of the ten days, see how we look compared to the other young men who are eating the king's rich food. Then you can decide whether or not to let us continue eating our diet." [14]So the attendant agreed to Daniel's suggestion and tested them for ten days.

[15]At the end of the ten days, Daniel and his three friends looked healthier and better nourished than the young men who had been eating the food assigned by the king. [16]So after that, the attendant fed them only vegetables instead of the rich foods and wines. [17]God gave these four young men an unusual aptitude for learning the literature and science of the time. And God gave Daniel special ability in understanding the meanings of visions and dreams.

[18]When the three-year training period ordered by the king was completed, the chief official brought all the young men to King Nebuchadnezzar. [19]The king talked with each of them, and none of them impressed him as much as Daniel, Hananiah, Mishael, and Azariah. So they were appointed to his regular staff of advisers. [20]In all matters requiring wisdom and balanced judgment, the king found the advice of these young men to be ten times better than that of all the magicians and enchanters in his entire kingdom.

Chosen trainees were served only the best food and wine from the king's table. This was a problem for Daniel and his friends. You see, portions of the king's food and wine were offered to idols in pagan ceremonies. And according to God's law, any food that was offered to an idol was considered contaminated and forbidden.

Daniel finally convinced the official to feed him and his friends nothing but vegetables and water for ten days. At the end of that period, the official compared Daniel and his friends with those who had eaten from the king's table. Because God was **taking care** of Daniel and his friends, they finished the ten days looking healthier and better nourished than the other men did.

Interesting story, right? But what does it have to do with our lives today? After all, you'll probably never be served food that's been sacrificed to idols. The point here is that God is concerned with our **physical well-being**—even down to the food we eat. When we shovel a constant stream of junk food down our throats, we are mistreating our bodies. And because **our bodies are creations of God,** that's a pretty serious offense. So while it is certainly important for us to make sure that the poor and needy are nourished, it is also important for us to **maintain a healthy diet** for ourselves.

HERE'S WHAT I'M GOING TO DO

☐ _____

_____

_____

GET READY

DAY

140

Ready for vacation? Let's check the list. Windows closed? Check. Dog taken to kennel? Check. Lawn mowed? Check. Lights turned off? Check? Mail and newspaper delivery stopped? Whoops, forgot that one.

Big events, even ones meant for our enjoyment, require **preparation** if they are to happen smoothly. We must pay attention to details if we want to enjoy a carefree vacation. In a similar way, we must pay attention to our preparation for **meeting God.** If we enter his presence casually or impatiently, how will we be **ready** to listen? Let's look at Daniel's life. His example shows us why he was ready to receive an important message from God.

> Daniel 10:1-3: ¹In the third year of the reign of King Cyrus of Persia, Daniel (also known as Belteshazzar) had another vision. It concerned events certain to happen in the future—times of war and great hardship—and Daniel understood what the vision meant.
>
> ²When this vision came to me, I, Daniel, had been in mourning for three weeks. ³All that time I had eaten no rich food or meat, had drunk no wine, and had used no fragrant oils.

One of the most amazing truths about God is that **he desires to communicate with us.** Not only does he want us to listen when he speaks, he also wants us to **tell** him everything—our thoughts, fears, sins, and hopes. The fact that God listens to us is especially important when we ask him for help.

In order to communicate with God—to talk and listen to him—we don't have to follow some specific formula or ritual. What we do need to do is **set aside time** to focus our minds on him and his Word.

Let's say we want to bring a specific need to the Lord in prayer. What are we **willing to sacrifice** out of our daily routine in order to focus **all of our attention** on asking God for help?

Of course, our communication with the Lord is not limited to specifically scheduled quiet times. We have the opportunity to enjoy God's presence every day in many different ways. But just as we need focused time with any person with whom we want to have a relationship, so we need it with God. And there are times when that will take sacrificial preparation.

PRAYER POINT

Ask God to help you develop an effective prayer life by bringing to mind actions you can take to strengthen the lines of communication between you and him.

HERE'S WHAT I'M GOING TO DO

☐ _____

☐ _____

☐ _____

☐ _____

☐ _____

THE "EVER-GIVING" GIFT

"Give the gift that keeps on giving." Hundreds of advertisers have used this phrase to sell everything from diamond rings to college educations. The idea behind the slogan is that the gift will continue to have **value** (and perhaps even increase in value) as time goes on.

The prophet Hosea, however, learned of another gift that keeps on giving—though in a much different way than any advertiser could imagine. Let's see what God had to say to Hosea about **the gift of mercy.**

> Hosea 6:4-6: ⁴"O Israel¹ and Judah, what should I do with you?" asks the LORD. "For your love vanishes like the morning mist and disappears like dew in the sunlight. ⁵I sent my prophets to cut you to pieces. I have slaughtered you with my words, threatening you with death. My judgment will strike you as surely as day follows night. ⁶I want you to be merciful; I don't want your sacrifices. I want you to know God; that's more important than burnt offerings."

The Bible is filled with commandments that God expects us to follow and instructions for pleasing him. But few verses are as direct as Hosea 6:6 in explaining what God wants. "I want you to be merciful"—you can't get much plainer than that.

What exactly is mercy? It's showing **kindness, compassion,** and **love** to someone who has no reason to expect such treatment. Obviously the Lord is the ultimate gift-giver in this department. Because of sin, humans were destined to spend eternity apart from God. But the Lord showed mercy on us by sending his only Son to die for us to pay the penalty for our sin, thus giving us an opportunity to spend eternity with him. **No greater gift has ever been given.**

Now this is where the "keeps on giving" part comes in. Because we have received mercy from the Lord, we, in turn, have a responsibility to show mercy to those around us, particularly those who have hurt or offended us.

Unfortunately, **showing mercy is not as easy as talking about it.** If we're honest, we'll probably admit that our first thought in any given situation is for ourselves. Letting go of our anger, our desire to settle the score, takes time and effort.

Mercy is not simply an attitude; it's a **way of life.** We can't just "feel" mercy for another person; we have to show it in our actions. Mercy does not allow us to ignore the plight of someone who may have said something unkind about us. Mercy causes us to become **physically involved in the situation,** showing kindness, compassion, and love— through our actions—to people who have no reason to expect it from us.

We have received a tremendous gift from God—the gift of mercy. It's only natural that we should pass it on.

PRAYER POINT

Spend some time praising the Lord for the mercy he has shown to you. Then ask him to help you show the same type of mercy to others.

HERE'S WHAT I'M GOING TO DO

☐ _____

_____

☐ _____

_____

SLACKING OFF

If you follow sports, you're probably familiar with the "big contract syndrome." If you don't follow sports, here's what happens. An athlete—let's say a baseball player—starts showing signs of greatness. A team owner recognizes this and signs the player to a long-term, big-bucks contract.

After signing the contract, however, the player's performance starts to suffer and he rarely shows the promise that got him the contract in the first place. Some people say the drop-off is due to the pressure of trying to live up to the expectations that go with the new salary. Others say the problem is **complacency.** Let's say the player has a 5-year, $55 million guaranteed contract. Think about this: If the player hits 50 home runs and leads his team to the World Series, he's going to make $11 million a year. On the other hand, if he strikes out every time he goes to the plate and causes his team to finish in last place, he's going to make . . . $11 million a year. So what incentive does he have for doing well?

It's nice to be content and comfortable, but too often contentment and comfort lead to complacency, **being self-satisfied.** Complacency has no part in the lives of God's people, as the Israelites discovered during the time of the prophet Hosea.

Hosea 10:11-12: [11]"Israel[1] is like a trained heifer accustomed to treading out the grain—an easy job that she loves. Now I will put a heavy yoke on her tender neck. I will drive her in front of the plow. Israel[2] and Judah must now break up the hard ground; their days of ease are gone. [12]I said, 'Plant the good seeds of righteousness, and you will harvest a crop of my love. Plow up the hard ground of your hearts, for now is the time to seek the LORD, that he may come and shower righteousness upon you.'"

---

[1] **10:11a** Hebrew *Ephraim*, referring to the northern kingdom of Israel.
[2] **10:11b** Hebrew *Jacob*.

During the time of Hosea, Israel (referred to as "Ephraim" and "Jacob" in this passage) had become complacent. God compares the nation to a contented young cow that eats while it threshes grain. The Lord then warns that he will soon shake them from their complacency.

PRAYER POINT

Ask God to help rid yourself of any complacency in your life.

Why do you suppose God is so strongly against complacency? Perhaps the best explanation is that complacency is a **problem of the heart.** It indicates that we have become **detached** from God and his concerns. God has a tremendous plan for his people—a plan that requires **work** on our part.

As strange as it may sound, there's a fine line between being thankful and being complacent. If God has blessed us with material possessions, we must not forget that those blessings are not merely for our own enjoyment—they're for everyone. We have **a responsibility to use the blessings God has given us to help others.** When we forget or ignore that responsibility, we become complacent.

It's very, very easy to become complacent—often without even realizing it. That's why it's important to regularly check ourselves for signs of self-satisfaction.

HERE'S WHAT I'M GOING TO DO

☐ _____

_____

☐ _____

_____

NOTHING BUT A PRAYER

DAY

143

Prayers come in all shapes, sizes, and varieties. Some, like public prayers in church, are well thought out and elegantly spoken. Others, like the Lord's Prayer or "Now I lay me down to sleep" are recited from memory. Still others are more urgent. In these prayers, people simply drop to their knees and cry, "Lord, help me!"

The prophet Joel offers an example of **an urgent prayer** in the first chapter of his Old Testament book. Let's take a look at what Joel was praying about.

Joel 1:16-20: [16]We watch as our food disappears before our very eyes. There are no joyful celebrations in the house of our God. [17]The seeds die in the parched ground, and the grain crops fail. The barns and granaries stand empty and abandoned. [18]How the animals moan with hunger! The cattle wander about confused because there is no pasture for them. The sheep bleat in misery.

[19]Lord, help us! The fire has consumed the pastures and burned up all the trees. [20]Even the wild animals cry out to you because they have no water to drink. The streams have dried up, and fire has consumed the pastures.

The situation outlined in this passage is pretty bleak. The people's food has been cut off. The ground is dry and hard. The storehouses and granaries are in bad shape because they haven't been used. Herds of cattle and flocks of sheep are starving to death because they have no pastures in which to graze. The land is suffering from a drought so severe that entire streams have dried up.

The situation is so hopeless that Joel recognizes there is only one thing to do—**call to the Lord for help.** Joel was a wise man. Not only could he recognize when things were beyond human capabilities, he also understood that **nothing**

is beyond God's capability.

This is a principle we need to recognize today. Any calamity we face forces us to make a decision. Do we worry ourselves sick with the thought that we will be left shattered and hopeless? Do we try to take the world on our shoulders and solve our own problems? Or do we fall back on the promises of God and trust him to lead us out of the darkness?

We will encounter situations in which we are powerless to help. Everyone has seen the devastating effects of drought and civil war in Third World countries. Maybe we have seen a loved one suffer from an incurable disease. Maybe we have lost our home in a flood or mudslide. We've all asked ourselves, "What can I do?"

Sometimes our only option is **prayer.** Thankfully, prayer is a pretty good option to have. Even when we don't exactly know what to ask for, we can still pray for the Lord's will to be done. It is important to remember that God **hears** and **answers** our prayers—often without our even knowing it. As a result, we are never helpless, no matter how hopeless a situation may seem.

Prayer Point

Spend some time in prayer asking God to intervene in situations that seem to be beyond human control.

Here's What I'm Going to Do

☐ _____

☐ _____

_____

BIG FAT COWS

If you were going to preach an effective sermon, how would you begin? With a joke? With an amazing story? How about by calling the women in your audience "big fat cows"?

You laugh, but that's exactly what the prophet Amos did when he came riding into town.

Amos 4:1-5: ¹Listen to me, you "fat cows" of Samaria, you women who oppress the poor and crush the needy and who are always asking your husbands for another drink! ²The Sovereign LORD has sworn this by his holiness: "The time will come when you will be led away with hooks in your noses. Every last one of you will be dragged away like a fish on a hook! ³You will leave by going straight through the breaks in the wall; you will be thrown from your fortresses.¹ I, the LORD, have spoken!

⁴"Go ahead and offer your sacrifices to the idols at Bethel and Gilgal. Keep on disobeying—your sins are mounting up! Offer sacrifices each morning and bring your tithes every three days! ⁵Present your bread made with yeast as an offering of thanksgiving. Then give your extra voluntary offerings so you can brag about it everywhere! This is the kind of thing you Israelites love to do," says the Sovereign LORD.

As prophets go, Amos was a no-nonsense kind of guy. He wasn't worried about hurting feelings or ruffling feathers. On the contrary, he bashed the Israelites for trusting more in their wealth and religious acts than they did in **living godly lives.**

How did the women "crush the needy"? Probably by being stingy with food to poor slaves. In punishment, these "cows" would become like fish. Archaeological evidence confirms that Israel's Assyrian captors actually did hook prisoners through the nose, attach a rope, and tow them away. Israel's strong fortresses would not be able to protect them from this fate (v. 3). Nor would her religious activities, done

---

¹ 4:3 Hebrew *thrown out toward Harmon*, possibly a reference to Mount Hermon.

mainly to "brag . . . everywhere" (v. 5).

How does all this Old Testament history apply to us? Just like the Israelites, it is possible for North American Christians to rely on their vast wealth. Isn't it odd that in a culture in which food is so plentiful, eating disorders are also common? For many, food and drink become the central controlling force in life. God's gifts are often taken for granted. Where is the **gratitude?**

Also, like the Israelites, we can sometimes fall into the trap of thinking that religious activity done for God can replace spiritual intimacy with him. This is a great mistake! **God doesn't want our empty actions.** He wants our **hearts.**

Let the hard words of a straight-shooting prophet penetrate your heart today. You won't find ultimate security or self-worth eating a lot or a little, having a good time on the weekend, or only going to church every Sunday. Look for your **security** in a God who loves you and wants you to love him.

PRAYER POINT

Pray that you will find your security in an intimate relationship with God. Ask him to make you less worried about your own comfort and more sensitive to those in need.

HERE'S WHAT I'M GOING TO DO

☐ _____

_____

☐ _____

_____

☐ _____

_____

TRAMPLED

On your way to school today, you probably stepped on grass, dirt, cement, asphalt, litter, and the floor mat of the car or bus. As long as the way is safe, sturdy, and somewhat clean, we usually give little thought to what's underfoot. In contrast, we avoid items not designed to be trampled and then feel the loss when we accidentally step on and break something of value.

In this passage, God, through Amos, accuses the people of **treating some people like dirt** and **walking all over them.** And God's not very happy.

Amos 5:10-15: [10]How you hate honest judges! How you despise people who tell the truth! [11]You trample the poor and steal what little they have through taxes and unfair rent. Therefore, you will never live in the beautiful stone houses you are building. You will never drink wine from the lush vineyards you are planting. [12]For I know the vast number of your sins and rebellions. You oppress good people by taking bribes and deprive the poor of justice in the courts. [13]So those who are wise will keep quiet, for it is an evil time.

[14]Do what is good and run from evil—that you may live! Then the LORD God Almighty will truly be your helper, just as you have claimed he is. [15]Hate evil and love what is good; remodel your courts into true halls of justice. Perhaps even yet the LORD God Almighty will have mercy on his people who remain.[1]

Poor people have few resources and thus few recourses when they are being oppressed. They have no power in society, no influential friends in high places, and no money to hire lawyers. Thus, they are vulnerable to being oppressed even further.

This is exactly what God is condemning in this passage.

---

[1] **5:15** Hebrew *on the remnant of Joseph.*

The wealthy and powerful (owners of "beautiful stone houses" and "lush vineyards") were taking advantage of those less fortunate, **using them** to maintain their opulence; in effect, the rich were "trampling" the poor, stepping on them to move on down the road to wealth and worldly success. Even worse, the oppressors were Jews in Israel. God's chosen people were oppressing fellow Jews. So God told them to turn from these evil ways and to "do what is good" instead.

Justice is close to God's heart. He cares deeply that all people are treated with **dignity** and **respect,** regardless of their social standing. You can share God's passion for justice by doing good, especially by **standing up for people who are treated unfairly.**

HERE'S WHAT I'M GOING TO DO

☐ _____

_____

☐ _____

_____

☐ _____

_____

☐ _____

_____

SPIRITUAL JOURNEY TRAVEL LOG

A FLOOD AND A RIVER

In the spring of 1997, the Red River inundated Grand Forks, North Dakota, forcing some 45,000 people from their homes to higher ground. This **flood** was devastating, causing damage in the billions of dollars. And yet there is a kind of flood that is NOT disastrous. In fact, it's **desirable!** Consider the words of the prophet Amos:

Amos 5:18-27: ¹⁸How terrible it will be for you who say, "If only the day of the LORD were here! For then the LORD would rescue us from all our enemies." But you have no idea what you are wishing for. That day will not bring light and prosperity, but darkness and disaster. ¹⁹In that day you will be like a man who runs from a lion—only to meet a bear. After escaping the bear, he leans his hand against a wall in his house—and is bitten by a snake. ²⁰Yes, the day of the LORD will be a dark and hopeless day, without a ray of joy or hope.

²¹"I hate all your show and pretense—the hypocrisy of your religious festivals and solemn assemblies. ²²I will not accept your burnt offerings and grain offerings. I won't even notice all your choice peace offerings. ²³Away with your hymns of praise! They are only noise to my ears. I will not listen to your music, no matter how lovely it is. ²⁴Instead, I want to see a mighty flood of justice, a river of righteous living that will never run dry.

²⁵"Was it to me you were bringing sacrifices and offerings during the forty years in the wilderness, Israel? ²⁶No, your real interest was in your pagan gods—Sakkuth your king god and Kaiwan your star god—the images you yourselves made.¹ ²⁷So I will send you into exile, to a land east of Damascus," says the LORD, whose name is God Almighty.

What does God mean by "a flood of justice"? Well, we know that floods wash over everything in their path. The

---

¹ **5:26** Greek version reads *You took up the shrine of Molech, and the star of your god Rephan, and the images you made for yourselves.*

waters seep into every crack and crevice. Even when the "wet stuff" recedes, the residue of the flood remains. God is saying that in the same way he desires **fairness** and **rightness** to cover the world—washing over and in and through the lives of his people.

PRAYER POINT

Ask God to flood your life with a passion for him and compassion for those hurt by injustice. Pray that you and your believing friends can join together to be a river of righteousness.

What is meant by "a river of righteous living"? If you've ever seen a fast-flowing river, you know that it doesn't let anything stand in its way; it chisels away at everything it encounters. Fast or slow, every river flows relentlessly to its destination, bringing life to the land in the process. God wants us to be like that—**faithfully working** with other believers to provide refreshment, even as we slowly but surely **erode the sin in our culture.**

Practically speaking, we become human floods of justice and rivers of righteousness by helping the victims of injustice. As we allow God's Spirit to **change** our attitudes, values, and priorities, we begin to recognize every person as **important** and **special.**

HERE'S WHAT I'M GOING TO DO

☐ _____

☐ _____

_____

_____

WHOM DO YOU TRUST?

Are you sitting down? Then you're **trusting** that chair to keep you from falling. Do you have an alarm clock? Then you're **trusting** it to make sure you wake up. The only problem with those things is that chairs can break and alarm clocks **can fail** to go off. So who or what is left? Read the first nine verses of Obadiah to find out.

Obadiah 1-9: ¹This is the vision that the Sovereign LORD revealed to Obadiah concerning the land of Edom. We have heard a message from the LORD that an ambassador was sent to the nations to say, "Get ready, everyone! Let's assemble our armies and attack Edom!"

²The LORD says, "I will cut you down to size among the nations, Edom; you will be small and despised. ³You are proud because you live in a rock fortress and make your home high in the mountains. 'Who can ever reach us way up here?' you ask boastfully. Don't fool yourselves! ⁴Though you soar as high as eagles and build your nest among the stars, I will bring you crashing down. I, the LORD, have spoken!

⁵"If thieves came at night and robbed you, they would not take everything. Those who harvest grapes always leave a few for the poor. But your enemies will wipe you out completely! ⁶Every nook and cranny of Edom¹ will be searched and looted. Every treasure will be found and taken.

⁷"All your allies will turn against you. They will help to chase you from your land. They will promise you peace, while plotting your destruction. Your trusted friends will set traps for you, and you won't even know about it. ⁸At that time not a single wise person will be left in the whole land of Edom!" says the LORD. "For on the mountains of Edom I will destroy everyone who has wisdom and understanding. ⁹The mightiest warriors of Teman will be terrified, and everyone on the mountains of Edom will be cut down in the slaughter."

¹ 6 Hebrew *Esau*; also in 8b, 9, 18, 19, 21.

Obadiah was a prophet from the nation of Judah. He was called by God to declare judgment on the nation of Edom. God was angry at the Edomites because they had rejoiced over the dismal fate of Israel and Judah.

Edom was located just south of Judah. The capital at this time was Sela, a city that the Edomites proudly felt couldn't be attacked. It was cut into rock cliffs and could only be approached through a narrow gap in a canyon.

They **trusted** their high city to be safe, but God said they would fall from its heights. They also trusted in their own self-sufficiency, in their wealth, in their allies, and in their own wise men.

But every single thing the Edomites put their trust in would be **totally destroyed** by God. They had put their trust in the **wrong** things. **Don't make the same mistake.**

HERE'S WHAT I'M GOING TO DO

☐ _____

_____

☐ _____

_____

_____

WALKING IN THE DARKNESS

When Wayne Gordon, now the pastor of Chicago's Lawndale Community Church, taught inner-city high schoolers, one of his best students was fatally shot. Reflecting on the other students' reaction to this senseless death, Gordon explains: "They gave me the news as if it were a weather report. Their young lives had already been numbed to violence and death." How do we account for such **callousness to evil?**

God calls it "spiritual darkness."

Jonah 4:11: [11]"But Nineveh has more than 120,000 people living in spiritual darkness,[1] not to mention all the animals. Shouldn't I feel sorry for such a great city?"

Literally, God says that the Ninevites don't know their right hands from their left. Most likely, he was declaring that the Assyrian people had lost all sense of good and bad. Right and wrong. They were hopelessly lost, cut off from the truth of a heavenly perspective.

Which explains why God sent Jonah to them. He wanted the people of Nineveh to have a basis by which to measure their lives and actions. And what was that standard? The light of **God's holiness** and **righteousness.** If the people turned from their sin and turned to God in mercy, they would be spared destruction.

For darkened hearts, like those of Gordon's high schoolers, life itself has little or no meaning or purpose. Existence is a short time in a shadowy world where right and wrong disappear. The goal of people living (or perhaps we should say dying) in darkness is not to please the God who created them but to live for themselves and for the gods of their own creation. For these people, satisfying immediate desires

---

[1] 4:11 Hebrew *people who don't know their right hands from their left.*

becomes the all-consuming goal. The **more** they pursue worldly desires, the **farther** away from God they move. And since he is the Light of the World, running from him only takes them **further into the darkness.**

What the book of Jonah teaches us is that God **loves** those in the darkness. He sees their plight and cares enough to send a reluctant prophet to invite them to turn back to the light. It's an amazing testimony to the **compassion and mercy of God.**

If you have a hard time believing that God would care that much about people living in spiritual darkness, fast-forward some 750 years. See a strange star twinkling above a ramshackle stable in Bethlehem. On a dark night comes an infant in a manger who would grow up to be the Light of the World to anyone who believes, no matter the darkness in life.

In this One lies **hope** for inner-city kids and for everyone else who stumbles in the dark.

PRAYER POINT

Ask God to help you shine for him "in a dark world full of crooked and perverse people" (Philippians 2:15). Pray for friends and classmates who still haven't come out of the darkness into the light of Christ.

HERE'S WHAT I'M GOING TO DO

☐ _____

_____

☐ _____

_____

_____

THE BOTTOM LINE

What does God want **most** from you? Your money in the offering plate? Your attendance at all church and youth group functions? Your faithfulness in wearing a Christian T-shirt everyday? Your listening to only Christian music? What is the bottom line?

We find the answer in the ancient prophetic book of Micah:

Micah 6:8: ⁸No, O people, the LORD has already told you what is good, and this is what he requires: to do what is right, to love mercy, and to walk humbly with your God.

Are you surprised by that list? It says nothing about wearing a cross around your neck or putting a Jesus fish on your car. There are no requirements about what books to read or stipulations about what kind of music is best.

This verse seems to say that God is more concerned with **internal** matters than **external** issues. His emphasis is more on the heart. Why? Because a heart that is humble, a heart that has been stunned by the mercy of God, will produce **a life filled with good things.**

Too often we neglect the inner qualities that shape our outward actions. We inventory our behavior and begin working from the outside in at tidying up and eliminating bad stuff. We plaster our lives with a lot of visible motion, but we never really deal with deeper issues like **attitudes, motives, and priorities.** In one sense, this is like slapping a coat of paint over an old rotten house. The paint looks good—for a while. It hides the bad stuff—for a while. But soon we have to do it again. And again. And again. Meanwhile, the whole house is caving in!

God (speaking through Micah) has a better way. We are to "do what is right." That is, we are to act justly and be fair in our dealings with others. "To love mercy" is to show kindness to the unlovable, even though they may scorn us and mock our ways. God, Micah says, delights in showing mercy (7:18), and he was kind to Israel even though the nation turned away from him. Finally, we are to "walk humbly" with our God. This conveys the idea of not being impressed with ourselves or concerned with our own glory, but rather relying totally on God.

PRAYER POINT

Ask God to teach you more and more what he really wants from you.

Get **radical** this week. Instead of buying another Christian CD, consider giving that money to someone in need. Rather than merely putting on a Christian T-shirt, remember that "the most important piece of clothing you must wear is **love"** (Colossians 3:14).

Love. Compassion. Humility. Faithfulness. **That's what God wants!**

HERE'S WHAT I'M GOING TO DO

☐ _____

_____

☐ _____

_____

☐ _____

_____

UNDERFOOT

One of the strangest and most popular events in the world is the "running of the bulls" in Pamplona, Spain. Every year thousands of people gather in this city for the opportunity to try to outrun several bulls through the streets. The lucky ones are those who manage to stay away from the bulls' horns. The **unlucky** ones are those who get too close and are gored or gouged by the animals. Perhaps the most unlucky of all are those who **stumble** or **lose their balance** in the melee and are trampled by the crowd behind them. If you've ever seen clips of the event, you've probably seen these panic-stricken people trying to get up while hundreds of others run over them. Often these tramplings result in severe injuries and sometimes even death.

Can you imagine what it must be like to have hundreds of people stepping all over you—and not being able to do anything about it? The prophet Habakkuk recognized that the poor were being stepped on by the well-off people of Israel—specifically rulers and other leaders.

> Habakkuk 2:9-11: [9]"How terrible it will be for you who get rich by unjust means! You believe your wealth will buy security, putting your families beyond the reach of danger. [10]But by the murders you committed, you have shamed your name and forfeited your lives. [11]The very stones in the walls of your houses cry out against you, and the beams in the ceilings echo the complaint."

Habakkuk lived thousands of years ago. How has the situation changed since then? Are the poor, needy, and weak still being pressed down today?

Our society places a great deal of importance on **getting ahead.** In every area of life, we're told, there are winners and losers. Those who have the power, money, and glory are the winners; those who don't are the losers. It's a dog-eat-dog world. It's either kill or be killed. To get to the top of the company ladder, you have to step on a lot of people on the way. Only the strong survive. Many have unfortunately taken these messages to heart.

The problem for Christians is that the people we have to step over—and on—to get ahead (according to the world's philosophy) are the very people **God instructs us to protect and care for.** Does that mean that Christians who work in the corporate world are doomed to fail? Absolutely not. It simply means that we **choose** to play by a **different** set of rules.

Thousands of Christian businesspeople have become successful without grinding down those who are weaker or less fortunate than they are. They operate ethical companies that show **compassion** for employees and **a burden for the well-being of others.** Such blessings await anyone else who chooses to play by God's rules and refuses to press down others.

PRAYER POINT

Ask God to point out any areas of your life in which you may be stepping on others in order to get ahead. Ask him to help you see people as he does.

HERE'S WHAT I'M GOING TO DO

☐ _____

_____

☐ _____

_____

_____

WAITING FOR HOPE

In 1972, a young woman from a wealthy family was abducted from her apartment. Her kidnappers devised a harrowing hideout for their victim—an underground compartment with barely enough room to sit up, a scant supply of food and water, and a narrow pipe for an air supply. This living coffin was the only place she knew for several days. When police finally discovered the underground hideout, they feared the worst. Would she be hysterical? Paralyzed with fright? Perhaps even dead? To their amazement, the woman was remarkably calm and composed. She later told an interviewer that her **faith in God** had sustained her through her nightmarish circumstances.

Habakkuk speaks of hope in the midst of devastation, the dark night of uncertainty. His message rings with **the certainty of God's deliverance.**

> Habakkuk 3:15-18: [15]You trampled the sea with your horses, and the mighty waters piled high. [16]I trembled inside when I heard all this; my lips quivered with fear. My legs gave way beneath me,[1] and I shook in terror. I will wait quietly for the coming day when disaster will strike the people who invade us. [17]Even though the fig trees have no blossoms, and there are no grapes on the vine; even though the olive crop fails, and the fields lie empty and barren; even though the flocks die in the fields, and the cattle barns are empty, [18]yet I will rejoice in the LORD! I will be joyful in the God of my salvation.

Habakkuk prophesied at a time when Judah was rebelling against God. He wanted God to do something to get the sinful nation back on track. Yet when Habakkuk was told that the evil, godless Babylonians would be the "broom" God would use to sweep the nation clean, well, Habakkuk sort of lost it. And so God set about helping the confused prophet get a right

---

[1] **3:16** Hebrew *Decay entered my bones.*

perspective. He promised that Babylon would eventually be punished too. "If [their punishment] seems slow, wait patiently, for it will surely take place" (2:3).

"Wait" is a key word in the book of Habakkuk. The prophet was still waiting for God even at the end of the book. But through a vision depicting God's past and future deliverance of his people, Habakkuk gained **confidence in God's promises.**

Once he trusted in the sure promises of a good God, Habakkuk couldn't help but "rejoice in the LORD" (v. 18). Though the situation appeared bleak from a human perspective, Habakkuk didn't let his circumstances dictate his way of looking at life. He looked **confidently** and **joyfully** beyond the land and the people to the Lord of the land and the people.

In a similar way, we need to learn to **trust in the promises God has given** to us his children through faith in Christ. When everything seems hopeless, God tenderly assures us that he cares. He will deliver us, but it's up to us to take him at his word.

PRAYER POINT

Ask God to give you the right perspective of what he's up to in the world. Find a pertinent promise in the Word and tell God you are trusting him to fulfill it in his time.

HERE'S WHAT I'M GOING TO DO

☐ _____

_____

☐ _____

_____

_____

LIVING FOR YOURSELF

The novelist Susan Howatch once told an interviewer about the spiritual crisis that led her to God. A bright, talented student, she attended law school but soon discovered a flair for writing. In her early thirties, she won both critical acclaim and a popular audience with her epic novels and gothic romances. She soon acquired houses in several countries, drove a Mercedes and a Porsche, and lived a life of luxury.

But not all was well. Her marriage failed, and she became angry and depressed. She remarked, "By the time I was forty, I had everything I wanted, and I woke up one morning and realized I was very, very miserable. By **serving myself,** I had actually made myself very unhappy. That was the beginning of my conversion."

The prophet Haggai knew that **living for one's own pleasure** led only to unhappiness. Listen to what he tells the people of Judah:

> Haggai 1:3-6: ³So the LORD sent this message through the prophet Haggai: ⁴"Why are you living in luxurious houses while my house lies in ruins? ⁵This is what the LORD Almighty says: Consider how things are going for you! ⁶You have planted much but harvested little. You have food to eat, but not enough to fill you up. You have wine to drink, but not enough to satisfy your thirst. You have clothing to wear, but not enough to keep you warm. Your wages disappear as though you were putting them in pockets filled with holes!"

These words of the Lord were directed specifically at the Israelites who had built fancy houses for themselves but had neglected to rebuild the Temple of the Lord. God urged the people to **rethink their perverted priorities, abandon their self-centeredness,** and **make him first** in their lives again.

Even though God's words in Haggai were intended for Israel, they might also apply to any Christian today whose priorities are out of whack. **The Lord's priorities** should be **our** priorities. Because the Lord places a special emphasis on the poor and needy, we should make ministry to the disadvantaged one of our **principal** concerns.

To do this requires a radical shift in thinking, from **self-focus** to **others-focus.** We need to honestly assess what we have (including time, money, and energy), what we would like to have, and what we can give to others. Rather than taking for granted the blessings we have been given, we can share those blessings with others.

PRAYER POINT

Ask the Lord to make you aware of things in your life that you take for granted. As he brings these things to your mind, thank him for them and ask his forgiveness for your attitude.

HERE'S WHAT I'M GOING TO DO

☐ _____

_____

☐ _____

_____

WISE WHYS

Think you're pretty smart? The following questions are guaranteed to cut you down to size. You have thirty seconds to answer each one.

1. Did Adam have a belly button? If so, why?
2. If God is all-powerful, could he create a rock so large that he couldn't lift it?
3. If you do what is **right** for the **wrong** reasons, is it still right?

The first two questions are merely brainteasers. The answers aren't really important (assuming that they're answerable at all). The answer to the third question, though, is extremely important. If the answer is no, it requires Christians to **examine their motivations** for being involved in God's work in the world.

The Lord confronted the Israelites on the issue of motivation during the time of Zechariah the prophet.

Zechariah 7:4-10: ⁴The LORD Almighty sent me this message: ⁵"Say to all your people and your priests, 'During those seventy years of exile, when you fasted and mourned in the summer and at the festival in early autumn,¹ was it really for me that you were fasting? ⁶And even now in your holy festivals, you don't think about me but only of pleasing yourselves. ⁷Isn't this the same message the LORD proclaimed through the prophets years ago when Jerusalem and the towns of Judah were bustling with people, and the Negev and the foothills of Judah² were populated areas?' "

⁸Then this message came to Zechariah from the LORD: ⁹"This is what the LORD Almighty says: Judge fairly and honestly, and show mercy and

---

¹ **7:5** Hebrew *fasted and mourned in the fifth and seventh months.* The fifth month of the Hebrew lunar calendar usually occurs in July and August. The seventh month usually occurs in September and October; both the Day of Atonement and the Festival of Shelters were celebrated in the seventh month.
² **7:7** Hebrew *the Shephelah.*

kindness to one another. [10]Do not oppress widows, orphans, foreigners, and poor people. And do not make evil plans to harm each other."

"Did you do it for me, or did you do it for yourselves?" That's the question the Lord asked the Israelites concerning their fasting, and that's the question Christians involved in ministry must answer today. Do we minister to others out of our love for them and for the Lord? Do we gather for worship hoping to impress others with our musical abilities or our gifts for speaking? Do we involve ourselves in service to others because it might look good to a college admissions board? These are questions that must be tackled with **brutal honesty** and **self-evaluation.**

The best—and most basic—reason for worship and for ministering to others is **obedience to God.** God's instructions in Zechariah 7:9-10 are pretty straightforward: Administer true justice; show mercy and compassion to one another; do not oppress the widow, the fatherless, the alien, or the poor; do not think evil of one another. If we follow these instructions, we do what is pleasing to God; if we don't, we disobey him. It's that simple.

HERE'S WHAT I'M GOING TO DO

The Tithes That Bind

One of the touchiest and most confusing issues in all of Christianity is **giving**—specifically, how much Christians should give to the church and to other ministries. Some people say that "tithing," giving ten percent of one's income, is what God requires. Other people say that tithing is the bare minimum and that Christians should give "offerings" on top of that. **How much of an offering, you may ask?** There is no agreed-on amount. Still others suggest that believers should simply give "what they can." But that doesn't really clarify anything, does it?

Do you see why giving is such a touchy issue? Too many unanswered questions and too many divided opinions. The only opinion that really matters, of course, is the Lord's. Based on his words in Malachi 3, we might conclude that if God were asked the question, "How much should a Christian give?" his answer would be, "More."

Malachi 3:6-12: [6]"I am the LORD, and I do not change. That is why you descendants of Jacob are not already completely destroyed. [7]Ever since the days of your ancestors, you have scorned my laws and failed to obey them. Now return to me, and I will return to you," says the LORD Almighty.

"But you ask, 'How can we return when we have never gone away?'

[8]"Should people cheat God? Yet you have cheated me!

"But you ask, 'What do you mean? When did we ever cheat you?'

"You have cheated me of the tithes and offerings due to me. [9]You are under a curse, for your whole nation has been cheating me. [10]Bring all the tithes into the storehouse so there will be enough food in my Temple. If you do," says the LORD Almighty, "I will open the windows of heaven for

[1] **3:11** Hebrew *from the devourer.*

you. I will pour out a blessing so great you won't have enough room to take it in! Try it! Let me prove it to you! [11]Your crops will be abundant, for I will guard them from insects and disease.[1] Your grapes will not shrivel before they are ripe," says the LORD Almighty. [12]"Then all nations will call you blessed, for your land will be such a delight," says the LORD Almighty.

This seems like an odd test, doesn't it? "Go ahead and give everything you can," the Lord dares. "See if I don't reward you beyond your wildest imagination!"

Quite simply, **the more we give, the more we receive.** God has an entire warehouse full of blessings that he's just waiting to pour out on those who are **not afraid to give** to him and his ministry.

The more **time, energy,** and **money** we dedicate to the Lord and his work, **the more blessings we can expect**—in this world and in the next.

HERE'S WHAT I'M GOING TO DO

☐ _____

_____

☐ _____

_____

☐ _____

_____

_____

ONLY THE BEST

One of the most beloved of all Christmas carols is "The Little Drummer Boy," which tells the story of a young man who is brought to the manger of Jesus. The fact that the story is fictional does little to detract from its poignancy. Recognizing that he has nothing of worth to present to the newborn king, the young man offers the only thing he possesses—his musical talent: "I played my drum for him/I played my best for him." The only explanation the Drummer Boy offers for his actions is that he wanted "to honor" Jesus. His musical gift was an act of worship.

The Magi, the wise men who brought gold, frankincense, and myrrh to Jesus, also recognized that **giving can be an act of worship.**

Matthew 2:9-12: 9After this interview the wise men went their way. Once again the star appeared to them, guiding them to Bethlehem. It went ahead of them and stopped over the place where the child was. 10When they saw the star, they were filled with joy! 11They entered the house where the child and his mother, Mary, were, and they fell down before him and worshiped him. Then they opened their treasure chests and gave him gifts of gold, frankincense, and myrrh. 12But when it was time to leave, they went home another way, because God had warned them in a dream not to return to Herod.

The fact that **giving and worship** are closely related is not exactly a news flash. After all, most churches collect tithes and offerings during their worship services. But unless we're careful, our giving may become a lifeless routine or a legalistic ritual. When we refuse to give beyond what's expected—be it a tithe or a standard we've set for ourselves—we may fall into the trap the Pharisees failed to see. Extraordinary needs may arise that require more time, energy, or money than we're used to giving. Our reaction to such circumstances will tell us a lot about the state of our hearts. Do we worship God because we want to or because we're expected to?

If we seek to honor the Lord, we'll do so by **giving without thought** for the cost. Whether we have much or little does not matter as much as our **willingness** to give what we have. If we maintain a joyful spirit and always consider the needs of others, God will look on our acts as a delightful offering of worship.

We may feel like the Little Drummer Boy—that we have no gifts fit to give the King. But God asks us to give our **best.** We can take comfort, however, in the fact that the Lord accepts as precious gifts our efforts on his behalf.

PRAYER POINT

Spend a few minutes in worshipful prayer, during which time you do nothing but praise God for who he is and what he has done. Offer to give him all that you have.

HERE'S WHAT I'M GOING TO DO

☐ _____

_____

☐ _____

_____

☐ _____

_____

☐ _____

_____

THE TEMPTATION

Food is a source of **temptation** for a large percentage of our nation's population. Bulimics and chronic overeaters are constantly tempted to consume unbelievable amounts of food. People with high blood pressure or heart conditions are often tempted to eat "off-limits" foods high in fat and sodium. Serious dieters have been known to empty their refrigerators, pantries, and cabinets completely to keep from being tempted to eat. Even so-called moderate eaters are often tempted to grab a bite at a fast-food restaurant rather than eating a more healthy meal at home.

It's probably safe to say, however, that no one has ever faced a food temptation quite like the one Jesus faced in Matthew 4.

> Matthew 4:1-4: ¹Then Jesus was led out into the wilderness by the Holy Spirit to be tempted there by the Devil. ²For forty days and forty nights he ate nothing and became very hungry. ³Then the Devil¹ came and said to him, "If you are the Son of God, change these stones into loaves of bread." ⁴But Jesus told him, "No! The Scriptures say, 'People need more than bread for their life; they must feed on every word of God.'² "

Satan was trying to get Jesus to use his supernatural powers for his own benefit. Knowing that Jesus hadn't eaten in forty days, Satan chose a basic human need to undermine Jesus' work. Hungry as he was, Jesus chose **spiritual nourishment** over physical sustenance. As the Son of God, Jesus had the power to turn the stones into bread, as Satan suggested. Jesus had the power to turn an entire mountain into a giant submarine sandwich if he had wanted to! Satan knew that and urged him on. Yet, as hungry as he was, Jesus refused to turn the stones into bread. He **refused** to satisfy his hunger **apart from God's will.**

[1] **4:3** Greek *the tempter.*
[2] **4:4** Deut. 8:3.

The point Jesus made to Satan is still valid today: Humans do not live on food alone, but by **spiritual feeding from God.** Sadly, many people live on spiritual starvation diets. They find their nourishment from a good sermon, an inspiring movie, a fascinating magazine article, or a television newsmagazine. Like people who have neglected their eating habits for years, they find themselves in real trouble when they face sudden crisis. To stay fit in God's Kingdom, we must thrive on **constant study in his Word.**

PRAYER POINT

Ask the Lord to give you strength and to help you rely on his Word as you face temptations in your daily life.

HERE'S WHAT I'M GOING TO DO

☐ _____

☐ _____

☐ _____

☐ _____

☐ _____

☐ _____

HOME SWEET HOME

The short-term missions team christened it The Palace. A layer of dirt and mold on the floors and walls, various "creature" comforts (salamanders and spiders), one leaking toilet, a rubber-hosed shower that gave warmth for maybe . . . ten minutes (if no one flushed the toilet), and rock-hard mattresses. This place was definitely, well, *rough.*

Yet the team quickly forgot those inconveniences. Why? Because they recognized a greater need: **the need for God.** It was what had brought them thousands of miles from steady jobs and a comfortable home. It was a need so strong that no obstacle would keep them from sharing the love of God with others who longed to hear his words of help and salvation.

Jesus told his followers that those who recognized their need for God would find salvation:

Matthew 5:1-3: ¹One day as the crowds were gathering, Jesus went up the mountainside with his disciples and sat down to teach them. ²This is what he taught them: ³"God blesses those who realize their need for him,¹ for the Kingdom of Heaven is given to them."

The unsaved people of the world would judge Christians insane for traveling around the earth . . . to serve the poor and needy. To build a cement block church, replacing a thatch one. To put in a water purification system, providing clean drinking water. To share with the elderly in a nursing home. To teach English as a second language to schoolchildren. To carry Bibles into China for distribution. Yes, in the world's view, these are ridiculous activities. They don't sound fun, entertaining, or personally profitable. But by God's standards, they are **right on target!**

Notice also that Christ teaches us that "God blesses" those who **do** what he calls them to. Another translation of this

---

¹ **5:3** Greek *the poor in spirit.*

could be *"happy* are those who realize their need for him."* In other words, when we're **fulfilling his purpose in our lives,** he gives us tremendous joy. That means that building, digging, sharing, teaching, and transporting can provide a happiness that only God can supply!

Christ has called his people to respond to the needy of this world like he did, with compassion and action. We can't all travel around the world, but we must **do what we can,** where we are, with the **resources** we have. Is there a "palace" where you can minister in your community? Joy awaits you!

PRAYER POINT

Pray for compassion and sensitivity to the poor in your neighborhood. It's easy to pray for the "poor around the world." But what about those in your community?

HERE'S WHAT I'M GOING TO DO

☐ _____

_____

☐ _____

_____

☐ _____

_____

☐ _____

_____

☐ _____

_____

SIMPLY SIMPLE

DAY

158

Being labeled **simple** is obviously not a compliment these days. Simple-minded, simpleton, and simple head certainly aren't given out with tender best wishes. And what about the poor guy named Simon?

But Jesus seems to put a **priority on simpleness.** He called himself the Bread of Life, the Living Water, the Rock. Pretty simple, everyday words. And Jesus labeled us sheep, one of the more intellectually challenged animals of his creation. In this passage, he asks us to ponder deeper issues with, once again, simple terms.

> Matthew 5:13-16: ¹³"You are the salt of the earth. But what good is salt if it has lost its flavor? Can you make it useful again? It will be thrown out and trampled underfoot as worthless. ¹⁴You are the light of the world—like a city on a mountain, glowing in the night for all to see. ¹⁵Don't hide your light under a basket! Instead, put it on a stand and let it shine for all. ¹⁶In the same way, let your good deeds shine out for all to see, so that everyone will praise your heavenly Father."

Isn't the strength of Christ's description in his simplicity? First he compares us to salt. It's so basic, so essential for the preservation of food, so needed for boosting receptive taste buds. Can you imagine french fries or spaghetti or steak without it? Now, Christ asks you to picture the world without *your* saltiness. **You have incredible potential!**

Next he directs our attention to light, comparing us to a city on a mountain. Now, that's a glow everybody notices! And why on earth would anyone light a lamp to then hide it under a basket? The glow's use is also so basic: to show the way, to help the world see, to point to God.

Maybe Christ instinctively knew we'd get so buried in our efforts to understand why he came—and our part in this magnificent plan—that we would lose the unaffected beauty of why he did what he did. So over and over again, Jesus attempted to make the idea of salvation understandable and . . . *simple.* Maybe simplicity is not such a bad thing after all.

We are the salt of the earth. We are the light of the world. Simple? Yes . . . and no. For in Jesus' mind, the simple become tools, the weak become strong, the foolish become wise. How simple can you be?

PRAYER POINT

Pray for specific direction in how you can be a testimony to your family and friends.

HERE'S WHAT I'M GOING TO DO

☐ _____

_____

☐ _____

_____

☐ _____

_____

☐ _____

_____

☐ _____

_____

☐ _____

_____

SO WHO'S IN CONTROL?

DAY 159

You're standing in line, waiting for tickets for the biggest concert of the year. You've been at the stadium since 5 a.m., hoping for some choice seats. Then you see them. A group of five students walks past you and starts up a conversation with some friends ahead of you in line. They talk and talk, and gradually work themselves into the line, as if they had been there all along.

Now you're angry. What should you do? You start scanning the faces of the line ahead of you, seeing if you can find a new "friend" to talk to.

This is when the **bargaining with God** usually begins. After all, we have to stand up for ourselves, don't we? And those cheaters shouldn't be allowed to get away with it! So the rationalizing goes.

But Jesus has something else in mind:

Matthew 5:38-48: [38]"You have heard that the law of Moses says, 'If an eye is injured, injure the eye of the person who did it. If a tooth gets knocked out, knock out the tooth of the person who did it.'[1] [39]But I say, don't resist an evil person! If you are slapped on the right cheek, turn the other, too. [40]If you are ordered to court and your shirt is taken from you, give your coat, too. [41]If a soldier demands that you carry his gear for a mile,[2] carry it two miles. [42]Give to those who ask, and don't turn away from those who want to borrow. [43]You have heard that the law of Moses says, 'Love your neighbor'[3] and hate your enemy. [44]But I say, love your enemies![4] Pray for those who persecute you! [45]In that way, you will be acting as true children of your Father in heaven. For he gives his sunlight to both the evil and the good, and he sends rain on the just and on the unjust, too. [46]If you love only those who love you, what good is that?

[1] **5:38** Greek 'An eye for an eye and a tooth for a tooth.' Exod. 21:24; Lev. 24:20; Deut. 19:21.
[2] **5:41** Greek *milion* [4,854 feet or 1,478 meters].
[3] **5:43** Lev. 19:18.
[4] **5:44** Some manuscripts add *Bless those who curse you, do good to those who hate you.*

Even corrupt tax collectors do that much. 47If you are kind only to your friends, how are you different from anyone else? Even pagans do that. 48But you are to be perfect, even as your Father in heaven is perfect."

Kind of puts a crimp in the revenge plans, doesn't it? So much of what Jesus is saying comes down to the issue of **control.** Which will you decide to do: allow your anger to control *you?* Or will *you* take control of your anger by demonstrating **strength of character** as you decide to forgive?

Here's the ironic part: If we allow our hatred to take charge, then we're also giving that person—the one we're so intent on seeing punished for what he's done—control over us too. Essentially, we're giving him permission to make us miserable! That's why **it's so important to forgive.** Forgiving is for *our* sake, for our contentment, for our ability **to grow spiritually.**

PRAYER POINT

Ask God to help you deal with the feeling of revenge you may be holding toward someone. Then seek reconciliation with that person.

HERE'S WHAT I'M GOING TO DO

☐ _____

_____

☐ _____

_____

☐ _____

_____

DEPENDENCY

Guangzhou, China. Picture a bustling, crammed city with pedestrians, buses, motorcycles, bicycles, and taxis—all jockeying for position. Sound like America? Not quite, for in Guangzhou there are essentially no traffic laws. No street-lights. Direction and U-turns are decided at will. We're talking a free-for-all, something like bumper cars on a grand scale. So when you climb into the front seat of a taxi, you learn quickly what it means to be **totally dependent** on that driver.

Puts dependence in a whole new category, doesn't it? That's like what Jesus was trying to get across to his listeners when he first taught what we've entitled "The Lord's Prayer."

Matthew 6:10-13: [10]May your will be done here on earth,
just as it is in heaven.
[11]Give us our food for today,[1]
[12]and forgive us our sins,
just as we have forgiven those who have sinned against us.
[13]And don't let us yield to temptation,
but deliver us from the evil one.[2]

Because we've heard it so many times and have a tendency to repeat it in monotoned voices, we've stripped this incredible prayer of the heart and depth of its meaning. To help restore this, picture your hands outstretched, palms up and open. In this position, we're vulnerable to him, waiting, accepting, totally dependent on him to fill, take away, lead, and direct.

Unfortunately, though, we're not always open to him or his will; we don't act or respond with this kind of posture. Instead, we have a tendency to **wrestle with God,** attempting to force him to do what we want, our way, in our timing. We face him with closed fists, ones already filled with

---

[1] **6:11** Or *for tomorrow.*
[2] **6:13** Or *from evil.* Some manuscripts add *For yours is the kingdom and the power and the glory forever. Amen.*

our wants and desires. Isn't it funny, though, considering the messes we make of our lives, that we still insist on attempting to take charge? To do what *we* want? When we take a close look at what we've accomplished—as compared to God's plans for our lives—generally we realize that we don't really want to be in charge after all. **He knows what we need.** He knows what's best for us. And he will provide.

PRAYER POINT

Ask God to point out areas in which you're wrestling with him about who's in control. How are you attempting to drive your "taxi"?

Just like riding in that taxi, we might as well sit back and **depend on him.** Sometimes, with palms up . . . and sometimes, hanging on for the ride!

HERE'S WHAT I'M GOING TO DO

☐ _____

_____

☐ _____

_____

☐ _____

_____

☐ _____

_____

☐ _____

_____

Peter Greyshock, 18, is a freshman at the University of San Diego, majoring in international relations. He was one of three 30 Hour Famine Study Tour participants in 1994 and wants to return to Africa one day and serve with World Vision. Peter loves surfing, volleyball, and "anything with peanut butter." But he no longer focuses as much on material things as he once did.

One thing I've learned by seeing others in need is that I don't need as much as I want. My friends would always say, "I need a new pair of ski pants" or "I need this new CD," but they really don't need those things. And I'd call

them on it. (Of course, now they've begun to call me on it if I say something like that.)

Growing up, I used to look at people differently. I always thought of other people as being the rich ones. Now I realize that we're actually the rich ones. That's just in a materialistic sense, not even getting into the God part and how rich in God we are.

I want to return to Africa someday and reach out to those in need. But in the meantime, there are plenty of opportunities for me and everyone else in all our communities to help people who are less fortunate. There are soup kitchens, gathering clothes, and collecting food for the needy. There are poverty-stricken areas all over America, not just overseas. And helping people here can be just as gratifying and accomplish just as much.

In Matthew 25, God tells us to give food and drink to the hungry and thirsty, help strangers, clothe people in need, take care of the sick, and visit prisoners. I don't think he says that just for the heck of it. He wants us to do something with it.

First, we need to identify with those in need. Then we have to follow Christ's teachings and act on the needs we see.

Kelly Polacek, 23, visited Kenya in 1992 as World Vision's first 30 Hour Famine Study Tour participant. She is currently studying for her master's degree in cellular biology at California Polytechnic State University, San Luis Obispo. After all those years away at school, it's no wonder that her favorite food is "anything of Mom's." God uses different things to speak to people. While her heart is touched by the misery she sees in the world, Kelly's life is most affected by the beauty.

One thing that I remember being out there in the middle of nowhere was that there was nothing but God's earth. And I thought how small we really are. So many things I had thought were important became irrelevant because I just felt like I was part of the natural world, of the animal kingdom, of God's creation. And I saw so much beauty. It was very touching and humbling.

I was very lucky to have been placed somewhere that was so beautiful. I think the best piece of advice I can give is to try to see beautiful things every day.

I know it's hard to do—to appreciate things when there's so much negativity. But you don't

In the Eyes of the Beholder

have to be on a safari to see the beauty of the earth and the things that God has done.

When I see unlovely things, I remind myself that everything is beautiful to God. All of his children are beautiful to him. He doesn't like what we do, and I don't like what we do, but we're all beautiful.

And as discouraging as it is to see starving children in Africa or another shooting in our cities, remember that all things are beautiful because all things are from God. It can give you the strength to find ways to help people who are in unlovely, hopeless, and even deadly situations.

"And now, dear friends, let me say one more thing as I close this letter. Fix your thoughts on what is true and honorable and right. Think about things that are pure and lovely and admirable. Think about things that are excellent and worthy of praise. Keep putting into practice all you learned from me and heard from me and saw me doing, and the God of peace will be with you" (Philippians 4:8-9).

VISION

Steve Wiggins

Big Tent Revival

Several months ago, I was part of a group visiting the Dominican Republic. We were traveling from village to village, and I was amazed that our cultures could differ so greatly. I had never seen such extreme poverty! I wanted so much to return and tell everyone about the great needs that exist in this country and around the world today. I especially felt deep sorrow for the children, as I imagined my own child living in such impoverished conditions. I wished that I could bring those children back home with me and let them live a "better" life.

In one village, we met a woman whose husband had left her to care for her three children alone. She was working very hard, but through various jobs she could only raise $30 a month. I walked into her house, looked up, and saw the sky through her rusted roof. Actually, to call it a house would be an exaggeration. Standing in the middle of the place and stretching out my arms, I could touch all four walls. The floor was muddy earth.

Through a Dominican translator, one of the members of our team said to the woman, "I have never met anyone living in such conditions. Is there any happiness in your life?"

Looking puzzled, the woman simply replied, "Yes."

The person questioned further, "Where do you find happiness in a place like this?"

The woman answered confidently: "I have the love of Jesus in my heart. He has shown kindness to me and my children through his people. Yes, I am happy. Very happy."

We all were shocked and very humbled. We had gone to their country thinking that their problems would be solved by raising their standard of living. But at best that would make them more like North Americans. Jesus didn't call us to make Americans; he called us to make disciples. How? By our *love*. Show them that you love them, and they will want to know the source of that love . . . as this lady did.

When we see all people as brothers and sisters, we will see God's vision for the world.

RIGHT FOR THE WRONG REASO

DAY 161

People sometimes do good deeds for the wrong reasons. A doctor produces a new cancer treatment so that more people will rely on *his* expertise. A prominent historian exposes what he calls the "plagiarism" of a rival's book so he can grab headlines. A politician proposes a new program to fight crime so he can tip the scales in a close election.

Only God **knows our deepest motivations.** Like the attention we really want when doing something virtuous. Or the applause we were really after for a job well done. And even the thank yous we were seeking after for a supposedly unselfish act. Jesus gets real close to home when he says:

Matthew 6:16-18: ¹⁶"And when you fast, don't make it obvious, as the hypocrites do, who try to look pale and disheveled so people will admire them for their fasting. I assure you, that is the only reward they will ever get. ¹⁷But when you fast, comb your hair and wash your face. ¹⁸Then no one will suspect you are fasting, except your Father, who knows what you do in secret. And your Father, who knows all secrets, will reward you."

Going without food for one whole day calls for self-denial, something that we might be pretty eager to let others know about. But Jesus makes it quite clear that if we're doing this publicly, if we're intent on others' knowing we're fasting, then we've missed the point *and* missed out. That praise will be the only reward we receive. **The blessing comes from keeping it secret.**

Likewise, anything we do for others should not be a reason for publicity and applause. That should not be our motivation.

It kind of comes down to showmanship, doesn't it? Are we doing religious things for applause from others? Are we merely performing? Essentially, we've circled back to where we started, for once again we're called to evaluate: *Why am I doing this?* If we do any religious or unselfish act, including fasting, for selfish reasons, **we need to be changed from within.**

So what are your motivations? Why do you do religious things? Why do you do *any* unselfish act? If it's for the praise, ask God to change your heart. Ask for God's help to always do right for the *right* reasons.

HERE'S WHAT I'M GOING TO DO

☐ _____

☐ _____

☐ _____

_____

_____

Heaven's Bank and Trust

DAY 162

No one in her aging neighborhood knew her very well. But they were becoming increasingly frustrated with the way the old woman was letting her house deteriorate. It badly needed a paint job. Shutters were rotting. The roof had holes birds could fly through. She let newspapers rot in her scraggly, small front yard, which was littered by rusting junk.

Her neighbors figured she was old, poor, and helpless. But none of them offered to help. And she apparently had no close family. Who would take care of things when she died?

Imagine the neighbors' surprise when the old woman finally died and police found cash stuffed under mattresses, behind couches, in cupboards and closets. The woman was hoarding nearly a half million dollars in cash. And a note found indicated that, since she had no family, she planned to give it to any neighbors who had helped her.

Where do you keep your riches? What will you do with them? Read Jesus' **investment advice** and then decide.

Matthew 6:19-21, 24: [19]"Don't store up treasures here on earth, where they can be eaten by moths and get rusty, and where thieves break in and steal. [20]Store your treasures in heaven, where they will never become moth-eaten or rusty and where they will be safe from thieves. [21]Wherever your treasure is, there your heart and thoughts will also be.

[24]"No one can serve two masters. For you will hate one and love the other, or be devoted to one and despise the other. You cannot serve both God and money."

In a world that seems consumed by money and possessions, Jesus' words are kind of shocking, aren't they? He simply says, "Don't store up treasures here on earth." What's the use? It'll just rust, be eaten by moths, or stolen by thieves. And you certainly **can't take it with you.**

So Jesus says, spend your time not creating earthly wealth, but heavenly wealth. Nothing can hurt those treasures, and you can enjoy them forever. So how do we store up heavenly treasures? **Giving money regularly to God's Kingdom** is one way. Set aside a portion of every paycheck or allowance to give back to God, recognizing that it's all his anyway and he's just letting you use it.

But that's not the only way to store up treasures in heaven. Every **good deed** you do, every act of **obedience,** every gift of your **time** and **energy** in service to others who need it is an eternal investment.

Jesus says you can't serve two masters. In this world, you'll be continually tempted to pursue money and possessions. To some people, that's all there is to life. They spend their time collecting things only to leave them all behind when they die.

Which master do you follow? What's the main thing that takes up your thoughts, your activities, your dreams? Jesus calls us to make a decision to live contentedly with whatever we have. It's a decision we'll benefit from forever and ever.

HERE'S WHAT I'M GOING TO DO

☐ _____

_____

☐ _____

_____

DON'T WORRY, JUST TRUST

Are you a worrier? Everyone is, to one degree or another. Unfortunately, life on this planet gives you **plenty to worry about.** Your homework assignments. Your boyfriend or girlfriend (or lack thereof). What you're going to wear. Getting your chores done. How to save money for the summer youth trip. Where to find money for lunch tomorrow. And what about college? Career? Future?

It's easy to **find something to worry about every waking moment,** isn't it?

Is that good? Let's hear what Jesus has to say.

Matthew 6:25-34: [25]"So I tell you, don't worry about everyday life—whether you have enough food, drink, and clothes. Doesn't life consist of more than food and clothing? [26]Look at the birds. They don't need to plant or harvest or put food in barns because your heavenly Father feeds them. And you are far more valuable to him than they are. [27]Can all your worries add a single moment to your life? Of course not.

[28]"And why worry about your clothes? Look at the lilies and how they grow. They don't work or make their clothing, [29]yet Solomon in all his glory was not dressed as beautifully as they are. [30]And if God cares so wonderfully for flowers that are here today and gone tomorrow, won't he more surely care for you? You have so little faith!

[31]"So don't worry about having enough food or drink or clothing. [32]Why be like the pagans who are so deeply concerned about these things? Your heavenly Father already knows all your needs, [33]and he will give you all you need from day to day if you live for him and make the Kingdom of God your primary concern.

[34]"So don't worry about tomorrow, for tomorrow will bring its own

worries. Today's trouble is enough for today."

The people Jesus was talking to had to worry about the basics of life—food, clothing, and shelter. Life was pretty rough then. But Jesus knew that **worry doesn't help.** Why waste time and energy worrying about the needs God has already promised he'd meet? Besides, it's unhealthy and unproductive, and it keeps us from trusting God. **Nothing good comes from worry.** So how do we break the bonds of worry in our life?

It boils down to **faith.** Jesus pointed to the birds of the air and the flowers of the field. He said God cares for their needs.

Pagans—people who don't believe in God—have every reason to worry. They haven't put their trust in the God who cares for them. But Jesus challenges us to live differently. He says, "Your heavenly Father already knows all your needs, and he will give you all you need from day to day if you live for him and make the Kingdom of God your primary concern" (vv. 32-33).

PRAYER POINT

Pray that your faith will increase in the God who seeks to provide everything you need forever.

HERE'S WHAT I'M GOING TO DO

☐ _____

_____

☐ _____

_____

☐ _____

_____

HEAVENLY HOSPITALITY

DAY

164

When you go to a friend's house, you like to be well received, don't you? Welcomed in. Offered a soft drink. **Made to feel at home.** Even invited to dinner! After all, that's the way you treat your friends who visit your home—right?

But what if you don't know the person at all? Or what if the person you're visiting doesn't know you? The experience is probably very different. What are Christians supposed to do? How are we supposed to **reach out to others?**

Matthew 10:5-10: 5Jesus sent the twelve disciples out with these instructions: "Don't go to the Gentiles or the Samaritans, 6but only to the people of Israel—God's lost sheep. 7Go and announce to them that the Kingdom of Heaven is near.[1] 8Heal the sick, raise the dead, cure those with leprosy, and cast out demons. Give as freely as you have received!

9"Don't take any money with you. 10Don't carry a traveler's bag with an extra coat and sandals or even a walking stick. Don't hesitate to accept hospitality, because those who work deserve to be fed.[2]"

Hospitality means making somebody—anybody, friend or not—feel at home, comfortable, enjoyed, wanted, welcomed. Jesus encouraged his disciples to take advantage of any hospitality offered to them. After all, they were out and about doing good stuff—praying, healing, declaring the coming Kingdom, ministering in Jesus' name. So they deserved whatever good they received in return. And what was the standard for them to follow? "Give as freely as you have received!" (v. 8b).

As Jesus' best friends, they had certainly received incredible blessings. Now they were given the opportunity from their Master to go out into a hurting, sick, scared world

[1] **10:7** Or *has come* or *is coming soon.*
[2] **10:10** Or *the worker is worthy of support.*

and pass those blessings along.

Of course, Jesus also encouraged the disciples to be discerning (vv. 11-15). If someone was antagonistic to them, they were to move on. But if someone received them and their message, they were to give that home a blessing.

We can learn a lot from the example of the disciples.

1. We are called to reach out to the world in Jesus' name, but we need to be smart about it.

2. We should freely accept any hospitality offered to us as we minister. Not only is that a **blessing** to us, but it is to the giver too.

3. Looking at it from the flip side, anytime a guest preacher, youth leader, youth group, singer, missionary, or other minister comes to our church, we should do all we can to make sure that **person's needs are provided** and that he or she feels right at home.

HERE'S WHAT I'M GOING TO DO

☐ _____

_____

☐ _____

_____

_____

PROOF POSITIVE

When things don't go right and we start feeling down about life, it's **easy to doubt** that **God is really in control.** Sometimes the doubts freak us out—after all, we shouldn't be questioning God!

But don't be afraid of your doubts. Just look through the Bible. You'll meet Doubting David, Doubting Peter, Doubting Moses . . . and of course, Doubting Thomas. There is no shortage of doubt in the Bible. So if you've ever struggled with doubt, you're in good company.

Today, we'll read about a time when John the Baptist doubted whether Jesus really was the One God had sent.

> Matthew 11:1-6: ¹When Jesus had finished giving these instructions to his twelve disciples, he went off teaching and preaching in towns throughout the country.
>
> ²John the Baptist, who was now in prison, heard about all the things the Messiah was doing. So he sent his disciples to ask Jesus, ³"Are you really the Messiah we've been waiting for, or should we keep looking for someone else?"
>
> ⁴Jesus told them, "Go back to John and tell him about what you have heard and seen—⁵the blind see, the lame walk, the lepers are cured, the deaf hear, the dead are raised to life, and the Good News is being preached to the poor. ⁶And tell him: 'God blesses those who are not offended by me.'¹"

John the Baptist was a wild guy. He lived out in the desert wearing a rough hair shirt, eating bugs, and preparing the way for the Messiah to come. He was bold. He was unorthodox. He was totally obedient to God. And he attracted mobs of people with his clear, strong message of repentance. In the Jordan River, John baptized Jesus whom he recognized as the Messiah

¹ **11:6** Or *who don't fall away because of me.*

sent by God. But soon after, he was imprisoned after he got into trouble with Herod. As he sat in that lonely, dark, disgusting prison, he started to doubt. Was Jesus really the One?

He sent his disciples to ask Jesus if he was indeed the Messiah. And Jesus answered with the words you read today. The evidence was all around—blind people who could see, lame who could walk, deaf who could hear, dead who were made alive. Yes, the Good News was being preached and put into action, Jesus said.

There's nothing wrong with doubt . . . unless you get **stuck** in it and let it **harden into unbelief.** Consider all the Bible characters who doubted: Each one ultimately realized that God was who he said he was.

So whenever you get worn down by the responsibilities you carry as a child of God, think of John in that prison cell. Whenever you get made fun of or even hurt because of your faith, remember Jesus' words. God will bless you when you take no offense because of Jesus, when you stand strong in your faith.

HERE'S WHAT I'M GOING TO DO

☐ _____

_____

☐ _____

_____

Spiritual Journey Travel Log

BREAKING THE RULES

R ules were made to be broken." You may have heard somebody say that. (Probably just before or after breaking a rule!) Some people just like to **break the rules.** They try to get away with everything they can. Sometimes they get caught, but often they don't.

That doesn't seem fair, does it? After all, you try to do the best you can to obey God's Word, to follow rules at school and at home. You know that **God calls us to be obedient to his Word.** And his principles are always for our **own good.**

But admit it, you've thought of breaking a few rules a time or two. Here's a time Jesus and his disciples broke some religious regulations . . . and got into trouble.

Matthew 12:1-8: [1]At about that time Jesus was walking through some grainfields on the Sabbath. His disciples were hungry, so they began breaking off heads of wheat and eating the grain. [2]Some Pharisees saw them do it and protested, "Your disciples shouldn't be doing that! It's against the law to work by harvesting grain on the Sabbath."

[3]But Jesus said to them, "Haven't you ever read in the Scriptures what King David did when he and his companions were hungry? [4]He went into the house of God, and they ate the special bread reserved for the priests alone. That was breaking the law, too. [5]And haven't you ever read in the law of Moses that the priests on duty in the Temple may work on the Sabbath? [6]I tell you, there is one here who is even greater than the Temple! [7]But you would not have condemned those who aren't guilty if you knew the meaning of this Scripture: 'I want you to be merciful; I don't want your sacrifices.'[1] [8]For I, the Son of Man, am master even of the Sabbath."

Busted! It was the Sabbath—Saturday, the Jewish day of rest. Jesus and his disciples were walking through a wheat

[1] **12:7** Hos. 6:6.

field grabbing at the heads and eating the grain. Some of the religious leaders caught the disciples in the act. They pointed out that it was against the Jewish law to "work" on the Sabbath.

Jesus answered them boldly. Of course the Sabbath is supposed to be kept holy. It's intended to be a time to set aside **your work** and **worship God.** The Pharisees kept the **letter** of the law but forgot the **purpose** of the law.

Jesus reminds us that the intent of the law—the **real meaning** behind the letter of the law—was that God wants our honest, meaningful worship and obedience. He calls us to make room for compassion and understanding. Only when our **hearts are right** with God can we truly obey him and do his will.

Jesus shook up the religious establishment of his time. It was an establishment that had fallen way off base. Yet he never sinned. He never broke a single law of God. He was able to live a life of perfect obedience. Let Jesus be the Lord of your Sabbath—and the Lord of every day of your life as you rely on him for strength and direction.

PRAYER POINT

Ask God to show you where you are just going through the motions of keeping rules rather than obeying out of the right motivations.

HERE'S WHAT I'M GOING TO DO

☐ _____

_____

☐ _____

_____

IMPOSSIBLE!

The task that lies before you is, frankly, impossible. When you consider the many people who need help in this world, it's obvious that it just can't be done. No way. How can you possibly feed all the hungry people? Help all the sick and hurting? Tell the world about Jesus Christ?

It's **overwhelming** for sure. But think back to an **"impossible" challenge** that had the disciples shaking their heads with disbelief.

Matthew 14:13-21: [13]As soon as Jesus heard the news, he went off by himself in a boat to a remote area to be alone. But the crowds heard where he was headed and followed by land from many villages. [14]A vast crowd was there as he stepped from the boat, and he had compassion on them and healed their sick.

[15]That evening the disciples came to him and said, "This is a desolate place, and it is getting late. Send the crowds away so they can go to the villages and buy food for themselves."

[16]But Jesus replied, "That isn't necessary—you feed them."

[17]"Impossible!" they exclaimed. "We have only five loaves of bread and two fish!"

[18]"Bring them here," he said. [19]Then he told the people to sit down on the grass. And he took the five loaves and two fish, looked up toward heaven, and asked God's blessing on the food. Breaking the loaves into pieces, he gave some of the bread and fish to each disciple, and the disciples gave them to the people. [20]They all ate as much as they wanted, and they picked up twelve baskets of leftovers. [21]About five thousand men had eaten from those five loaves, in addition to all the women and children!

The people had followed Jesus, hungry for his word and

his touch. Though he was tired and wanted some time alone, he had compassion on them and healed their sick. By evening, everyone had become hungry for food as well. The disciples urged their Master to send the people away so they could buy food and eat.

Imagine their shock when Jesus said, "That isn't necessary—you feed them" (v. 16).

Huh? There were only five loaves of bread and two fish—hardly enough to feed thousands. It was, in a word, "impossible!"

But Jesus took what they had and multiplied it **far beyond the need.** Thousands ate and were filled. There were even twelve baskets of leftovers. **Jesus had turned the impossible inside out.**

Today you face any number of "impossible" tasks. But don't let yourself get overwhelmed by the immense need you see when you look at the big picture. Focus on the specific areas in which you can play your part as God guides you. Remember, you follow the same Master the disciples did. He is all-powerful, all-knowing, and all-loving. He is the Master of the impossible!

HERE'S WHAT I'M GOING TO DO

GETTING IN GOD'S WAY

In the late 1950s in Britain, physicians began writing prescriptions for a potent new drug called Thalidomide to reduce the severity of morning sickness. The drug worked. But months later, many of the children born to these mothers suffered from severe birth defects. By the time scientists discovered that Thalidomide was a direct harm to developing fetuses, more than 10,000 infants had been born with physical deformities. The drug was immediately recalled, but not before thousands of families had experienced profound trauma.

Many **bad mistakes** result from people with **good intentions.** Peter, who had been with Jesus a while, thought he had God figured out by this point. So he let Jesus know, in a soothing and confidential way, that his mentor was probably taking things too seriously. But Peter found out that he didn't know the score as well as he thought.

Matthew 16:21-26: [21]From then on Jesus began to tell his disciples plainly that he had to go to Jerusalem, and he told them what would happen to him there. He would suffer at the hands of the leaders and the leading priests and the teachers of religious law. He would be killed, and he would be raised on the third day.

[22]But Peter took him aside and corrected him. "Heaven forbid, Lord," he said. "This will never happen to you!"

[23]Jesus turned to Peter and said, "Get away from me, Satan! You are a dangerous trap to me. You are seeing things merely from a human point of view, and not from God's."

[24]Then Jesus said to the disciples, "If any of you wants to be my follower, you must put aside your selfish ambition, shoulder your cross, and follow me. [25]If you try to keep your life for yourself, you will lose it.

[1] **16:26** Or *your life.*

But if you give up your life for me, you will find true life. ²⁶And how do you benefit if you gain the whole world but lose your own soul¹ in the process? Is anything worth more than your soul?"

What was Peter thinking when he rebuked the Lord for talking about the suffering that lay ahead for him? Maybe Peter was playing macho and saying, "I'll never let that happen to you, Lord!" Maybe he was uncomfortable with the thought of Jesus suffering. Or maybe he had no idea what the Lord was talking about and just said the first thing that popped into his mind. Whatever the reason, Peter said **the wrong thing.**

Like Peter, we who have lived the Christian life a while may think we have God figured out. But if we are honest, we will begin to see a pattern: **We are imposing our expectations on God.** And as Jesus reminded his disciples, that doesn't work. We have to **put aside selfish tendencies,** whatever the cost, to follow him. What wrong ideas and bad attitudes are keeping you from hearing what God is saying today?

PRAYER POINT

Ask the Lord to give you the strength to take up your cross and follow him. Then ask him to help you see things as he does.

HERE'S WHAT I'M GOING TO DO

☐ _____

_____

☐ _____

_____

_____

A NOT-SO-STRANGE IDOL

DAY 169

When was the last time you worshiped an idol? If you're like most people, when you hear the word **idol,** you probably think of weird-looking statues and pagan ceremonies—the kind of stuff you might see in an Indiana Jones movie. As a result, you probably feel safe in saying, "Never!"

The Gospel of Matthew, however, presents a much different view of idols and idolatry—one that hits a little closer to home. For more details, let's take a look at Jesus' encounter with a rich young ruler.

> Matthew 19:21-22: ²¹Jesus told him, "If you want to be perfect, go and sell all you have and give the money to the poor, and you will have treasure in heaven. Then come, follow me." ²²But when the young man heard this, he went sadly away because he had many possessions.

Can you spot any idols or idolatry in this passage? If not, look again—and think about this: **An idol is anything in our lives that takes a higher priority than God.** In the case of the rich young ruler, his idol was his wealth. He was unable to give up his riches—even if it meant receiving eternal life. He was trapped by his own idolatry.

Sometimes idols are hard to spot because they're not always obvious. In fact, many things that become idols—money, exercise, and sports, to name a few—are not necessarily bad in and of themselves. Money is not only necessary in today's world, it can also be used to help others. Exercise, in moderation, is recommended for good health. Sports provide great opportunities for relaxation and fun. However, when these things begin

to **consume** the majority of our **time, energy,** and **devotion,** we're in danger of committing idolatry.

Wealth seems to be the most popular idol of our day. The story of the rich young ruler is a sad reminder of what can happen to a person who places too much emphasis on worldly possessions. This young man cared so much for his earthly riches that he couldn't see the treasure Jesus offered. The same danger faces anyone who places a high priority on money and possessions. A person doesn't have to be rich to treat money as an idol.

Take this test: If you are not following God with all your heart, discover what it is you lack. You may be surprised to find an idol blocking the path. Determine to **remove** whatever is in the way so that you can serve God **wholeheartedly.**

PRAYER POINT

Ask the Lord to help you identify any idols in your life and to give you the strength to rid yourself of them.

HERE'S WHAT I'M GOING TO DO

☐ _____

☐ _____

☐ _____

☐ _____

_____

THE HARD WAY

The Chicago Cubs have a snowball's chance in Hades of winning the World Series." "It will be a cold day in July when Arnold Schwarzenegger wins a Best Actor Oscar." "There are two possibilities for winning the lottery—slim and none." If you think about it for a minute, you can probably come up with at least two or three other colorful expressions for something that seems **impossible.**

Jesus came up with a pretty good expression himself when he was talking to his disciples about the possibility of rich people entering the Kingdom of heaven. Let's take a look at what he had to say.

> Matthew 19:23-24: ²³Then Jesus said to his disciples, "I tell you the truth, it is very hard for a rich person to get into the Kingdom of Heaven. ²⁴I say it again—it is easier for a camel to go through the eye of a needle than for a rich person to enter the Kingdom of God!"

Unless you know of a species of microscopic camels (or a twenty-foot needle), Jesus' point is pretty obvious—it is extremely difficult for a rich person to become part of the Kingdom of heaven. This may not seem like much of a news flash to anyone who's read or heard about the wild, immoral lifestyles of the rich and famous in our society. However, for Jesus' disciples, this was a stunning idea.

Today many wealthy people believe that they are **better than others** simply because they have more money. In New Testament times, most people would have agreed with them. During the time of Jesus' ministry, wealth was seen as a reward from God for spiritual faithfulness. In other words, the more riches you had, the more godly you were considered to be. Jesus' words must have knocked his disciples for a loop. After all, if it was nearly impossible for a rich man to be saved, what hope was there for anyone else?

Jesus' comments came after seeing the rich young ruler walk away. If anyone had it made, it was this man. He had wealth, power, and a religious upbringing. But he could not part with any of them. His earnest questions and restlessness indicate the struggle he felt inside. He wanted **God's approval**—but not if it meant surrendering his wealth. And so he walked away, sad but still clinging foolishly to the riches that had kept him from God.

Sadly, many people want to strike a deal with God. They'll accept his comfort, wisdom, and guidance as long as their lives don't change too much—maybe not at all. But Jesus called his disciples to **surrender everything.** The ones who were blessed did just that. Peter and Andrew left their fishing boat to follow Jesus. Zacchaeus, certainly no stranger to riches, promised to give away most of what he had and to repay generously those he had cheated. We too will discover true wealth when we **put everything we have at God's disposal.** What are you holding back?

PRAYER POINT

Spend some time praying for God to reveal anything you may be holding back. Ask for the strength to surrender everything.

HERE'S WHAT I'M GOING TO DO

☐ _____

_____

☐ _____

_____

_____

THE BOTTOM LINE

In business today, everyone wants to know the bottom line. How much is it going to cost? How much am I going to make from it? What's in it for me? When people make investments of time, money, and energy, they want to be guaranteed **something worthwhile in return.**

Peter was a bottom-line kind of guy. He and his fellow disciples had given up their careers and almost everything else in their lives in order to follow Jesus. Now Peter was starting to wonder what kind of dividends he could expect to see from his investment. So, in typical fashion, he put the question to Jesus in the most blunt manner possible: "We have left everything to follow you! What then will there be for us?"

How do you suppose Jesus responded to Peter's interesting (but rather tacky) question? See for yourself.

Matthew 19:29-30: [29]And everyone who has given up houses or brothers or sisters or father or mother or children or property, for my sake, will receive a hundred times as much in return and will have eternal life. [30]But many who seem to be important now will be the least important then, and those who are considered least here will be the greatest then.[1]

If you had been one of Jesus' disciples, how would you have reacted to Jesus' words in Matthew 19? Would you have been excited about the possibility of receiving a hundred times as much as you already had? Would you have been disappointed to learn that you wouldn't be receiving much in this world, that you would have to wait until you got to heaven to be repaid for your efforts? Would you have asked Jesus for more details about what exactly you would be receiving in heaven?

Think about your answer carefully because the same situation applies to us today. The first in this world will be the

---

[1] **19:30** Greek *But many who are first will be last; and the last, first.*

last in God's Kingdom; the last in this world will be first in the Kingdom of heaven.

That's not to say that the Lord leaves us bankrupt in this world. In fact, he offers his followers **abundant life.** Of course, the Lord's idea of abundant life is much different than the world's view. Rather than material possessions, God offers us **peace, joy, security,** and **a passion for living**—things that have **long-lasting value.**

From a bottom-line point of view, no investment in this world can match the returns that God offers. Not only will we receive a hundred times what we have invested, we will also receive **eternal life with God in heaven.** What a combination!

Abundant life follows from an **obedient life,** however. God demands our very lives, but he also promises to restore them with an abundance we cannot imagine. We must invest ourselves in the work of his Kingdom, but we can look forward to the rich return that will never stop providing dividends.

HERE'S WHAT I'M GOING TO DO

☐ _____

_____

☐ _____

_____

_____

KING RALPH AND KING JESUS

I n the Hollywood movie *King Ralph,* Britain's entire royal family dies at once. The next-in-line for the throne just so happens to be a burly American rocker. When this crass, bumbling foreigner runs up against the expectations of royalty, the results are quite humorous.

In today's reading, Jesus **challenges the expectations** of those who would be part of his royal family and his Kingdom.

Matthew 20:20-28: ²⁰Then the mother of James and John, the sons of Zebedee, came to Jesus with her sons. She knelt respectfully to ask a favor. ²¹"What is your request?" he asked. She replied, "In your Kingdom, will you let my two sons sit in places of honor next to you, one at your right and the other at your left?" ²²But Jesus told them, "You don't know what you are asking! Are you able to drink from the bitter cup of sorrow I am about to drink?" "Oh yes," they replied, "we are able!" ²³"You will indeed drink from it," he told them. "But I have no right to say who will sit on the thrones next to mine. My Father has prepared those places for the ones he has chosen." ²⁴When the ten other disciples heard what James and John had asked, they were indignant. ²⁵But Jesus called them together and said, "You know that in this world kings are tyrants, and officials lord it over the people beneath them. ²⁶But among you it should be quite different. Whoever wants to be a leader among you must be your servant, ²⁷and whoever wants to be first must become your slave. ²⁸For even I, the Son of Man, came here not to be served but to serve others, and to give my life as a ransom for many."

The mother of James and John had it all wrong. She was convinced the Kingdom of Jesus would operate like every earthly kingdom—people scratching and clawing their way to the top. People pulling strings and making deals to get the positions of prominence. Her "power play" on behalf of her sons angered the other disciples because they shared her worldly view of "how to get to the top." They were probably irritated that she asked the question first. "Why didn't we think to ask that!"

But Jesus shattered all their wrong expectations with his topsy-turvy explanation of spiritual leadership. To become important in my Kingdom, Jesus explained, you have to give up your attempts at **self-promotion.** You have to be willing to be unimportant. If you want to be seen as a leader, be willing to be unseen as **a lowly servant who cares for others.** You want glory? Okay, but only after you have served and even suffered. These statements must have shocked the disciples as much as they surprise us.

Just as Hollywood's King Ralph turned the idea of royalty on its ear, King Jesus turned the idea of leadership upside-down. That's heaven's idea of fun and ultimate good times—**giving up our lives** for others, **leading by serving,** and **serving in obscurity.**

HERE'S WHAT I'M GOING TO DO

☐ _____

_____

☐ _____

_____

RISKY BUSINESS

Have you ever gone whitewater rafting? If so, you know how nerve-wracking it is to negotiate your boat past giant rocks and over sudden drops. Veteran rafters know how falling into the river can result in serious injury. But if you've ever done it, you also know how satisfying it is to make it safely to the takeout point. The feeling of accomplishment is worth all the risks.

In today's passage, Jesus encourages us **to take a big risk**—to **use all that we've been given for his glory:**

Matthew 25:14-15, 19-30: [14] "Again, the Kingdom of Heaven can be illustrated by the story of a man going on a trip. He called together his servants and gave them money to invest for him while he was gone. [15] He gave five bags of gold[1] to one, two bags of gold to another, and one bag of gold to the last—dividing it in proportion to their abilities—and then left on his trip.

[19] "After a long time their master returned from his trip and called them to give an account of how they had used his money. [20] The servant to whom he had entrusted the five bags of gold said, 'Sir, you gave me five bags of gold to invest, and I have doubled the amount.' [21] The master was full of praise. 'Well done, my good and faithful servant. You have been faithful in handling this small amount, so now I will give you many more responsibilities. Let's celebrate together!'

[22] "Next came the servant who had received the two bags of gold, with the report, 'Sir, you gave me two bags of gold to invest, and I have doubled the amount.' [23] The master said, 'Well done, my good and faithful servant. You have been faithful in handling this small amount, so now I will give you many more responsibilities. Let's celebrate together!' [24] Then the

---

[1] **25:15** Greek *talents;* also throughout the story. A talent is equal to 75 pounds or 34 kilograms.
[2] **25:29** Or *who have nothing.*

servant with the one bag of gold came and said, 'Sir, I know you are a hard man, harvesting crops you didn't plant and gathering crops you didn't cultivate. 25I was afraid I would lose your money, so I hid it in the earth and here it is.' 26But the master replied, 'You wicked and lazy servant! You think I'm a hard man, do you, harvesting crops I didn't plant and gathering crops I didn't cultivate? 27Well, you should at least have put my money into the bank so I could have some interest.

Prayer Point

Confess any ways you have failed to use your gifts to glorify God. Commit yourself (all that you have and are) to serving God faithfully today.

28Take the money from this servant and give it to the one with the ten bags of gold. 29To those who use well what they are given, even more will be given, and they will have an abundance. But from those who are unfaithful,2 even what little they have will be taken away. 30Now throw this useless servant into outer darkness, where there will be weeping and gnashing of teeth.' "

Our talents, abilities, opportunities, and gifts all come from God. He wants us to **use what we've been given** to forward his Kingdom. The issue is not what others have been given; the issue is **being faithful** with what we've been given.

Serving God is risky business. It calls us to **step out of our comfort zones** and do things that are hard or scary. But if we are willing to go for it, we will eventually find a fulfillment and joy we could never know otherwise.

HERE'S WHAT I'M GOING TO DO

GROWING PAINS

What do you want to do when you "grow up"? Do you plan to attend college and then climb a certain career-ladder? Do you have ambitions for starting your own business and making a lot of money? **Striving for excellence** can be a virtue and the desire to do something **great** can be noble, but aiming only at publicity or recognition is **dangerous,** according to the Bible. Listen to Jesus' words in today's reading:

> Matthew 23:11-12: 11The greatest among you must be a servant. 12But those who exalt themselves will be humbled, and those who humble themselves will be exalted.

In this situation, Jesus was condemning the Pharisees for the prideful way they wanted to be noticed by other men (vv. 6-7). Everything they did was selfish and "for show" (v. 5). We've seen in previous devotions that the most important (and the most rewarded!) members of God's Kingdom do not seek earthly (or even heavenly) notice. That's because they understand that Jesus is the one who should be our focus. He alone deserves all glory and honor and praise.

So what is the formula for greatness? According to Jesus, **we become great by serving others.** And these weren't just empty words from our Lord. He practiced what he preached! He was the ultimate servant.

Don't get caught up in all that superficial religious mumbo-jumbo! Jesus seemed to be saying, "Don't take yourself so seriously! Don't act high and mighty! Don't get the spiritual big head! You're just supposed to serve. You want to do something great? Do that. **Serve.** Period.

Do the things no **one else is willing to do.** Do the things **no one else will ever see."**

According to Jesus, that's the real test of greatness: the willingness to do things in secret, without ever getting any earthly recognition (Matthew 6:1-18). In so many words, Jesus challenges you to be a **secret servant.** How's that for a job description or for a career objective? Imagine the impact if every follower of Christ would make that his or her ambition in life: I'm going to quietly and faithfully serve God, with no fanfare, with no expectations, with no strings attached. Just because he is the great King of the universe and of my life and because he has loved and blessed me so much.

Will you make that your goal? There's not a greater ambition to be found.

HERE'S WHAT I'M GOING TO DO

☐ _____

_____

☐ _____

_____

☐ _____

_____

_____

SEEING THE FACE

Famine. Poverty. Drought. You hear the awful stories coming out of Third World countries. You sometimes see the pictures on TV or in magazines. But it's still hard to grasp the magnitude of **world hunger.**

Until God helps us see this problem, until we are able to "put a face" on it, our hearts will never be moved to action. In today's reading we learn that, for Christians, the "face" of poverty ultimately is **the face of Christ.**

Matthew 25:34-40: ³⁴"Then the King will say to those on the right, 'Come, you who are blessed by my Father, inherit the Kingdom prepared for you from the foundation of the world. ³⁵For I was hungry, and you fed me. I was thirsty, and you gave me a drink. I was a stranger, and you invited me into your home. ³⁶I was naked, and you gave me clothing. I was sick, and you cared for me. I was in prison, and you visited me.'

³⁷"Then these righteous ones will reply, 'Lord, when did we ever see you hungry and feed you? Or thirsty and give you something to drink? ³⁸Or a stranger and show you hospitality? Or naked and give you clothing? ³⁹When did we ever see you sick or in prison, and visit you?' ⁴⁰And the King will tell them, 'I assure you, when you did it to one of the least of these my brothers and sisters, you were doing it to me!' "

In this discourse about the end times, Jesus begins speaking figuratively about his intimate identification with mankind. In taking on human flesh, **Christ made himself subject to the pains and sorrows of this world.** Leaving the glory and riches of heaven, he lived most of his life dependent on the kindness of strangers. Jesus may not have literally experienced each of the trials listed in this passage, but he did experience rejection and a life devoid of most of the comforts enjoyed by others. Jesus is the **ultimate**

representative of the poor and downtrodden.

What can we learn from these questions posed by the righteous in this passage? First, we need to remember that our Savior, like the prisoners and sick people he mentions in these verses, "was acquainted with the bitterest grief" and "a man of sorrows" (Isaiah 53:3). Why was he willing to endure such suffering? To save us. Recalling this aspect of Jesus' life should increase our **appreciation** for what Christ has done for us. It should also increase our **compassion** for the hurting people we encounter.

Second, there is a very real sense in which we serve Jesus by serving others (2 Corinthians 4:5; Colossians 3:24). By ministering to our brothers and sisters, we are, in fact, bringing comfort to "the body of Christ" (Ephesians 5:30). Since we never know who we're coming in contact with and how God plans to enrich our life through them, we need to keep our eyes open for the neglected, the suffering, and the helpless around us. It's something of a mystery, but in helping those who are so closely identified with Christ, Jesus says we end up **ministering to him!**

HERE'S WHAT I'M GOING TO DO

☐ _____

_____

_____

THAT SWEET SMELL

DAY

176

O K, picture this scene. For a going-away gift at a farewell party, a friend walks up and pours a **whole bottle** of Polo or Chanel on you. We're talking a jumbo bottle from an exclusive store. What would you say? What would you do?

The odds are that this will never happen to you. But such a thing did happen to Jesus just days before his death.

Matthew 26:6-13: ⁶Meanwhile, Jesus was in Bethany at the home of Simon, a man who had leprosy. ⁷During supper, a woman came in with a beautiful jar¹ of expensive perfume and poured it over his head. ⁸The disciples were indignant when they saw this. "What a waste of money," they said. ⁹"She could have sold it for a fortune and given the money to the poor."

¹⁰But Jesus replied, "Why berate her for doing such a good thing to me? ¹¹You will always have the poor among you, but I will not be here with you much longer. ¹²She has poured this perfume on me to prepare my body for burial. ¹³I assure you, wherever the Good News is preached throughout the world, this woman's deed will be talked about in her memory."

Matthew doesn't mention the name of the woman who poured the fragrance on Jesus, but John identified her as Mary, the sister of Martha and Lazarus. In other passages, we learn of Mary's utter devotion to Jesus (Luke 10:38-42). So her perfuming incident should come as no surprise. But Matthew reports that the disciples were "indignant" (v. 8).

They accused Mary of wastefulness: "She could have sold it for a fortune and given the money to the poor" (v. 9). Isn't it interesting that the disciples got so hung up on the extravagance of the gesture that they missed **the love that prompted it?!** Perhaps they really were concerned about the poor. Maybe they just didn't understand Mary's love. Or

¹ **26:7** Greek *an alabaster jar.*

possibly, they just felt guilty because they had never demonstrated such affection. (It's natural to **criticize** others when you want to **feel better about yourself.**)

Whatever the case, the disciples learned a great lesson about worship from this incident. Mary offered the **very best gift** she had. It was costly. Based on historical and archaeological evidence, scholars are pretty certain that Mary had to break the jar to release the fragrant ointment inside. This meant Mary couldn't have saved any of the perfume for another occasion. She used it all on Jesus, and from the sound of the passage, she did so **gladly.**

Worship is all about declaring **the worth of the Lord.** He alone deserves our attention, our allegiance, our affection, and our resources. And when our worship stems from a heart full of love and gratitude, it produces **a pleasing aroma,** whether or not it involves perfume!

HERE'S WHAT I'M GOING TO DO

☐ _____

_____

☐ _____

_____

☐ _____

_____

HEALTHY PEOPLE

Pity the poor Pharisees of Jesus' day. These men were the religious leaders of the Jews, the experts in God's law. Highly educated, they spent every waking minute studying, debating, and making rulings on the law. These men were so **obsessed** with making sure that every aspect of the law was followed that they began **creating their own laws within the law.** The situation escalated until the Jewish people were faced with a system of rules that was impossible to keep. So rather than being an expression of devotion to God, the law became **a source of frustration** to the people. Only the most pious and obsessive Jews—the Pharisees, in other words—could possibly hope to be righteous in the eyes of the law. The Pharisees took pride in their self-determined righteousness and lorded their piety over the "common" Jews.

But then Jesus came and spoiled their fun. One of Jesus' favorite pastimes was **puncturing the self-righteous attitudes** of the Pharisees and other religious leaders, often using their **own words** against them. Look at the way he cuts through their indignation in Mark 2.

> Mark 2:15-17: [15]That night Levi invited Jesus and his disciples to be his dinner guests, along with his fellow tax collectors and many other notorious sinners. (There were many people of this kind among the crowds that followed Jesus.) [16]But when some of the teachers of religious law who were Pharisees[1] saw him eating with people like that, they said to his disciples, "Why does he eat with such scum[2]?"
>
> [17]When Jesus heard this, he told them, "Healthy people don't need a doctor—sick people do. I have come to call sinners, not those who think they are already good enough."

The Pharisees were looking to discredit Jesus, lest people

---

[1] **2:16a** Greek *the scribes of the Pharisees.*
[2] **2:16b** Greek *with tax collectors and sinners.*

begin to follow his teachings rather than theirs. When they saw Jesus enter the house of a tax collector, the Pharisees seized their opportunity. You see, tax collectors were considered outcasts. No self-respecting Pharisee would be caught speaking with a tax collector, let alone eating in his home! So when Jesus entered Levi's home, the Pharisees made a big deal of his eating with unclean sinners.

Jesus replied—in so many words—"You Pharisees claim to be righteous and to have no need for repentance and salvation. These tax collectors and admitted sinners, on the other hand, realize their need for repentance and salvation. So who do you think I'm going to spend my time with?" Not surprisingly, the Pharisees had no response to Jesus' explanation.

As followers of Christ, we have a similar responsibility to the outcasts of society: the poor, the "unwashed," the lower class, the ignored. **Jesus was not above mingling with and ministering to such people,** even going so far as visiting them in their homes. Should we then be any different? Are we above ministering to these people in need?

HERE'S WHAT I'M GOING TO DO

❏ _____

_____

❏ _____

_____

DON'T WAIT TO SERVE

Let's say you and three of your friends are going on a camping trip together in your family's minivan. "We don't have a lot of room in the van," you tell your friends, "so bring only what you need for the weekend." Depending on your friends' **definition of need,** one of them may show up with nothing more than a toothbrush and a sleeping bag, while another brings four suitcases, a portable TV, and a microwave.

When Jesus sent his disciples out to tell others about him, he gave a whole new meaning to the phrase "traveling lightly." He instructed his disciples to take only the barest of essentials with them. Let's look at the contents of the disciples' traveling kit.

> Mark 6:7-9: [7]And he called his twelve disciples together and sent them out two by two, with authority to cast out evil spirits. [8]He told them to take nothing with them except a walking stick—no food, no traveler's bag, no money. [9]He told them to wear sandals but not to take even an extra coat.

A staff (or walking stick) and a pair of sandals—that's all the disciples needed to take with them on their journeys. They didn't need food, money, or even a blanket, because all of those things would be **provided** for them.

How do you suppose the disciples felt as they embarked on their trips? Do you think they felt "naked" traveling with so little? Do you think they were at all apprehensive about where they were going to stay or how they were going to find food? It's hard to say, but we do know that they were taken care of.

If you had to make a list of the things necessary in order for you to go out and minister in your community, what would you include on it? Do you need some sort of transportation? Do you need someone to accompany you like the disciples did? Do you need money? Do you need a Bible? Who's to say what anybody "needs"? The Lord is, because he **can** and **does** supply us with **everything necessary** to serve him.

We don't need a lot to serve the Lord. In fact, all it really takes is the **willingness** to go where he sends us, to walk through the doors he opens for us in order to minister to others. So if you're waiting for a better time, more education, or more money in the bank, stop! God can use you **as you are** right now!

PRAYER POINT

Ask God to help you discern between your needs and wants as they relate to ministry. Ask him to supply everything you need in order to minister to others.

HERE'S WHAT I'M GOING TO DO

- ☐ _____
  _____

- ☐ _____
  _____

- ☐ _____
  _____

- ☐ _____
  _____

AN IMPROBABLE FEAST

The *Guinness Book of Records* lists some amazing feats involving food. For example, did you know that the longest banana split ever created was more than four-and-a-half miles long? Did you know that the largest burrito ever created weighed 3,960 pounds? Did you know that the biggest chocolate chip cookie ever made covered an area of 1,001 square feet? It makes you hungry just thinking about it.

However, all of these food feats pale in comparison to the events that occurred during an impromptu meal in Decapolis more than two thousand years ago.

Mark 8:1-9: ¹About this time another great crowd had gathered, and the people ran out of food again. Jesus called his disciples and told them, ²"I feel sorry for these people. They have been here with me for three days, and they have nothing left to eat. ³And if I send them home without feeding them, they will faint along the road. For some of them have come a long distance."

⁴"How are we supposed to find enough food for them here in the wilderness?" his disciples asked.

⁵"How many loaves of bread do you have?" he asked.

"Seven," they replied. ⁶So Jesus told all the people to sit down on the ground. Then he took the seven loaves, thanked God for them, broke them into pieces, and gave them to his disciples, who distributed the bread to the crowd. ⁷A few small fish were found, too, so Jesus also blessed these and told the disciples to pass them out.

⁸They ate until they were full, and when the scraps were picked up, there were seven large baskets of food left over! ⁹There were about four thousand people in the crowd that day, and he sent them home after they had eaten.

Believe it or not, the most interesting thing about Jesus' feeding of the four thousand is not the miracle itself but the between-the-lines details of the story. Think about this: Jesus did not simply create food to feed the crowd, although he certainly had the power to. Instead, he asked his disciples how much food they had and then used their loaves and fish to feed the multitude. **Jesus multiplied his disciples' limited resources to miraculous effect.**

The good news for us is that Jesus does the same thing for his disciples today. When we look at the big picture of world hunger and suffering, it's easy to be **overwhelmed,** to feel powerless and small. After all, what can **one** person do to affect such an enormous situation?

Our question should not be *What can I do?* but rather **What can Jesus do through me?** If he so desires, Jesus can take our small, individual efforts to help the needy in our community and expand those efforts to miraculous proportions, accomplishing **more** with them than we could ever imagine.

HERE'S WHAT I'M GOING TO DO

☐ _____

_____

☐ _____

_____

SACRIFICES

When you decided to become a Christian and follow Christ, did you **sacrifice** or **give up** anything in your life—maybe a habit, a group of friends, or an attitude? In the time you've been a Christian, have you ever faced any suffering or mistreatment because of your faith—perhaps taunting or derogatory jokes aimed your way?

Nobody said being a Christian would be easy, right? In fact, Jesus himself paints a rather stark portrait in Mark 8 of **what it means to follow him.**

> Mark 8:34-38: [34]Then he called his disciples and the crowds to come over and listen. "If any of you wants to be my follower," he told them, "you must put aside your selfish ambition, shoulder your cross, and follow me. [35]If you try to keep your life for yourself, you will lose it. But if you give up your life for my sake and for the sake of the Good News, you will find true life. [36]And how do you benefit if you gain the whole world but lose your own soul[1] in the process? [37]Is anything worth more than your soul? [38]If a person is ashamed of me and my message in these adulterous and sinful days, I, the Son of Man, will be ashamed of that person when I return in the glory of my Father with the holy angels."

Jesus wanted his followers to understand one thing: Just as suffering, rejection, and sacrifice were part of Jesus' life, they will also likely be part of the believer's life. Jesus gave a three-part explanation as to what it means to follow him. First, a person must **deny himself**—that is, shift his focus away from himself and toward Christ and his ministry. Second, a person must **pick up his cross,** demonstrating a willingness to suffer and die for the Lord's sake, if necessary. Third, a person must **follow Christ,** patterning his life, actions, and attitude after Jesus'.

---

[1] **8:36** Or *your life;* also in 8:37.

Jesus' words make it clear that following him is not a decision to be taken lightly. The possibility of actually dying for the Lord's sake underscores the **seriousness of our faith.** And yet it has been said that it is harder to live for the Lord than it is to die for him.

Anyone who has ever struggled to deny himself in order to minister to others knows how **hard** living for Christ can be. Placing the needs of someone else first—particularly those of the poor and "unlovable" of the world—goes completely against human nature. Yet that's what Christ calls us to do.

So, are you willing to die for Christ, if necessary? More important, are you willing to live for him?

PRAYER POINT

Ask the Lord to help you maintain an "others first" attitude as you minister to people in your community and church.

HERE'S WHAT I'M GOING TO DO

☐ _____

☐ _____

☐ _____

☐ _____

☐ _____

THE GREATEST

Our society seems to have an **obsession** with lists and rankings. No matter what the category, we want to know who's the best, what's the most popular, who's ranked number one, and what's the greatest of all time. Who was voted the funniest person alive? What professional sports team holds the record for the longest drought between championships? What is the most widely read magazine in North Dakota? Who has sold more albums in Paraguay than the Beatles and Elvis combined?

Of course, there are some areas in which terms like "the greatest" and "number one" have **little** or **no meaning.** Jesus' disciples found this out for themselves one day on the road to Capernaum.

> Mark 9:33-37: [33]After they arrived at Capernaum, Jesus and his disciples settled in the house where they would be staying. Jesus asked them, "What were you discussing out on the road?" [34]But they didn't answer, because they had been arguing about which of them was the greatest. [35]He sat down and called the twelve disciples over to him. Then he said, "Anyone who wants to be the first must take last place and be the servant of everyone else."
>
> [36]Then he put a little child among them. Taking the child in his arms, he said to them, [37]"Anyone who welcomes a little child like this on my behalf welcomes me, and anyone who welcomes me welcomes my Father who sent me."

Note what happened when Jesus asked the disciples what they'd been arguing about. No one answered him. Most likely the disciples were embarrassed about their argument. They may also have wanted to avoid being on the receiving end of one of Jesus' withering rebukes (see Mark 8:33).

The disciples had been arguing about which one of them would be greatest in the coming kingdom. Jesus took this opportunity to teach his followers about **true greatness.**

Jesus' strategy for finishing first is certainly unique. Can you imagine using this same technique for a sporting event? "OK, kid, the best way to win the Indianapolis 500 is to let every car on the track pass you. When you come across that finish line in thirty-third position, you'll know you've won the race."

But in God's arena, **serving others becomes a path to greatness.** Becoming a servant means making a deliberate decision to put others' needs before your own. When we put others first, when we concentrate on helping others, we lose our inclination to seek the honor and fame the world clamors for. Remember, greatness in the Christian faith is not determined by status but by **service.**

HERE'S WHAT I'M GOING TO DO

❑ _____

_____

❑ _____

_____

❑ _____

_____

LOSING EVERYTHING

Suppose you're watching the evening news. Your attention is drawn to a "hidden camera" investigation of a local carnival that you were going to visit this weekend. A reporter, posing as a new employee, asks his boss about safety inspections for some risky-looking rides. "Are you crazy?" he booms. "But what if someone gets hurt?" the reporter asks. "If someone gets hurt, we can probably settle for a lot less than the cost of a new roller coaster," his boss replies.

After the news report airs, attendance at the carnival falls dramatically, even after the owner claims he is "misquoted." The owner of this carnival probably ended up losing far more than he bargained for. His greed and lack of concern for others will likely cost him everything he put into his business.

Mark's Gospel tells us about another man who **lost everything** trying to hold on to what he had.

Mark 10:17-22: [17]As he was starting out on a trip, a man came running up to Jesus, knelt down, and asked, "Good Teacher, what should I do to get eternal life?" [18]"Why do you call me good?" Jesus asked. "Only God is truly good. [19]But as for your question, you know the commandments: 'Do not murder. Do not commit adultery. Do not steal. Do not testify falsely. Do not cheat. Honor your father and mother.'[1]" [20]"Teacher," the man replied, "I've obeyed all these commandments since I was a child."

[21]Jesus felt genuine love for this man as he looked at him. "You lack only one thing," he told him. "Go and sell all you have and give the money to the poor, and you will have treasure in heaven. Then come, follow me." [22]At this, the man's face fell, and he went sadly away because he had many possessions.

So you think this is only about the wealthy of this world? And how these people—merely because they're rich—can't get

[1] **10:19** Exod. 20:12-16; Deut. 5:16-20.

into heaven? Let's take another look. First of all, it wasn't the possessions themselves that kept the Rich Man from following God. Jesus had this incredible skill to see directly into a person's heart, knowing that person's motivations, deepest desires, and loves. This man's sin was not that he had money but that he **_loved_ his money more than he loved God.**

Now to the next important point: You don't have to be rich to love money. As a matter of fact, you can be upper middle class, lower middle class . . . or poor. Whenever the desire for obtaining and keeping our money becomes an obsession, we're putting that before God. The remedy is not that we need to sell all we have, but instead that we put money in its proper place: **_after_ trusting God.** Even if the Rich Man had sold all his goods at that very moment, the core problem would still remain if he had continued to be preoccupied with money.

If Jesus were standing before you and pointed out the deepest desires of your life in relation to money, just what would he see? What would he say? So where _is_ your heart?

HERE'S WHAT I'M GOING TO DO

☐ _____

_____

☐ _____

_____

_____

THE COST

He was a humble man, soft-spoken and preferring to talk about his God rather than himself. Living in a communist country, this man risked all to be an underground pastor. He had served nearly nineteen years in prison; while there, his entire family died. He had no citizenship. Denied even this by his government, he was literally a man with no country to call his own.

He did not own his apartment. In truth, he owned essentially nothing. Still, he gave abundantly to the churches he pastored, to those whom he sought to train to preach God's message.

Poor? Oh, definitely, by the world's measurement. But this man was like the woman whom Jesus observed in the temple. They both understood that **generous giving goes far beyond monetary limits.**

Mark 12:41-44: 41Jesus went over to the collection box in the Temple and sat and watched as the crowds dropped in their money. Many rich people put in large amounts. 42Then a poor widow came and dropped in two pennies.1 43He called his disciples to him and said, "I assure you, this poor widow has given more than all the others have given. 44For they gave a tiny part of their surplus, but she, poor as she is, has given everything she has."

She gave **everything.** All that she had. It boggles the mind, doesn't it, to think of that kind of faith and generosity? So our inner voice probably responds, *I can't be like her! And I can't be like this pastor who puts his very life in danger to give to his God.* Or can I?

Jesus doesn't share this with his disciples to merely make them feel guilty. And he isn't asking us to empty our savings, sell our possessions, and give away everything. But he is

1 **12:42** Greek *2 lepta, which is a kodrantes.*

calling us to **evaluate our giving.** How generous are we? What is the spirit of our giving? Joyful? Or reluctant? Do we give first, demonstrating a trust in God's provision? Do we give regularly? Do we follow a plan that allows us to give joyfully and with **increasing generosity?** And finally, does it *cost* us something?

It certainly cost the poor widow. And the underground pastor. How about you?

PRAYER POINT

Pray for the ability to trust God even more with your finances, and consider the possibility of giving more than you do now.

HERE'S WHAT I'M GOING TO DO

☐ _____

_____

☐ _____

_____

☐ _____

_____

☐ _____

_____

☐ _____

_____

☐ _____

_____

CRAVINGS

Don't you just hate it when you're **hungry** and you can't figure out what it is you want? You probably end up shuffling through the cupboards, rejecting the two remaining Girl Scout cookies scrunched in the bottom of the box, the stale graham crackers, and a piece of candy from last Christmas.

Next stop: the pantry. Soup? Nah. Ravioli? No way. Cereal? Well, a definite maybe. The last resort is the refrigerator, where you might stare at its depressing contents: leftovers (probably green by now), wilted lettuce (please! no healthy stuff!), and lunch meat (ugh). Sigh. So what *are* you craving anyway?

That's one type of hunger, but it does not begin to compare to the deep craving that much of the world experiences today. Jesus told his disciples about this other hunger—and how we should respond.

Mark 16:15: ¹⁵And then he told them, "Go into all the world and preach the Good News to everyone, everywhere."

Just like we may crave something and not know what it is, the unsaved people of this world have a craving too. They know **the deepest void** possible within their hearts . . . and have no answers for the **emptiness** and **pain.** They desire a Savior whom they haven't met. They long for a forgiveness and cleansing that knows no substitute. They thirst for Living Water when their spiritual lives are dry. They hunger for the Bread of Life because they have **no fulfillment in their lives.** And they won't find any of this . . . unless we tell them.

Around the world, people are literally dying from spiritual

hunger. They cover up the symptoms with materialism, political solutions, new ideologies, and twisted ideas, but the hunger remains. "Go into all the world," Jesus said. He didn't suggest. He didn't ask. He commanded.

PRAYER POINT

Ask God to give you a passion for those who are physically and spiritually hungry.

As a follower of Jesus, the responsibility rests squarely on your shoulders. But you are not alone—**God has promised his Spirit to help you** every step of the way.

It's a big world out there. Think you could start with a hungry neighbor?

HERE'S WHAT I'M GOING TO DO

☐ _____

_____

☐ _____

_____

☐ _____

_____

☐ _____

_____

☐ _____

_____

☐ _____

_____

WHAT REALLY MATTERS

Nicaragua is a beautiful country, but living conditions there can be brutally hard. Julio knew this, firsthand. Living with his family on a mountain by the sea, he daily reckoned with the relentlessness of the wind. It covered everything—and everyone—with a layer of dirt. The bamboo and plastic hut in which his family sought shelter did little to keep out the gritty dust. They had no running water. Six lived in an area the size of a small room. And the only clothes they owned were those they wore.

Certainly Julio would be bitter and miserable, right? Wrong. Instead, he was **eager to share the little he had.** Intense joy radiated from him and his family. It's a miracle, really, that type of **contentment.** And Mary echoes this same satisfaction in her song of praise to God:

> Luke 1:53: 53"He has satisfied the hungry with good things and sent the rich away with empty hands."

Finding the words *satisfaction* and *hungry* and *good* in the same sentence certainly seems incongruous. If we're not satisfied, things certainly are not good. Only good things tend to satisfy us. And it's definitely not a good thing if we're hungry! So putting those three words together just can't be possible, can it? Somehow you get the feeling that God's performing another small miracle here.

For indeed, Mary was satisfied and content before her God. Poor and single, she still responded to her Lord's call with amazing faith and trust. And among the poorest of the poor in the heart of Nicaragua, Julio is profound evidence that this same kind of contentment can still happen. For when someone knows the **joy of the Lord,** satisfaction comes through relationship. And love. And eternal life. These are the things that really matter in this world. And when you have essentially nothing else, you *know* **what really matters.**

But living in a culture that clamors for material goods, pleasure, indulgence, and instant gratification can lead us away from spiritual riches. To discover what Mary sang about, we need to make a determined effort to detach ourselves from *things* and **attach ourselves to *people.*** And if we trust God, he will help us remove the clutter from our lives.

Julio, poor? Actually, he probably has just about everything.

HERE'S WHAT I'M GOING TO DO

☐ _____

_____

☐ _____

_____

☐ _____

_____

☐ _____

_____

☐ _____

_____

THE SMELL OF HOPELESSNESS

DAY

186

Sierra Leone, Africa, 1995—Refugees from ravaged Liberia camped in a dense area, seeking one thing: survival. The smell of hopelessness and meaninglessness and victimization hung in the air like a fog. The loss of dignity hovered there too, coupled with the loss of identity. The loss of significance. The loss of hope. Their desperation was almost touchable.

A refugee camp certainly commands the attention of every one of our senses, smell included. We might nearly be overwhelmed by this despair. Fortunately, however, **Christ brings hope** to the refugees of this world!

Luke 6:20-26: ²⁰Then Jesus turned to his disciples and said, "God blesses you who are poor, for the Kingdom of God is given to you. ²¹God blesses you who are hungry now, for you will be satisfied. God blesses you who weep now, for the time will come when you will laugh with joy. ²²God blesses you who are hated and excluded and mocked and cursed because you are identified with me, the Son of Man. ²³When that happens, rejoice! Yes, leap for joy! For a great reward awaits you in heaven. And remember, the ancient prophets were also treated that way by your ancestors.

²⁴"What sorrows await you who are rich, for you have your only happiness now. ²⁵What sorrows await you who are satisfied and prosperous now, for a time of awful hunger is before you. What sorrows await you who laugh carelessly, for your laughing will turn to mourning and sorrow. ²⁶What sorrows await you who are praised by the crowds, for their ancestors also praised false prophets."

In Christ, and often in him alone, the Christians of this camp knew and exhibited a miraculously different spirit. They still experienced sorrow and pain, but beyond that was an incredible trust and determination to make the best of the situation. They had nothing but the clothes they wore. Their shacks were made from plastic tarps. They traded everything they owned simply to arrive at this place. And their only source of food came from relief agencies. But in their eyes existed a glimmer of hope because **the Kingdom of God had been given to them.** And he has promised blessings, satisfaction, laughter, and joy!

PRAYER POINT

Pray for the refugees of this world! So many are completely dependent on relief agencies and on your support for material food and spiritual nourishment.

God can, and does indeed, provide **blessings** for the poor and hungry of this world. Many of those promises will come true only in the future heavenly Kingdom. But even today, on this often cruel earth, his inner riches can make an intolerable situation tolerable. Among poverty and pain, **God can still provide satisfaction and joy.** The refugees and poor only need to know the One who provides these gifts. Through one who cares enough to tell them.

The smell of hopelessness is horrible. But the glimmer of hope brings joy. Only Christ can provide that glimmer . . . through you.

HERE'S WHAT I'M GOING TO DO

☐ _____

_____

☐ _____

_____

_____

RUSH HOUR

Rush hour traffic can bring out the worst in people. Traveling at a snail's pace (even bumper-to-bumper), blaring horns, aggressive and impatient, many drivers tend to be incredibly irritating, annoying, and often just plain obnoxious! The result: Often we respond with the same bullying spirit. We become just as pushy. Just as **intolerant.** Generally out for *me*.

But what if we determine to stay courteous, looking out for the other guy and giving him a break? What if we try to operate even our cars by Jesus' charge to **love the unlovable?**

Luke 6:27-36: [27]"But if you are willing to listen, I say, love your enemies. Do good to those who hate you. [28]Pray for the happiness of those who curse you. Pray for those who hurt you. [29]If someone slaps you on one cheek, turn the other cheek. If someone demands your coat, offer your shirt also. [30]Give what you have to anyone who asks you for it; and when things are taken away from you, don't try to get them back. [31]Do for others as you would like them to do for you.

[32]"Do you think you deserve credit merely for loving those who love you? Even the sinners do that! [33]And if you do good only to those who do good to you, is that so wonderful? Even sinners do that much! [34]And if you lend money only to those who can repay you, what good is that? Even sinners will lend to their own kind for a full return.

[35]"Love your enemies! Do good to them! Lend to them! And don't be concerned that they might not repay. Then your reward from heaven will be very great, and you will truly be acting as children of the Most High, for he is kind to the unthankful and to those who are wicked. [36]You must be compassionate, just as your Father is compassionate."

Now, quite honestly and realistically, this is a definite challenge. Loving someone who's lovable can be pretty tough sometimes, because even the best of us have days when we're cranky and unbearable. Still, that presents no insurmountable problem. But what about loving those who are *always* like some rush hour drivers? Always pushy? Irritating? And mean?

Doing good to those who do good things for us doesn't take **a lot of effort** on our part. But it takes someone special to **love** the *unlovable*. To do good things for people who have been cruel to us. To lend money to someone who we know can't repay the loan. To love an enemy. These efforts aren't easy or effortless; they take sacrifice, determination, and power from the Holy Spirit.

At this point, you might also be asking *why* you should even attempt this. Well, **Jesus loved you when *you* were unlovable.**

So will you accept the challenge? How about determining to love and allowing that driver to pull out ahead of you during the peak of rush hour traffic? Quite honestly, the look of shock on his face will be worth it!

HERE'S WHAT I'M GOING TO DO

☐ _____

_____

☐ _____

_____

GOOD NEIGHBORS

Who is your **neighbor?** The people who live next door? Check. The guys whose lockers are on either side of yours? Check. Okay . . . who else? Check out what Jesus says in today's reading.

Luke 10:25-37: [25]One day an expert in religious law stood up to test Jesus by asking him this question: "Teacher, what must I do to receive eternal life?" [26]Jesus replied, "What does the law of Moses say? How do you read it?" [27]The man answered, " 'You must love the Lord your God with all your heart, all your soul, all your strength, and all your mind.' And, 'Love your neighbor as yourself.' "[1] [28]"Right!" Jesus told him. "Do this and you will live!"

[29]The man wanted to justify his actions, so he asked Jesus, "And who is my neighbor?" [30]Jesus replied with an illustration: "A Jewish man was traveling on a trip from Jerusalem to Jericho, and he was attacked by bandits. They stripped him of his clothes and money, beat him up, and left him half dead beside the road.

[31]"By chance a Jewish priest came along; but when he saw the man lying there, he crossed to the other side of the road and passed him by. [32]A Temple assistant[2] walked over and looked at him lying there, but he also passed by on the other side.

[33]"Then a despised Samaritan came along, and when he saw the man, he felt deep pity. [34]Kneeling beside him, the Samaritan soothed his wounds with medicine and bandaged them. Then he put the man on his own donkey and took him to an inn, where he took care of him. [35]The next day he handed the innkeeper two pieces of silver[3] and told him to take care of the man. 'If his bill runs higher than that,' he said, 'I'll pay the difference the next time I am here.'

[1] **10:27** Deut. 6:5; Lev. 19:18.
[2] **10:32** Greek *A Levite*.
[3] **10:35** Greek *2 denarii*. A denarius was the equivalent of a full day's wage.

³⁶"Now which of these three would you say was a neighbor to the man who was attacked by bandits?" Jesus asked. ³⁷The man replied, "The one who showed him mercy." Then Jesus said, "Yes, now go and do the same."

The man who asked the question was Jewish. The one who got beaten on the road was Jewish. Jewish people passionately hated the Samaritans (and the Samaritans returned the feeling). In the story, one Jewish person after another walked past the hurting man. Only the despised Samaritan treated his "enemy" as a human being who needed help—a person worth loving and caring for.

Jesus' story gives us three truths to keep in mind when it comes to loving our neighbor: (1) Our neighbor is **anyone**—no matter what their race, color, creed, or social background—**who needs help.** (2) We can always justify or rationalize not helping someone, but doing so is never right. (3) Loving our neighbor means acting in order to meet that person's need. Now, ask yourself again: Who is your neighbor?

HERE'S WHAT I'M GOING TO DO

☐ _____

_____

☐ _____

_____

GREAT VALUE

Does God really **know** you? Does he even **care?** Does it matter to him how you did on that math test? Does he care that you're feeling lonely today? Does he even look at your feeble attempts to live as a Christian? It's easy to feel small. You look at a NASA photograph of the earth from space, and you can hardly see your state, let alone your city, your house, yourself.

How can God keep everything straight? How does he ever have time to even acknowledge your existence, let alone listen to your prayers and answer them in his wisdom?

If you're feeling lost in the cosmos, let Jesus bring you down to earth today.

Luke 12:4-7: 4"Dear friends, don't be afraid of those who want to kill you. They can only kill the body; they cannot do any more to you. 5But I'll tell you whom to fear. Fear God, who has the power to kill people and then throw them into hell. 6What is the price of five sparrows? A couple of pennies? Yet God does not forget a single one of them. 7And the very hairs on your head are all numbered. So don't be afraid; you are more valuable to him than a whole flock of sparrows."

Jesus was speaking to his followers. Already they were attracting the attention of the people in charge, who didn't like the waves Jesus was making in their very comfortable system. Jesus knew that whoever followed him ran the risk of upsetting the authorities. Even today in various places around the world, Christian faith is a good excuse to lose your life.

But Jesus said not to worry about the people who could kill your body. **We ought to be more concerned about God.** He has ultimate authority over every single person's soul—and where it winds up in the end. Naturally, that raised a question about God. Could a God this powerful, this authoritative, really know and care about us as individuals?

Jesus set his listeners' minds at ease. Hey, God knows every single sparrow—and they only cost a couple cents for five at the Temple! If a simple bird is known by God, certainly we are. In fact, Jesus said, God knows exactly how many hairs are growing out of your head. That may sound kind of ridiculous. The point isn't that God has a thing about hair; it's that **he knows every single solitary detail of your life.** "So don't be afraid," Jesus says, "you are more valuable to him than a whole flock of sparrows" (v. 7).

Prayer Point

Spend some time in prayer just thanking God for his infinite love and care for you. He is worthy of your praise, isn't he? Pray a psalm back to him in his honor (consider using Psalm 145, 146, 147, or 148).

God values you. You are important to him. He knows everything about you—every wart and freckle, every sin and doubt, everything. And still **he loves you.** Amazing! A God like that is worth praising and serving, don't you think?

Here's What I'm Going to Do

☐ _____

☐ _____

☐ _____

_____

_____

THE MEASURE OF REAL LIFE

If you only bought a certain brand of soft drink, you would be cool. If you only drove a certain kind of car, you would be sexy. If you only wore this kind of jeans, you'd be truly admired.

Advertisers spend billions of dollars every year trying to make you think you need whatever their product is in order to be happier, more fulfilled, more accepted, more satisfied. And yet can carbonated sugar water, a bunch of metal and plastic parts, or a collection of woven threads really have that much power over our lives?

Silly, isn't it? But think about it. Do you have an unconscious list of things you really **need** to get in order to be **truly happy?** Thought so. So what does Jesus have to say about all this?

> Luke 12:13-21: 13Then someone called from the crowd, "Teacher, please tell my brother to divide our father's estate with me." 14Jesus replied, "Friend, who made me a judge over you to decide such things as that?" 15Then he said, "Beware! Don't be greedy for what you don't have. Real life is not measured by how much we own."
>
> 16And he gave an illustration: "A rich man had a fertile farm that produced fine crops. 17In fact, his barns were full to overflowing. 18So he said, 'I know! I'll tear down my barns and build bigger ones. Then I'll have room enough to store everything. 19And I'll sit back and say to myself, My friend, you have enough stored away for years to come. Now take it easy! Eat, drink, and be merry!' 20But God said to him, 'You fool! You will die this very night. Then who will get it all?' 21Yes, a person is a fool to store up earthly wealth but not have a rich relationship with God."

Jesus uses the opportunity of a family squabble that a man

brings to his attention in order to make a broader point to his listeners: "Don't be greedy for what you don't have. **Real life is not measured by how much we own"** (v. 15).

You see, the "good life"—the life that is fulfilling, exciting, satisfying, and real—has nothing to do with how much money we have or what possessions we own. Our society wants us to believe differently, but Jesus is speaking **the truth.** He tells the story of a rich man who owned so much, his barns wouldn't hold everything. He decided to tear down his old barns and build barns that were *New! Improved! Bigger!*

PRAYER POINT

Ask God to make your relationship with him richer and richer. That may involve rethinking your finances—and your giving to him. Talk to him about how you can be more giving on earth . . . and more "wealthy" in heaven.

Better! Then he'd really have everything he needed.

But first, a word from this man's sponsor—God: "Surprise! You fool! Tonight you're going to die. And there's no time left to enjoy your barn full of possessions. You're out of here!"

The tagline? Jesus put it this way: "Yes, a person is a **fool** to store up earthly wealth but not have a rich relationship with God" (v. 21).

HERE'S WHAT I'M GOING TO DO

☐ _____

_____

☐ _____

_____

_____

THE HEART'S TREASURE

Look around your room at the little treasures you have on a shelf, desk, or table. As you look at each object, take note of why you keep it—why it's **special** to you, what it means to you.

The old rag doll you had as a baby. The stuffed bear you slept with as a toddler. The photos of you and your friends. The cartoon mug your best friend gave you that makes you laugh every time you read it. The beautiful seashell you found on the beach when you and your friend were walking and talking. The cross you made out of Popsicle sticks at vacation Bible school. The trophy you won when your team made it to the soccer finals. On and on the memories flood your mind. **You treasure those things because they are dear to you.** You think about them. You feel certain things about them. They are precious to you.

With that idea in mind, read today's passage.

Luke 12:33-34: ³³"Sell what you have and give to those in need. This will store up treasure for you in heaven! And the purses of heaven have no holes in them. Your treasure will be safe—no thief can steal it and no moth can destroy it. ³⁴Wherever your treasure is, there your heart and thoughts will also be."

Jesus makes a bold statement to emphasize a very important point: Heavenly treasure is **far more valuable** than earthly treasure. To get that across, he goes so far as to suggest that you sell everything you have and give to those in need.

What would happen if you did that? You could get by with very little on earth, and you would be storing up vast treasure in heaven. Jesus challenges us to decide *now* to **make God first.**

Then Jesus explains, "Wherever your treasure is, there your heart and thoughts will also be" (v. 34). Whatever we value will become the center of our lives. If we choose God above all else, our thoughts will dwell constantly on him. And the treasure that comes from life in God cannot be taken from us. Money, on the other hand, is a relentless master. When it becomes our reason for living, it consumes our thoughts, our plans, our interests, our time, and our energy, but it does not satisfy. An obsession with money also **keeps us from using God's gifts as he intended.**

Jesus isn't saying there's anything wrong with having things that are meaningful and precious to you. But he is challenging you to think about **what your heart and mind routinely dwell on.**

Is it money and earthly possessions or heavenly treasures earned by obedient, sacrificial acts of service?

PRAYER POINT

Let those meaningful objects around your room prompt your prayer time today. Pray for your friends and family members who are connected to those objects. Then ask God to give you treasures in heaven that are just as meaningful and important to you as these objects are. Ask him for an opportunity today to store up some treasure in heaven.

HERE'S WHAT I'M GOING TO DO

☐ _____

_____

☐ _____

_____

_____

ARE YOU READY FOR THIS?

DAY

192

Have you ever been caught doing something you **weren't** supposed to be doing? Be honest now!

Say your parents were out for the evening, and you thought you'd have a little fun. Maybe you rented a movie you knew you shouldn't be watching or invited a friend over to get into a little "harmless" mischief. Only your parents decided to make a short night of it and came home a lot earlier than you'd expected. It was a pretty bad scene. Of course, you've learned a lot from that and will never do anything like it again, right?

Jesus tells a story very similar to that one—but the **consequences** are much more devastating. They are eternal.

Luke 12:35-47: 35"Be dressed for service and well prepared, 36as though you were waiting for your master to return from the wedding feast. Then you will be ready to open the door and let him in the moment he arrives and knocks. 37There will be special favor for those who are ready and waiting for his return. I tell you, he himself will seat them, put on an apron, and serve them as they sit and eat! 38He may come in the middle of the night or just before dawn.[1] But whenever he comes, there will be special favor for his servants who are ready!

39"Know this: A homeowner who knew exactly when a burglar was coming would not permit the house to be broken into. 40You must be ready all the time, for the Son of Man will come when least expected." 41Peter asked, "Lord, is this illustration just for us or for everyone?"

42And the Lord replied, "I'm talking to any faithful, sensible servant to whom the master gives the responsibility of managing his household and feeding his family. 43If the master returns and finds that the servant has done a good job, there will be a reward. 44I assure you, the master will put that servant in charge of all he owns. 45But if the servant thinks, 'My

---

[1] **12:38** Greek *in the second or third watch.*

master won't be back for a while,' and begins oppressing the other servants, partying, and getting drunk—⁴⁶well, the master will return unannounced and unexpected. He will tear the servant apart and banish him with the unfaithful. ⁴⁷The servant will be severely punished, for though he knew his duty, he refused to do it."

Jesus often told his disciples that he would leave this world only to return at some future time—a time only the Father knows. In the meantime, he wants his followers to be ready for his return.

If we adopt the attitude that the unfaithful servant demonstrated, thinking, "My master won't be back for a while," and then waste time pursuing frivolous and ungodly activities—then we may be in for an unwanted surprise.

Jesus promises to reward those who live **faithfully** while they wait for his return. Our rewards in eternity will reflect our activities done in his name on earth.

God has given you a lot. And as he explains, "Much is required from those to whom much is given, and much more is required from those to whom much more is given" (v. 48). Wouldn't it be great to "get caught" doing something meaningful and wonderful for somebody who needs it?

PRAYER POINT

Do you need to confess any activities and behaviors that have been keeping you from living a responsible, mature life with God? Ask God to cleanse you, forgive you, and fill you with his Spirit to help you be ready for Jesus' return.

HERE'S WHAT I'M GOING TO DO

THE GUEST LIST

If you were throwing a dinner party and could invite any ten people who ever lived, whom would you choose? Think of it—any ten people, living or dead, famous or infamous. Depending on how creative you wanted to get, you could have some fun with your guest list. Why not invite Abraham Lincoln and Julius Caesar just to see what kind of conversation they might have?

Dinner parties in New Testament times usually had very specific guest lists. In the middle of one such party, Jesus proposed some rather **radical changes** to these guest lists. Let's see what he had to say.

> Luke 14:12-14: ¹²Then he turned to his host. "When you put on a luncheon or a dinner," he said, "don't invite your friends, brothers, relatives, and rich neighbors. For they will repay you by inviting you back. ¹³Instead, invite the poor, the crippled, the lame, and the blind. ¹⁴Then at the resurrection of the godly, God will reward you for inviting those who could not repay you."

Reciprocity is a fancy term for doing something for another person and then expecting something of equal value in return. Reciprocity was a **key concept** in the Middle Eastern culture of Jesus' day. Dinner party hosts usually restricted their guest lists to include only people who could "repay" them by hosting a dinner party for them.

Jesus pointed out that it's no great sacrifice to invite someone to dinner when you know that you will be repaid for it later. A **more generous** and **loving** act would be to invite the poor, the crippled, the lame, and the blind—**people who cannot repay the generosity.**

The same concept holds true today—even without a dinner party. Let's say, for instance, that the most popular kid in school asked for help on a homework assignment. What would you say? Most people would probably say yes because they would see it as an opportunity to get in good with the popular crowd at school. On the other hand, what if the least popular kid in school asked for homework help? Most would probably find an excuse not to do it.

This is the kind of attitude Jesus is addressing. We must learn to help those who **really need us**—those who can't offer us anything in return. True generosity is **one-sided.** It involves doing things for others simply because we care about them and because God expects us to—without any thought about what's in it for us.

Ultimately, true generosity is not one-sided. Eventually we will be repaid—and then some—for everything we do on behalf of the poor and needy. We may never see any evidence of this repayment in this world, but we can certainly expect it in heaven.

PRAYER POINT

Ask God to make you aware of someone in your community to whom you can show some one-sided generosity, doing things for that person without expecting anything in return.

HERE'S WHAT I'M GOING TO DO

- [ ]
- [ ]
- [ ]

A Distorted Image

Day

194

Imagine that you grew up in a house with funhouse mirrors—the kind that **distort** your features. Every time you looked in a mirror, the reflection you saw was that of an oversized Mr. Potato Head. You probably would grow up thinking that's what you really look like. If nobody ever told you the truth, you'd live your entire life believing that you were different from other people, simply because you had a **distorted self-image.**

Although the Pharisees didn't have funhouse mirrors, they definitely had distorted opinions of themselves and others. Let's see what Jesus had to say about their views.

Luke 15:1-7: 1Tax collectors and other notorious sinners often came to listen to Jesus teach. 2This made the Pharisees and teachers of religious law complain that he was associating with such despicable people—even eating with them! 3So Jesus used this illustration: 4"If you had one hundred sheep, and one of them strayed away and was lost in the wilderness, wouldn't you leave the ninety-nine others to go and search for the lost one until you found it? 5And then you would joyfully carry it home on your shoulders. 6When you arrived, you would call together your friends and neighbors to rejoice with you because your lost sheep was found. 7In the same way, heaven will be happier over one lost sinner who returns to God than over ninety-nine others who are righteous and haven't strayed away!"

Tax collectors in Jesus' day worked for the Roman government; the Jews branded them as traitors. Furthermore, they had a reputation for being corrupt. It's probably safe to say that in New Testament times tax collectors were considered to be the scum of the earth. That's why the Pharisees and teachers of the law complained when Jesus shared a meal with such "sinners."

The Pharisees wondered why Jesus associated with sinners—people who admitted that they needed him—when he could have been hanging around religious leaders and teachers of the law—people who believed that they didn't need him.

This parable shows just how deeply **God cares for those who are lost.** No matter how far a person strays into sin, the Lord will look for him or her. If and when that person is found, all heaven rejoices. That's why it's important for us to join the "search party."

PRAYER POINT

Ask God to help you expand your circle of acquaintances to include people you normally might not associate with, while at the same time maintaining a strong Christian commitment.

Like the Pharisees, some Christians today have a tendency to isolate themselves from "obvious sinners"—despite the fact that these are the people who need to hear of Jesus' love the most.

Jesus set the example. He didn't spend his time on earth preaching to the Pharisees and other religious leaders; he met "sinners" where they lived. In order to follow Christ's example, we need to **break out of our comfort zones** and learn to approach people we normally would avoid. We need to **carry the Lord's message of hope** to those who need—and want—to hear it most.

HERE'S WHAT I'M GOING TO DO

☐ _____

_____

☐ _____

_____

THE MONEY TEST

Imagine that you've just become the manager of a new music store. Business is sluggish. So you decide on an aggressive sales campaign: You discount every title to the bone for one weekend only. You're anxious to get customers and willing to take the risk. And it works! People come from miles around to get their favorite titles. The owner is so encouraged he gives you a big raise.

Jesus also told a story about a **risk-taking** manager who was anxious to keep his customers coming back.

Luke 16:1-9: ¹Jesus told this story to his disciples: "A rich man hired a manager to handle his affairs, but soon a rumor went around that the manager was thoroughly dishonest. ²So his employer called him in and said, 'What's this I hear about your stealing from me? Get your report in order, because you are going to be dismissed.' ³The manager thought to himself, 'Now what? I'm through here, and I don't have the strength to go out and dig ditches, and I'm too proud to beg. ⁴I know just the thing! And then I'll have plenty of friends to take care of me when I leave!'

⁵"So he invited each person who owed money to his employer to come and discuss the situation. He asked the first one, 'How much do you owe him?' ⁶The man replied, 'I owe him eight hundred gallons of olive oil.' So the manager told him, 'Tear up that bill and write another one for four hundred gallons.¹ ' ⁷'And how much do you owe my employer?' he asked the next man. 'A thousand bushels of wheat,' was the reply. 'Here,' the manager said, 'take your bill and replace it with one for only eight hundred bushels.² ' ⁸The rich man had to admire the dishonest rascal for being so shrewd. And it is true that the citizens of this world are more shrewd than the godly are. ⁹I tell you, use your worldly resources to

¹ **16:6** Greek *100 baths . . . 50 [baths].*
² **16:7** Greek *100 korous . . . 80 [korous].*
³ **16:9** Or *Then when you run out at the end of this life, your friends will welcome you into eternal homes.*

benefit others and make friends. In this way, your generosity stores up a reward for you in heaven.[3]

The parable Jesus told may be a little confusing, but the main point of the story is that the manager **wisely prepared** for his future by creating a situation in which his master's debtors would actually be in debt to him for reducing the amount they owed. Jesus used this story to illustrate for his disciples the importance of being **wise users of material possessions.**

We can use money in three basic ways: (1) **We can spend it** to fulfill our basic needs, such as food, shelter, and clothing; (2) **we can use it** to satisfy needs, some of them important (a new business computer, books for school), some trivial (concert tickets, junk food); or (3) **we can give it away** to help others. With that in mind, carefully examine in the days ahead the way you spend your money. Here are a couple of questions to ask: First, do you demonstrate with your money that you can be trusted with greater responsibilities? Second, what changes can you make in your spending in order to invest more in God's Kingdom?

HERE'S WHAT I'M GOING TO DO

☐ _____

_____

☐ _____

_____

SPIRITUAL JOURNEY TRAVEL LOG

Rich Man, Poor Man

Have you ever seen the bumper stickers that read, "He who dies with the most toys wins" or "Hearses don't have luggage racks." These **opposite views** of the value of **money** and **possessions** are powerfully illustrated in Jesus' parable of the rich man and Lazarus in the Gospel of Luke.

Day 196

Luke 16:19-31: [19]Jesus said, "There was a certain rich man who was splendidly clothed and who lived each day in luxury. [20]At his door lay a diseased beggar named Lazarus. [21]As Lazarus lay there longing for scraps from the rich man's table, the dogs would come and lick his open sores. [22]Finally, the beggar died and was carried by the angels to be with Abraham.[1] The rich man also died and was buried, [23]and his soul went to the place of the dead.[2] There, in torment, he saw Lazarus in the far distance with Abraham.

[24]"The rich man shouted, 'Father Abraham, have some pity! Send Lazarus over here to dip the tip of his finger in water and cool my tongue, because I am in anguish in these flames.' [25]But Abraham said to him, 'Son, remember that during your lifetime you had everything you wanted, and Lazarus had nothing. So now he is here being comforted, and you are in anguish. [26]And besides, there is a great chasm separating us. Anyone who wanted to cross over to you from here is stopped at its edge, and no one there can cross over to us.'

[27]"Then the rich man said, 'Please, Father Abraham, send him to my father's home. [28]For I have five brothers, and I want him to warn them about this place of torment so they won't have to come here when they die.' [29]But Abraham said, 'Moses and the prophets have warned them. Your brothers can read their writings anytime they want to.' [30]The rich man replied, 'No, Father Abraham! But if someone is sent to them from

[1] **16:22** Greek *into Abraham's bosom.*
[2] **16:23** Greek *to Hades.*

the dead, then they will turn from their sins.'
³¹But Abraham said, 'If they won't listen to Moses and the prophets, they won't listen even if someone rises from the dead.' "

The rich man had it made in this world, strutting around in expensive clothes, eating the best foods, traveling first class all the way. Lazarus, on the other hand, lived a life of misery. He was so **desperate for food** that the crumbs from the rich man's table looked good to him. He had nothing.

When the two men died, however, their situations **changed—drastically.** Lazarus was carried away by angels. The rich man found himself in hell, the place of eternal torture. Can you imagine the horror the rich man must have felt when he realized that his riches could do him no good anymore?

This story should stand as a strong warning to anyone who allows material possessions to rule life. These things will vanish like smoke when our lives end. When we stand before God, we will have to answer for **the things we have done** and **the priorities we have set** in this life.

HERE'S WHAT I'M GOING TO DO

UP A TREE

People are innately **curious.** What else can explain the way we slow down to stare at car wrecks? Why else would so many buy tabloid newspapers? You've heard the saying "Curiosity killed the cat." Maybe today's reading should be headlined "Curiosity saved the tax collector."

Luke 19:1-10: ¹Jesus entered Jericho and made his way through the town. ²There was a man there named Zacchaeus. He was one of the most influential Jews in the Roman tax-collecting business, and he had become very rich. ³He tried to get a look at Jesus, but he was too short to see over the crowds. ⁴So he ran ahead and climbed a sycamore tree beside the road, so he could watch from there. ⁵When Jesus came by, he looked up at Zacchaeus and called him by name. "Zacchaeus!" he said. "Quick, come down! For I must be a guest in your home today." ⁶Zacchaeus quickly climbed down and took Jesus to his house in great excitement and joy. ⁷But the crowds were displeased. "He has gone to be the guest of a notorious sinner," they grumbled.

⁸Meanwhile, Zacchaeus stood there and said to the Lord, "I will give half my wealth to the poor, Lord, and if I have overcharged people on their taxes, I will give them back four times as much!" ⁹Jesus responded, "Salvation has come to this home today, for this man has shown himself to be a son of Abraham. ¹⁰And I, the Son of Man, have come to seek and save those like him who are lost."

Imagine being Zacchaeus.

You have heard all about the miracle-working carpenter from Nazareth and got word he was coming to your town. Something—curiosity, desire, emptiness—drew you to go see for yourself. Then it happened. Jesus stopped and spoke to you. To you! You were so shocked, you almost fell out of the tree! When he invited himself to your home, you shifted nervously amidst the leaves. Everyone was watching and whispering. But somehow you didn't care anymore.

As you climbed down and walked away with the teacher, you felt a cataclysmic change take place in your heart. You forgot the buzzing crowds around you. In that moment, you were engulfed by love. Despite being short and insecure, dishonest and despised, Jesus had **accepted you completely and unconditionally.** You know at last you're free. This man talked to you not because of your money or status but because he wanted to.

Zacchaeus' story reminds us of a simple truth: Jesus accepts *you* just as he accepted a despised tax collector. Let that fact cause you to **respond joyfully to others** the way Jesus responds to you.

HERE'S WHAT I'M GOING TO DO

☐ _____

_____

_____

BORROWERS

A friend calls you one day because she's heard that you have a terrific novel she wants to borrow. You're a little reluctant because she has a tendency to be **careless** with her belongings. Eventually, you agree to lend her the book.

Almost two months later, she finally returns the novel. The cover is torn. The binding is cracked. Worst of all, every page has underlining and comments—in pen.

Some people are just as **careless with the gifts God has given them,** as Jesus once told in this parable:

Luke 19:12-26: [12]He said, "A nobleman was called away to a distant empire to be crowned king and then return. [13]Before he left, he called together ten servants and gave them ten pounds of silver[1] to invest for him while he was gone. [14]But his people hated him and sent a delegation after him to say they did not want him to be their king.

[15]"When he returned, the king called in the servants to whom he had given the money. He wanted to find out what they had done with the money and what their profits were. [16]The first servant reported a tremendous gain—ten times as much as the original amount! [17]'Well done!' the king exclaimed. 'You are a trustworthy servant. You have been faithful with the little I entrusted to you, so you will be governor of ten cities as your reward.' [18]The next servant also reported a good gain—five times the original amount. [19]'Well done!' the king said. 'You can be governor over five cities.' [20]But the third servant brought back only the original amount of money and said, 'I hid it and kept it safe. [21]I was afraid because you are a hard man to deal with, taking what isn't yours and harvesting crops you didn't plant.'

[22]" 'You wicked servant!' the king roared. 'Hard, am I? If you knew so much about me and how tough I am, [23]why didn't you deposit the money

---

[1] **19:13** Greek *10 minas;* 1 mina was worth about 3 months' wages.
[2] **19:26** Or *who have nothing.*

in the bank so I could at least get some interest on it?' ²⁴Then turning to the others standing nearby, the king ordered, 'Take the money from this servant, and give it to the one who earned the most.' ²⁵'But, master,' they said, 'that servant has enough already!' ²⁶'Yes,' the king replied, 'but to those who use well what they are given, even more will be given. But from those who are unfaithful,² even what little they have will be taken away.' "

Jesus wants us to see several truths through this parable: (1) He has given each of us certain **resources** to use for his glory. All come from him, and all should be used for him. (2) He is coming back one day. We should live with an **awareness of his return.** (3) We will one day be assessed for how well we have **served God** with the resources he has given (2 Corinthians 5:10). (4) Our future rewards will be determined by how faithfully we are serving him in the **present** (2 Timothy 4:8; James 1:12; 1 Peter 5:4).

PRAYER POINT

Pray for faithfulness in managing all God has entrusted to you. Pray for opportunities to multiply your "allowances." Trust God for opportunities to share the gift of the gospel with those who have yet to receive it.

HERE'S WHAT I'M GOING TO DO

☐ _____

_____

☐ _____

_____

☐ _____

_____

GIVE ME ALL YOUR MITE

In his book *Real Hope in Chicago*, pastor Wayne Gordon remembers the time the members of his congregation began building a gymnasium, even though they were unsure how to completely fund the project. "One day I heard a knock on the door. . . . It was [senior citizen] Mary Rhodes. She reached out to hand me an envelope. . . . I opened up this envelope to find a money order in the amount of $1,000. Reminded of the biblical account of the widow's mite, I could not help but start to cry."

This is the story to which Pastor Gordon was referring:

Luke 21:1-4: ¹While Jesus was in the Temple, he watched the rich people putting their gifts into the collection box. ²Then a poor widow came by and dropped in two pennies.[1] ³"I assure you," he said, "this poor widow has given more than all the rest of them. ⁴For they have given a tiny part of their surplus, but she, poor as she is, has given everything she has."

This account of a woman dropping a Roman lepta or mite (a coin worth about two cents) into a Temple treasury box reveals that Jesus has an interesting way of **measuring giving.** According to this story, affluent people who give their leftovers do not touch the heart of God so much as an old woman on Social Security who drops a dollar bill into the offering plate. Apparently, Jesus is saying the **real issue** isn't the amount we give but **the attitude with which we give it.**

Think about it. If a millionaire gives $50,000 to the church missions fund, everyone oohs and aahs. Certainly that's a sizable amount of money, but it's not a very sacrificial gift. (It's not real hard to imagine living on $950,000!) But suppose a retiree with only $10 to his name (cash that needs to last until the end of the week) gives that money to the missions campaign. Do you see that he has made **an incredible**

[1] **21:2** Greek *2 lepta.*

offering to God? Not big in terms of sheer monetary value, but huge in terms of devotion and love. And that's the kind of gift God wants.

PRAYER POINT

Ask God to make you like the widow in Luke 21: a selfless, sacrificial, generous giver.

Sacrifice means being willing to do without. It also means giving up control. Mary Rhodes gave $1,000 to help build an inner-city gym. This sum was a drop in the bucket in terms of the total amount needed, but it was (nearly) everything she had. And when she gave her money to the building effort, she gave up her say on how it was to be used from that point on. That kind of "no-strings-attached" giving **pleases God.**

According to Jesus, what we do with our material wealth is **a very good test of our spiritual health** (Matthew 6:19-21). How we handle money speaks volumes about what we truly believe. Merely giving God our leftovers (whether money, time, or energy) shows that he is not the ultimate priority in our lives.

When we give sacrificially to God, however, he always fills us with enough to go on. And often he **blesses** us beyond what we ever imagined (Luke 6:38; Acts 20:35).

HERE'S WHAT I'M GOING TO DO

☐ _____

☐ _____

_____

_____

SACRIFICING

You stare out at the pitching mound, wave the aluminum bat across a sand-covered plate, and glance at your teammate standing on third base. The score is tied 3-3 with one out. You see the pitch, as if in slow motion. You swing, hear a firm clink, and watch the ball soar up into the blue sky. Though the center fielder easily catches your fly ball, you turn around in time to see your teammate tag up and trot home with the winning run.

In baseball, that play is called a *sacrifice* because the hitter, thinking only about the good of the team, does whatever he can to advance the runner. In today's reading, Jesus talks about the **personal sacrifice** he will make for the good of the world.

John 3:13-17: ¹³"For only I, the Son of Man¹ have come to earth and will return to heaven again. ¹⁴And as Moses lifted up the bronze snake on a pole in the wilderness, so I, the Son of Man, must be lifted up on a pole,² ¹⁵so that everyone who believes in me will have eternal life.

¹⁶"For God so loved the world that he gave his only Son, so that everyone who believes in him will not perish but have eternal life. ¹⁷God did not send his Son into the world to condemn it, but to save it."

The idea of sacrificing means **letting go of personal goals and working selflessly for larger purposes.** Christ is the ultimate example of this. As the Creator (Colossians 1:16), all of life is under his control. But by offering himself as the ultimate sacrifice, Jesus put the needs of his creatures **above** his own desires. He surrendered his chance for quick fame and glory (Matthew 4:8-11; John 6:15). He humbly and willingly complied with the wishes of his Father (Philippians 2:5-8). All of his energies were focused on "advancing us" to heaven. What else can explain the cruel

¹ **3:13** Some manuscripts add *who lives in heaven.*
² **3:14** Greek *must be lifted up.*

agony he endured at the cross on our behalf? **He laid down his life** that we might find **eternal life with God in heaven.**

Speaking on another occasion, Jesus said, "The greatest love is shown when people lay down their lives for their friends" (John 15:13). This is the essence of what we're talking about. To sacrifice is to "lay down your life." It means letting go of your own ambitions, exchanging your agenda for God's plan. And so the question is, "In view of the great sacrifice that Christ has made on your behalf, how much do you sacrifice for him? For others?"

According to Paul, your **whole life** should be one "living and holy sacrifice" (Romans 12:1). Is it?

PRAYER POINT

Take a moment to thank God for his sacrificial love. Pray for the selflessness and strength to follow Christ as a "living sacrifice" (Romans 12:1), loving others no matter how different, odd, or far-out they may seem.

HERE'S WHAT I'M GOING TO DO

☐ _____

☐ _____

☐ _____

☐ _____

A Gift of Quiet Confidence

Brooke Kolconay, 19, spent two weeks in Mozambique in 1994 on the 30 Hour Famine Study Tour. Today, she is a sophomore at Boston College in Massachusetts, where she majors in international studies. She plays volleyball, basketball, and softball and is actively involved in community services. Brooke loves chocolate and Marvin Gaye and is considering Peace Corps service after graduation.

Two weeks after my World Vision trip to Africa, my best friend died in a car accident. Then, two weeks after that, my parents announced they were getting divorced. At the same time, my sister, who is the closest person to me, left for college.

I felt alone—like my world was crashing down. All the strength I thought I had was depleted.

That was when I fell from my Christian walk. I didn't understand why things were happening. It took a complete year-and-a-half to get back up again and feel confident that God wasn't trying to hurt me.

My faith has just grown so much since then. Now I witness to people without having to say as much. It's more part of my life. I don't know if my faith would have ever been this strong if those circumstances hadn't happened.

And I think back to how God spoke to me in a very special way during those first weeks after my trip. Maybe it was to prepare me for what I would be going through. It was a sermon at church on Psalm 46:10—"Be silent, and know that I am God!"

That just rocked my world. After the trip, I was overwhelmed, thinking, "I need to do this, and I need to do that, and I need to . . . whatever, to fix everything." Then came the death, divorce, and my sister's departure.

Now I know that some way or other, God will put paths in my life and work things out so that whatever needs to be done, I can do. Today, I encourage you to keep your faith—and know that he is God.

When the
eyes of the
soul looking
out meet the
eyes of God
looking in,
heaven has
begun right
here on this
earth.

A. W. Tozer

THE STANDARD FOR GIVING

I think that everyone needs to experience, at least once, going overseas and helping better the lives of those less fortunate than we are. You never know how fortunate you are until you see the struggles that so many others have to endure daily just to survive. The experience is one that you will treasure and certainly never forget.

In August 1996, I left my comfort zone of friends and music to see if there was any way that God could use me in Haiti. I spent a lot of time in prayer and felt that I was ready for anything. Two things really hit me hard when I landed in Port-au-Prince: the extreme poverty and the heat! Never before had I seen such a rundown and

Reality Check

destroyed city. When we got through customs and I was able to see more of the city up close, things didn't look any better. So many people looked depressed—my heart began to hurt for them.

We drove to a tiny village called Flammand, where I was to spend the majority of my 10 days in Haiti. There we worked with the people of the village to build a wall around their church and school. A few days earlier, some kids were reported missing—no one knew where they were. A missionary who lived in the village explained that most likely these kids had been kidnapped and sold into slavery and prostitution.

In Haiti everything is for sale. The average annual income there is $400. Most families live in little thatched huts, often with six to eight people in each one. Most villages, including Flammand, have virtually no business.

Despite these disheartening facts, the Haitians in this poor village were the most giving people I have ever met. This made a tremendous impact on me.

Many times we get so possession-oriented. We want things so that other people will think we look good. But then we don't want to share. Basically it comes down to selfishness. Americans, myself included, tend to be very selfish. In contrast, Haitians will give you anything that they can simply to ensure your happiness. There is a very important lesson here. Christ gave everything he had and kept nothing for himself when he died on the cross to pay the penalty for our sins. He did that to give us the opportunity to have eternal life.

Christ set the standard for giving, and many times I fall short of that standard. When I don't follow Christ, I let him down. But he continues to give.

WASTE NOT

Two weeks before Bryan's family was to move to a new town, a lady from his church told him and his sisters that she wanted to make them a farewell meal. She instructed the kids to write down all of their favorite foods on a sheet of paper, so they did. Only their list didn't fit on one page, so they gave her two.

Two weeks later, when they arrived at her house for lunch after church, they were stunned to discover that she had prepared almost everything on their list! Fried chicken, hamburgers, bologna sandwiches, chocolate chip cookies, ice cream, potato chips, Twinkies, and at least six different kinds of pop stood on the long table. There was just one problem: Bryan and his sisters weren't hungry because they had devoured an entire box of cereal before church! Most of the food the woman had prepared **went to waste.**

The Gospel of John provides a more thoughtful example of dealing with leftover food.

> John 6:10-13: [10]"Tell everyone to sit down," Jesus ordered. So all of them—the men alone numbered five thousand—sat down on the grassy slopes. [11]Then Jesus took the loaves, gave thanks to God, and passed them out to the people. Afterward he did the same with the fish. And they all ate until they were full. [12]"Now gather the leftovers," Jesus told his disciples, "so that nothing is wasted." [13]There were only five barley loaves to start with, but twelve baskets were filled with the pieces of bread the people did not eat!

Most people, when they read this passage, focus on the miraculous feeding of the five thousand—as well they should. However, we should be careful not to overlook the example Jesus sets for believers at the end of this story. "Let nothing be wasted," he instructed, as his disciples collected every piece of bread that was left over after the five thousand had been fed.

What would happen if our society adopted the motto "Let nothing be wasted"? We live in a land of abundance. Unfortunately, one of the things that seems to go along with **abundance** is **waste.**

Perhaps with some careful planning, we can begin to take **small steps** toward **correcting this situation.** What if we reduced our grocery bills—and thus, the amount of food we bring home—by, say, fifteen dollars a month and donated the extra money to a local homeless shelter? What if, rather than spending money to eat out, we eat the food we have at home and use the extra bucks to support a needy child overseas? These are just two suggestions to get you thinking. If you put your mind to it, you'll probably be able to come up with a much better plan for **reducing the amount of food you waste and wisely distributing your resources.**

HERE'S WHAT I'M GOING TO DO

☐ _____

☐ _____

☐ _____

FIRST THINGS FIRST

How impulsive are you in your everyday life? Are you the type of person who would shave off all of your hair just because you got the urge to do it? Or are you the type of person who prefers a three-week advance notice before making any decision?

One of the most (seemingly) **impulsive acts of faith** in all of Scripture is found in John 12. In this passage, Mary, the sister of Martha, does something that draws an unusual reaction from one of Jesus' disciples.

John 12:1-8: ¹Six days before the Passover ceremonies began, Jesus arrived in Bethany, the home of Lazarus—the man he had raised from the dead. ²A dinner was prepared in Jesus' honor. Martha served, and Lazarus sat at the table with him. ³Then Mary took a twelve-ounce jar¹ of expensive perfume made from essence of nard, and she anointed Jesus' feet with it and wiped his feet with her hair. And the house was filled with fragrance.

⁴But Judas Iscariot, one of his disciples—the one who would betray him— said, ⁵"That perfume was worth a small fortune.² It should have been sold and the money given to the poor." ⁶Not that he cared for the poor—he was a thief who was in charge of the disciples' funds, and he often took some for his own use.

⁷Jesus replied, "Leave her alone. She did it in preparation for my burial. ⁸You will always have the poor among you, but I will not be here with you much longer."

Not only was Judas the most notorious traitor in history, he was also a fledgling scam artist. Check out his supposed concern for the poor in this passage. As the keeper of the

---

1 **12:3** Greek *took 1 litra* [327 grams].
2 **12:5** Greek *300 denarii.* A denarius was equivalent to a full day's wage.

money bag for the disciples, Judas was the one who collected the offerings given by Jesus' followers. Despite his pious behavior, Judas had apparently made a habit of skimming money from the bag for his own personal use. Of course, he couldn't very well have said, "Hey, I could have sold that perfume and kept the money for myself!" So instead he objected on behalf of the poor—but he really cared little about them.

PRAYER POINT

Spend some time in prayer,

showing the same type of adoration

for the Lord that Mary showed

when she washed Jesus' feet.

Despite the fact that Judas was insincere in his concern for the poor, we can use this passage to make an important point about **priorities.** Mary's unusual—and very expensive—gesture was not very "religious" according to the custom of the day, but it showed clearly that her **heart** was in the **right place.** So even if Judas' objections concerning the poor were sincere, he still would have been wrong to question Mary.

Mary's unmistakable devotion should cause us to examine ourselves. **Are we willing to give all to Christ?** If we minister to others for any other reason than our love for God, we will always miss the mark.

HERE'S WHAT I'M GOING TO DO

☐ _____

_____

☐ _____

_____

☐ _____

_____

LOVE ONE ANOTHER HOW?!

DAY

203

Did you know that more songs have been written about **love** than any other topic? In fact, music has quite a bit to say on the topic. Let's see . . . Love can make you happy. Love changes everything. Love hurts. Love is a battlefield. Love is a hurtin' thing. Love is a many-splendored thing. Love is a wonderful thing. Love is a stranger. Love is all you need. Love is like oxygen. Love is alive. Love is all around. Love is forever. Love is in control. Love is in the air. And of course, love is like a rock.

As informative as music may be, perhaps the **most important thing** we need to know about love is found in John 13.

> John 13:34: ³⁴"So now I am giving you a new commandment: Love each other. Just as I have loved you, you should love each other."

This is really a two-part command that Jesus gives. The first part is a piece of cake: "Love one another." Yeah, OK, no sweat. We Christians can show love to one another. We'll worship together in church. We'll pray for each other. We'll eat fellowship dinners together. We'll control our tempers in church-league basketball and softball games.

The second part of the command is more difficult—a lot more difficult: "As I have loved you, so you must love one another." Whoa. **Love each other as Jesus loved us?** Now you're talking about sacrificial love, love that manifests itself not only through words but through actions. It's love that is **unconditional.**

Think about how Christ demonstrated his love for us. Because there was no other way for us to be reconciled to God, Jesus left his glory in heaven to assume human form. He allowed himself to be tortured and executed in order to pay the price for our sins. **There is no greater example of love in human history.** And we're supposed to have that kind of love for one another? How? Sacrifice, sacrifice, sacrifice.

If we are to love somebody the way that Christ loved us, we've got to be prepared to **give up** our time, our energy, our comfort, and our material possessions for that person. That's a serious relationship, one that requires a **tremendous commitment.** That's the kind of relationship Jesus calls you to!

PRAYER POINT

Take a few minutes to praise the Lord for his example of sacrificial love. Identify the aspects and demonstrations of his love that you most appreciate.

HERE'S WHAT I'M GOING TO DO

❑ _____

_____

❑ _____

_____

❑ _____

_____

❑ _____

_____

❑ _____

_____

❑ _____

_____

A WORLDWIDE IMPACT

A side from Jesus, name five people whose actions, accomplishments, or lives have **changed the world.** Can you think of five off the top of your head? How about Alexander the Great? Christopher Columbus? Copernicus? Galileo? Thomas Edison? Albert Einstein? Dr. Martin Luther King Jr.? It would be interesting to compare lists with other people. Of course, it's quite possible that we're not even aware of the five people who have changed the world most profoundly. After all, who's to say what actions are actually responsible for a change?

Jesus calls us to impact the world around us. In John 17, he offers a fairly detailed prayer for his disciples and their work in this world.

> John 17:9-19: 9"My prayer is not for the world, but for those you have given me, because they belong to you. 10And all of them, since they are mine, belong to you; and you have given them back to me, so they are my glory! 11Now I am departing the world; I am leaving them behind and coming to you. Holy Father, keep them and care for them—all those you have given me—so that they will be united just as we are. 12During my time here, I have kept them safe.[1] I guarded them so that not one was lost, except the one headed for destruction, as the Scriptures foretold.
>
> 13"And now I am coming to you. I have told them many things while I was with them so they would be filled with my joy. 14I have given them your word. And the world hates them because they do not belong to the world, just as I do not. 15I'm not asking you to take them out of the world, but to keep them safe from the evil one. 16They are not part of this world any more than I am. 17Make them pure and holy by teaching them your words of truth. 18As you sent me into the world, I am sending them into the world. 19And I give myself entirely to you so they also might be

[1] **17:12** Greek *I have kept in your name those whom you have given me.*

entirely yours."

In praying for his disciples, Jesus clarifies the Christian's relationship with and responsibility to the world. Even though believers live in the world, **we are not of this world.** Such a contrast may seem confusing. Our eternal home is in heaven, but our work as believers is right here on earth. Jesus sends his followers into the world to proclaim his truth and to model his love and compassion.

Jesus spoke this prayer as he anticipated his arrest and crucifixion. Aware of his approaching suffering, he nonetheless poured out his concerns for his beloved disciples and prayed for their safety and faithfulness. Jesus gave himself **entirely** so that we might belong to the Father. Knowing that, we should have great incentive to **be faithful** to the commands of Jesus. Such faithfulness may have a bigger impact than the most exciting scientific discoveries ever made.

HERE'S WHAT I'M GOING TO DO

☐ _____

_____

☐ _____

_____

☐ _____

_____

SHEEP FEEDERS

Talk about your world-class blunders! In 1631, a couple of printers in London left one word out of an official version of the Bible. No big deal, right? Well, the word they left out was "not"; the verse from which it was omitted is Exodus 20:14. So because of the printers' error, the seventh commandment read, "Thou shalt commit adultery."

The apostle Peter was certainly no stranger to **blunders.** Yet despite Peter's penchant for sticking his foot in his mouth, the Lord **never gave up** on him. Let's take a look at the last recorded encounter between Jesus and Peter.

John 21:15-17: ¹⁵After breakfast Jesus said to Simon Peter, "Simon son of John, do you love me more than these?" "Yes, Lord," Peter replied, "you know I love you." "Then feed my lambs," Jesus told him. ¹⁶Jesus repeated the question: "Simon son of John, do you love me?" "Yes, Lord," Peter said, "you know I love you." "Then take care of my sheep," Jesus said. ¹⁷Once more he asked him, "Simon son of John, do you love me?" Peter was grieved that Jesus asked the question a third time. He said, "Lord, you know everything. You know I love you." Jesus said, "Then feed my sheep."

This is one of the most poignant reunions in all of Scripture. The last time Jesus and Peter spoke before Jesus' crucifixion, Peter had vowed to lay down his life for the Lord. Jesus told Peter that not only would he (Peter) not lay down his life, on three separate occasions that very night, he would actually deny even knowing Jesus! Shortly thereafter, Jesus was arrested and tried. During the trial, Peter was confronted three times by people who claimed he was one of Jesus' followers. Three times Peter denied knowing Jesus, just as Jesus had predicted. When Peter realized what he had done, the Bible says he "wept bitterly" (Luke 22:62).

Imagine Peter's emotional state, then, as he is confronted by the resurrected Jesus near the Sea of Tiberias. Three times the Lord asks Peter if he loves him. Three times Peter answers yes. Three times Jesus instructs Peter to feed or take care of his sheep. With this symbolic gesture, Jesus **forgave** Peter for his three denials and **restored him to ministry.**

Christians today are also called to feed Jesus' sheep—that is, take care of his people. Sometimes that care involves actually feeding people or providing food for needy families and the homeless. Sometimes it involves protecting and standing up for the rights of those who are exploited or powerless in our society. Whatever the responsibility, we are called to **get involved personally** with Jesus' flock. After all, you can't feed sheep unless you're right there next to them.

PRAYER POINT

Ask God to give you the wisdom and opportunity to serve as a "shepherd" to someone else, feeding (whether physically or spiritually) and taking care of that person according to Jesus' instructions to Peter in John 21.

HERE'S WHAT I'M GOING TO DO

☐ _____

_____

☐ _____

_____

☐ _____

_____

_____

Spiritual Journey Travel Log

BRAND GAMES

Advertisements can be pretty slick. They often don't simply provide for our needs; instead, they create needs—or better put, what we *think* are needs. Like sneakers. Sure, you need a decent pair. But a name brand for a couple hundred dollars? Jeans are a must too, but designer ones? We're paying how much for that company's name on the pocket? The problem is, just where do we **draw the line?**

Figuring out **needs** versus **wants** can be pretty tough, and advertisements generally don't help an already difficult process. But this view of the early church is a revealing snapshot of what we're supposed to be about and **what our goals should be.**

> Acts 2:44-45: 44And all the believers met together constantly and shared everything they had. 45They sold their possessions and shared the proceeds with those in need.

Did you catch all that? They shared, they worshiped, they praised, and they added! What a cause for rejoicing! Obviously, they were practicing what we must still do today: Sort through needs versus wants, put our priorities in order, and decisively act on them. These early Christians made the decision to **be poor** and **make others rich** in the Lord . . . rather than seek to be materially rich while making others poor.

Does that mean we must literally be poor? No, of course not, but it does mean that we must choose to live a lifestyle that ultimately **serves God rather than ourselves and our wants.** No, it won't be easy; it will be a constant struggle. But note once again the result of their commitment: People were saved every day (Acts 2:47)! In many ways, it comes down to a clear question and decision. **What will I invest in?** We must constantly evaluate. **Things?** Or **people?**

Picture in your mind that new pair of overpriced sneakers or treating a friend to lunch. Now, which will it be? The right decision sounds like a bargain to me!

PRAYER POINT

When you are alone, consider what wants you have that are not in line with God's desires for your life. Confess these and ask God to change your heart.

HERE'S WHAT I'M GOING TO DO

☐ _____

☐ _____

☐ _____

☐ _____

☐ _____

FIVE FEET OF COURAGE

All of five feet tall, petite and unimposing, Lydia doesn't appear to pose a threat to anyone. Yet she's one courageous woman. Standing firm with the armor of truth, peace, faith, salvation, and the power of the Holy Spirit, Lydia's a valiant warrior for the Lord she humbly serves.

In America, we take for granted the **freedom to obtain and read Bibles,** but China doesn't enjoy these privileges. Therefore, Lydia continually puts herself in great danger by carrying into China a backpack full of Bibles and tracts. Dangerous? Absolutely. Risky for possible imprisonment? Certainly. But does this deter her? Not for one moment.

Read about others who purposefully put themselves in danger:

> Acts 4:1-3: ¹While Peter and John were speaking to the people, the leading priests, the captain of the Temple guard, and some of the Sadducees came over to them. ²They were very disturbed that Peter and John were claiming, on the authority of Jesus, that there is a resurrection of the dead. ³They arrested them and, since it was already evening, jailed them until morning.

Just like these disciples, Lydia knows the risks quite well. She's already been interrogated several times; the authorities know her name. Yet every trip into China finds her seeking ways to carry more (even though that backpack weighs nearly

as much as she does!), to stuff another pocket, to provide yet one more Bible for a seeking soul in a land she loves. For Lydia, **taking risks** is a lifelong ministry, a lifestyle, a passion.

So how do we develop that same

kind of passion? I suppose when we truly grasp the importance of what we're doing, then the risk will not seem so great. And the **rewards** will become crystal clear in their significance. When we actually believe that those rewards far **outweigh the risks,** we'll become valiant Christians like Peter and John and Lydia. Then when we're given the opportunity to share the gospel, we'll exhibit **courage.** When we're called to exchange comfort for sacrifice, we won't refuse. And when we're asked to trust God with great risk, we'll take that step.

If one tiny woman named Lydia can, **so can you.**

PRAYER POINT

Ask God to give you courage to share the gospel today.

HERE'S WHAT I'M GOING TO DO

☐ _____

☐ _____

☐ _____

☐ _____

☐ _____

☐ _____

BIG WHEELS

A 21-speed bike is a great picture of what working together is all about. Sprockets, derailleurs, shifters, control cables, and chains work together (hopefully!) in perfect unison. The result is a smooth transition uphill and down, one that gives endurance, fitness benefits, and sustained power. Now, that's a ride!

Sometimes, however, **one** part of the system gets out of adjustment or breaks. When that happens, obviously the whole mechanism comes to an abrupt stop. And that's pretty much what happened to the early church.

Acts 6:1-7: ¹But as the believers¹ rapidly multiplied, there were rumblings of discontent. Those who spoke Greek complained against those who spoke Hebrew, saying that their widows were being discriminated against in the daily distribution of food. ²So the Twelve called a meeting of all the believers. "We apostles should spend our time preaching and teaching the word of God, not administering a food program," they said. ³"Now look around among yourselves, friends,² and select seven men who are well respected and are full of the Holy Spirit and wisdom. We will put them in charge of this business. ⁴Then we can spend our time in prayer and preaching and teaching the word."

⁵This idea pleased the whole group, and they chose the following: Stephen (a man full of faith and the Holy Spirit), Philip, Procorus, Nicanor, Timon, Parmenas, and Nicolas of Antioch (a Gentile convert to the Jewish faith, who had now become a Christian). ⁶These seven were presented to the apostles, who prayed for them as they laid their hands on them. ⁷God's message was preached in ever-widening circles. The number of believers greatly increased in Jerusalem, and many of the Jewish priests were converted, too.

---

¹ **6:1** Greek *disciples;* also in 6:2, 7.
² **6:3** Greek *brothers.*

Often in Scripture we're taught about the church and how this body is intended to **function smoothly** as **each person takes a part.** When we come together as Jesus instructed, he is glorified. And when we don't, we're distracted from our purpose. The mechanism—the organism we call the church—comes to an abrupt stop just like that busted bike. This group of believers faced just such a dilemma and solved the problem in a creative and God-designed way.

First, they **organized** themselves. After agreeing on a plan, they divided the workload. And last, responsible people **stepped up** to the tasks at hand. A difficult process? Not really—unless just one part of the body fails in its contribution. Note that rumblings, discontent, and complaining occur if we don't all carry our weight. But **when we share the work, God is glorified,** and "the number of believers greatly increases." Now that's a reward for teamwork!

HERE'S WHAT I'M GOING TO DO

❏ _____

❏ _____

❏ _____

_____

FINAL WORDS

The stories of the bizarre last requests of the dying often find their way into tabloids and news clips. A man wants to be buried in the uniform of a Civil War general. An elderly woman leaves all her worldly possessions to a cat. A rabid football fan wants his ashes scattered on the turf of his team's stadium. As Christians, we can easily dismiss these as examples of what the unsaved would do as a legacy.

The question is **what kind of legacy *will* we leave behind?** How will we be remembered? What relationships will we have invested in? We learn about a woman named Dorcas—and her life—in the book of Acts. Now here's someone worth knowing.

> Acts 9:36-41: ³⁶There was a believer in Joppa named Tabitha (which in Greek is Dorcas¹). She was always doing kind things for others and helping the poor. ³⁷About this time she became ill and died. Her friends prepared her for burial and laid her in an upstairs room. ³⁸But they had heard that Peter was nearby at Lydda, so they sent two men to beg him, "Please come as soon as possible!"
>
> ³⁹So Peter returned with them; and as soon as he arrived, they took him to the upstairs room. The room was filled with widows who were weeping and showing him the coats and other garments Dorcas had made for them. ⁴⁰But Peter asked them all to leave the room; then he knelt and prayed. Turning to the body he said, "Get up, Tabitha." And she opened her eyes! When she saw Peter, she sat up! ⁴¹He gave her his hand and helped her up. Then he called in the widows and all the believers, and he showed them that she was alive.

Note the possible inscription for her headstone: "She was always doing kind things for others and helping the poor." But eulogies weren't needed for long as friends begged Peter to

---

¹ 9:36 The names *Tabitha* in Aramaic and *Dorcas* in Greek both mean "gazelle."

come and he prayed over her dead body. Once again this much-beloved woman was used by God as many were saved through her miraculous raising. And somehow, you just know that she continued to **serve God** through acts of kindness. Here was a woman who was given a second chance when she never needed one to begin with!

Undoubtedly she did not collect material goods to impress others. Nor did she seek the company of the movers and shakers. Instead, she helped the poor. Finally, note that she had friends who cared for her physical body after she had died rather than scavengers who snatched up an inheritance of collected wealth. What was the legacy she left behind? **Kindness. Relationships. Love.** Pretty impressive, huh?

Dorcas' beloved legacy went from life to death to life again. She didn't waste a moment. And she knew what was important. Do you? What legacy will you leave behind?

HERE'S WHAT I'M GOING TO DO

☐ _____

_____

☐ _____

_____

☐ _____

_____

GET NOTICED

Many people who feel inferior resort to outlandish behavior so they will **get noticed.** They may dye their hair pink or get a tattoo. They may drink heavily so they can be the "life of the party." They may shop for exclusive designer clothes that will set them apart from the crowd.

It's comforting to realize that we don't have to depend on attention-getting antics so that God will notice us. Check out Cornelius, a **humble** man whose **kindness** brought him some unexpected heavenly attention:

Acts 10:4-8, 30-33: 4Cornelius stared at him in terror. "What is it, sir?" he asked the angel. And the angel replied, "Your prayers and gifts to the poor have not gone unnoticed by God! 5Now send some men down to Joppa to find a man named Simon Peter. 6He is staying with Simon, a leatherworker who lives near the shore. Ask him to come and visit you." 7As soon as the angel was gone, Cornelius called two of his household servants and a devout soldier, one of his personal attendants. 8He told them what had happened and sent them off to Joppa. . . .

30Cornelius [told Peter], "Four days ago I was praying in my house at three o'clock in the afternoon. Suddenly, a man in dazzling clothes was standing in front of me. 31He told me, 'Cornelius, your prayers have been heard, and your gifts to the poor have been noticed by God! 32Now send some men to Joppa and summon Simon Peter. He is staying in the home of Simon, a leatherworker who lives near the shore.' 33So I sent for you at once, and it was good of you to come. Now here we are, waiting before God to hear the message the Lord has given you."

All too often, we are impressed by professional athletes who can dunk a basketball, hit a curveball, or sprint down a field. We're awed by the beauty of a model, the power of the wealthy, or the genius of the gifted. Those are things that attract our attention. But God has **different priorities** and **holy (set apart) ideals:** He notices the one who gives to the lowly poor. That's the type of person, a Gentile man with a tender heart, that God points out to Peter.

PRAYER POINT

Ask God to help you begin

to stand out through acts of

kindness for others.

Cornelius became one **incredible tool** in God's hands, all because *he noticed* the poor around him!

God does indeed notice when we give to the needy—through money, time, or effort. The return? **A blessing far outdistancing our expectations or dreams.**

Want to get noticed? Don't rely on athletic abilities, knowledge, or beauty products and regimens. Instead, work on a **tender and giving heart.** God does notice. And he will honor your care for others.

HERE'S WHAT I'M GOING TO DO

☐ _____

_____

☐ _____

_____

☐ _____

_____

☐ _____

_____

_____

WHAT A RELIEF!

DAY

211

A fter his history teacher talked about civil war and famine in Africa, fifteen-year-old Justin became concerned. "What can I do to help end all the suffering? I'm just one person!"

A lot of people feel **overwhelmed** like this when they see what shape the world is in. "God doesn't call us to alleviate all the world's suffering by ourselves," Justin's youth pastor said. "He calls us to start together and where we are." Pastor Bob suggested the youth group "adopt" a child or family in Africa, sending letters to the kids and money for food. The rest of the group agreed. As in the Antioch church in Acts, the whole project got under way because of **concern for the needy.**

> Acts 11:27-30: 27During this time, some prophets traveled from Jerusalem to Antioch. 28One of them named Agabus stood up in one of the meetings to predict by the Spirit that a great famine was coming upon the entire Roman world. (This was fulfilled during the reign of Claudius.) 29So the believers in Antioch decided to send relief to the believers in Judea, everyone giving as much as they could. 30This they did, entrusting their gifts to Barnabas and Saul to take to the elders of the church in Jerusalem.

In today's passage, we see that the young church in Antioch sent "relief" to the mother-church in Jerusalem. Note that it was **the Holy Spirit** who **prompted the believers to give.** This reminds us of the importance of making sure that we are being **led by God.**

One way to discern the Spirit's prodding is to talk about the need with other prayerful Christians (as Justin did). If others share your passion and urgency, then begin to prayerfully develop a plan of action for how you can meet the need together. The desire to help the poor in Jerusalem was apparently felt by the whole Antioch church (v. 29). Unity like this can be a confirmation of God's will. And when there is a sense that a particular project is "of God," people are motivated to give as much as they can (see v. 29). Nobody gives because they "have" to; they give because they "want" to!

The final step of the Christians in Antioch was to "entrust" their gifts to reliable carriers (v. 30). Barnabas and Saul (i.e., Paul) were men of complete integrity. If you decide to give money to a particular ministry or charity, make sure they really do what they say they do. And if you're ever asked to carry a gift or message for someone, realize that others are trusting you to **finish the job right.**

Like Justin, you may be inclined to think, *I'm just* **one** *teenager, what could I do to help?* If so, you need to remember the church at Antioch. The Christians there **banded** together, **followed** the leading of the Spirit, and **contributed** as much as they could. When the individual gifts were added up, the total was sizable!

HERE'S WHAT I'M GOING TO DO

☐ _____

_____

☐ _____

_____

WORLD OF WONDERS

DAY

212

On his album *Winds of Heaven, Stuff of Earth*, Rich Mullins sings to God: "You've filled this world with wonders and now I'm filled with the wonders of your world." Whether he glories in the "spills and sputters and spurts" of the world or its "rattles and patters," Mullins **praises God** for a wild world, just as Paul does in today's reading:

> Acts 14:11-17: [11]When the listening crowd saw what Paul had done, they shouted in their local dialect, "These men are gods in human bodies!" [12]They decided that Barnabas was the Greek god Zeus and that Paul, because he was the chief speaker, was Hermes. [13]The temple of Zeus was located on the outskirts of the city. The priest of the temple and the crowd brought oxen and wreaths of flowers, and they prepared to sacrifice to the apostles at the city gates.
>
> [14]But when Barnabas and Paul heard what was happening, they tore their clothes in dismay and ran out among the people, shouting, [15]"Friends,[1] why are you doing this? We are merely human beings like yourselves! We have come to bring you the Good News that you should turn from these worthless things to the living God, who made heaven and earth, the sea, and everything in them. [16]In earlier days he permitted all the nations to go their own ways, [17]but he never left himself without a witness. There were always his reminders, such as sending you rain and good crops and giving you food and joyful hearts."

In this passage, Paul and Barnabas were in Lystra, a city in Greece. Their healing of a crippled man had caused the people to think that Paul was the god Hermes in a human body and that Barnabas was the god Zeus!

Bizarre? No doubt! But also the perfect opportunity for the missionaries to **share the Good News** about the one, true God (in contrast to the Greek belief of many gods—Acts 17:23).

---

[1] **14:15** Greek *Men.*

As Paul explained, there have been times in history when God has allowed people to "go their own ways" (v. 16) and believe all sorts of wrong things about him. But to those honestly seeking the truth, the God of the Bible has "never left himself without a witness" (v. 17).

There have always been reminders of his goodness (v. 17). Everyday life is full of hints about **God's power** and **majesty.** A sunny day. A booming thunderstorm. A dazzling mountain peak. Each of these is a good gift from above (James 1:17). Each wonderful facet of creation points to a wonderful Creator.

In Romans 1:20, Paul says much the same thing: "From the time the world was created, people have seen the earth and sky and all that God made. They can clearly see his **invisible qualities**—his **eternal power** and **divine nature.** So they have no excuse whatsoever for not knowing God."

It's undeniable. God has placed within each and every soul a longing to know him. In Rich Mullins' words, God has left "winds of heaven" and "stuff of earth" to evidence his handiwork. Everything points back to him.

PRAYER POINT

Ask God to make you more aware of his goodness, evident in creation, and then thank him for the wonders of his love, shown to you.

HERE'S WHAT I'M GOING TO DO

☐ _____

_____

☐ _____

_____

THE RIGHT GIFT

Yesterday Josh agonized in the floral shop about what kind of flower would best complement Amy's black dress. Now the night of the Christmas banquet had arrived. In a box on the passenger seat of his parents' car lay a beautiful rose corsage. Josh pulled into the driveway, got out, and nervously rang the doorbell. She opened the door, and Josh stood speechless—Amy looked amazing! Josh handed her the box and watched a broad smile brighten her face as she stared at the flawless flowers.

If you've ever given something special to a special friend, you know by experience what today's passage teaches: **It really is better to give than to receive.**

Acts 20:33-35: ³³"I have never coveted anyone's money or fine clothing. ³⁴You know that these hands of mine have worked to pay my own way, and I have even supplied the needs of those who were with me. ³⁵And I have been a constant example of how you can help the poor by working hard. You should remember the words of the Lord Jesus: 'It is more blessed to give than to receive.'"

In this passage, Paul was meeting with the leaders of the church at Ephesus. He was reminding them of his **unselfish behavior.** Even though he was a missionary chosen and approved by God, Paul refused to take their money. Instead he worked extra hard so that he might have some funds to give to them! Paul did this gladly. Why? Because he deeply loved the Ephesian Christians (a simple reading of his letter to the Ephesians will confirm this!).

This explains why we feel so good when we **give a gift to a friend.** We love our friends, and it is the very nature of love to "give" (see John 3:16). A so-called "love" that only takes is not love.

According to Paul, Jesus never said, "It's better to give . . ."; he said, "It is more blessed to give . . ." (v. 35b). Giving doesn't cause God to love us more than he loves another Christian who doesn't give as much. However, **our giving pleases God.** Not because God needs our gifts, but because our giving shows God we **love** and **value** him. How we handle money is always an accurate monitor of our spiritual health. Giving helps focus our minds on God as the source of all the good things in our lives. And oddly enough, when we give *we* are blessed.

We need to be **generous** as Paul was. And not only to our friends to make ourselves and them feel good but to anyone around us who has a need. And like Josh, we need to put special thought into our gifts. The right gift offered with the **right attitude** results in tremendous blessing: God is honored; others are helped; and we find unearthly joy!

PRAYER POINT

Thank God for the many blessings he's given you. Pray about the ways you can give these gifts (time, talents, spiritual gifts) back to him. Confess any ways in which you are guilty of being stingy instead of generous.

HERE'S WHAT I'M GOING TO DO

☐ _____

_____

☐ _____

_____

☐ _____

_____

HOLIER THAN THOU

DAY

214

It's not hard to walk down the hallway of your school and look at various people with a **judgmental attitude.** That guy's a druggie. That girl sleeps around.

Well, if you've ever **judged people** like that—even rightfully—Paul the apostle would like to have a word with you.

Romans 2:1-10: ¹You may be saying, "What terrible people you have been talking about!" But you are just as bad, and you have no excuse! When you say they are wicked and should be punished, you are condemning yourself, for you do these very same things. ²And we know that God, in his justice, will punish anyone who does such things. ³Do you think that God will judge and condemn others for doing them and not judge you when you do them, too? ⁴Don't you realize how kind, tolerant, and patient God is with you? Or don't you care? Can't you see how kind he has been in giving you time to turn from your sin?

⁵But no, you won't listen. So you are storing up terrible punishment for yourself because of your stubbornness in refusing to turn from your sin. For there is going to come a day of judgment when God, the just judge of all the world, ⁶will judge all people according to what they have done. ⁷He will give eternal life to those who persist in doing what is good, seeking after the glory and honor and immortality that God offers. ⁸But he will pour out his anger and wrath on those who live for themselves, who refuse to obey the truth and practice evil deeds. ⁹There will be trouble and calamity for everyone who keeps on sinning—for the Jew first and also for the Gentile. ¹⁰But there will be glory and honor and peace from God for all who do good—for the Jew first and also for the Gentile.

Imagine the first Christians who listened as Paul's words were read. After some opening words of encouragement, he jumped right in, talking about the **sinfulness of humanity without God.**

The people listening to these strong words about sinners were no doubt shaking their heads as they heard Paul's arguments. And Paul read their minds: "You may be saying, 'What terrible people you have been talking about!' " (v. 1a). But he doesn't stop there: "But you are just as bad, and you have no excuse!" (v. 1b). Yikes!

He was pointing out that they were doing **many** of the things they **condemned in other people.** The fact that they weren't being judged—yet—was due solely to God's **kindness,** tolerance, and patience with them.

PRAYER POINT

If you have been engaging in persistent sin—sin that you know can cause you ultimate harm—now is the time to get right with God. Confess your sin—agree with God that you're doing wrong. Ask him to cleanse and forgive you and to fill you with the Holy Spirit.

Christians can rejoice that Jesus paid the penalty for their sins. **We can be assured of heaven.** But we can also be assured that **persistent sin** leads only to great harm.

HERE'S WHAT I'M GOING TO DO

☐ _____

☐ _____

☐ _____

_____

FREE TO SERVE

Imagine a job in which you had to accomplish 475 things every day perfectly. And if you missed doing one single thing or did it incorrectly, you would be put to death. Do you think you'd actually make it to retirement?

Hopefully when you get out into the workforce, you won't have a job like that. But the Jewish people had to live under a system kind of like that. They had to obey a long list of laws, rules, and regulations in order to be **right with God.**

Thank goodness for you, things have changed. Paul explains how.

Romans 7:1-6: ¹Now, dear friends¹—you who are familiar with the law—don't you know that the law applies only to a person who is still living? ²Let me illustrate. When a woman marries, the law binds her to her husband as long as he is alive. But if he dies, the laws of marriage no longer apply to her. ³So while her husband is alive, she would be committing adultery if she married another man. But if her husband dies, she is free from that law and does not commit adultery when she remarries.

⁴So then, dear friends, the point is this: The law no longer holds you in its power, because you died to its power when you died with Christ on the cross. And now you are united with the one who was raised from the dead. As a result, you can produce good fruit, that is, good deeds for God. ⁵When we were controlled by our old nature, sinful desires were at work within us, and the law aroused these evil desires that produced sinful deeds, resulting in death. ⁶But now we have been released from the law, for we died with Christ, and we are no longer captive to its power. Now we can really serve God, not in the old way by obeying the letter of the law, but in the new way, by the Spirit.

Paul uses the illustration of marriage to explain believers'

¹ **7:1** Greek *brothers;* also in 7:4.

relationship to **the law of God.** When two people are married, they are subject to the laws of marriage. But if one of them dies, the other is free of those laws and can remarry.

In the same way, **Christians today are free of the power of the law.** We have **a new way of living.** As Paul puts it, "The law no longer holds you in its power, because you died to its power when you died with Christ on the cross" (v. 4).

Some people try to keep a set of rules—whether it's going to church every week or even doing good deeds—in order to gain acceptance by God. But the only thing they get for their troubles is frustration. People simply **can't** make it to God **on their own.**

By dying on the cross, Jesus opened the way to God. **He makes believers perfect in God's sight.** And now, rather than trying to follow all those rules, we can live in the power of God's Spirit. We can become more and more like Jesus **by living for him every day.**

PRAYER POINT

Thank God for freedom from the power of the law. Praise him that he has given you freedom to live, freedom to serve, and freedom to reach out to others. Ask him to give you an opportunity to exercise that freedom in the power of the Spirit today. Ask him to make you more like Jesus every day.

HERE'S WHAT I'M GOING TO DO

☐ _____

_____

☐ _____

_____

LOVE BEYOND MEASURE

DAY 216

You lose your after-school job. Your boyfriend/girlfriend breaks up with you. Somebody steals your clothes out of your gym locker. All in all, **it's a pretty bad day.**

When bad things happen, it's **natural** to think that God must not love you. But today's passage claims the opposite.

Romans 8:28-39: ²⁸And we know that God causes everything to work together[1] for the good of those who love God and are called according to his purpose for them. ²⁹For God knew his people in advance, and he chose them to become like his Son, so that his Son would be the firstborn, with many brothers and sisters. ³⁰And having chosen them, he called them to come to him. And he gave them right standing with himself, and he promised them his glory.

³¹What can we say about such wonderful things as these? If God is for us, who can ever be against us? ³²Since God did not spare even his own Son but gave him up for us all, won't God, who gave us Christ, also give us everything else?

³³Who dares accuse us whom God has chosen for his own? Will God? No! He is the one who has given us right standing with himself. ³⁴Who then will condemn us? Will Christ Jesus? No, for he is the one who died for us and was raised to life for us and is sitting at the place of highest honor next to God, pleading for us.

³⁵Can anything ever separate us from Christ's love? Does it mean he no longer loves us if we have trouble or calamity, or are persecuted, or are hungry or cold or in danger or threatened with death? ³⁶(Even the Scriptures say, "For your sake we are killed every day; we are being slaughtered like sheep."[2]) ³⁷No, despite all these things, overwhelming victory is ours through Christ, who loved us.

[1] **8:28** Some manuscripts read *And we know that everything works together.*
[2] **8:36** Ps. 44:22.

PRAYER POINT

³⁸And I am convinced that nothing can ever separate us from his love. Death can't, and life can't. The angels can't, and the demons can't. Our fears for today, our worries about tomorrow, and even the powers of hell can't keep God's love away. ³⁹Whether we are high above the sky or in the deepest ocean, nothing in all creation will ever be able to separate us from the love of God that is revealed in Christ Jesus our Lord.

If you are struggling with something bad that's happened to you lately, ask God to let his truths transform your thinking and build your faith.

Let's pick out the highlights of this passage:

1. God causes everything to work together for good (v. 28). He does cause even bad stuff to work together for **ultimate good,** for all who "love God and are called according to his purpose for them."

2. God is on our side, and nobody can ever condemn us (v. 31). God is the all-powerful king of the universe. He will give us **everything** we need to be victorious in life.

3. Nothing can ever separate us from God's love (v. 35). And if bad things happen—that doesn't mean he no longer loves us. No matter what happens, "**overwhelming victory is ours through Christ,** who loved us" (v. 37).

God's love for you is **beyond measure.** Even in the midst of bad times, you can hold on to that truth, because God is hard at work to do something wonderful in your life.

HERE'S WHAT I'M GOING TO DO

☐ _____

_____

_____

WILLING SACRIFICE

It's a real shame, isn't it? All those needy people around you. You see them in news photos in the papers and magazines and on videotape on TV. You walk past them on the street. The lost. The blind. People without Christ. They may be rich or poor, hungry or fat. But they are going to hell. And that's a real shame.

But you walk on. Or turn your glance away. There's nothing you can do. You may even have some family members in that situation. You pray for them; you may even cry for them. But what else would you be **willing to do** that they would be saved?

Take a look at Paul's example today.

Romans 9:1-5: ¹In the presence of Christ, I speak with utter truthfulness— I do not lie—and my conscience and the Holy Spirit confirm that what I am saying is true. ²My heart is filled with bitter sorrow and unending grief ³for my people, my Jewish brothers and sisters. I would be willing to be forever cursed—cut off from Christ!—if that would save them. ⁴They are the people of Israel, chosen to be God's special children. God revealed his glory to them. He made covenants with them and gave his law to them. They have the privilege of worshiping him and receiving his wonderful promises. ⁵Their ancestors were great people of God, and Christ himself was a Jew as far as his human nature is concerned. And he is God, who rules over everything and is worthy of eternal praise! Amen.¹

Paul was raised a good Jew. He became influential in the synagogues. He was a leader. He was thoroughly Jewish. And then one day, on the road to Damascus, Jesus intervened. And the world has never been the same.

Paul became a new man. An apostle. A missionary. A man of zeal for the Lord. But he was still Jewish. So his heart was

---

¹ **9:5** Or *May God, who rules over everything, be praised forever. Amen.*

"filled with bitter sorrow and unending grief" (v. 2) for his people. They were lost, blind to the light of Christ. And they were destined for eternal destruction.

Paul emphatically declares that he "would be willing to be forever cursed—cut off from Christ!—if that would save them" (v. 3). That would be the ultimate sacrifice, wouldn't it: to set aside eternity with Jesus if that would help some other people experience it for themselves.

Of course, the **only one** who can take someone else's punishment is Jesus. Yet Paul is showing **a depth of love and concern** for a group of people that can't be matched. Like Jesus, Paul was willing to **sacrifice everything dear to him so others could be saved.**

With that example in mind, ask yourself: How concerned am I about people who don't know Jesus? Am I willing to sacrifice even my time, my money, my efforts to introduce them to the Lord of eternity?

PRAYER POINT

Ask God to give you a heart willing to sacrifice in order to reach out to others in Jesus' name. Ask him for wisdom to determine just how to do that today. And be sure to pray for your friends and family members who don't know Jesus—yet.

HERE'S WHAT I'M GOING TO DO

☐ _____

_____

☐ _____

_____

_____

OPEN YOUR GIFT

Someone you love is having a birthday. You know this person very well, and you thought long and hard about what gift to give. You shopped carefully, being sure to get just the right color, size, and style. It's perfect. You can't wait to give your present. You can't wait to see your friend enjoy it and use it.

At the party, your eyes dance with joy as your friend rips the paper open. "Oh! Isn't that nice," your friend says and then puts the gift aside. Last time you checked, your gift was still stuck in your friend's closet. Never used. Never enjoyed. How do you feel? Well, read today's Scripture and then ask yourself how God must feel.

> Romans 12:3-8: ³As God's messenger, I give each of you this warning: Be honest in your estimate of yourselves, measuring your value by how much faith God has given you. ⁴Just as our bodies have many parts and each part has a special function, ⁵so it is with Christ's body. We are all parts of his one body, and each of us has different work to do. And since we are all one body in Christ, we belong to each other, and each of us needs all the others.
>
> ⁶God has given each of us the ability to do certain things well. So if God has given you the ability to prophesy, speak out when you have faith that God is speaking through you. ⁷If your gift is that of serving others, serve them well. If you are a teacher, do a good job of teaching. ⁸If your gift is to encourage others, do it! If you have money, share it generously. If God has given you leadership ability, take the responsibility seriously. And if you have a gift for showing kindness to others, do it gladly.

God gives his children gifts in order to **build up his church.** When everyone exercises their gifts—of service, administration, giving, teaching, and so on—then a church operates smoothly, meets needs regularly, and grows continually.

To use your gift **effectively,** you have to:

- Realize that all gifts and talents come from God.
- Recognize that people have been given different gifts.
- Know what gift or gifts you've been given.
- Commit yourself to use your gifts to serve God, not to promote yourself.
- Determine to use your gift wholeheartedly, whenever you can.

God doesn't expect any one person to do all the work himself or herself. He wants the body of Christ to work **together**—just as the parts of a human body must work together—for his glory.

Don't let your gift gather dust stuffed away somewhere. Use it! Enjoy it! The Giver will be very happy when you do. And he will give you **all the faith and power you'll need** to succeed.

PRAYER POINT

Ask God to use your gifts to balance other people's weak areas and to use their gifts to balance your weaknesses. Ask him to help you work together in unity and harmony to build up his church in the world.

HERE'S WHAT I'M GOING TO DO

☐ _____

_____

☐ _____

_____

_____

THE BILL OF (DOING) RIGHTS

Y ou know the type. Very, very nice. As friendly as they can be. In fact, a little too nice and friendly. You can't help but feel they have an ulterior motive. They **pretend** to show concern. They may even promise to pray for you about something. But as soon as they leave you, they totally forget all about you.

It's hard to feel close to people like that. Because they're **not real.** The things they do and say don't have much power because they don't really mean them. As you read today's Scripture passage, keep in mind the difference between **doing right**—and **really meaning it.**

Romans 12:9-18: ⁹Don't just pretend that you love others. Really love them. Hate what is wrong. Stand on the side of the good. ¹⁰Love each other with genuine affection, and take delight in honoring each other. ¹¹Never be lazy in your work, but serve the Lord enthusiastically.

¹²Be glad for all God is planning for you. Be patient in trouble, and always be prayerful. ¹³When God's children are in need, be the one to help them out. And get into the habit of inviting guests home for dinner or, if they need lodging, for the night.

¹⁴If people persecute you because you are a Christian, don't curse them; pray that God will bless them. ¹⁵When others are happy, be happy with them. If they are sad, share their sorrow. ¹⁶Live in harmony with each other. Don't try to act important, but enjoy the company of ordinary people. And don't think you know it all!

¹⁷Never pay back evil for evil to anyone. Do things in such a way that everyone can see you are honorable. ¹⁸Do your part to live in peace with everyone, as much as possible.

Did you catch verse 9? "Don't just pretend that you love

others. **Really love them!"** That's key. Paul goes on from there with a whole list of practical pointers for the Christian walk—it's kind of like the Christian's Bill of Doing Rights. And yet Paul clearly points out that if people do all those things without meaning it, it's really a waste of their time and energy.

Notice the words Paul uses: "really . . . genuine . . . enthusiastically . . ." We're supposed to put our heart into this stuff!

These verses sum up **the whole core of Christian life.** If we love and serve someone as Christ has loved and served us, we will be living just the way he wants us to. That means loving, serving, and reaching out to others sincerely.

To love someone sincerely takes **concentration** and **effort.** It demands time, money, and energy. It means helping without ulterior motives. Giving without expecting anything back. Serving just because God wants us to.

Does that sound too hard? It's not, if you **trust God** to give you the wisdom and guidance you need to do it.

PRAYER POINT

Ask God for a genuine heart: one that longs to really love and honor people, stands up for what's right, lives in harmony and humility with others, and does good. Then ask him for an opportunity today to put that heart into action for someone else.

HERE'S WHAT I'M GOING TO DO

☐ _____

_____

☐ _____

_____

A DEBT OF LOVE

A friend reveals an embarrassing incident about you in front of a school convocation. A coach cracks a joke about your last-place finish at yesterday's track meet. A fellow employee at your after-school job accuses you of taking money from the cash register—despite the fact that you haven't stolen a thing in your life. Stuff like this happens in life all the time. What are you going to do about it?

You can get back at the other person. You can throw a fit. You can just ignore the person but keep stewing in your anger. Or you can take **a whole different approach.** Let's see what Paul would suggest.

Romans 13:8-14: [8]Pay all your debts, except the debt of love for others. You can never finish paying that! If you love your neighbor, you will fulfill all the requirements of God's law. [9]For the commandments against adultery and murder and stealing and coveting—and any other commandment—are all summed up in this one commandment: "Love your neighbor as yourself."[1] [10]Love does no wrong to anyone, so love satisfies all of God's requirements.

[11]Another reason for right living is that you know how late it is; time is running out. Wake up, for the coming of our salvation is nearer now than when we first believed. [12]The night is almost gone; the day of salvation will soon be here. So don't live in darkness. Get rid of your evil deeds. Shed them like dirty clothes. Clothe yourselves with the armor of right living, as those who live in the light. [13]We should be decent and true in everything we do, so that everyone can approve of our behavior. Don't participate in wild parties and getting drunk, or in adultery and immoral living, or in fighting and jealousy. [14]But let the Lord Jesus Christ take control of you, and don't think of ways to indulge your evil desires.

"Love your neighbor as yourself." Such a simple

[1] **13:9** Lev. 19:18.

statement. One we're so familiar with that it really doesn't even register in our brain cells. But Paul—like Jesus before him—summarizes the whole law of God with those simple words.

No matter who offends us, the right thing to do is to **respond in love.** To let God work his love through us.

PRAYER POINT

Ask God to help you forgive those who offend and hurt you. Ask Jesus to love others through you as only he can.

A lot of people have the idea that loving yourself is wrong. But if it were, then the idea of loving your neighbor as yourself wouldn't make any sense.

How do you love yourself? Think about it: You feed yourself, clothe yourself, take care of your body. You protect yourself from pain and hurt and need. That's exactly what we need to be doing for our neighbors. We need to do what we can to see they are fed, clothed, and housed as well as possible. We need to be concerned with issues of social justice. That's what loving your neighbor as yourself is all about.

How do you do all this? "Let the Lord Jesus Christ take control of you, and don't think of ways to indulge your evil desires" (v. 14). The truth is, we can't continually live a life of loving our neighbors in our own power. But Jesus can, and he lives inside you. So **let him work through you today.**

HERE'S WHAT I'M GOING TO DO

❑ _____

_____

❑ _____

_____

SPIRITUAL JOURNEY TRAVEL LOG

A Team Effort

Michael Jordan is probably the greatest basketball player of all time. He's so good, in fact, that people occasionally refer to him as a "one-man team." But as good as Michael Jordan is, he's not a one-man team. The truth is that Michael Jordan—like the rest of us—needs **teammates.**

The apostle Paul recognized a Christian's need for "teammates," especially in the areas of support, encouragement, and unity.

> 1 Corinthians 1:10-17: [10]Now, dear brothers and sisters, I appeal to you by the authority of the Lord Jesus Christ to stop arguing among yourselves. Let there be real harmony so there won't be divisions in the church. I plead with you to be of one mind, united in thought and purpose. [11]For some members of Chloe's household have told me about your arguments, dear friends.[1] [12]Some of you are saying, "I am a follower of Paul." Others are saying, "I follow Apollos," or "I follow Peter,[2]" or "I follow only Christ." [13]Can Christ be divided into pieces?
>
> Was I, Paul, crucified for you? Were any of you baptized in the name of Paul? [14]I thank God that I did not baptize any of you except Crispus and Gaius, [15]for now no one can say they were baptized in my name. [16](Oh yes, I also baptized the household of Stephanas. I don't remember baptizing anyone else.) [17]For Christ didn't send me to baptize, but to preach the Good News—and not with clever speeches and high-sounding ideas, for fear that the cross of Christ would lose its power.

In the early days of the church, several Christian leaders traveled throughout the Roman Empire (and beyond), teaching people in various churches along the way. As you might expect, the people who listened to these evangelists began to develop favorites, preferring one leader's style over another. The church in Corinth, however, began to take this to

[1] **1:11** Greek *my brothers.*
[2] **1:12** Greek *Cephas.*

an extreme. Little cliques were forming in the church, based on which leader people followed. Some identified with Paul. Others preferred Apollos. Still others followed Peter. Some even believed that they were the only ones who truly followed Christ.

This issue was so troublesome to Paul that he discussed it immediately in his first letter to the Corinthians. Paul emphasized the need for **unity** among Christian brothers and sisters. In fact, he used the image of a family to let the Corinthians know that Christians are bound by more than a common belief—**we are all part of the family of God.** And in God's family, there is no room for division.

One committed individual can have a **tremendous impact** when he or she determines to serve the Lord by ministering to others. When joined by two or three Christian "teammates"—people who support, pray for, and accompany that ministry—the results can be **incredible.** When that group of teammates is working in conjunction with the church as a whole, the impact can **rock** a community to its core.

PRAYER POINT

Confess any attitude that has kept you from being a team player. Ask God to provide an opportunity for you to begin or develop a relationship with at least a couple other people from your church—people who are interested in the same type of ministry that you're interested in.

HERE'S WHAT I'M GOING TO DO

❑ _____

_____

❑ _____

_____

ROLE PLAYERS

Each member of a football team has a **specific role.** No player's role is more important than another player's because if anyone fails to do his job, the whole play breaks down, and the entire team suffers. The best teams function as a unit.

Believe it or not, this same principle holds true for churches. The strongest churches are those whose members recognize their **individual roles** and perform them to the **best** of their ability, as the apostle Paul explains in his first letter to the Corinthians.

1 Corinthians 3:1-9: [1]Dear brothers and sisters, when I was with you I couldn't talk to you as I would to mature Christians. I had to talk as though you belonged to this world or as though you were infants in the Christian life.[1] [2]I had to feed you with milk and not with solid food, because you couldn't handle anything stronger. And you still aren't ready, [3]for you are still controlled by your own sinful desires. You are jealous of one another and quarrel with each other. Doesn't that prove you are controlled by your own desires? You are acting like people who don't belong to the Lord. [4]When one of you says, "I am a follower of Paul," and another says, "I prefer Apollos," aren't you acting like those who are not Christians?[2]

[5]Who is Apollos, and who is Paul, that we should be the cause of such quarrels? Why, we're only servants. Through us God caused you to believe. Each of us did the work the Lord gave us. [6]My job was to plant the seed in your hearts, and Apollos watered it, but it was God, not we, who made it grow. [7]The ones who do the planting or watering aren't important, but God is important because he is the one who makes the seed grow. [8]The one who plants and the one who waters work as a team

---

[1] **3:1** Greek *in Christ*.
[2] **3:4** Greek *aren't you merely human?*

with the same purpose. Yet they will be rewarded individually, according to their own hard work. [9]We work together as partners who belong to God. You are God's field, God's building—not ours.

The church in Corinth was caught up in petty bickering and jealousy. As we discovered yesterday, rather than pulling together to work as a team, the Corinthians were splitting apart, choosing sides, and blaming others for the disunity. By the tone of his letter, it's pretty obvious that Paul was getting frustrated with the people at Corinth.

In order to emphasize the need for church members to work as a team, Paul used an example that hit close to home with the Corinthian believers. Paul pointed out that the various leaders whom the Corinthians singled out and looked up to were actually part of one team. Paul's role on the team was to plant the seed of faith, to spread the news of Christ. Apollos' role was to water the seed that Paul planted. Neither role was more important than the other. After all, it was **God alone** who could make the seed grow.

The same principle holds true for modern believers. Teamwork among Christians is every bit as important today as it was in Corinth two thousand years ago. No matter what our ministry role is, you need to remember that it is no more or less important than the roles of other believers.

HERE'S WHAT I'M GOING TO DO

❑ _____

_____

_____

LIVING EXPENSES

DAY

223

Most of us have heard stories about divorces of the rich and famous. They are often messy, petty episodes and often include one of the partners demanding a living allowance based on the lifestyle he or she has grown accustomed to. Such "necessities" can include a $10,000 a month budget for clothes, a new car every year, several vacations, and a palatial estate.

In contrast, Paul made the case for his **necessities** with great humility. Still, he spoke with great authority and truth when he reminded the Corinthians of what he had done for them.

1 Corinthians 9:1-7: ¹Do I not have as much freedom as anyone else?¹ Am I not an apostle? Haven't I seen Jesus our Lord with my own eyes? Isn't it because of my hard work that you are in the Lord? ²Even if others think I am not an apostle, I certainly am to you, for you are living proof that I am the Lord's apostle.

³This is my answer to those who question my authority as an apostle.² ⁴Don't we have the right to live in your homes and share your meals? ⁵Don't we have the right to bring a Christian wife³ along with us as the other disciples and the Lord's brothers and Peter⁴ do? ⁶Or is it only Barnabas and I who have to work to support ourselves? ⁷What soldier has to pay his own expenses? And have you ever heard of a farmer who harvests his crop and doesn't have the right to eat some of it? What shepherd takes care of a flock of sheep and isn't allowed to drink some of the milk?

Paul reminds us that **the church must take the responsibility to support God's workers.** Christians should provide financial, material, and spiritual assistance to

---

¹ **9:1** Greek *Am I not free?*
² **9:3** Greek *those who examine me.*
³ **9:5a** Greek *a sister, a wife.*
⁴ **9:5b** Greek *Cephas.*

people in service to the Lord. Even if you have only a couple of dollars a week to give, the important thing is that you provide **regular support.** What kind of material help could you provide for the missionaries who are sponsored by your church? A clothing (or toy) drive could be very beneficial. Depending on the missionary's situation, a Bible or Christian resource drive could also be very helpful.

These ideas may take a bit of **time** and **effort** on your part, but they're well worth it. What kind of financial assistance could you offer a Christian service organization in your community?

Finally, what kind of **spiritual encouragement** could you offer the Christian leaders in your community? Prayer is perhaps the most powerful encouragement tool available. What kind of difference could you make in your community simply by **praying regularly for Christian leaders?**

Obviously these are only suggestions. Carefully (and prayerfully) consider how you can support God's workers in your community and around the world.

HERE'S WHAT I'M GOING TO DO

☐ _____

_____

☐ _____

_____

_____

COME TO THE PARTY

Nothing beats a **good party,** right? Laughing with friends, meeting new people—you know, generally having a good time. Unfortunately, parties often have a way of getting out of hand. All it takes is a couple of people getting drunk, starting a fight, or getting too rowdy to bring a celebration to a screeching halt, ruining the party for everyone else.

The first-century Corinthians were world-class party people. In fact, more often than not their festivities went out of control. This was a big problem, you see, because these parties tended to happen at the worst times—such as when the church gathered for communion. As you can probably imagine, the apostle Paul had a few things to say about these **out-of-control celebrations.**

> 1 Corinthians 11:33-34: ³³So, dear brothers and sisters, when you gather for the Lord's Supper, wait for each other. ³⁴If you are really hungry, eat at home so you won't bring judgment upon yourselves when you meet together.

Before their communion service, the Corinthians would hold an agape (love) feast. This was probably like a modern-day potluck dinner, with church members bringing food and drink to share with everyone else. Obviously the rich people in the church could bring more than the poor people, but everyone usually brought something. In addition to bringing more, however, the wealthy people ate and drank more at these dinners. In fact, the rich people of the church were such drunken gluttons at these parties that the poor people

often went home hungry.

You can imagine what this type of celebration did to the **fellowship in the church**—especially right before the Lord's Supper. Paul offered a rather simple solution to the problem: If the Corinthians had such a hard time controlling their appetites at the agape feast, perhaps they should eat at home and not bring their self-centered practices into the church. The Lord's Supper is a time for Christians to **remember the Lord's sacrifice** and to **celebrate the fact that we are all part of the body of Christ.** It is certainly not a time to create divisions in the church.

PRAYER POINT

Ask God to help you prepare for your church's next communion service. And look for ways to meet the needs of others in your congregation.

We can learn from the experience of the Corinthian church. First, we can learn the importance of **unity** among believers. As members of the body of Christ, believers are called to **support** each other. Second, and perhaps most important, we can learn that the church should be a place where we **look out for others first.** We should not go primarily to have our needs met but to meet the needs of others.

HERE'S WHAT I'M GOING TO DO

☐ _____

_____

☐ _____

_____

☐ _____

_____

LOVE, LOVE, LOVE

Let's start off with a quick multiple-choice quiz:
1. What is your favorite primary color—red, blue, or yellow?

2. What's the best flavor in Neapolitan ice cream—chocolate, vanilla, or strawberry?

3. Who is the funniest stooge—Moe, Larry, or Curly?

4. Which is the greatest of these—faith, hope, or love?

The first three questions call for opinions, so obviously there are no right or wrong answers (although if you chose anyone but Curly for the third question, one point will be deducted from your score). Paul answers the fourth question in the last verse of 1 Corinthians 13.

1 Corinthians 13:4-13: ⁴Love is patient and kind. Love is not jealous or boastful or proud ⁵or rude. Love does not demand its own way. Love is not irritable, and it keeps no record of when it has been wronged. ⁶It is never glad about injustice but rejoices whenever the truth wins out. ⁷Love never gives up, never loses faith, is always hopeful, and endures through every circumstance.

⁸Love will last forever, but prophecy and speaking in unknown languages¹ and special knowledge will all disappear. ⁹Now we know only a little, and even the gift of prophecy reveals little! ¹⁰But when the end comes, these special gifts will all disappear.

¹¹It's like this: When I was a child, I spoke and thought and reasoned as a child does. But when I grew up, I put away childish things. ¹²Now we see things imperfectly as in a poor mirror, but then we will see everything with perfect clarity.² All that I know now is partial and incomplete, but then I will know everything completely, just as God knows me now.

¹³There are three things that will endure—faith, hope, and love—and the

¹ **13:8** Or *in tongues.*
² **13:12** Greek *see face to face.*

greatest of these is love.

The apostle Paul, in this one chapter of the Bible, gives us the most complete description of **true love** ever.

Don't be fooled, however. This isn't the mushy, hearts-and-flowers kind of love that you might read in a greeting card. This kind of love doesn't come easily. In fact, love like this takes a lot of **work** and **sacrifice** to achieve. This love comes only from God, and this is the love that **Christians** are **instructed to show to one another.** More than a feeling, this love is an action.

How do we start to show love for those around us? Paul spells things out pretty clearly in his description of love in verses 4-7. We can **show patience** by not losing our temper when other people do things we don't agree with. We can **show kindness** by doing small things to help others. We can **avoid envy** by learning to be truly happy when good things happen to others. We can **avoid boasting** simply by keeping our mouths shut at the right time.

These are just some ideas to get you thinking. If you put your mind to it, you'll probably be able to come up with dozens of better ways to show love to those around you.

HERE'S WHAT I'M GOING TO DO

❑ _____

_____

_____

SPIRITUAL JOURNEY TRAVEL LOG

GOD'S COMFORT

DAY

226

Someone close to you is diagnosed with cancer. Or you break an arm. Or your cat gets hit by a car. Or you get turned down for the part-time job you were hoping to get. Or . . . or . . . or . . . **Life is full of painful events,** ranging from a paper cut to the loss of a loved one.

At times like these, our **faith** can really grow. How do you respond when something bad happens to you? Do you get angry and sulk? Do you withdraw in sadness? Do you give up or press on? Paul suffered incredible difficulties and pains for his faith. And he offers a different way to **deal with troubles.**

2 Corinthians 1:3-7: [3]All praise to the God and Father of our Lord Jesus Christ. He is the source[1] of every mercy and the God who comforts us. [4]He comforts us in all our troubles so that we can comfort others. When others are troubled, we will be able to give them the same comfort God has given us. [5]You can be sure that the more we suffer for Christ, the more God will shower us with his comfort through Christ. [6]So when we are weighed down with troubles, it is for your benefit and salvation! For when God comforts us, it is so that we, in turn, can be an encouragement to you. Then you can patiently endure the same things we suffer. [7]We are confident that as you share in suffering, you will also share God's comfort.

When troubles arise, the first thing to do is **ask God for his comfort.** Of course, that doesn't necessarily mean that the troubles will suddenly vanish. If that were the case, people would turn to God just as an occasional pain reliever. Instead of popping a couple of aspirin, they'd shoot up a prayer. But our relationship with God is based on **a desire to love and serve him**—it's not just a "gimme" thing to do when we need help.

Being comforted by God means getting the strength, the hope, the encouragement we need to get through our troubling

---

[1] **1:3** Greek *the Father.*

situation. And the more we suffer for the sake of Christ, the more God will "shower us with his comfort through Christ" (v. 5). But receiving God's comfort isn't the end of the matter. There's an even more exciting part to Paul's advice. "He comforts us in all our troubles so that we can comfort others. When others are troubled, we will be able to give them **the same comfort God has given us"** (v. 4).

Think about the opportunities you have to reach out to someone with God's comfort. What a privilege that can be. When someone comes to you hurting, lonely, or frustrated because of their troubles, you can offer them understanding, acceptance, and love in Jesus' name. You can be **the channel for God's comfort** in their lives. And there's no greater blessing than that.

HERE'S WHAT I'M GOING TO DO

☐ _____

_____

☐ _____

_____

☐ _____

_____

_____

Farsighted Faith

A h, summer vacation. Freedom from school. Sun and fun. Time to hang out with friends. The family vacation. The youth group trip. Maybe a summer romance. The beach. The lake. The river. Whatever it is, it's going to be great.

Do you look forward to your summer vacation? Of course you do. It helps get you through the last few months of school. The tests. The papers. The early morning alarm clocks. The late night homework sessions. Hey, you can put up with just about anything if you keep that summer of fun in mind.

Well, Paul gives the Corinthians some relevant advice. (And it's **even better** than summer vacations.)

2 Corinthians 4:17-18: [17]For our present troubles are quite small and won't last very long. Yet they produce for us an immeasurably great glory that will last forever! [18]So we don't look at the troubles we can see right now; rather, we look forward to what we have not yet seen. For the troubles we see will soon be over, but the joys to come will last forever.

Paul encourages **farsighted faith.** By looking forward to what waits for us—joyful, eternal life with our Lord and Savior—we can get through anything now.

When we put things in that perspective, looking at the big picture, "our present troubles are quite small and won't last very long" (v. 17). So **we can survive the troubles and toil and temptations** now because they don't really amount to anything.

Yet those present troubles "produce for us an immeasurably great glory that will last forever" (v. 17). What did Paul mean by that? If we don't let our pains and troubles decrease our faith or disillusion us, we'll discover there's always **a purpose for the suffering** or **something good** that God can bring out of it.

Our human problems can give us opportunities to:

- Remember that Christ suffered for us.
- Stay humble and dependent on God.
- Look beyond life on earth and count on life in heaven.
- Grow in our faith as we trust God more.
- Identify with others and comfort them with God's comfort.
- See God's power at work in our lives.

So think of your problems as **growth opportunities.** Look beyond them to what waits for you, a child of God, in heaven forever.

PRAYER POINT

Thank God for the gift of eternal life in heaven that he has already given you. Ask him to help you keep heaven on your mind as you live on earth today. And ask him to give you some opportunities to grow through your hassles and heartaches.

HERE'S WHAT I'M GOING TO DO

☐ _____

☐ _____

☐ _____

☐ _____

HAVING IT ALL

What would you think if your life featured one trouble, hardship, and calamity after another? What would you do if you were beaten, put in jail, attacked by angry mobs, forced to go without sleep and food—all for the sake of **your faith?** What if people despised you and said evil things about you—all because of what you believe? What if you were beaten within an inch of your life, your heart ached, and you owned nothing—all because you followed Jesus and wanted others to know him? Would all of that affect your faith? Would you quit living for Christ? Before you answer, read how Paul responded to those very circumstances.

2 Corinthians 6:3-10: ³We try to live in such a way that no one will be hindered from finding the Lord by the way we act, and so no one can find fault with our ministry. ⁴In everything we do we try to show that we are true ministers of God. We patiently endure troubles and hardships and calamities of every kind. ⁵We have been beaten, been put in jail, faced angry mobs, worked to exhaustion, endured sleepless nights, and gone without food. ⁶We have proved ourselves by our purity, our understanding, our patience, our kindness, our sincere love, and the power of the Holy Spirit.¹ ⁷We have faithfully preached the truth. God's power has been working in us. We have righteousness as our weapon, both to attack and to defend ourselves. ⁸We serve God whether people honor us or despise us, whether they slander us or praise us. We are honest, but they call us impostors. ⁹We are well known, but we are treated as unknown. We live close to death, but here we are, still alive. We have been beaten within an inch of our lives. ¹⁰Our hearts ache, but we always have joy. We are poor, but we give spiritual riches to others. We own nothing, and yet we have everything.

Paul never gave up. Despite horrifying circumstances and

---

¹ **6:6** Or *the holiness of spirit.*

trouble on top of trouble, his attitude never wavered. He knew he was doing right. He knew the One he believed. The One he followed day by day. The One he wanted to share with others, regardless of the cost.

Paul remained **faithful to God** whether people praised him or trashed him. He remained joyful and content in the toughest circumstances. Even though he was poor, he was able to give spiritual riches to others. "We own nothing, and yet we have everything" (v. 10). Can you say that too?

The **same power** that gave Paul the strength to stand up and do right dwells within you. Don't let tough circumstances or people's expectations affect the way you live and believe. **God is able and ready to give you all the strength you need** to deal with life's hassles. Stand firm. Stand true. **Refuse to compromise** what you believe and how you live. You, too, can have everything that's worth having.

HERE'S WHAT I'M GOING TO DO

❑ _____

_____

❑ _____

_____

_____

GUIDELINES FOR GIVING

Have you ever given your friend a gift just because you care? It's **a gift of love** with no strings attached.

You love God, right? So how do you give him gifts of love? Read Paul's counsel carefully and find out.

2 Corinthians 8:1-5, 9, 11b-15: [1]Now I want to tell you, dear friends,[1] what God in his kindness has done for the churches in Macedonia. [2]Though they have been going through much trouble and hard times, their wonderful joy and deep poverty have overflowed in rich generosity. [3]For I can testify that they gave not only what they could afford but far more. And they did it of their own free will. [4]They begged us again and again for the gracious privilege of sharing in the gift for the Christians in Jerusalem. [5]Best of all, they went beyond our highest hopes, for their first action was to dedicate themselves to the Lord and to us for whatever directions God might give them. . . .

[9]You know how full of love and kindness our Lord Jesus Christ was. Though he was very rich, yet for your sakes he became poor, so that by his poverty he could make you rich.

[11b]Give whatever you can according to what you have. [12]If you are really eager to give, it isn't important how much you are able to give. God wants you to give what you have, not what you don't have. [13]Of course, I don't mean you should give so much that you suffer from having too little. I only mean that there should be some equality. [14]Right now you have plenty and can help them. Then at some other time they can share with you when you need it. In this way, everyone's needs will be met. [15]Do you remember what the Scriptures say about this? "Those who gathered a lot had nothing left over, and those who gathered only a little had enough."[2]

---

[1] **8:1** Greek *brothers*.
[2] **8:15** Exod. 16:18.

Paul complimented the believers in the city of Corinth for their great faith, strong teaching, and beautiful service to one another. But there was an important area they were neglecting: giving to the cause of God. Paul wanted them to "excel also in this gracious ministry of giving." Because they were missing out on **a great blessing.**

Giving is always a touchy subject in the church. **How much is enough?** Paul really doesn't address that question specifically, but he gives general guidelines that we would do well to follow:

- Give in response to God's love, not to get something in return.
- Give whatever you can according to how much you have.
- Give sacrificially but responsibly.
- If you give to others in need, they will help you out when you're in need. In this way, Paul says, everyone's needs will be met (v. 14).

Giving to God can be a real blessing—especially for the giver. But there's only one way to find out!

HERE'S WHAT I'M GOING TO DO

☐ _____

_____

_____

SOWING SEEDS OF LOVE

Remember the old grade school project—planting seeds in little Styrofoam cups filled with potting soil? You stuck those seeds in that dark, rich dirt and watched and waited for the sprout to push through. You'd watch the progress day by day until the plant was too large to fit in the little cup; then you'd transplant it into a bigger pot. It was so cool!

Maybe you've helped your parents with a backyard garden. Or maybe you've even visited or lived on a farm. If so, you know the wonder, the miracle of **sowing seeds and reaping a harvest.** You also know that certain things need to happen in order to get that harvest: seeds, planted properly; enough nutrients, water, sun, and protection from pests; and patience as you wait for the harvest.

Keep those principles in mind as you read Paul's words today.

2 Corinthians 9:9-10: ⁹As the Scriptures say, "Godly people give generously to the poor. Their good deeds will never be forgotten."¹ ¹⁰For God is the one who gives seed to the farmer and then bread to eat. In the same way, he will give you many opportunities to do good, and he will produce a great harvest of generosity² in you.

In the context of advice to the Corinthian Christians about giving, Paul expands the concept beyond giving money. Giving to the poor is just another kind of good deed. The principle Paul quotes (from Psalm 112:9) says, "Godly people give generously to those in need. Their good deeds will never be forgotten."

Giving is a mark of godliness. Giving to the poor is like planting seeds that will bear great fruits of blessing—not only to the poor you help but to yourself. Because God will always remember **every** good deed you do **in his name.**

¹ **9:9** Ps. 112:9.
² **9:10** Greek *righteousness*.

The really neat part of this, however, comes in verse 10: "For God is the one who gives seed to the farmer and then bread to eat. In the same way, he will give you many opportunities to do good, and he will produce a great harvest of generosity in you."

You see, God gives you the **resources,** the **opportunities,** everything you need to do good deeds. **It's your responsibility** to plant them, care for them, and harvest them. You cultivate the opportunities that God gives you in order to produce more

crops. So when you invest what God gives you in his work, he'll provide you even more opportunities to give in his name. God stands ready to start **this growing process in you.** So get ready for a great harvest.

HERE'S WHAT I'M GOING TO DO

☐ _____

_____

☐ _____

_____

☐ _____

_____

SPIRITUAL JOURNEY TRAVEL LOG

THE RIPPLE EFFECT

Somewhere in West Africa, a young woman dives headfirst into the Atlantic Ocean. Her small splash creates a slight ripple on the surface of the water. That ripple extends outward, joining with other ripples, and starts to get bigger. The Gulf Stream current guides the ripple westward, then northward. The ripple begins to rise and then starts rolling in on itself, becoming a wave. Gathering momentum and height, the wave rolls over and under swimmers on the east coast of America before shifting direction and heading northeastward. Sometime later on the southeastern coast of Greenland, thousands of miles away from West Africa, a twenty-foot wave crashes spectacularly onto the shore.

One small movement—one slight ripple—has the potential to produce a **tremendous eventual impact.** Strangely enough, the apostle Paul emphasizes this very principle in his second letter to the Corinthians.

2 Corinthians 9:11-15: [11]Yes, you will be enriched so that you can give even more generously. And when we take your gifts to those who need them, they will break out in thanksgiving to God. [12]So two good things will happen—the needs of the Christians in Jerusalem will be met, and they will joyfully express their thanksgiving to God. [13]You will be glorifying God through your generous gifts. For your generosity to them will prove that you are obedient to the Good News of Christ. [14]And they will pray for you with deep affection because of the wonderful grace of God shown through you.

[15]Thank God for his Son—a gift too wonderful for words![1]

The church in Corinth apparently was sending financial support to the struggling church in Jerusalem. Paul wanted the Corinthians to recognize the enormous impact their generosity

---

[1] **9:15** Greek *Thank God for his indescribable gift.*

was producing. Not only did their support meet the immediate needs of the people in Jerusalem, it resulted in widespread prayer and praise being offered to God. The impact of such prayer and praise, in turn, is **immeasurable.**

The same principle holds true today, although we may never recognize it. Befriending an immigrant family in your neighborhood and helping them adjust to life in this country may not seem like a big deal. Sending a portion of your monthly income to support a child overseas may seem like a small sacrifice. Organizing a coat-collection drive for the homeless in your community seems hardly worth mentioning. In fact, all of these examples of **individual ministry** are nothing more than tiny ripples in the vast ocean of world needs. But sometimes a tiny ripple can eventually produce a tremendous impact.

Look for opportunities to impact a person's life—to create the tiny ripple that can make the difference in hundreds of lives someday.

PRAYER POINT

Ask God to show you the opportunities for ministry and to multiply your ministry efforts so that countless people may benefit.

HERE'S WHAT I'M GOING TO DO

☐ _____

_____

☐ _____

_____

☐ _____

_____

BOASTER SHOTS

In our world of **information overload,** it takes a particularly vivid image or character to stick in our minds. As a result, people looking to stand out are forced to go to more and more extreme lengths to promote themselves. This climate has produced a culture in which boasting thrives. Watch any NBA or NFL game (including pre- and postgame interviews), and you'll see more trash talking, posturing, chest-thumping, and rampant egomania than you ever thought humans capable of.

That's not to say that boasting is a new phenomenon, of course. The Bible, for one, certainly contains its share of boasters. In New Testament times, the apostle Paul faced off against some especially troublesome boasters in the Corinthian church.

2 Corinthians 10:12-18: [12]Oh, don't worry; I wouldn't dare say that I am as wonderful as these other men who tell you how important they are! But they are only comparing themselves with each other, and measuring themselves by themselves. What foolishness!

[13]But we will not boast of authority we do not have. Our goal is to stay within the boundaries of God's plan for us, and this plan includes our working there with you. [14]We are not going too far when we claim authority over you, for we were the first to travel all the way to you with the Good News of Christ. [15]Nor do we claim credit for the work someone else has done. Instead, we hope that your faith will grow and that our work among you will be greatly enlarged. [16]Then we will be able to go and preach the Good News in other places that are far beyond you, where no one else is working. Then there will be no question about being in someone else's territory. [17]As the Scriptures say, "The person who wishes to boast should boast only of what the Lord has done."[1] [18]When people

---

[1] **10:17** Jer. 9:24.

boast about themselves, it doesn't count for much. But when the Lord commends someone, that's different!

Apparently false teachers had invaded the church in Corinth. Even worse, these false teachers were a rather cocky group, boasting of their ministry and behaving as though there was no higher standard than themselves. Paul, in contrast, recognized that if any boasting was to be done concerning his work, it would have to be **boasting in the Lord.** Paul understood that it is the Lord who deserves credit for **any good that results from our work.**

The other principle that Paul makes crystal clear is that "When people boast about themselves, it doesn't count for much." What does count? The Lord's commendation. So don't seek the spotlight. And trust God to commend your work as you serve him in your life.

HERE'S WHAT I'M GOING TO DO

☐ _____

☐ _____

☐ _____

☐ _____

A SECOND OPINION

One of the basic tenets of the medical profession is "First do no harm." All medical caregivers—physicians, surgeons, nurses, emergency medical technicians, psychiatrists—are bound by this principle. The idea is that before any treatment is administered to a patient, the caregiver must determine to the best of his or her ability that the treatment will not injure or put the patient at risk.

Although no such official guideline governs the actions of Christian servants, this principle is one that we should adopt. Before we do something to care for or protect a person in need, we should consider the **implications of our action.** In our eagerness to minister, we may end up doing unintentional harm.

Recognizing dangers such as this, the apostle Paul set up a system to safeguard his ministry. He gave his advice to a troubled Galatian church, which was insisting on observing Jewish customs.

Galatians 2:1-5: ¹Then fourteen years later I went back to Jerusalem again, this time with Barnabas; and Titus came along, too. ²I went there because God revealed to me that I should go. While I was there I talked privately with the leaders of the church. I wanted them to understand what I had been preaching to the Gentiles. I wanted to make sure they did not disagree, or my ministry would have been useless. ³And they did agree. They did not even demand that my companion Titus be circumcised, though he was a Gentile.¹

⁴Even that question wouldn't have come up except for some so-called Christians there—false ones, really²—who came to spy on us and see our freedom in Christ Jesus. They wanted to force us, like slaves, to follow their Jewish regulations. ⁵But we refused to listen to them for a single

¹ **2:3** Greek *a Greek.*
² **2:4** Greek *some false brothers.*

moment. We wanted to preserve the truth of the Good News for you.

Paul guarded against losing his ministry focus by surrounding himself with people who would **prevent him from going astray.** Note the importance that Paul placed on **companionship** and

fellowship with Barnabas and Titus joining him. This is not to suggest that we must have someone with us at all times in order to minister to others. What it does suggest is that we not adopt a "Lone Ranger" mentality to ministry. We need to find **mature Christians** who will be willing to serve as "sounding boards" and advisors (of sorts) to us. They will keep us from the overzealous behavior that caused many in the Galatian church to burden others with needless regulations.

It also means that who we choose as "companions" *is* important. Who are your friends? Can they be trusted to give you sound advice? That needed "second opinion"? Make it a point to surround yourself with mature and trustworthy friends.

HERE'S WHAT I'M GOING TO DO

☐ _____

_____

☐ _____

_____

☐ _____

_____

FORGET-ME-NOT

If you've ever sat through an Academy Awards telecast, you'll probably recognize this scenario: The winner stands behind the podium, grasping his or her Oscar, and begins to thank every person he or she has ever worked with. After naming half of the people in Hollywood, the excited winner adds this little blurb at the end of the speech—"and anyone else whose name I've forgotten." How do you suppose those **forgotten people** feel when they hear that?

Galatians 2 records a meeting between two of the most important figures in the early church—the apostles Peter and Paul. Interestingly enough, one of the main topics of their conversation is forgotten people.

> Galatians 2:6-10: [6]And the leaders of the church who were there had nothing to add to what I was preaching. (By the way, their reputation as great leaders made no difference to me, for God has no favorites.) [7]They saw that God had given me the responsibility of preaching the Good News to the Gentiles, just as he had given Peter the responsibility of preaching to the Jews. [8]For the same God who worked through Peter for the benefit of the Jews worked through me for the benefit of the Gentiles. [9]In fact, James, Peter,[1] and John, who were known as pillars of the church, recognized the gift God had given me, and they accepted Barnabas and me as their co-workers. They encouraged us to keep preaching to the Gentiles, while they continued their work with the Jews. [10]The only thing they suggested was that we remember to help the poor, and I have certainly been eager to do that.

During the early days of the church, Jesus' disciples were looked to as the leaders of the Christian movement. Because Paul had not been one of the Twelve, it was important that he be accepted by James, Peter, and John. If these men recognized

---

[1] **2:9** Greek *Cephas;* also in 2:11, 14.

Paul's ministry as legitimate, so would other believers. The three disciples were only too happy to welcome Paul into a position of leadership in the church.

PRAYER POINT

Ask God to help you focus your thoughts regularly on the poor and not forget the needy.

They had just **one request** for Paul. Now keep in mind, these were the early days of the church. Believers were facing a multitude of issues and problems—persecution, growth, false teachers, and squabbles among various factions, just to name a few. With all of these serious situations to consider, what did James, Peter, and John want Paul to remember more than anything? The poor.

Taking care of the needy is every bit as important today as it was in the early church. Yet many Christians fail to heed the advice that James, Peter, and John gave to Paul. Unfortunately, the poor of our society are often **forgotten by God's people.**

Before you conclude this devotion, ask yourself three questions: (1) On a scale of one to ten, how well do you do at remembering the poor? (2) What are some things that tend to occupy your mind and cause you to forget about the poor? (3) What specific steps can you take to ensure that you will **continue to remember** the poor?

HERE'S WHAT I'M GOING TO DO

☐ _____

_____

☐ _____

_____

BEARING A BURDEN

In the motion picture *The Mission*, a slave trader named Mendoza is overcome with **remorse** over his life of sin, which includes murder, thievery, and adultery. In jail, he encounters the news of God's forgiveness and decides to join a religious order. Still haunted by his sin, he decides to do penance by dragging a net full of armor and weapons through a treacherous jungle terrain. Through rivers, swamps, and steep paths he marches, refusing to let go of his burden. At last he scales a hill and encounters one of the natives he had enslaved. The man comes at Mendoza with a knife. But instead of attacking, he cuts the net from Mendoza's back and hurls it into the falls below. Overwhelmed by the man's kindness and God's grace, Mendoza begins to sob uncontrollably.

Paul knew the **relief** that comes when **God lifts our burden of sin.** He instructs Christians to imitate God's example by bearing each other's burdens.

> Galatians 6:3-5: ³If you think you are too important to help someone in need, you are only fooling yourself. You are really a nobody. ⁴Be sure to do what you should, for then you will enjoy the personal satisfaction of having done your work well, and you won't need to compare yourself to anyone else. ⁵For we are each responsible for our own conduct.

In these verses, Paul explains that before we can be burden-bearers, we need to **rid ourselves of conceit.** The problem with conceit, which is believing that we're better than others, is that it causes us to be intolerant of other people's shortcomings. It's tough to carry others' burdens without having a proper attitude toward them.

The remedy for conceit is a good old-fashioned self-examination. Rather than comparing ourselves with other people and their ministries, we need to take **an objective**

look at ourselves and our ministry. This objective look will reveal not what we have accomplished but **what God has accomplished through** us. That's what we can take pride in—the work of God.

Carrying another person's burdens is a huge responsibility. It's a task that requires a proper attitude. Perhaps the best way to sum it up is to put it in physical terms. If we are going to respond to God's call to carry the burdens of the poor and needy, we need to make sure that we are in **good enough (spiritual) shape** to do some heavy lifting. Are you?

PRAYER POINT

Spend some time in prayer thanking the Lord for others whose help keeps you from carrying your burdens alone.

HERE'S WHAT I'M GOING TO DO

☐ _____

_____

☐ _____

_____

☐ _____

_____

☐ _____

_____

☐ _____

_____

_____

WHAT A DIFFERENCE!

After you've traveled in a Third World country, you're no longer the same. You appreciate space and quiet and leisure. You're grateful for uncrowded sidewalks, the independence of your car, spacious rooms, backyards, and *Western* toilets! And you recognize the luxury of an unhurried and hot shower, your own comfortable bed, and clean clothes. Customs officials note an almost unanimous response from returning Americans: They're glad to be back home.

As **grateful** as we may be for such **comforts,** we should be infinitely more thankful for the way **God has welcomed us** into his presence. When we consider how terrible our situation was before God rescued us, our response should be praise and awe. Listen to what Paul tells the Ephesians:

> Ephesians 2:1-10: ¹Once you were dead, doomed forever because of your many sins. ²You used to live just like the rest of the world, full of sin, obeying Satan, the mighty prince of the power of the air. He is the spirit at work in the hearts of those who refuse to obey God. ³All of us used to live that way, following the passions and desires of our evil nature. We were born with an evil nature, and we were under God's anger just like everyone else.
>
> ⁴But God is so rich in mercy, and he loved us so very much, ⁵that even while we were dead because of our sins, he gave us life when he raised Christ from the dead. (It is only by God's special favor that you have been saved!) ⁶For he raised us from the dead along with Christ, and we are seated with him in the heavenly realms—all because we are one with Christ Jesus. ⁷And so God can always point to us as examples of the incredible wealth of his favor and kindness toward us, as shown in all he has done for us through Christ Jesus.

[8]God saved you by his special favor when you believed. And you can't take credit for this; it is a gift from God. [9]Salvation is not a reward for the good things we have done, so none of us can boast about it. [10]For we are God's masterpiece. He has created us anew in Christ Jesus, so that we can do the good things he planned for us long ago.

Gratefulness should be the norm in our lives, not the occasional or rare outburst. And even though we tend to concentrate on our physical blessings, these are mere *things.* Nothing in this world—nothing!—can begin to compare with the greatest gift God has given us: **eternal life.** Blessings like wealth and health may come and go, but our salvation is **secure, constant,** and **reserved** for us forever in heaven. We see God's incredible work in redeeming us when we deserved nothing but his anger. And for that reason alone we have a reason to be forever thankful!

He gave us life! How can we help but praise him? How can we help but sing? How can we help but live a life of thankfulness? Lord, stir us from complacency . . . and move us toward gratefulness. It's the **only perspective** through which we should view the world.

HERE'S WHAT I'M GOING TO DO

DON'T CHEAT!

A missionary in Africa was teaching an adult Bible class, and when it came time for the examination, he reminded the students: Don't cheat! Soon after he handed out the exams, however, he found that the pupils almost immediately turned to one another, sharing answers. The teacher was confounded by their actions—astounded, most of all, that they would ignore his instructions and violate such an important code of ethics. But after warning them yet again, the pupils still talked among themselves. Finally, a national missionary came to his aid to explain the mystery.

Don't cheat to them meant: **Don't withhold valuable knowledge from one another!** In one way, the students were merely exhibiting what Paul says:

> Ephesians 4:11-16: [11][God] is the one who gave these gifts to the church: the apostles, the prophets, the evangelists, and the pastors and teachers. [12]Their responsibility is to equip God's people to do his work and build up the church, the body of Christ, [13]until we come to such unity in our faith and knowledge of God's Son that we will be mature and full grown in the Lord, measuring up to the full stature of Christ.
>
> [14]Then we will no longer be like children, forever changing our minds about what we believe because someone has told us something different or because someone has cleverly lied to us and made the lie sound like the truth. [15]Instead, we will hold to the truth in love, becoming more and more in every way like Christ, who is the head of his body, the church. [16]Under his direction, the whole body is fitted together perfectly. As each part does its own special work, it helps the other parts grow, so that the whole body is healthy and growing and full of love.

Notice that Christ gave the "gifts" to the church, and those gifts are given to apostles, prophets, evangelists, pastors, and teachers—in other words, people just like you. Other gifts listed elsewhere in Scripture include those given for hospitality and service and prayer. Each one is of infinite value and absolutely necessary for the church to properly function. The design, fitted together by God, hinges on **cooperation, commitment,** and **contribution.**

PRAYER POINT

Ask God to point out specific ways you can contribute to your local church. Prayerfully consider: *Do I have a servant's heart?*

Therefore, if someone withholds his or her gift, the church suffers. So when the teacher doesn't teach, there's a void for the learners. When those with friendly hospitality don't host others, there's a need that's not filled. And when evangelists don't reach out with the gospel, the unsaved go untold. **Each believer must do his or her part** or the body suffers. In other words, the church is cheated of that needed contribution!

The reward for full participation, Paul tells us, is harmony and maturity. We will not be deceived by wrong ideas. We grow together in Christ.

The church is indeed miraculous and living, formed of many parts to create the whole. Are you contributing **your part** to the living body? Remember, *don't cheat!*

HERE'S WHAT I'M GOING TO DO

☐ _____

_____

☐ _____

_____

_____

WALK IT OUT

There's an old saying that challenges us **not to judge another** until we've walked a mile in his or her shoes. In other words, we need to view life from another's perspective before we become critical or patronizing or egocentric. Well, that sounds easy enough, doesn't it? But more and more we find that having the ability to step out of our own perceptions—and into another's—is the true mark of maturity. And it's *not* easy.

Take a look at how God (through Paul) describes this:

Philippians 2:3-4: ³Don't be selfish; don't live to make a good impression on others. Be humble, thinking of others as better than yourself. ⁴Don't think only about your own affairs, but be interested in others, too, and what they are doing.

That's a lot of maturity in just a few words, isn't it? Don't be selfish. Don't live merely to impress others. Be humble. Think of others more highly than yourself. And don't be self-centered, but instead focus on what others are doing. That sounds more like walking a million miles in another's shoes!

How does all this work out, specifically? Well, say we were quick to judge another's aloofness. *Isn't she the snobby one?* we might casually comment to ourselves. And then later we learn that she's merely shy, the product of a home that constantly demeans her. Or maybe we thought a new acquaintance pushy and controlling; eventually we might realize that he merely had an intense desire to help and please. *Oh Lord, forgive us. And help us begin to learn what it is to* **love—with genuine love!**

Genuine love—now that's what we're aiming for. Paul tells us that it involves **working together with one heart and purpose.** It's unselfish, not attempting to merely make a good impression or to cultivate *me*. And it's humble, thinking of others first. When Christ freely demonstrated all of this to us—when we deserved nothing—shouldn't we attempt to **do this for each other?** And finally, genuine love does indeed mean walking in another's shoes—before I form an impression, before I make a snap judgment, and definitely before I might wound another's heart.

By the way, what size shoe do you wear?

HERE'S WHAT I'M GOING TO DO

☐ _____

_____

☐ _____

_____

☐ _____

_____

☐ _____

_____

☐ _____

_____

☐ _____

_____

THE SECRET OF LIVING

Malcolm Muggeridge, the famous British journalist who became a Christian late in life, spent several years in India. His keen eye noticed a quality of life among the people in India that contrasted sharply with those who live in the West. He wrote: "They were all so poor; they all had so very little. Anyone from the West was a sort of millionaire by comparison, even nuns and monks and vagrants. When floods came and they had to leave their homes, they could comfortably carry all they possessed on their heads: a tin box, a mat, some cooking vessels, no more. . . . They had no sales potential; the siren voices recommending eating this, wearing that, urging them to consume, consume would be wasted on their air. Their poverty immunized them against the chief sickness of the age. Perhaps it is in this that the **blessedness of the poor**—the least appreciated of the Beatitudes today—resides."

The apostle Paul knew the blessedness of **having little.** He shared the secret of his contentment with the Philippians:

Philippians 4:10-14: [10]How grateful I am, and how I praise the Lord that you are concerned about me again. I know you have always been concerned for me, but for a while you didn't have the chance to help me. [11]Not that I was ever in need, for I have learned how to get along happily whether I have much or little. [12]I know how to live on almost nothing or with everything. I have learned the secret of living in every situation, whether it is with a full stomach or empty, with plenty or little. [13]For I can do everything with the help of Christ who gives me the strength I need. [14]But even so, you have done well to share with me in my present difficulty.

Whether he was living with a full stomach or empty,

whether he had much or little, whether he had everything or nothing—Paul was happy and grateful. Obviously, he discovered and practiced the **secret of contentment.** And you know what that is? The power of **decision.** That's it. Such a little thing . . . such a major jump.

It's all **a matter of perspective,** isn't it? You can whine and complain that you don't have enough . . . or you can decide to be content. You can be bitter and resentful that your friend has a new car when you're stuck with an old junker . . . or you can decide to be content. And you can even be angry and defensive about the lack of advantages you had as a child growing up . . . or you can decide to be content.

Where do we find **the strength** to make those kinds of decisions? Paul tells us that too: "For I can do everything with the help of Christ who gives me the strength I need" (v. 13). He lives within you. And he's able and waiting. **So make the decision.**

That's the secret.

PRAYER POINT

Prayerfully evaluate: In what areas of life are you unsatisfied? Confess these and ask God to help you decide to be content.

HERE'S WHAT I'M GOING TO DO

☐ _____

_____

☐ _____

_____

☐ _____

_____

CARING FOR OTHERS

She sits alone in her small, tidy house watching game shows. Occasionally she glances at the phone sitting beside her on a lacy white doily, wondering why it never rings. Is it broken? Has the phone company cut off her service? Sometimes she even picks up the receiver to listen to the dial tone. Still droning.

Then she notices the mail truck out front, depositing her mail. She works hard to get up out of her easy chair and walk to the mailbox, her arthritic hips nagging at her all the way. Perhaps there'd be a letter today or a card from a friend. But no. She grimaces as she looks through the few envelopes. Junk mail. A couple of bills. Not even a Social Security check.

Slowly, even more painfully, she returns to her house. Perhaps she will take a nap. And escape.

1 Timothy 5:3-8: 3The church should care for any widow who has no one else to care for her. 4But if she has children or grandchildren, their first responsibility is to show godliness at home and repay their parents by taking care of them. This is something that pleases God very much.

5But a woman who is a true widow, one who is truly alone in this world, has placed her hope in God. Night and day she asks God for help and spends much time in prayer. 6But the widow who lives only for pleasure is spiritually dead. 7Give these instructions to the church so that the widows you support[1] will not be criticized.

8But those who won't care for their own relatives, especially those living in the same household, have denied what we believe. Such people are worse than unbelievers.

Paul sets forth some guidelines about **caring** for widows and the elderly to his son in the faith, Timothy, a young pastor.

---

[1] **5:7** Or *so the church;* Greek reads *so they.*

First and foremost, a widow's family is to take responsibility to care for her. But if a widow has no family, it is the church's responsibility. As the church helps **supply** her physical and emotional needs, she in turn is able to **serve** the church as she can.

The principle is clear: The church is designed by God **to support those who have no families.**

Often, families who must care for their ill or elderly members are placed under a heavy financial burden. They may need extra money. Encouraging support. A helping hand. And **the church should be there for them.** Something very interesting usually happens as the church shares as a truly caring community. Those who receive the blessing of support often become a blessing to others. That's the way it's supposed to work.

HERE'S WHAT I'M GOING TO DO

☐ _____

_____

☐ _____

_____

☐ _____

_____

☐ _____

_____

_____

Righteous Riches

DAY 241

Everybody would love to get rich quick. Admit it. Wouldn't it be great to have that magazine sweepstakes van wake you up with a knock on your door and a check for ten million buckaroonies? Or maybe some long-lost rich uncle you never even knew existed dies and leaves you his entire estate of ten billion smackeroos? You could deal with that, couldn't you? But then, how much is really enough? If you had the ten million, or even the ten billion, would that really bring contentment? **What really brings contentment?** Paul tells his young friend Timothy:

> 1 Timothy 6:6-10: ⁶Yet true religion with contentment is great wealth. ⁷After all, we didn't bring anything with us when we came into the world, and we certainly cannot carry anything with us when we die. ⁸So if we have enough food and clothing, let us be content. ⁹But people who long to be rich fall into temptation and are trapped by many foolish and harmful desires that plunge them into ruin and destruction. ¹⁰For the love of money is at the root of all kinds of evil. And some people, craving money, have wandered from the faith and pierced themselves with many sorrows.

When John D. Rockefeller died, a reporter was determined to find out how much money he left behind. He made an appointment with one of Rockefeller's highest aides and asked him. The aide replied, "How much did he leave? All of it!"

Paul says, "We didn't bring anything with us when we came into the world, and we certainly **cannot carry anything with us** when we die" (v. 7). So what are we supposed to do? "Let us be content" with what we have. Contentment is an elusive thing in our culture. After all, our whole society is built on the idea of **having more.** We must make more money to buy more things. But that philosophy is totally foreign to the way of Christ. When is it so bad to want money and things? When they **force our attention away from God and his will for us.** We get on a treadmill that's very difficult to get off. It's a treadmill that leads to "ruin and destruction."

Money itself is not bad. But the love of money is the root, the source, the cause of all kinds of sin. Greed. Lust. Stealing. All of that evil is sourced in wanting more. And many who fall into the money trap "have wandered from the faith and pierced themselves with many sorrows." Ouch.

PRAYER POINT

Offer to God all your things. Your money. Your savings account. Your possessions—even your favorites. Give him control of them all. Ask him for a contented heart that's free of the love of money. And full of the love of the Lord.

Don't get on that treadmill. **Be content with what you have.** God will bless you with everything you need. Then you can spend your time and energy pursuing ways to love and serve others. And that's the richest wealth a human being can experience.

HERE'S WHAT I'M GOING TO DO

☐ _____

_____

☐ _____

_____

☐ _____

_____

CLEAN UTENSILS

Does your family have a nice set of silverware or stainless steel utensils? It's the "good stuff." The forks and spoons and knives you use for big dinners at Thanksgiving, Christmas, Easter, maybe family birthdays and other special occasions. If so, you probably keep this silverware in a beautiful wooden box. Occasionally someone will lovingly polish every piece so it's shiny and beautiful and ready to use. Now compare that silverware with the plastic "sporks" you get at a fast-food restaurant, wrapped in plastic with a cheap napkin. They're used once and then tossed. Nothing special.

If you were a utensil, which would you rather be: treasured silver or tossed-away plastic?

2 Timothy 2:20-21: 20In a wealthy home some utensils are made of gold and silver, and some are made of wood and clay. The expensive utensils are used for special occasions, and the cheap ones are for everyday use. 21If you keep yourself pure, you will be a utensil God can use for his purpose. Your life will be clean, and you will be ready for the Master to use you for every good work.

Paul uses picture language to get an important point across to Timothy. In those days, of course, they didn't have plastic utensils. But they did have wood or clay ones that were cheap and not used for anything special. His point is that in the world—and even in the church—there are **faithful** people

whom God uses, and there are **unfaithful** people. Followers of Jesus should aim to be the kind of people that God uses for special occasions: utensils—**vessels for his Spirit**—that are clean and ready to use for joyful, loving purposes. That can happen only when they are pure. Clean. Ready to use.

Of course, something clean and set apart for special use can easily become grungy and contaminated. When a spoon is gross with old food on it—even if it's a beautiful silver spoon—it is set aside and left unused until it can be cleaned up properly.

Don't let that happen to you. **Be careful with whom you hang out** and **what you do in your spare time.** Strive to keep yourself clean and ready for God to use. Be the kind of person Jesus can work through for his noblest purposes. Then God can use you as **an instrument of his blessing** in every good work.

PRAYER POINT

Are you all cleaned up and ready for God to use for every good work? If not, spend some time in prayer confessing your sins and thanking God for cleansing you and filling you. Ask God to give you an opportunity to be used for his glory today.

HERE'S WHAT I'M GOING TO DO

☐ _____

_____

☐ _____

_____

☐ _____

_____

☐ _____

_____

THE NEW YOU

People who have endured an unexpected trauma or who have made major changes often discover **a new outlook on life.** Some hospital patients who have had a near-death experience develop a much greater appreciation for life. People who have lost a lot of weight often become more outgoing. A family that loses a house in a fire often discovers a new sense of unity.

Nothing, however, can bring about a more **radical shift** than when a person **gives his or her life to Christ.** The apostle Paul describes the changes that occur when a person becomes a Christian. Let's take a look.

Colossians 3:1-10: ¹Since you have been raised to new life with Christ, set your sights on the realities of heaven, where Christ sits at God's right hand in the place of honor and power. ²Let heaven fill your thoughts. Do not think only about things down here on earth. ³For you died when Christ died, and your real life is hidden with Christ in God. ⁴And when Christ, who is your¹ real life, is revealed to the whole world, you will share in all his glory.

⁵So put to death the sinful, earthly things lurking within you. Have nothing to do with sexual sin, impurity, lust, and shameful desires. Don't be greedy for the good things of this life, for that is idolatry. ⁶God's terrible anger will come upon those who do such things. ⁷You used to do them when your life was still part of this world. ⁸But now is the time to get rid of anger, rage, malicious behavior, slander, and dirty language. ⁹Don't lie to each other, for you have stripped off your old evil nature and all its wicked deeds. ¹⁰In its place you have clothed yourselves with a brand-new nature that is continually being renewed as you learn more and more about Christ, who created this new nature within you.

¹ **3:4** Some manuscripts read *our.*

The way Paul describes it, turning away from the old self and embracing the new self—**going from sinfulness to righteousness**—is almost like changing clothes. Christians should be recognizable by the "clothing" of the new self—compassion, kindness, humility, gentleness, patience, forgiveness, and love. We all know what it means to be compassionate, kind, humble, and so on. The key is making **a conscious decision to demonstrate** these qualities to others every day.

If you're at a loss as to how and to whom you can demonstrate these qualities, start with simple gestures. Befriend the lonely student. Show kindness to family members. Be a visible light of compassion in a world of darkness. It's a style that **never** goes out of fashion.

HERE'S WHAT I'M GOING TO DO

☐ _____

☐ _____

☐ _____

☐ _____

_____

_____

A Source of Comfort

Is there anything tougher than trying to **comfort** someone at a funeral? Often the best we can hope for in a situation like that is not to say something that causes even more pain. If you've ever lost a loved one, you probably know that people can say some pretty dumb things when they're trying to "comfort" you.

The apostle Paul, interestingly enough, strongly encourages Christians to **comfort each other in the face of death.** His first letter to the Thessalonians includes this comforting wisdom:

> 1 Thessalonians 4:13-18: 13And now, brothers and sisters, I want you to know what will happen to the Christians who have died so you will not be full of sorrow like people who have no hope. 14For since we believe that Jesus died and was raised to life again, we also believe that when Jesus comes, God will bring back with Jesus all the Christians who have died.

> 15I can tell you this directly from the Lord: We who are still living when the Lord returns will not rise to meet him ahead of those who are in their graves. 16For the Lord himself will come down from heaven with a commanding shout, with the call of the archangel, and with the trumpet call of God. First, all the Christians who have died will rise from their graves. 17Then, together with them, we who are still alive and remain on the earth will be caught up in the clouds to meet the Lord in the air and remain with him forever. 18So comfort and encourage each other with these words.

Paul was explaining a Christian's eternal destiny to the Thessalonians. Believers who die—or "fall asleep," as Paul put it—will be brought first to heaven by God as a result of Jesus' resurrection. Believers who do not die—those who are still alive when Christ returns—will meet the Lord in the air on their way to heaven. Either way, all believers can look forward to **spending eternity with the Lord**—and we can't even imagine how incredible that will be.

These are the words that Paul instructs believers to use as they comfort one another in the face of death. Christ's resurrection opened the door for all believers to be resurrected, so death is certainly not the end. There's never been a grave dug that could hold the spirit of a believer. The trite saying still rings true: Christians who have died are in **a much better place** than we are.

Let's not kid ourselves, though. As incredible as Paul's words in today's passage are, they cannot erase the pain and sorrow of losing a loved one. Those of us who try to comfort others with Paul's words need to keep this in mind. Grieving people may not always respond to our efforts to comfort them in the way we hope.

After time has passed, God may give you the opportunity to speak to the person who has lost a loved one and is looking for **true comfort.** If you're a person who wants to be able to provide real comfort to others, Paul's words in 1 Thessalonians 4 should be a great help to you.

HERE'S WHAT I'M GOING TO DO

☐ _____

_____

☐ _____

_____

SPIRITUAL LEADERS

DAY

245

What are the **attributes** and **characteristics** you look for in a friend? Is loyalty important to you? How about compassion? Do you prefer people who have a sense of humor or people who are more serious-minded? Do you care whether the person is popular or not? Is it important that you share the same interests? If you could design your own friend, what would he or she be like?

Now, what if we asked you to list the attributes and characteristics that are important for a **church leader** to have? What things might be on your list? Go ahead and make a list. Then compare your ideas with those of the apostle Paul in his letter to Titus.

> Titus 1:6-9: [6]An elder must be well thought of for his good life. He must be faithful to his wife,[1] and his children must be believers who are not wild or rebellious. [7]An elder[2] must live a blameless life because he is God's minister. He must not be arrogant or quick-tempered; he must not be a heavy drinker, violent, or greedy for money. [8]He must enjoy having guests in his home and must love all that is good. He must live wisely and be fair. He must live a devout and disciplined life. [9]He must have a strong and steadfast belief in the trustworthy message he was taught; then he will be able to encourage others with right teaching and show those who oppose it where they are wrong.

After Paul introduced Christianity to the island of Crete, he left his fellow worker Titus there to oversee the spiritual growth of the new believers. Among his other duties, Titus was responsible for selecting elders to organize and lead churches in the area.

Obviously Titus couldn't appoint just anyone to be an elder. That's why Paul gave Titus some specific requirements

---

[1] **1:6** Or *have only one wife*, or *be married only once*; Greek reads *be the husband of one wife.*
[2] **1:7** Greek *overseer.*

for the position. Many of the characteristics Paul listed have to do with the elder's **reputation** in the community. He had to be faithful to his wife. His children not only had to be believers, they also had to be obedient. He could not be a hothead, a drunkard, or a cheat. In other words, an elder was required to **live an upright life.**

Why do you suppose God places such strict standards on **spiritual leaders?** Well, for one thing, they're responsible for teaching others about the Lord and his will. And **one of the best ways to lead others is by example.** When we look at a Christian leader, we should see attributes and characteristics that we would like to develop in our own lives. (By the same token, we should learn to model those attributes so that others will learn from **our example.**)

It is very important to have the right people in church leadership positions today. Do you have what it takes to become such a person—specifically, the **desire** to develop the attributes of an effective leader?

HERE'S WHAT I'M GOING TO DO

☐ _____

_____

☐ _____

_____

SPIRITUAL JOURNEY TRAVEL LOG

RUNAWAY

Your dad has given you special permission to take his restored 1966 Mustang to your school graduation. You're delighted because many of your friends have admired the car for years, and you know how much your dad treasures that car. But as you enter the school parking lot, you get a little goofy and start honking the horn, waving to friends, not looking at the road. You hear a sickening crunch before you realize you've plowed the car into a light pole. You are not hurt, but you are overwhelmed with fear and disgust with yourself. What are you going to say to your dad? What is he going to say when he learns *how* the accident happened?

Asking yourself these questions will help you get in the proper mind-set for today's devotion. In the shortest book of the New Testament, the apostle Paul tells the story of a man named Philemon who was betrayed by one of his slaves, a man named Onesimus. Let's take a look at Paul's surprising request of Philemon on behalf of Onesimus.

> Philemon 10-12: ¹⁰My plea is that you show kindness to Onesimus. I think of him as my own son because he became a believer as a result of my ministry here in prison. ¹¹Onesimus¹ hasn't been of much use to you in the past, but now he is very useful to both of us. ¹²I am sending him back to you, and with him comes my own heart.

The situation was cut-and-dried. Onesimus was a slave, the lowest rung on society's ladder. Apparently Onesimus had run away from Philemon, his master, and had stolen some things on his way out the door. Bad idea. You see, under Roman law, these offenses were punishable by death.

While on the run, however, Onesimus had crossed paths with Paul and had become a Christian. Philemon, whom Paul apparently knew, was also a Christian. Onesimus was willing to return to his master to **make things right,** but he was

¹ **11** *Onesimus* means "useful."

probably nervous about what Philemon would do to him.

That's why Paul wrote this letter on Onesimus' behalf. The apostle urged Philemon to **receive** Onesimus not as a slave but as a Christian brother. He wanted Philemon to **forgive** Onesimus the way he would forgive any other member of his church. He wanted Philemon to **welcome** Onesimus with the same respect and affection that he would give Paul himself.

The book of Philemon is not just a lesson in **forgiveness,** however. It also shows the importance of **recognizing people's true worth.** In the world's eyes, Onesimus was just a slave—an unimportant, "disposable" servant. In Paul's eyes, however, Onesimus was a **valuable** Christian brother.

How do you regard your brothers and sisters in Christ? Do you spend more time remembering their liabilities, their faults, their past slipups? Or do you love them as Christ would, encouraging them in their faith and helping them do good? If we follow Paul's example, we will nurture Christians who will come to maturity and mentor others in the same way.

HERE'S WHAT I'M GOING TO DO

☐ _____

_____

_____

WORK TO BE DONE

What is the most difficult job you could imagine? A police officer patrolling a gang-infested neighborhood of a major city? A window-washer balancing a hundred stories above the ground? A construction worker smoothing asphalt on a scorching summer day? A doctor in a refugee camp with few supplies and an endless stream of new patients? Some jobs require a daily dose of **courage** to complete the work at hand. The jobholder well deserves—or more than deserves—the compensation he or she gets for his or her efforts.

God recognizes that those who labor on his behalf merit their rewards too. The writer of the book of Hebrews reminds his audience that God will not forget how hard they have labored for him.

> Hebrews 6:9-12: ⁹Dear friends, even though we are talking like this, we really don't believe that it applies to you. We are confident that you are meant for better things, things that come with salvation. ¹⁰For God is not unfair. He will not forget how hard you have worked for him and how you have shown your love to him by caring for other Christians, as you still do. ¹¹Our great desire is that you will keep right on loving others as long as life lasts, in order to make certain that what you hope for will come true. ¹²Then you will not become spiritually dull and indifferent. Instead, you will follow the example of those who are going to inherit God's promises because of their faith and patience.

God is the perfect boss. He knows everything about his workers, including which jobs will best suit their abilities. He never gives his laborers any task that is **too difficult** for them, and he is **always available** to help them complete their work. In addition, he's extremely **generous** in his rewards for a job well done.

It may involve physical labor, but sometimes a Christian's work involves nothing more than **persevering.** Unfortunately, that is often the most difficult work of all. Although most of us will never face physical persecution or death because of our faith, we live in a society that **does not respond well to Christians.** In fact, many people actively oppose Christian beliefs and those who hold them. Sometimes that opposition is so intense that we're tempted to give up, to stop defending our faith and living it openly. That's when the work starts. That's when we have to motivate ourselves—and others—**to continue to live according to God's will, regardless of the opposition.**

Work is extremely important to God. There is no room for laziness among his people. Fortunately for us, God recognizes how difficult it can be for us to carry out his work. That's why he's created such an incredible incentive program for us. Unlike our work on earth, which often goes unnoticed, God will reward **everything**—*every little thing*—we do for him. God, the perfect boss, sees all and rewards all.

HERE'S WHAT I'M GOING TO DO

☐ _____

_____

☐ _____

_____

STRANGE BLESSING

You've heard the stories. There's the one about the couple driving on a lonely road late one night who stop to pick up a mysterious hitchhiker. He sits quietly in the backseat as they drive on. Then he says, "His lips are on the trumpet! Jesus is coming soon!" Shocked, they turn around to look—but the hitchhiker has vanished!

Then there's the story about the elderly gentleman in the soup line at a homeless shelter who lets everyone else go before him. The line was long, and the soup was running low. The volunteers were fretting about how they would feed so many. Finally, the man accepted his bowl of soup and crust of bread. But then he turned, saw the long line of hungry people still waiting to be served, and turned back to the volunteer. "Here," he said, "pour my soup back in the pot for these others." The volunteer smirked—what good would one bowlful do?—but did so. The next time she dipped into the pot, it was full again! And the elderly man was gone.

Whether or not these stories are true, have you ever considered that you may have **entertained an angel** without realizing it?

Hebrews 13:1-2: [1]Continue to love each other with true Christian love.[1] [2]Don't forget to show hospitality to strangers, for some who have done this have entertained angels without realizing it!

There are a lot of "urban legends" about angelic visitations. Whether they're true or not is hard to tell. But the writer of Hebrews leaves no doubt that believers are to **show hospitality to strangers,** "for some who have done this have entertained angels without realizing it!"

The Bible has at least three Old Testament stories of people entertaining angels unaware: Abraham (in Genesis 18), Gideon

---

[1] **13:1** Greek *with brotherly love.*

(Judges 6), and Manoah (Judges 13). But encountering God's messengers in amazing ways isn't the point here. The point is, we're to "continue to love each other with true Christian love" (v. 1). That means showing hospitality to strangers in need. Hospitality is simply making other people **feel comfortable** and **at home.** And there are a lot of people in this world who would love to experience some warm hospitality.

Consider these: a new family in the community that comes to visit your church. Elderly people who live in retirement centers or nursing homes. Single young adults whose families live far away. Single mothers with young children. Traveling missionaries. The list is endless.

Make hospitality a regular part of your life.
Whether you encounter an angel or just another human being, you'll be miraculously blessed.

PRAYER POINT

Thank God for the many times that you have been shown hospitality. And ask him to increase your capacity to help others with true Christian love. Ask him for more opportunities to show hospitality to others.

HERE'S WHAT I'M GOING TO DO

☐ _____

_____

☐ _____

_____

☐ _____

_____

FADING RICHES

How do you feel when you meet people who are very wealthy? Do you admire them? Are you jealous of what they possess—their clothes, their "toys," their cars? Do you hope you'll become their friend? And that they'll spoil you rotten?

How do you feel when you meet someone who's poor? Do you feel jealous then? The funny thing is, the Bible says the poor are **the ones we should be jealous of,** because they're the ones God has honored! Want proof? Read today's Scripture.

James 1:9-11: [9]Christians who are[1] poor should be glad, for God has honored them. [10]And those who are rich should be glad, for God has humbled them. They will fade away like a flower in the field. [11]The hot sun rises and dries up the grass; the flower withers, and its beauty fades away. So also, wealthy people will fade away with all of their achievements.

James clearly points out that the thing about wealth is that it's easy come, easy go. In the short term, if the stock market goes down a few points, a wealthy stockholder can lose millions of dollars—just like that. And in the long 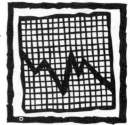 term—the eternally long term—wealth isn't even a factor because money doesn't exist in heaven. That's why James says poor Christians should be glad. They are great in God's eyes. While they may be looked down on by a society that worships the almighty buck, God **raises them up** and **honors** them.

That's quite a contrast with the rich. James says they should be glad too—but for a different reason. God has humbled them! After all, they and all their possessions will wither away like the

---

[1] **1:9** Greek *The brother who is.*

grass in the hot sun. Whether you're rich or poor, or somewhere in between, **your attitude is what counts.**

If you're poor, be glad that riches don't mean anything to God. Because you're worthy of God's attention and love, even without money! If you're rich, be glad that riches don't mean anything to God. True wealth is found in **growing your spiritual life,** not your assets. You see, God's more concerned with the **eternal** (our souls) than the **temporary** (our money and possessions). So no matter how much money you have in your bank account, keep your priorities straight. Know God. Serve him. And use whatever you have to bring him glory.

PRAYER POINT

Pray for the wealthy people you know. Ask God to reveal the truth about money and possessions to them and help them keep a proper perspective. Pray for the poor people you know. Ask God to meet every need they have. And ask God to keep the rich and the poor free from the love of money.

HERE'S WHAT I'M GOING TO DO

☐ _____

☐ _____

☐ _____

☐ _____

PURE RELIGION

A summary of our culture's messages would read as follows:

- Seek pleasure—it's the most important thing in life!
- Success comes when you have plenty of money and stuff!
- You've got to control your destiny—you're nothing if you don't have power and prestige!
- Look out for yourself—nobody else will!
- Do what you want to do, be what you want to be—because you're the most important person in the world!

Few people would actually say they believe these statements, but it's clear that they express **the philosophy of our world system.** So where do we as believers fit in with all this? Read James' simple statement and figure it out.

James 1:27: 27Pure and lasting religion in the sight of God our Father means that we must care for orphans and widows in their troubles, and refuse to let the world corrupt us.

Did you catch that last phrase? "Refuse to let the world corrupt us." Refuse! Just don't do it. Don't buy into it. Don't let it seep into your thinking.

You see, for us believers to keep ourselves from letting the world's influence and philosophy corrupt us—or mess us up—we have to **commit ourselves to the way of Jesus.** To his ethics. His moral system. His philosophy.

The world's system is based on money, power, and pleasure. Jesus' system is totally the opposite. In fact, it's expressed simply in its essence here by James: "Pure and lasting religion in the sight of God our Father means that we must care for orphans and widows in their troubles" (v. 27).

Is he saying that that's all we have to do—take care of widows and orphans? Of course not. But that **simple effort** reveals **tons of truth.** Being willing to serve others in need demonstrates you aren't putting yourself first. You're putting the needs of others before your own. You're serving and loving in Jesus' name. You've got the needy on your heart, just like God has them on his heart.

If that's your lifestyle, it proves that **your faith is pure and lasting.** It's for real. And the world can't touch you.

PRAYER POINT

Ask God for a faith that's pure and lasting, for a heart that seeks to help others in need, for a life that shows you're walking closely with your heavenly Father. Pray for the widows, orphans, and other needy and poor people in your community and look for a way to help them. This is a great first step in building a real faith.

HERE'S WHAT I'M GOING TO DO

☐ _____

_____

☐ _____

_____

_____

PLAYING FAVORITES

Imagine this scene. Your youth group is getting ready to meet at church. Two new guys show up. One drives up in a shiny new Miata convertible. The other walks. One is wearing cool clothes, obviously just purchased from an upscale men's store. The other is wearing what look like hand-me-downs from a few generations ago. One is clearly rich. The other is obviously poor.

How do you and your fellow youth group members **respond?** Which one do you gravitate toward and talk with the most? Which one feels more **"at home," welcomed,** and **wanted** by you?

As you think about that scenario, read today's Scripture.

James 2:1-9: ¹My dear brothers and sisters, how can you claim that you have faith in our glorious Lord Jesus Christ if you favor some people more than others?

²For instance, suppose someone comes into your meeting¹ dressed in fancy clothes and expensive jewelry, and another comes in who is poor and dressed in shabby clothes. ³If you give special attention and a good seat to the rich person, but you say to the poor one, "You can stand over there, or else sit on the floor"—well, ⁴doesn't this discrimination show that you are guided by wrong motives?

⁵Listen to me, dear brothers and sisters. Hasn't God chosen the poor in this world to be rich in faith? Aren't they the ones who will inherit the kingdom God promised to those who love him? ⁶And yet, you insult the poor man! Isn't it the rich who oppress you and drag you into court? ⁷Aren't they the ones who slander Jesus Christ, whose noble name you bear?

⁸Yes indeed, it is good when you truly obey our Lord's royal command

---

¹ **2:2** Greek *synagogue*.
² **2:8** Lev. 19:18.

found in the Scriptures: "Love your neighbor as yourself."² ⁹But if you pay special attention to the rich, you are committing a sin, for you are guilty of breaking that law.

It's natural to show favoritism toward someone who's rich. Why?

First, we don't feel real comfortable around poverty—partly because we know we're responsible to help the poor as best we can. Second, deep down, most of us want to be rich ourselves. We think that if we hang around someone who's rich, maybe it will rub off on us!

Of course, those motives are **selfish.** They indicate that we think we're better than poor people. We're not. In fact, James says, "Hasn't God chosen the poor in this world to be rich in faith? Aren't they the ones who will inherit the kingdom God promised to those who love him?" (v. 5). If we really believe in Jesus and want to follow him, then **we need to show favoritism . . . to no one!** We need to **love everyone** regardless of whether they are rich or poor.

God looks at all people as **equals.** Follow his example.

PRAYER POINT

If you realize you've been playing favorites, especially with people who are rich, confess your sin to God. Ask him to give you a heart that sees all people as equals— regardless of their economic status, race, color, neighborhood, clothes, or hairstyle. And ask him to help you love them all equally—just as his Son does.

HERE'S WHAT I'M GOING TO DO

☐ _____

_____

_____

THE POOR RICH

L ife is serious business. **The way you live here and now** on earth will determine **the way you live forever.** Every attitude, every action, every word, every deed matters. What you believe, and how you put those beliefs into action, matters. Sometimes the reality of all this escapes us. We just coast through life, trying to do the right things here and there, whenever we feel like it.

Our faith is something we do on Sundays. The rest of the time, we're really looking out for ourselves. Doing what we want to do. Treating others indifferently or worse. Pursuing money, people, things, or other dreams of happiness.

Let James shake you up a bit today. Let his words grab you and rattle your thinking. Let him help you **get back on track.**

James 5:1-6: ¹Look here, you rich people, weep and groan with anguish because of all the terrible troubles ahead of you. ²Your wealth is rotting away, and your fine clothes are moth-eaten rags. ³Your gold and silver have become worthless. The very wealth you were counting on will eat away your flesh in hell.¹ This treasure you have accumulated will stand as evidence against you on the day of judgment. ⁴For listen! Hear the cries of the field workers whom you have cheated of their pay. The wages you held back cry out against you. The cries of the reapers have reached the ears of the Lord Almighty.

⁵You have spent your years on earth in luxury, satisfying your every whim. Now your hearts are nice and fat, ready for the slaughter. ⁶You have condemned and killed good people who had no power to defend themselves against you.

OK, so James is addressing self-centered, clueless rich people. But be honest. Sometimes we fit very neatly into that

---

¹ **5:3** Or *will eat your flesh like fire.*

category, don't we? James doesn't beat around the bush when it comes to explaining his—and God's—views on money. He says the money you hold on to and grab after today will be **worthless** when Jesus comes back. So there's no point in trying to build up bank accounts here. Instead we should be accumulating the kind of riches and treasures **found only in God's heavenly Kingdom.**

Of course, money isn't the problem. You need money to live. Churches and ministries need money to serve effectively. Missionaries need money to spread the Good News. It's **the *love* of money** that brings about all kinds of evil (see 1 Timothy 6:10). It's the *love* of money that causes some people to stomp all over others in order to get more.

So James warns all believers not to follow **the world's standards** of success but rather **God's standards** of service. **Are you?**

PRAYER POINT

Let James' stern words lead you in a prayer of confession over any wrong attitudes you've held on to about money, about poor people, about possessions. Open up to God about your life. Your need for more boldness and direction. Your desire to walk closer with him. And your opportunities to serve him by reaching out to others.

HERE'S WHAT I'M GOING TO DO

WHAT'S IT LIKE?

One of the most common accusations people hurl at each other today is "You don't know what it's like." Some kids argue that their parents have no idea what it's like to be young in today's society. Some physically challenged adults point out that the rest of us don't know what it's like to be handicapped. Some people who have lost loved ones contend that no one knows what it's like to experience the grief they're feeling. In short, our distinctions have a tendency to **divide us** because we **underestimate** the ability of others to sympathize with us.

Jesus, though, has no trouble empathizing with suffering people. He was subject to so much suffering during his short time on earth that he is called "man of sorrows."

1 Peter 2:21-24: 21This suffering is all part of what God has called you to. Christ, who suffered for you, is your example. Follow in his steps. 22He never sinned, and he never deceived anyone. 23He did not retaliate when he was insulted. When he suffered, he did not threaten to get even. He left his case in the hands of God, who always judges fairly. 24He personally carried away our sins in his own body on the cross so we can be dead to sin and live for what is right. You have been healed by his wounds!

Part of God's plan for Christians is to **patiently endure suffering.** Jesus modeled this endurance throughout his life—especially during the events leading up to his crucifixion. Facing vicious taunts, insults, physical abuse, and other forms of persecution, Jesus refused to retaliate. Instead he placed himself in God's hands, recognizing that God is **the ultimate source of justice.** When we face persecution or suffering today, we too should place ourselves in God's hands with the **confidence** that he will eventually make things right.

If we attempt to look at suffering in terms of fairness or unfairness, we'll become frustrated very quickly. No matter how much we suffer in life, we may encounter people who suffer even more. Some do bear hardships that the rest of us can't even imagine. But we must **stay focused** on the great truth that no matter our situation, God understands fully how much we hurt. He remains the One who will put an end to all grief and injustice. He gave us his own Son, who suffered an agonizing death beyond the experience of any human. He remains our comfort when all else is empty and cold.

God also charges us with **a responsibility to follow Christ's example** in assisting others in their times of suffering. We may not be able to prevent sorrows from happening, but we can be the **agents of healing** made possible through the incredible work of Christ. Follow in his steps!

PRAYER POINT

Praise God not only for the fact that he suffered and gave his life for us but also for the fact that he understands our suffering, having suffered himself.

HERE'S WHAT I'M GOING TO DO

☐ _____

_____

☐ _____

_____

☐ _____

_____

_____

A Good Manager

What's so hard about being a baseball manager? It's simple, right? All you do is fill out a starting lineup card every day, put your best players on the field, go to the bullpen when your starting pitcher gets tired, and yell at an umpire occasionally. Seems pretty easy.

Those who know the game, however, will tell you that good managers can make the difference between a mediocre season and a championship team. Good managers study the game and know the best players to use in a given situation. They experiment with new strategies to get the most out of their team. They rein in the big egos of star athletes and win the respect of bench players. They

exploit the weaknesses of other teams and compensate for their team's own shortcomings. In short, they **make the best of the resources that are given to them.**

In a similar way, Peter encourages Christians to be good managers of the gifts God has entrusted to them.

> 1 Peter 4:10-11: [10]God has given gifts to each of you from his great variety of spiritual gifts. Manage them well so that God's generosity can flow through you. [11]Are you called to be a speaker? Then speak as though God himself were speaking through you. Are you called to help others? Do it with all the strength and energy that God supplies. Then God will be given glory in everything through Jesus Christ. All glory and power belong to him forever and ever. Amen.

Peter encourages us, first of all, to take stock of what we have. Just as the baseball manager may study his team to discover that his starting pitching is his strongest asset, you need to find out what talents God has entrusted to you. If you are not sure, many churches and Christian organizations have **spiritual gift surveys,** which can help you pinpoint your talents more precisely.

Second, **act on those gifts!** Part of being a good manager is **using what you have to the best possible advantage.** Notice, too, that once you act, God himself intervenes to help you. His generosity flows through you. He speaks through you. He supplies "all the strength and energy" you need (v. 11).

With such help available, there is no reason why you can't be a world-class manager. Take God at his word and **act on his promises today.**

PRAYER POINT

Ask God to help you manage your gifts wisely, using them to glorify him and to minister to others.

HERE'S WHAT I'M GOING TO DO

☐ _____

_____

☐ _____

_____

☐ _____

_____

☐ _____

_____

☐ _____

_____

INSTANT GENERATION

You've heard all of this before. How we're the generation of microwaves, drive throughs, and computers. We're **impatient** and proud of it. Take a computer, for instance: Can you believe how long it can take to connect to an Internet site? Must be several seconds! Do these people think we have all day or what? We're the **instant generation,** all right, and finger drumming's a practiced habit.

Often we apply you these same attitudes to Christianity as **we desire immediate spiritual growth.** After all, we should expect maturing to be quick, easy, and efficient, right? Maybe not, according to Peter.

> 2 Peter 1:5-7: 5So make every effort to apply the benefits of these promises to your life. Then your faith will produce a life of moral excellence. A life of moral excellence leads to knowing God better. 6Knowing God leads to self-control. Self-control leads to patient endurance, and patient endurance leads to godliness. 7Godliness leads to love for other Christians, and finally you will grow to have genuine love for everyone.

Now compare these verses with today's prevalent attitudes and solutions: Having problems with relationships? We read a book. That should do it, shouldn't it? Trying to decide how to respond to an ethical dilemma? We take one class on decisions concerning morality. Plenty of time on that one, surely. Need more Bible study? Hey, that's no problem; we sign up for one class at church and consider that void conquered. Like it advertised . . . "Five Easy Steps to Practicing Theology." Right? Well, like we pointed out earlier, maybe not quite.

Peter does indeed make it sound like it will take a little bit longer. As a matter of fact, he presents a case for "spiritual bodybuilding." This is something that's not going to be accomplished in one day, one class, one push. Instead, effort upon effort, day after day, **consistent** and **decisive** work builds a life of faith, moral excellence, knowledge, self-control, patience, godliness, and finally, love. That doesn't appear instant *or* easy.

You know what? You might as well accept that growing spiritually, learning to "do unto others," and reaching out to our world are going to comprise **a lifelong journey.**

Impatient finger drummers need not apply.

PRAYER POINT

Reflect on the qualities listed in this passage. Are you making progress in your spiritual growth? Pray for God's strength and the wisdom to grow.

HERE'S WHAT I'M GOING TO DO

☐ _____

☐ _____

☐ _____

☐ _____

☐ _____

THE BREATH OF GOD

One of the greatest tenets of our faith is that the original manuscripts are **inspired.** That means they're **infallible,** directly given from God through his people. Another way to say it is that Scripture is "carried along by the Holy Spirit" or "God-breathed." Miraculously, the writers' personalities and uniqueness still came through, but the driving force, the Truth that was to be revealed—all of this came **from God** and **God alone.**

Could this be one of the greatest examples of unselfishness and committed love? These men were not about developing their own agendas; they willingly **allowed themselves to be used**—for another's goal—by the Holy Spirit. And we're not talking about one small act of sacrifice. These men actually allowed the breath of God to push their pens.

Read what importance Peter places on this:

2 Peter 1:14-21: [14]But the Lord Jesus Christ has shown me that my days here on earth are numbered and I am soon to die.[1] [15]So I will work hard to make these things clear to you. I want you to remember them long after I am gone.

[16]For we were not making up clever stories when we told you about the power of our Lord Jesus Christ and his coming again. We have seen his majestic splendor with our own eyes. [17]And he received honor and glory from God the Father when God's glorious, majestic voice called down from heaven, "This is my beloved Son; I am fully pleased with him." [18]We ourselves heard the voice when we were there with him on the holy mountain.

[19]Because of that, we have even greater confidence in the message proclaimed by the prophets. Pay close attention to what they wrote, for

---

[1] **1:14** Greek *I must soon put off this earthly tent.*
[2] **1:19** Or *until the day dawns and the morning star rises in your hearts.*
[3] **1:20** Or *is a matter of one's own interpretation.*

their words are like a light shining in a dark place—until the day Christ appears and his brilliant light shines in your hearts.[2] [20]Above all, you must understand that no prophecy in Scripture ever came from the prophets themselves[3] [21]or because they wanted to prophesy. It was the Holy Spirit who moved the prophets to speak from God.

This entire passage is a model of unselfishness for us—beginning with Peter's admission that he's about to die as well as his chief concern for those he leaves behind. He isn't concerned about their remembering him; instead, he desires that they not forget the inspired words—**the Word**—that God has used him to pen. Peter also takes or claims no glory for himself but constantly points toward the Lord he serves. With great love and obvious worship, he recalls the events of Christ's baptism. And last, Peter speaks of the **confidence** we have in Scripture because of the **miraculous way** it came about.

God-breathed? Amazing, yes, but no less so than the fact that the Holy Spirit resides in you and me. He doesn't push your pen . . . but he does want to **direct** you in **a life of unselfish love.**

PRAYER POINT

Picture the Holy Spirit's involvement in your life like a glove in which you need to insert each finger to be fully directed and used. Prayerfully ask: How much control do I give him?

HERE'S WHAT I'M GOING TO DO

☐ _____

_____

_____

In the Light of Love

That church down the street from yours is a little different, isn't it? They may not quite have it right. In fact, they could really be messing some people up. Another one is too emotional. Another is too rigid. Another is too liberal. And the one across town is just way too boring.

Ever have thoughts like that? You know some of the **other Christian kids** in your school, but you have them "pegged" according to your understanding of their church or denomination. In fact, some of them may not even really be Christians, you think smugly. At least not as good a Christian as you are.

You may not even realize that you have such thoughts. So think about it. Then read what John has to say about such an **attitude.**

> 1 John 2:3-8: ³And how can we be sure that we belong to him? By obeying his commandments. ⁴If someone says, "I belong to God," but doesn't obey God's commandments, that person is a liar and does not live in the truth. ⁵But those who obey God's word really do love him. That is the way to know whether or not we live in him. ⁶Those who say they live in God should live their lives as Christ did.
>
> ⁷Dear friends, I am not writing a new commandment, for it is an old one you have always had, right from the beginning. This commandment—to love one another—is the same message you heard before. ⁸Yet it is also new. This commandment is true in Christ and is true among you, because the darkness is disappearing and the true light is already shining.

John assures us, his "dear children," that we belong to Christ. How do we know? "By obeying his commandments" (v. 3). That's the test.

And what are these commandments? John summarizes

them in the familiar phrase, **"love one another."** He concedes they've heard that commandment before. And yet it's still a new and fresh idea. **If we really love God, then we'll follow his way of life.** "Those who say they live in God should live their lives as Christ did" (v. 6). Sacrificially and lovingly.

This kind of love has no room for **judgmentalism.** If you say you're a Christian but reject another Christian, you're revealing your own ignorance and lack of true faith. Is John saying that if you dislike someone you aren't a Christian? No. Other Christians may be hard to get along with. That's just a fact of life. But that doesn't mean you can ignore them, say negative things about them, or treat them as enemies.

You see, Christian love isn't a feeling. **It's a choice.** You can choose to be concerned about someone else and treat them with respect without feeling affectionate toward them. When you make that choice, God will honor it and help you show real love.

HERE'S WHAT I'M GOING TO DO

☐ _____

_____

☐ _____

_____

FINDING YOUR FIRST LOVE

DAY 258

Have you ever seen someone who was just "going through the motions"? You may have even suffered from this lack of **motivation** yourself. It's usually pretty easy to spot these people and their **lack** of enthusiasm, passion, and excitement.

In the book of Revelation, the Lord confronts a church that had **lost its motivation and passion.** Let's see what Jesus has to say to the church in Ephesus.

Revelation 2:1-6: [1]"Write this letter to the angel of[1] the church in Ephesus. This is the message from the one who holds the seven stars in his right hand, the one who walks among the seven gold lampstands:

[2]"I know all the things you do. I have seen your hard work and your patient endurance. I know you don't tolerate evil people. You have examined the claims of those who say they are apostles but are not. You have discovered they are liars. [3]You have patiently suffered for me without quitting. [4]But I have this complaint against you. You don't love me or each other as you did at first! [5]Look how far you have fallen from your first love! Turn back to me again and work as you did at first. If you don't, I will come and remove your lampstand from its place among the churches. [6]But there is this about you that is good: You hate the deeds of the immoral Nicolaitans, just as I do."

On the surface, it would appear that the church in Ephesus was doing pretty well. Its members were **hard workers** who had **persevered** through trying times. Unlike other churches, the people in Ephesus had refused to tolerate wicked men and false teachers. They had **endured hardships** without growing weary. In fact, as far as we can tell, the church lacked only one thing. Unfortunately, it was the most important quality of all—**love.** The church in Ephesus had lost something extremely important—its motivation for good works.

[1] **2:1** Or *the messenger for;* also in 2:8, 12, 18.

God is interested in our work, but he is just as interested in **our motivation** for doing it. Work that is done grudgingly or with a grumbling attitude is unacceptable to him. It does us no good, for example, to drag ourselves down to the local homeless shelter three times a week and "put in our time" helping the poor and needy if we're only doing it out of a sense of obligation. The only reason we should commit ourselves to helping others is because we love God and his people.

God doesn't expect us always to be "up" and excited about our work. For imperfect humans who go through mood swings and bad days, that would be unreasonable. However, God does expect us to hold on to our "first love." The only way to keep that first love is to set aside time to pray, to read his Word, and to think about Jesus, who saved us and sustains us every day. If we're burned out or just going through the motions, it's a sign that we need to return to our **first love.**

PRAYER POINT

Ask the Lord to help you honestly evaluate the motivation behind your actions. If you believe that you've lost your first love, ask him to help you rekindle that old flame. Be honest. He wants you to turn back!

HERE'S WHAT I'M GOING TO DO

☐ _____

_____

☐ _____

_____

☐ _____

_____

JUDGMENT AND MERCY

Nonbelievers can ask a lot of tough questions. You may have heard this statement yourself: *How can a loving God judge and punish people?* We can't really give an adequate answer unless we shake off any flawed ideas we have about **God's love, mercy, and justice.**

Revelation 7 gives us a clear portrait of God as both a loving heavenly Father and a stern, frightening Judge. More important, it allows us to see how these **two sides** of his nature **fit together.**

Revelation 7:1-3, 9-17: [1]Then I saw four angels standing at the four corners of the earth, holding back the four winds from blowing upon the earth. . . . [2]And I saw another angel coming from the east, carrying the seal of the living God. And he shouted out to those four angels who had been given power to injure land and sea, [3]"Wait! Don't hurt the land or the sea or the trees until we have placed the seal of God on the foreheads of his servants. . . ."

[9]After this I saw a vast crowd, too great to count, from every nation and tribe and people and language, standing in front of the throne and before the Lamb. They were clothed in white and held palm branches in their hands. [10]And they were shouting with a mighty shout, "Salvation comes from our God on the throne and from the Lamb!"

[11]And all the angels were standing around the throne. . . . And they fell face down before the throne and worshiped God. [12]They said, "Amen! Blessing and glory and wisdom and thanksgiving and honor and power and strength belong to our God forever and forever. Amen!"

[13]Then one of the twenty-four elders asked me, "Who are these who are clothed in white? Where do they come from?" [14]And I said to him, "Sir, you are the one who knows." Then he said to me, "These are the ones

coming out of the great tribulation. They washed their robes in the blood of the Lamb and made them white. ¹⁵That is why they are standing in front of the throne of God, serving him day and night in his Temple. And he who sits on the throne will live among them and shelter them. ¹⁶They will never again be hungry or thirsty, and they will be fully protected from the scorching noontime heat. ¹⁷For the Lamb who stands in front of the throne will be their Shepherd. He will lead them to the springs of life-giving water. And God will wipe away all their tears."

PRAYER POINT

Ask the Lord to give you the wisdom and courage to tell an unbelieving friend or family member about him and the salvation he offers.

In the minds of most people, **love** and **judgment** do not go together. God judges sin because he is holy and perfect. Sin, on the other hand, is destructive. Therefore, **because God is a loving God, sin must be judged.**

But God demonstrates his love by **protecting** the people who have chosen to follow him. He marks them with a seal that sets them apart from those who will be judged.

This is the same **promise** given to those of us who believe in Jesus Christ. We will escape the wrath of his judgment. What a motivation—and responsibility—to tell others about **the good news of Jesus Christ!**

HERE'S WHAT I'M GOING TO DO

☐ _____

_____

_____

This Must Be Heaven

Travel agencies and airlines make a business of selling **paradise on earth.** They lure you with images of tropical islands with white sand beaches, deep blue water, and a gentle breeze that refreshes a weary businessman as he lies in a hammock, sipping an ice-cold fruit drink. Or maybe you are tempted by the scene of a perfectly powdered Alpine slope whose virgin snow swooshes beneath your skis while a brisk wind reddens your cheeks.

Try as they might, travel agencies could never dream up a place that compares to the **paradise God has prepared** for those who **receive him.** In the book of Revelation, John gives believers a very brief taste of what their **eternal home** will be like.

Revelation 21:1-4: ¹Then I saw a new heaven and a new earth, for the old heaven and the old earth had disappeared. And the sea was also gone. ²And I saw the holy city, the new Jerusalem, coming down from God out of heaven like a beautiful bride prepared for her husband.

³I heard a loud shout from the throne, saying, "Look, the home of God is now among his people! He will live with them, and they will be his people. God himself will be with them.¹ ⁴He will remove all of their sorrows, and there will be no more death or sorrow or crying or pain. For the old world and its evils are gone forever."

Perfect! **No more pain, death, sorrow, or crying!** And heaven will be a place of incomparable beauty because it is **filled with God's presence.** In heaven, God will dwell among his people. He will not be separated from us—he will be present at all times! Imagine what it will be like to live in the presence of **pure goodness, joy, and happiness!**

Heaven will also be beautiful for what it *doesn't* have.

---

¹ **21:3** Some manuscripts read *God himself will be with them, their God.*

Think about what our world would be like today if we found a way to end hunger and drought. Think about what things would be like if everyone on earth learned to live together peacefully—**no more wars,** no more skirmishes, no more armies. Imagine what the world would be like if the medical community discovered a cure for every sickness known to man. Think about what it would mean if **no one ever died.** Even if you try to imagine such a world, you're still a long, long way from what eternity will be like for those who trust in Christ.

It's important for believers—especially those who are struggling—to remind one another of our **eternal future.** Christians who suffer hardship now in this dark world can find strength in **the bright, glorious hope of heaven.** Let this thought fill your mind with joy as you commit your life to serving God.

PRAYER POINT

Pray for the resolve to bring

heaven to earth by doing

everything you can to relieve those

who suffer in the name of Christ.

HERE'S WHAT I'M GOING TO DO

☐ _____

_____

☐ _____

_____

☐ _____

_____

_____

SPIRITUAL JOURNEY TRAVEL LOG

change your direction

Vertical Landing
'98

The *Every Day God Experience* calls you into a living relationship with God. One that moves you to share his love with a broken world.

Just flip on the evening news and you'll see people in desperate need of God's love. Famine, war, and poverty—both physical and spiritual—seem to be everywhere. For many, life is just one constant struggle for survival.

As you consider the scope of the world's problems . . . and the fact that you're *just one person* . . . you may feel like throwing your hands into the air and saying, "What can *I* possibly do to make a difference?"

Plenty. Especially when you understand that you can change the world—one person at a time. Just follow the theme that runs through your *Every Day God Experience* . . . and **act on your faith.**

As Christians, we are called to follow the example of Jesus Christ, who exhorts us to share life's necessities and provide comfort, encouragement, and counsel. Because he cares for the poor, we must too.

That's why World Vision was a natural ministry partner for the *Every Day God Experience.*

For more than 47 years, World Vision has reached out—from Finland to Fiji, from Australia to Zimbabwe—to meet the dire physical needs of the poor.

Yet this food, care, and relief are shared around the world not only because World Vision is a relief and development organization. *It's done because World Vision is a Christian organization.*

"BE READY TO PREACH THE WORD IN SEASON AND OUT OF SEASON; AND IF NECESSARY USE WORDS."
UNKNOWN

World Vision represents the hands and feet of God to approximately 50 million people in 95 countries. And today, you are invited to join an international partnership of Christians who offer compassion and hope to the hurting.

You can participate through World Vision's 30 Hour Famine—the worldwide event to k*now hunger.* Or maybe you can become personally involved in the life of a precious child through sponsorship. (Check out the last page in this section to learn how you can take part in one of these exciting World Vision programs.)

You'll discover that you *can* make a difference in our world when you act on your faith.

Make your impre

Partner with World Vision and sha

■ One of every three children under age 12 is hungry or at risk in the United States.

Source: Bread for the World

United States

Photo: P. Diederich

World Vision's *Project Home Again* helps the homeless in several major U.S. cities find permanent housing.

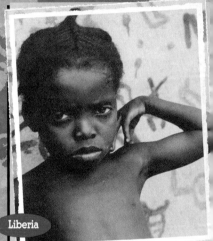

Liberia

Photo: Karen Homer

Five-year-old Larkpor has lived most of her short life in a displaced persons camp in war-torn Liberia. 30 Hour Famine funds help to feed and care for the hundreds of families in this camp.

Bolivia

Photo: R. Miller

Thanks to caring Famine participants, four-year-old Israel has clean water to drink. World Vision is able to dig wells that provide clean water for families in her village of Villcapujio in Bolivia. Contaminated water is suspected in the deaths of six of her brothers and sisters.

■ Africa has the greatest proport of hungry people Two in five are undernourished.

Source: Bread for the World

ion on the world.

mpassion, hope, and life with the needy.

■ Asia and the Pacific have the greatest number of undernourished people—528 million.

Source: Bread for the World

Ethiopia

ve Reynolds

rt from the 30 Hour Famine brings nutritious and smiles to the faces of hungry kids in pia and other needy countries around the world.

The victim of a land mine in her native Cambodia, Ros is a 17-year-old amputee. Yet she has hope and health today because of World Vision's work in Southeast Asia.

Photo: Sanjay Sojwal

Cambodia

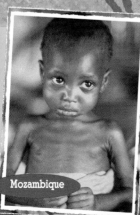

Funds raised through the 30 Hour Famine support scores of feeding centers in Muturara, Mozambique, that provide nutrition for hundreds of children—like little Rose.

Photo: Alastair Crombie

Mozambique

Highlights from World Vision's worldwide ministry include:

◆ Undertaking more than 4,500 projects in 95 countries

◆ Helping more than 1.1 million children around the world through child sponsorship

◆ Providing more than 8.4 million people in places like Bosnia, Zaire, North Korea, and Sierra Leone with vital lifesaving assistance through 331 relief and rehabilitation projects

◆ Bringing life-changing assistance to more than 37.5 million people through community development projects

◆ Allocating more than 77 percent ($234 million) of total support and revenue to fund relief, development, and evangelism efforts around the world

The 30 Hour Famine

Put your faith into action with World Vision's 30 Hour Famine, the worldwide event to k*no*w **hunger.**
The 30 Hour Famine allows students to reach out to the world's needy children by fasting—that's right, by going without food for 30 hours. By raising money in support of their fast, participants help provide food for hungry children. And they're having an incredible impact on world hunger.

In 1997, Famine groups and individuals across the United States raised more than $5 million—funds that gave hundreds of thousands of hungry children the chance to eat . . . and live.

More than 500,000 students in the United States are expected to unite in the fight against hunger in 1998.

The 30 Hour Famine is a powerful way to show your compassion for those in need—and to personally know what it's like to save a child's life. It's an unforgettable experience!

Child Sponsorship

You can begin a life-changing relationship with a child in need through World Vision's child sponsorship program.

When you do, you'll make a lasting difference in the life of a child, as well as in his or her family and community. You'll help provide tools for self-reliance—like improved health, nutrition, education, and the chance to know God's love.

Plus, you'll have the chance to build a meaningful relationship with your sponsored child.

We'll send you a photograph and background information so you can get to know your child. You can also exchange letters and pictures, and you'll receive periodic progress reports to show how you are changing your child's life.

It's a rich and rewarding way to share the love of Christ with a precious child.

To learn more about how you can partner with World Vision and make a difference in our world,
call 1-800-7-FAMINE.